The Irish Theatres Series 8
Edited by Robert Hogan, James Kilroy *and* Liam Miller

The Modern Irish Drama, *a documentary history*
III: The Abbey Theatre: The Years of Synge 1905–1909

The Modern Irish Drama
a documentary history III

The Abbey Theatre:
The Years of Synge
1905-1909

by Robert Hogan and James Kilroy

The Dolmen Press

Humanities Press Inc.

*Set in Times Roman type and printed
and published in the Republic of Ireland
by The Dolmen Press Limited
North Richmond Industrial Estate, North Richmond Street, Dublin 1*

*Published in the United States of America and in Canada
by Humanities Press Inc.,
171 First Avenue, Atlantic Highlands, N.J. 07716*

First published 1978

ISBN 0 85105 280 0: The Dolmen Press
ISBN 0 391 00754 8: Humanities Press Inc.

Library of Congress Cataloging in Publication Data

Hogan, Robert Goode, 1930–
    The Abbey Theatre.
    (Their The modern Irish drama; 3) (The Irish theatre series; 8)
    Includes bibliographical references.
    1. Dublin. Abbey Theatre.   2. English drama — Irish authors — History
and criticism.   3. English drama — 20th century — History and criticism.
I. Kilroy, James, joint author.   II. Title.
PR8789.H62 vol. 3 [PN2602.D82] 792'.09415s
ISBN 0-391-00754-8 [792'.09418'35]   77-19197

219783

Contents

Acknowledgements

Estate of Daniel Corkery, for quotations from article in *The Leader*.

Srimati Rukmini Devi, for quotations from *We Two Together* and manuscripts by James Cousins.

Stephen Fay, for quotations from manuscripts and published writings of F. J. Fay.

Desmond Fay, for quotations from manuscripts and published writings of W. G. Fay.

Nevin Griffith, for quotations from *The United Irishman* and *Sinn Fein*, and writings of Arthur Griffith.

Harcourt, Brace and World, Inc., for quotations from W. G. Fay and Catherine Carswell, *The Fays of the Abbey Theatre*.

Rupert Hart-Davis, Ltd., for quotations from James Agate, *Anthology*.

The Irish Independent, for quotations from *The Daily Nation, The Freeman's Journal* and *The Irish Daily Independent*.

The Irish Times for quotations from *The Daily Express, The Dublin Evening Mail* and *The Irish Times*.

Gerald MacDermott, for quotations from the journals of Joseph Holloway.

J. C. Medley, for quotations from published works and manuscripts of George Moore.

Oxford University Press and Dr. Ann Saddlemyer for quotations from writings of J. M. Synge.

Diarmuid Russell, for quotations from the manuscripts and published works of Æ (George Russell).

Sidgwick & Jackson, Ltd., for quotations from Lennox Robinson, *Ireland's Abbey Theatre*.

The Sunday Times.

A. P. Watt and Son, for quotations from Wade edition of W. B. Yeats's *Letters*, with permission of Michael Yeats.

National Library of Ireland, for quotations from manuscript collections.

Introduction

This five-year period begins with the first full year of the Irish National Theatre Society in its new home in Abbey Street. It contains the account of the extraordinary riots which occurred on the first production of J. M. Synge's masterpiece, *The Playboy of the Western World*. It sees the departure of Frank and Willie Fay from the Abbey, and the development of new actors, such as Arthur Sinclair and Fred O'Donovan. It sees also the emergence of significant new playwrights, such as George Fitzmaurice, Seumas O'Kelly, W. F. Casey, Lennox Robinson, T. C. Murray, Daniel Corkery, Rutherford Mayne, and Gerald MacNamara. It sees the strengthening of the Ulster Literary Theatre and the abortive beginnings of a national theatre in Cork. And finally, two events in 1909 — the premature death of J. M. Synge and the Abbey production of Bernard Shaw's *The Shewing Up of Blanco Posnet* — bring the period of this volume to a dramatic conclusion.

Shaw's play had been banned in England by the Lord Chancellor, and the announcement that the Abbey would stage it in Dublin caused Dublin Castle to exert great pressure upon the theatre's directors to cancel the production. However, Yeats and Lady Gregory persisted, despite the very real threat of losing their patent, in producing the piece. They were, of course, triumphantly vindicated by the applause and admiration of audience and critics; and their persistance shows that even such a blow as the death of Synge had not impaired the vitality of the theatrical movement. The masterpieces of Synge had brought fame to the theatrical movement, but the combined and dedicated efforts of many people had given it strength and endurance. That strength and endurance would be sorely tested in the years to come.

In this volume, as in our previous two, we have attempted to recreate the flavour of the period by allowing the story to be told, as much as possible, by the players and playwrights and playgoers themselves. For the most part in these three initial volumes, we have refrained from overt critical comment. The important plays of these early years — by Yeats, Synge, Lady Gregory and Shaw particularly — are so well-known and easily available that it would have been an impertinence to comment briefly on work that has received so much distinguished and thorough analysis elsewhere. However, in the years covered in this volume, as well as in the years to come, we are faced with a swiftly increasing number of plays that will be unfamiliar even to the most dedicated of our readers. Many of the scripts have never been published, and many that have been are long out of print and difficult to obtain. As our history is an attempt at a comprehensive survey of the modern Irish theatre, we have felt it necessary, then, to rely sometimes upon contemporary summaries of plots, so that the modern reader may have at least some indication of what these many lost plays were about. This procedure occasionally necessitates an amount of space given to some work greater than its merit warrants. In such instances we have, when we have read the plays in old editions or in manuscripts, intruded as a critical counterbalance our own assessments of their worth.

ROBERT HOGAN
JAMES KILROY

1905

1905 was the first full year of the Irish National Theatre Society in the new theatre in Abbey Street. If the theatre did not play constantly, it did play regularly — at least one week in each month. During the year, at the insistence of Miss Horniman, it began to establish itself on a more businesslike basis. Its producer, its voice coach, and its principal actors were put on contract and on salary. The salaries were far from princely, but in comparison with what a manual labourer received they provided a living wage. In addition to revivals of older pieces, the theatre produced five new plays, of which at least four have proved of lasting merit. The company again visited England, playing in Oxford, Cambridge, and London, and its reception there enhanced its reputation.

But there were also divisive and weakening influences. Some players were dissatisfied at the growing accumulation of power in the hands of the three directors, Yeats, Synge, and Lady Gregory. Before the year was out, some of the principal players had left. Animosity toward the plays of John Synge increased. Yeats and Arthur Griffith held a lengthy debate in the press about Synge's earlier play, *In the Shadow of the Glen*, while his new play, *The Well of the Saints*, was generally regarded as offensive to patriotism and morals. Although the other new plays by Lady Gregory, Padraic Colum, and William Boyle were for the most part admired, the distrust of Synge made people suspicious of the whole theatre.

Despite its title of the Irish National Theatre Society, the theatre was not regarded as a National Theatre by the large and influential group of middle-class patriots. Consequently, there rose up a rival group affiliated with the Gaelic League and called the National Players, which gave several enthusiastically received performances. The National Players were never a serious artistic challenge to the Abbey, for they produced no new plays with any claim to enduring merit. Their acting and staging were amateurish, and they often played in small, cramped quarters.

Outside of Dublin, there was much dramatic activity, the most significant being centred in Belfast and Cork. The Ulster Literary Theatre and the Cork National Theatre Society, both modelled on the Dublin group, produced a number of new plays, and the Ulster group was already strong enough in 1905 to bear some comparison with the Abbey Theatre itself.

*   *   *

In January, controversy over Synge's *In the Shadow of the Glen* again broke out, with the following letter from Yeats to Griffith in *The United Irishman*:

You say of Mr. Synge's *Shadow of the Glen* in one of your paragraphs on the performances at the Abbey Theatre, "The story is two thousand years old — it was invented by the decadent Greeks — the reputation of womankind has suffered in every century from it. Mr. Synge heard the story, he called the Greek dame Nora Burke; her husband, Dan Burke; and the robber with whom in the original, she goes away, while the Greek husband and the Greek lover remain, 'a Tramp.' He calls Ephesus a Wicklow Glen, and lo! the thing is staged and dubbed an Irish play." If the names have been changed from Greek to Irish, they have not been changed by him, but by the unknown Irish peasant who first told the story in Ireland. You will find the Irish form of the story in Mr. Synge's forthcoming book on the Aran Islands. You, yourself, once suggested that it was imported by the hedge schoolmasters. I do not, myself, see any evidence to prove what country it first arose in, or whether it may not have had an independent origin in half-a-dozen countries. The version of the Widow of Ephesus that I know differs from Mr. Synge's plot, and also from the Irish folk-story on which he has founded his play. I would be very much obliged if you would give me the reference to the story referred to by you in the paragraph I have quoted. I do not remember it in the *Decameron*, which I have lately read. This story may, however, be exactly the same as some Greek or Italian story, and we be no nearer its origin.

Among the audience at the last performance of *On Baile's Strand* there was a famous German scholar who had just edited the old German version of the world-wide story of the king who fights with his own son. Yet, no man can say whether that story came from Ireland to Germany or from Germany to Ireland, or whether to both countries from some common source.

There is certainly nothing in the accounts that travellers give of mediaeval Ireland or in Old Irish or Middle Irish literature to show that Ireland had a different sexual morality from the rest of Europe. And I can remember several Irish poems and stories in which the husband feigns death for precisely the reason that the husband does in Mr. Synge's play; one of them a very beautiful ballad found in the Aran Islands by Mr. Fournier.

10

But after all, if Mr. Synge had found the story in some Greek writer and had changed the names into Irish names, or even if he had found it in the *Decameron* itself, as you suggest, he would have precedents to encourage him. Shakespeare laid the scene of *Cymbeline* in his own country, but he found the story in the *Decameron*.

I do not reply to the matters of opinion in dispute between us, for to do so would be to repeat what I have already written in my introduction to *A Book of Irish Verse*, in the Irish part of *Ideas of Good and Evil*, and in the last number of *Samhain*. It is no bad thing that our two so different points of view should find full and logical expression, for as William Blake says: "All progress is by contraries"; but differences that arise out of mistakes of fact are useless.[1]

To which, Griffith replied:

If Mr. Yeats' account of how Mr. Synge first came to hear the story of the Widow of Ephesus be correct, we are forced to believe Mr. Synge unacquainted with the classics and with modern French literature. It is indeed astonishing that Mr. Synge should have to journey from Paris to the Aran Islands to hear a story which is a stock one in the Quartier Latin, and which he could have purchased in the Palais Royal. We do not understand how Mr. Yeats came to think that we suggested a story which is 2,000 years old had been taken from the *Decameron*, and Mr. Yeats is mistaken in believing the story of the Ephesian Widow a folk-story. It is a story invented by the wits of decadent Greece, and introduced, with amendments, into Latin literature by the most infamous of Roman writers, Petronius Arbiter, the pander of Nero. But Mr. Synge could not have ventured to produce Petronius' version on the stage of any civilised country. Unless it be in the lying pages of Giraldus Cambrensis, we are ignorant of any mediaeval writer who slanders the women of Ireland, and we know of nothing in old or middle Irish literature which would confirm Mr. Yeats's impression that the mediaeval Irishwoman was of the same class with the Ephesian Dame. Mr. Yeats does not say whether he considers taking a Greek story, dramatising it, and changing the names of the characters into Irish names constitutes Irish drama, but he says Mr. Synge has precedents, and instances Shakespeare's *Cymbeline*. Shakespeare's *Cymbeline* is an English national play — a work of English genius. Imogen is a glory, not a slander on her countrywomen. Mr. Synge's Norah Burke is not an Irish Norah Burke — his play

11

is not a work of genius — Irish or otherwise — it is a foul echo from degenerate Greece. His absurd ignorance of the Irish peasant is shown in every line of the play. Mr. Yeats never heard an Irish tramp in Wicklow or elsewhere address a peasant-woman as "Lady of the House," nor did he, Mr. Synge or any other human being, ever meet in Ireland a peasant-woman of the type of Norah Burke—a woman devoid of all conception of morality, decency and religion. She is a Greek — a Greek of Greece's most debased period, and to dress her in an Irish costume and call her Irish is not only not art, but it is an insult to the women of Ireland.[2]

In the following week, Yeats replied:

You have wasted some of my time. There is no such story in Petronius, and I must again ask you for your reference. He does, indeed, tell the well-known story of the Ephesian widow. You will find a rather full paraphrase of his version in chapter 5 of Jeremy Taylor's *Holy Living*. It is an admirable fable. It has been described by a good scholar and masterly writer as "the very model of its kind, and withal the perfection of ironic humour," but it is not Mr. Synge's story nor the story of your paragraph.

Here it is: "A widow mourning on the tomb of her husband surrenders to the love of a soldier who has been sent to watch over the hanged body of a robber. In the night the robber's friends steal his body away, and the widow hangs her husband's body in its place to save the life of the soldier who had otherwise been executed for neglect of duty." This is a bare summary, and does no justice to a fable that has gone through the whole world. It was not invented by the decadent Greeks, for you will find, if you look in Dunlop's *History of Fiction*, that it is one of the oldest of Eastern tales. It is in that most ancient book of fables, *The Seven Wise Masters*, and is extant in a very vivid form in old Chinese writings. Ireland may, I think, claim all the glory of Mr. Synge's not less admirable tale. The only parallels I can remember at this moment to the husband who pretends to be dead that he may catch his wife and his wife's lover, are Irish parallels. One is in a ballad at the end of *The Love Songs of Connacht*, and the other in a ballad taken down in Tory Island by Mr. Fournier.

In everything but the end of the play Mr. Synge has followed very closely the Aran story, which he has, I believe sent to you; but it is precisely the end of the play that puts him at once among the men of genius. For this there is no parallel in any story that I know of. The sitting down together of the husband and the lover is certainly "the perfection of ironic humour."

It is not my business to dispute with you about the character of Petronius. I know little about him, but I do know that his identification with Arbiter Elegantiarum is considered very uncertain by good scholars, and that little that is certain is known of either Petronius or Arbiter. Mr. Charles Whibley, a sound critic and, as I have always understood, a sound scholar, has said of Petronius, "One thing only is certain, he was a gentleman, and incomparably aristocratic."

The Aran story and the Ephesian story are alike stories of wrong-doing; and so, too, is Bluebeard, and we are none of us a penny the worse.[3]

And Griffith answered:

Mr. Yeats is wasting his time, but he is doing so voluntarily. It is not at our request he indulges in log-rolling. If Mr. Yeats refers again to our reply to his question, Where he may procure the prurient Greek story Mr. Synge has dubbed *In a Wicklow Glen* he will find the answer, in the Palais Royal. Mr. Yeats, who informs us there is no such story in Petronius, has never read Petronius. He has learned, however, from one Whibley that it is doubtful whether Petronius was Petronius, but that it is certain he was a gentleman and an aristocrat. We advise Mr. Yeats not to trust too implicitly in Mr. Whibley's scholarship and his definitions. If Mr. Yeats had read Petronius and his editors he would not have been put to the necessity of referring to Dunlop's *History of Fiction*, which takes equal rank for accuracy and learning with Chambers's *Book of Days*. He would have found that Petronius brought the story out of Greece, where it had been invented by the decadents, and altered it. Mr. Yeats fails to tell us who the "mediaeval travellers" were he spoke of in his last letter, who led him to believe that Irishwomen were of the same class with the Ephesian dame, and where in Old or in Middle Irish literature he found confirmation for the impression these "mediaeval travellers" made upon him. In future we advise him to catch his traveller before quoting him for fear his imagination has carried him away in this matter as it did in America when he told his audiences the Castle lived in fear of his theatre and sent forty baton-bearing myrmidons down to its each performance. Mr. Synge forwards us a tale he states he took down in Aran, which is essentially different to

13

the play he insolently calls *In a Wicklow Glen*. In the Aran story the wife appears as a callous woman — in Mr. Synge's play the wife is a strumpet. In the interests of the National Theatre Society, we advise its writers to leave that kind of "drama" to the "Theatre of Commerce," where Mr. Synge's "genius" may entitle him to a seat beside the author of *Zaza*.[4]

The next week, Yeats wrote:

I don't see how we can go on with the controversy about the origin of the *Shadow of the Glen* until you have printed Mr. Synge's letter to you, with its enclosure giving the Irish original, and given me a more definite reference than "The Palais Royal." I must, however, contradict a statement you have made about myself. You say, "In America he told his audience the Castle lived in fear of his Theatre, and sent forty baton-bearing myrmidons down to its each performance." This is as true as the statement made to me by an American journalist that you were paid by the British Government to abuse the Irish Party. I described in many of my American lectures the attack made upon the *Countess Cathleen* by Mr. F. H. O'Donnell and the *Nation* newspaper. I have my exact words among my papers in London. This seems to be the origin of your extravagant charge, doubtless sent to you by some imaginative correspondent, or copied from some inaccurate newspaper. I mentioned neither Dublin Castle nor politics of any kind.[5]

Griffith then replied:

In declining to continue the controversy he began, we think Mr. Yeats is acting wisely. To remove the misapprehension Mr. Yeats' letter is calculated to create, we may say that this is the first intimation we had that Mr. Synge intended his letter for publication, and not for our personal enlightenment. Since we find we have erred, we subjoin it:

Sir — I beg to enclose the story of an unfaithful wife which was told to me by an old man on the Middle Island of Aran in 1898, and which I have since used in a modified form in *The Shadow of the Glen*. It differs essentially from any version of the story of the "Widow of Ephesus" with which I am acquainted. As you will see, it was told to me in the first person, as not infrequently happens in folktales of this class.—
Yours,
J. M. SYNGE.

14

Mr. Synge's story, which, as we said last week, depicts the wife as a callous woman, whilst his Ephesian play depicts her as a strumpet, is, we regret to say, of insufficient merit to entitle it to a place in our columns. We presume Mr. Yeats' "American journalist" is a blood relation of those "mediaeval travellers" from whom he learned that the mediaeval Irishwomen were akin to the Ephesian dame, and that we shall request his name from Mr. Yeats with the same ill-success we have requested the names of the mediaeval slanderers. The statement which Mr. Yeats contradicts is taken from one of those English papers which latterly Mr. Yeats delights to quote — the *Daily News*. Mr. Yeats will notice that it purports to give his exact words, and that, therefore, if untrue, it is a deliberate forgery. This is the paragraph:

Mr. W. B. Yeats has been lecturing in America upon the intellectual revival in Ireland under the auspices of the Irish Literary League of America. In the course of his remarks he said about the Irish National Theatre: "There is a deeper and bitterer tone in the new Irish literature than there ever was in the old Irish ballads. The Gaelic League has developed passion where there was once apathy. Our dramatists now study what the people want, and then we give it to them in such form that thirty or forty police must often be stationed inside the theatre to prevent riots. You can do something with people like that." That Mr. Yeats never mentioned Dublin Castle nor politics of any kind in America is all the more wonderful in view of the fact that he delivered a public address to a Nationalist audience on Robert Emmet there. An address on Robert Emmet with all reference to the Castle and politics left out eclipses the record of the stage-manager who successfully produced *Hamlet* with the part of the Prince of Denmark omitted.[6]

And there the controversy rested.

*   *   *

The suspicion of Synge, however, was increased by his new play. On 6 January, Joseph Holloway wrote in his journal:

I saw the entire play of *The Well of the Saints* gone through at the rehearsal at the Abbey Theatre and came to the conclusion that Mr. Synge is a complete master of picturesque strong language and sometimes brutal coarseness, not to say sheer repulsiveness. . . . If a good deal of the dialogue as it at

15

present stands be not toned down, or omitted on the night of public performance, I feel sure the piece will meet with a very hostile reception (and justly, in my opinion be it said) that may injure the society permanently.[7]

On 11 January Holloway wrote:

J. M. Synge conducted the rehearsal of . . . *The Well of the Saints* . . . and though he has made some cuts in the text much yet remains to be erased before an Irish audience is likely to swallow it. Parts of it suggest to the mind a picturesque setting of the slang dictionary. . . . Having written so far, a thought struck me to drop a line of warning to Frank J. Fay re the matter, and this was the result — 21 Northumberland Road, Dublin, January 12, 1905: Dear Mr. Fay, Just a word in your ear as a sincere friend and well-wisher of the Irish National Theatre Society. Please use all your power to have certain passages, such as that about the priest and the pair in the ditch, and the two or three coarse references to bringing all sorts of monstrosities into the world, indulged in by the Douls and Timmy the Smith, erased from *The Well of the Saints*. For, if they are allowed to remain they will undoubtedly give unnecessary offence to most of those who witness the play, and probably ruin the Society's chance of future success in Dublin. Billingsgate no matter how clothed in imagery of diabolical cleverness remains Billingsgate and never can become anything else; and when linked with irreverence it becomes quite intolerable to an Irish audience. Be warned by me, who knows the pulse of audiences fairly well by this time, and cut out as much of the nastiness as possible out of the piece. Having said so much, as a sincere friend, I leave the rest to your good sense to see my warning fall not on deaf ears. Your commonsense friend, Joseph Holloway.[8]

To this letter, Fay replied:

Thanks for your kind letter. I cannot help thinking that you are needlessly alarmed over *The Well of the Saints*. Surely the Dublin public who crowd to hear *The Geisha* and the other musical comedies full of eroticism conveyed to the audience by that subtle minister music, who go to *Faust* and revel in *Tristan and Isolde*, to say nothing of Shakespear, will not be affronted when they hear two or three people on our stage speaking after their kind. You must close your ears to the language of our city if you think Irish people don't say such things; and I personally like plain speaking. It is only

16

suggestion that does harm. If we ever play a Shakespearian play, I shall certainly try to get it played exactly as it is printed. Plain, blunt words hurt no one. You remember the row over *The Countess Cathleen* and *Diarmuid and Grania* and *In the Shadow of the Glen.* Well, if you take the trouble to read Hyde's *Literary History of Ireland* and turn to the story of Deirdre, you will see what the real thing was like. When I was at Rosses I met a young priest who praised *In the Shadow of the Glen*; so does Father O'Donovan, and so did my other brother who is a very pious man who knows the Catholic religion and its philosophy. I spoke to Synge long ago about the passage about the priest; but he saw the incident and won't alter it, and I am sorry I ever spoke about it. Have you read Shakespear lately? I have and Synge is mild compared to him. Shakespear has of course become a religion. Well, I claim that Synge be allowed as much liberty as Shakespear or Sophocles. If the Irish public were reverent, they would not turn one's blood cold with their use of words that really religious people — the orientals for instance — scarcely dare breathe. You may say it is the lower classes who do so; well, they are principally Catholics; and Synge's play deals with their like. Why should the stage have less liberty than the press? We do not put on a play for the sake of such passages; but they are as legitimate surely as, say, Othello's "Be sure you prove my love a whore." I know the kind motive that actuates you and what a good friend you have been to us; but in this matter we think differently. Even if I did not agree with the Society on this point, I will sink or swim with it because I wish it to be seen that there is at least one body in Ireland that knows its own mind. You have seen that there are people in Ireland who don't like Hyde's Nativity Play; many of our supporters would like us to leave what they call politics — that is, the expression of Ireland's desire for separation — out of our bill. We have probably lost friends over *In the Shadow of the Glen* and we may over the next piece, but I think they will come back to us. We have set out to produce a sincere and vigorous drama such as the ordinary theatre couldn't and wouldn't produce; a lot of people would support us if we gave them what they get in the other theatres, laying the scene in Ireland; but if we did that we should have no *raison d'être.* I think you will agree with most of what I have said and that your objections are not so much your own as looking at the matter from the point of view of others. I have always fought against the "Island of Saints" view of

17

this country. When Guaire broke the law (the Guaire whose acquaintance you made in *The King's Threshold*), he was supported by the Saints against the King of Ireland, his chief, and we have been paying the penalty ever since. I prefer to think that this is a country of men and women with virtues and vices (especially the latter, or what would we do for our Drama?) like others, and I would see them get rid of the sentimentalism that they probably learnt from Davis whose wretched "kindly Irish of the Irish" is not at all true of to-day. Look around you, read *The Leader* and the *U.I.* [*The United Irishman*], and listen to the way we abuse each other in public and private, and you will see how little we deserve the epithet "kindly." Synge is not a "kindly" dramatist, but I think he may yet be a great one that will make this country talked of again, and we mustn't try to clip his wings even if he splash us now and then. Read *King Lear* again.[9]

Holloway's prediction about the typical Dublin playgoer's reaction to Synge's play was fairly accurate, as may be seen by the review of the first production on 4 February, which appeared in *The Freeman's Journal*:

The Irish National Theatre Society produced a new play — *The Well of the Saints* — by Mr. J. M. Synge, on Saturday evening. An audience that did not quite fill the Abbey Theatre gave the play an encouraging, but not an enthusiastic reception. Mr. Synge's plays are somewhat baffling. How are they to be interpreted? Are they designed as a contribution to Irish national drama, and if so, what is meant by Irish national drama? Is it an attempt to hold the mirror up to Irish nature? Are we to look to it for a treatment of the facts of Irish life, present or past, in accordance with the commonly accepted Irish ideals? Or is the drama to be Irish and national merely because of the place of its production, the scenes in which the action is laid, and the dialect in which the dialogue is spoken? Whence is it to derive its philosophy of life? From what source its psychology of character? Upon the answer to these questions depends the judgment of Mr. Synge's claims to be regarded as an Irish national dramatist, if, indeed, he makes any claim to be so regarded. This is the third of Mr. Synge's contributions to the repertoire of the Irish National Theatre; and his point of view as a dramatist is pretty clearly defined. The point of view is not that of a writer in sympathetic touch with the people from whom he purports to draw his characters. To begin with, he knows nothing of Irish peasant religion.

18

The widow in *Riders to the Sea*, who consoles herself with the thought that her prayers to Providence may cease, leaves off her praying just when the Irish peasant's prayers would really begin. The wife in *The Shadow of the Glen* shows never a trace of the conscience that even the vagabond carries somewhere in Ireland. With Martin Doul — the principal character, in fact, the only character in *The Well of the Saints* — religion is only a decayed mythology, useful for incantation or imprecation, but having no further concern with soul or body. Behind this representation of the popular religion is the subtle irony of the latter-day French school satirising a Providence that has ceased to be paternal, and is shadowed forth merciless as the Destiny of the Greek drama. Such a presentation of the peasant religion, lacking in reverence and expressed in a jargon of profane familiarity, is an artistic blunder and a constant offence. Again Mr. Synge is as preoccupied with the sex problem as any of the London school of problem playwrights. . . . Add to all this, or rather a result of all this, Mr. Synge's leading characters repel sympathy. . . .

The analysis of the blind man's feelings and frenzies is not without power; and in the dialogue beauty of thought and felicity of phrase are not lacking. The monologue of the lonely blind man after darkness has fallen upon him a second time is quite searching in its pathos. But the roughness of the peasants' passion is exaggerated, the ferocity of their rage excessive, and the hell-wrath of their imprecations repulsive. Here and there are touches of cynicism that make an ugly impression, and help to deepen the conviction that as a painter of Irish life and manners Mr. Synge is either too incredulous of its main health or too much attracted by the problems suggested by unhealthy elements that no society is free from, to give a typical picture. . . .

The players did excellently in the measure of their opportunity. Mr. W. G. Fay is a comedian of rare powers, and in the subtler touches of his part was excellent. His explosions were not convincing, but that, perhaps, was not his fault. Miss Emma Vernon[10] as the blind woman was also admirable. Her brogue is perfect, and the peasant manner is given without strain or stiffness. The other characters afforded the actors little chance; but Mr. George Roberts's Timmy, the Smith, was made the most of, and Mr. F. J. Fay as a wandering Friar gave as much reality and sincerity to the part as could be put in it. . . .[11]

Arthur Griffith gave the new play a predictably slashing review:

The story — a well-known one — has been treated in our own time by an English novelist. Mr. Synge's localisation of it is a failure, and his dramatisation disappointing. His peasants are not Irish, and the language they use in strife is pure Whitechapel. The dialogue is most uneven, varying from passages of lyric beauty to violent eruptions of no real strength; the duologues are lengthy, iterative, and apt to become wearisome. The imperfections of the play are numerous, and it is dragged out to three times its natural length. A moment of possible fine tragedy when Martin Doul recovers his sight is overlooked by the author, and the blunder by which he confounds the loss of sight with the loss of imagination is so gross that even the "Theatre of Commerce" cannot produce its equal. One of the most amusing blunders which the author perpetrates is making the blind man immediately on recovering his sight recognise people by the colour of their hair. The atmosphere of the play is harsh, unsympathetic, and at the same time sensual. Its note of utter hopelessness evokes a feeling akin to compassion for the author. What there is "Irish," "national," or "dramatic" about it even Oedipus might fail to solve. How is it that the Irish National Theatre, which started so well, can now only alternate a decadent wail with a Calvinistic groan.[12]

The review in *The Irish Times* criticized the scenery:

It is, we know, heresy to suggest an amplification of the scenery. That, it is said, would unduly distract attention from the literary matter, but there were periods during the performance of Saturday when a little distraction from the long-drawn dialogues would have been a relief. . . . Saturday's play was particularly crude in its scenic equipment. It was a three act play, and in the first and last the background was a tolerably well-painted mountain, reminiscent more of the west than the east of Ireland.[13]

The Evening Herald criticized the characterization:

But perhaps the most serious defect in Mr. Synge's play is that it is more than doubtful whether in any part of Ireland are to be found such types of the Irish peasant as Martin and Mary Doul, who, as far as I can see, have nothing to recommend them. The old type of whiskey-drinking, jig-dancing, handy, rascal Irishman manifested a certain boisterous and

20

somewhat objectionable vivacity in and out of season — mostly out — but I question if in most respects he was not greatly the superior of the pessimistic loafer which there is a tendency to set up as the standard.[14]

And R.M. in *The Dublin Evening Mail* criticized nearly everything:

It seems to me, however, that it is hardly worth while analyzing Mr. Synge's intentions for the simple reason that out of such intangible and fantastic material it will never be possible to build up a national Irish drama. . . . Martin Doul is a well-drawn study, but he is the only character in the play which grips the audience and compels interest in spite of the fact that throughout the whole of the three Acts there is a singular dearth of action and incident.[15]

L. J. M'Quilland in *The Belfast Evening Telegraph* added further disagreements:

Mr. Synge's madness is not always the sanity of the theatre, but he has at last produced a live play, a play without corpses. . . . The comedy-drama contains many beautiful and poetic lines, the effect of which, however, is seriously marred by the squalor of the play's human nature. . . . With regard to the mounting of the play, really wonderful effects have been produced by the simplest means. Flat cloths and faint tints suggested surprising semblances of rugged lands and sombre skies.[16]

In this chorus of damns and faint praises, Synge had one eloquent defender, but one who would make him few converts in Ireland — George Moore:

I should like to call the attention of the readers of *The Irish Times* to an important event which has just happened in Dublin, and which very likely may be overlooked by them and to their great regret hereafter. The event I allude to is of exceeding rarity, it happens occasionally in Paris. I have never seen in London any play written originally in English that I can look upon as dramatic literature. I have not forgotten Oscar Wilde's plays — that delicious comedy *The Importance of Being Earnest* — but however much I admire them I cannot forget that their style is derived from that of Restoration comedy, whereas Mr. Synge's little play seems to me to be of a new growth. Its apparent orthodoxy reminds us of the painters who worked in the latter half of the 15th century. Filippo Lippi and Botticelli did not accept religious superstitions as easily as the monk of Fiesole. There are other points of comparison between Mr. Synge's writings and these pictures, but I must reserve my explanation for another occasion. In your paper I would call attention to the abundance and the beauty of the dialogue, to the fact that one listens to it as one listens to music and the ease with which phrase is linked into phrase. At every moment the dialogue seems to lose itself, but it finds its way out. Mr. Synge has discovered great literature in barbarous idiom as gold is discovered in quartz, and to do such a thing is surely a rare literary achievement.

The interpretation partakes of the literary quality, it is original and it is like itself. Mr. W. Fay was wholly admirable as the blind beggar; he was whimsical and insolent, and pathetic in turn; he was always in the key, and his love scene with Molly Byrne seemed to me a little triumph of distinguished acting. The close of the act was especially effective in intonation and in gesture. Mr. Frank Fay was very good as the saint; the part is a difficult one, and the ecclesiastical note might not have been caught as well by another actor. The part of the blind beggarwoman was so well played by Miss Vernon that I am afraid I shall regret having spoken of it, for I shall not find words wherewith to praise it enough. Above all I admired her reticence, and it seemed to me that she must have thought the part out from end to end, omitting nothing that might be included, including nothing that might be omitted. The age of the old woman is portrayed in every gesture, the walk and the bodily stiffness, and something of the mind of an old woman, for in her voice there is a certain mental stiffness. Her elocution was faultless. Some will say that she was not effective enough when she left the church, but I do not share this opinion. I think in seeking to be effective she would have been less true.[17]

Of course, Moore was hardly a typical member of the audience, and Holloway's reaction was closer to the general view:

Mr. Synge, I believe was not present at the performance on Friday night, and I happened to be in the Green Room on Saturday when he made his appearance and Lady Gregory asked him, "What happened to you last night? We thought you had committed suicide!" Which was the severest thing said of him or his play in my hearing during the week from one of the worshippers. Oh, it was shocking! [18]

*   *   *

In a preliminary notice of the Abbey's next new production, Lady Gregory's *Kincora*, on 25 March, *The Freeman's Journal* made some specific observations about 'the novel principles of staging and costume which have been adopted.'

> . . . the action leads down to the battle of Clontarf, which took place about A.D. 1015; so that Irish and Danish costumes are to be looked for, and in designing these Mr. Robert Gregory has gone as near as possible to the usages of the period without sacrificing effect to mere archaeological detail. The scenic treatment is practically a new departure here. It is merely decorative and suggestive — not realistic or spectacular at all. The object is to admit nothing on the stage calculated to distract the attention of the audience from the words and action of the personages who take part in the drama. A more thoroughly artistic motive could not be conceived. Then as to the costumes, a certain scheme of colour has been adhered to with the view of making dress and character accord with one another as much as possible. The background for the Prologue consists of hangings on which tree forms appear, thus suggesting without picturing a wood. The whole of the first act will take place in an interior of Kincora Palace, a little more realistic than the scene which preceded it, but still keeping to the suggestive, and ignoring all attempts at palatial representation. This interior does for the second act also. The third act is carried through a repetition of the wood scene, the interior of the palace, and a new scene which conveys the outside of Brian Boru's tent at the battle. The plot brings four Irish royal personages on the scene — namely, Brian Boru, King Malachy of Ireland, King Maelmore of Leinster, and Prince Murrogh, son of Brian. The costumes of all these are similar — red with a grey cloak and sword, and a minn or ancient Irish coronet on the head. No glaring embroidery or glittering jewellery. Chief amongst the female personages is Queen Gormleith; and she wears a very bright orange dress ornamented with black and gold. The costume of the Danish warriors, who appear at the end of the play, is to be black with yellow fringes. Attendants of the palace are clad in green and brown on grey green. As already mentioned, all the costumes and the scenic backgrounds have been designed by Mr. Robert Gregory, and made and painted in the theatre, assistance of indispensable value having been given by Mr. Fay as the producer of the piece.[19]

23

The Evening Herald, reviewing the production, thought that *Kincora* was 'not only a great advance on her previous tentative efforts at dramatic construction — *Twenty-Five* and *Spreading the News* — but in several respects the best play produced under the auspices of the National Theatre Society.' *The Evening Mail* was no less enthusiastic, remarking that, 'it is not too much to say that in their repertoire they have no play which is stronger, more dramatic in its story and in the manner of its telling, or more likely to win a lasting popularity.' Arthur Clery, writing under the pseudonym of 'Chanel' in *The Leader*, had some criticism of the acting, but little of the play:

> After the shallow cynicism of *The Well of the Saints*, Lady Gregory's *Kincora* came as a pleasant and wholesome change at the Abbey Theatre. *Kincora* is the vigorous product of a healthy mind that has an appreciation for art, and yet is not out of touch with reality. The first strictly historical drama (if I recollect aright) produced by this society, it was an unquestioned success, and seems to open out a new path on which our dramatist may tread with safety and success. The audience showed that it appreciated the purer atmosphere of the drama — an atmosphere neither dimmed by mist, nor tainted by foul vapours, and there was far more real enthusiasm shown than I have lately seen at any of this society's productions. . . . Mr. A. Power as Malachy, though he acted the more emotional scenes fairly well, was utterly lacking in dignity, and had not got his body under control.[20]

The *Freeman's* review was similarly generous:

> *Kincora*, the new Irish historical play by Lady Gregory, was produced by the players of the Irish National Theatre Society on Saturday evening. The performance had been looked forward to with great interest, and the house was more crowded than at any performance since the opening night of the Abbey Theatre. The interest was more than satisfied by the play, which roused the audience to great enthusiasm, and the applause when the curtain had fallen was sustained for several minutes, until the author bowed her acknowledgments. No play to which the new dramatic movement has given birth is so likely to achieve popularity. . . .
> To fit such a story and character into a prose play would have seemed an impossibility. But Lady Gregory's prose, in its best moments, offers new material to sustain the argument, that the distinction as to form between prose and poetry is an

unreal one. Some of the speeches have the afflatus of the best blank verse, without its measure. If she has failed to some extent to vitalise or build up with sufficient complexity the chief male characters of the play, she has utilised the minor characters skilfully to supply a chorus to her theme. They are as pertinent, if the comparison may be dared, as Shakespeare's fools. Some of the dialogue among them is full of wistful wisdom and the real poetry that so often emerges in the rustic speech. . . .

The play was well acted and staged with a simplicity that culminated in a scene of rare beauty. Miss Máire Nic Shiubhlaigh gave a rendering of Gormleith which, if slightly lacking in power, was entirely harmonious with the author's conception. Mr. F. J. Fay acted the part of King Brian with that dignity he can so well assume, though he could have used some more inches if they were his to dispose of.[21]

Even Arthur Griffith could hardly charge that this play was un-Irish:

It is always a pleasure to go to Miss Horniman's Theatre, if for no other reason than to admire its complete and beautiful arrangement. . . . Of all the plays which the Irish National Theatre Society has acted this is the most successful by reason of its interest and its spectacular effect. . . . Pre-eminent amongst them all, Miss Nic Shiubhlaigh acted in a way that alone would have made the play a success. Acting like hers has no precedent in this theatre. Mr. Roberts made a most difficult scene a success. The play, on the whole, was interesting, and held its audience from beginning to end. It is a pity that so much of its construction depended on the supernatural. It was a little too fayish and unnatural, and this detracted from the human interest. The stage management was somewhat at fault, but the playing of the pipes between the acts added to the evening's entertainment.[22]

Holloway went by the theatre on Monday evening, *Kincora's* second performance, and noted:

I had a look in at the Abbey Theatre on my way down to the lecture at the National Literary Society and found the house extremely slack considering the unanimity of the Press in praising *Kincora*. . . . In speaking to Mr. Yeats re the colour scheme of the piece, he remarked how beautifully the colour of the Queen's costume asserted itself in the opening scenes and how the background of the last scene blotted her out of importance at the same time as the dramatist ended her career of power.[23]

Of the staging, Yeats wrote in *Samhain*, 'Our staging of *Kincora*, the work of Mr. Robert Gregory, was beautiful, with a high grave dignity and that strangeness which Ben Jonson thought to be a part of all excellent beauty.' And Lady Gregory described the set specifically:

> The first acts of the play are laid in King Brian's great hall at Kincora. It was hung with green curtains, there were shields embossed with designs in gold upon the walls, and heavy mouldings over the doors. The last act showed Brian's tent at Clontarf; a great orange curtain filled the background, and it is hard to forget the effect at the end of three figures standing against it, in green, in red, in grey. For a front scene there was a curtain — we use it still in its dimness and age [in 1913] — with a pattern of tree stems interlaced and of leaves edged with gold. This was the most costly staging we had yet attempted: it came with costumes to £30. A great deal of unpaid labour went into it.[24]

*　　*　　*

The Abbey's next new play was William Boyle's *The Building Fund*. Born in 1853 and raised in County Louth, Boyle was older than the other Abbey writers, even older than Lady Gregory, and some of his subsequent asperity towards the theatre may have arisen because he felt himself scanted by people who were not only younger but also less popular dramatists. At the time of the production of *The Building Fund*, he was a civil servant in London. He had published in Irish magazines a good deal of light verse as well as some humorous prose sketches of country life, some of which were collected under the title of *A Kish of Brogues*. None of his prolific earlier writing which we have seen is of particular excellence, but his first play was a hard, rather Jonsonian comedy of humours. It was played for several years by the Abbey in both Ireland and England with great success, and was also played by the Fays in America. An unimaginative reading of the play today would hardly indicate the reasons for its popularity in 1905. Its dialogue, if compared to that of Synge or Lady Gregory, seems spare and flat, but it was workable stage dialogue which threw into effective relief his well-drawn and rather venomous comic characters. Despite the caustic quality of the character drawing,

26

the play was quite entertaining, and the reason was probably twofold — a couple of excellent theatrical situations and the opportunity given to the actors for caricature. Reading over reviews of the play, one is surprised to find Boyle compared to Molière, to Ibsen, and to Hauptmann. Such judgments we can now see are far-fetched, but the play was good in its time, and it, as well as Boyle's more farcical later work, was to prove a major drawing power for several years.

On 13 April Boyle wrote revealingly from London to George Roberts about his characters in *The Building Fund*:

> My wish to see a rehearsal springs from a desire to improve the language of the dialogue by changing a word here and there. . . . I am glad to see both the Fays are in it. W. G. Fay's acting suggested the character to me which he is to play. Of the other characters — Mrs. Grogan is intended to have tender moments against which she fights; Sheila is a scheming young woman with certain religious fervour bordering on hypocrisy; MacSweeny is a kind of rustic dandy fond of tall talk and quite a worthless person, while old O'Callaghan is a sincere, honourable and kindly old man. Mrs. Grogan's part is not an easy one to act as I imagine it.[25]

On 25 April the Abbey presented *The Building Fund*, as well as a revised version of Yeats's *The King's Threshold*. The next day *The Freeman's Journal* remarked that *The Building Fund*

> . . . is a most clever and amusing play, sure to succeed on any stage. . . . Mr. Boyle's dialogue is replete with humour and character — so much so that he is entitled to be described as a first-rate delineator of Irish character. There is a smack of reality about every word that everybody utters and the constant laughter of the audience showed how much entertained they were. The part of Mrs. Grogan was acted by Miss Emma Vernon with an uncommon amount of dramatic skill. She pictured the old lady with such vividness and fidelity to real life that it would have been difficult for any professional artist to have given a better portraiture. The part in her hands was one of the highest excellence. Mr. W. G. Fay was Shan Grogan, and made that part a capital companion-picture to that given by Miss Vernon of his hard, griping, relentless parent. His hypocritical conduct in reference to his niece and his trepidation when the contents of the will came to be disclosed were features capitally brought out.[26]

The Dublin Daily Express called it 'A notable success'; *The Dublin Evening Telegraph* called it 'most clever and amusing'; and *The Evening Mail's* reviewer called it 'One of the best comedies I have ever seen.'

Griffith's review of Boyle's play sounds rather as if he had enjoyed the performance and had then remembered that he disliked the Abbey:

> *The Building Fund*, by Mr. William Boyle, is the most recent addition to the repertoire of the Abbey Theatre, and its humour is undeniable, although it is wholly of the cynical order. The atmosphere of the play is a sordid one. Mr. Boyle has drawn no single character in his play which could command either esteem or affection. We have seen the play and laughed at it, but we are still convinced that there are to be found in contemporary Ireland men and women whose characters are noble characters, despite the fact that the writers for the Abbey Theatre seem to have never met them. Dr. Johnson's cynical observation that the Irish are an honest people, since they are never heard speaking well of one another, seems to be borne out by the plays produced in the Abbey Theatre. Mr. Boyle apparently attempted to make one of the characters in his play the possessor of a heart, but he eventually succumbed to that new law of art which seems to prevail in Abbey street, and deprecates the representation of a single virtue or ideal on its stage.[27]

A more typical summation was Holloway's:

> The splendid popular success of Mr. Boyle's comedy is a great step in advance for the Society — as it takes it out of its narrow groove of clique-ism and fluttered the dovecote of mutual admiration dramatists. . . . The Abbey Theatre dramatic quartette, Yeats-Synge-Gregory & Colum, sang anything but a glee on Tuesday when Mr. Boyle scored a number-one success with his *Building Fund*. The struggle it had to pass the committee of literary cranks — because forsoothe, it was nature that was depicted and not artifice — was not without its humours, when one comes to think that they failed to see that it was true to life; they knew so little of the real article themselves.[28]

Although Holloway's comment sounds malicious, it contained an element of truth, as may be seen in the following letter of Yeats to Synge:

28

. . . Boyle's play [undoubtedly an early version of his second play, *The Eloquent Dempsy*] came here last week, and I have no doubt it will be sent to you almost immediately. Both Lady Gregory and myself think that it is impossibly vulgar in its present form, though there is a play somewhere sunk in it. . . . if you agree with us about the vulgarity of the play protest as strongly as possible. It will need vehemence, for Russell and the two Fays are evidently for it. It is most likely Colum will vote for it through love of popularity and that we shall be beaten in the voting. I take a very serious view of the matter indeed, partly because I am not at all sure of the effect of a play of this kind on Miss Horniman who has spent four thousand pounds on us already. The only condition she makes is that we shall keep up the standard. I don't mind going against her where I know we are right, but if we produce this our position will be perfectly indefensible.[29]

Probably early in September, Synge wrote to Yeats about another play as well as Boyle's:

It is, of course, in many ways a very capable piece of work — both in dialogue and putting together, although there are points I do not like — but I think it is too near the conventional historical play and has too much conventional pathos to be the sort of thing we want. On the other hand, we seem to be short of plays, and it is hard to say on what pretext we should vote against this stuff, however little we may like it.

   I got Boyle from F. Fay last night and have read two acts of him. He sets one's teeth on edge continually, and yet I think it is certainly worth revising and playing. It hovers over being a good picture of the patriot publican, and yet it is never quite right and it is very often quite wrong. Your brother and I saw something of these kind of people when we were away for *The Manchester Guardian*. They are colossal in their vulgarity, but their vulgarity is as different from cockney vulgarity as the Mayo dialect is from the Cockney. Boyle does not seem able to distinguish between the two and sticks in English Music Hall vulgarity of the worst kind. I rather agree with Fay that you would be more likely to get Boyle to put it to rights than Colum. Boyle would be sure to resent in his heart having Colum appointed to direct him, besides Colum seems never to know his own mind and if Boyle was sulky Colum would give in at once.[30]

A few days later Synge wrote to Frank Fay from Kerry:

I am sorry I have been so long in answering your letter. I have had several moves, and in these places it is not easy to get a quiet place to write. I sent you Boyle's play some time ago and I hope it reached you safely. I also wrote Yeats my opinion of it in brief. I have not much more to say of it and I suppose by this time it has gone through the committee for good or bad. I think it has a good deal of vitality but it is not possible in its present state, though a little revision would make it possible. I have had no news of what took place at the general meeting.

There is the most terrible rain going on here now and the thatch is dripping and splashing about my ears, in spite of tin buckets stuck about the floor to catch the drops.[31]

* * *

Possibly around 20 April, Padraic Colum wrote from Coole Park to Máire Garvey about his own new play:

Here's from the Seven Woods. I'm working very hard here trying to finish the play this week. Lady Gregory is holding me up as an example to Yeats. Yeats and I have been fishing. We have had talks about the Society and I have put our point of view very strongly. He is quite aware of W.G.'s prejudices, and I do not think is much influenced by them.

Until I have the play finished I cannot insist on a cast. I want you and Roberts to play juveniles, if you would like. Yeats and Lady Gregory agree with me as far as that is concerned. W.G. may postpone the play, but I do not think W.B. will allow it to be shelved. He is very keen on it being played this season.[32]

The new play was first presented by the Abbey on 9 June. It was now titled *The Land*, and *The Freeman's Journal* gave the production one of the best reviews that the Abbey had yet received:

If there is one thing beyond dispute in Mr. Colum's work it is his power of creating individuals. All his characters are drawn with a clear, firm hand. But he has created individuals that are at the same time typical; and it is in this way, and in this way alone, that a theatre can be a criticism of life. . . . Mr. Colum's dialogue is admirable. It lives, which is everything. It is strong, coloured, subtle, and easily rises into lyricism, as when Murtagh rejoices over the redeemed land, or Ellen asks Matt for the sights of the cities, as in the song a man offers towns to his sweetheart. The play too has a curious formal excellence. It preserves absolutely the unity of time, the whole action being compressed into something less than two hours.

Miss Nic Gharbhaigh, as Ellen Douras, had a very exacting role, and on the whole she filled it adequately. But she was hardly as exuberant or abrupt as one would imagine the part, and at times she was on the borderline of melodrama. As Matt Cosgar, Mr Mac Siubhlaigh was almost painfully strong. He showed a soul flayed and quivering; and Mr. F. J. Fay's Martin Douras is one of the most careful and convincing studies we have ever had from him. Mr. W. G. Fay, as Murtagh Cosgar, seemed to be somewhat misinterpreted by the audience. He has made his reputation in humorous parts, and his very appearance on the stage seems to create a prima facie case of laughter. As a result of this, his Murty Cosgar seemed to be taken much too lightly, and the deep irony, the essential tragedy of the part, were hardly appreciated. Cornelius was delightfully played by Mr. Arthur Sinclair; and Sally, by Miss Sara Allgood. Both parts are broadly humorous — that must be granted; but humour is little more than a point of view; and when one changed the point of view and considered the relative social "fitness" of the two who go from the land, and of the two who stay, and remembered certain lunacy statistics, one began to see grave things behind the laughter.

No play yet produced in the Abbey Theatre has so gripped and held captive an audience. There have been fuller houses, but never more enthusiastic. What we have been waiting for was a play that should be at once good and popular. Mr. Yeats has proved a little too abstruse, and Mr. Synge a little too bizarre to get fully down to the hearts of the people. . . . Mr. Colum has caught up his play out of the mid-current of actual, Irish life. . . . *The Land* is a human, actual play; it stands in a definite, luminous relation to the Ireland in which we all live and move; but if the unusually warm reception which it had last night means anything, it means that the Abbey Theatre has at last given its audience a sort of play that they want. It is the type of play that will make the theatre popular and powerful.

At the fall of the curtain the author was called on stage, and received a tremendous ovation. In response to imperative demands for a speech, he briefly returned thanks, and said that, to his mind, the function of the theatre was to put before the public strong, great types, and so contribute to the evolution in Ireland of a great democracy.[33]

The Daily Express was more reserved:

> *The Land* reveals traces of immaturity, which possibly will disappear in later efforts of the author. This is most notable in the third act, where, after some inartistic wobbling, instead of the climax which one would anticipate one is treated to an anti-climax that is distinctly disappointing. The first great merit of the play is that it is distinctly original. The dramatic material is taken from what has to the present been an absolutely untapped source.[34]

The reviewer for *The Dublin Evening Mail* thought that, 'Mr. Walker's Matt and Mr. Sinclair's Cornelius were sufficiently good, but more care might be taken with advantage of the facial make-up of some of the minor characters.' W.M.R. in a letter to *The Irish Independent* referred to 'the perfect rendering of the part of Matt Cosgar by Proinsias Mac Siubhlaigh.' L. J. M'Quilland in *Ireland's Saturday Night* had praise for Máire Garvey who played Ellen Douras: 'It is astonishing that a girl so young should have achieved so thorough an artistic triumph in a far from sympathetic part. The intensity and force of her acting is extraordinary.' By contrast, it is interesting to note that he thought Sara Allgood's Sally 'was too vehemently voluble for even the comic relief of stage flirtation.'

Although some observers admired the simplicity of staging at the Abbey, there were others who felt that it was entirely too spare and untheatrical. For instance, in a joint notice of *The Land* and *The Building Fund*, *The Irish Times* remarked:

> It would seem, indeed, that dramatic art, in its naked National Theatre Society conception, is doomed to a struggle for existence. The scenic equipment of the building, we need hardly repeat, is almost disdainfully crude.
>
> Its whole scheme disclaims the influences of alien elements, and the audience are invited to surrender themselves to admire the pure in dramatic art — according to the Society's ideals — or nothing. Thus, in *The Building Fund* there is but one scene, a poor, untrimmed cottage interior. The whole action of the comedy is carried on in this scanty apparel. No lime-light shoots its mystical influence over actors or pierces into clefts and crannies. The jar of slow music never flits across the dramatically-absorbed minds of the audience.[35]

32

Despite the generally enthusiastic reviews of Colum's play, Holloway noted that the Abbey had a depressingly small house on 12 June, Whit Monday. However, by Friday business had picked up, and he could write:

. . . the poor houses of the opening nights were forgotten in the cheery ones of to-night and last night, but large or small there was no lack of enthusiasm for *The Land*. Young Colum must have his head screwed on properly, or it must have been turned by the avalanche of eulogy heaped on the child of his imagination. That he remained the shy retiring boy through the very trying ordeal of success shows what an unassuming genius he is. It took enthusiastic applause of many minutes' duration at the conclusion of the piece to attract him on to the stage to bow his acknowledgment to the audience, and then he merely summoned up sufficient courage to give a half-frightened nod in the direction of the auditorium and retire like a frightened rabbit at the approach of the hounds. . . . He has a large following of admirers who pin their faith on him and look forward with confidence to the time when he will be the dramatist of Ireland.[36]

*   *   *

The Abbey's last new play of 1905 was another historical drama by Lady Gregory, *The White Cockade*. The play treated the aftermath of the Battle of the Boyne, in which James II ignominiously fled and left the field to William of Orange. According to Lady Gregory, writing in *Our Irish Theatre*, James Stuart was regarded in her time by the country people as a figure not only despicable, but also somewhat foolish. In her play he is a contemptible and pompous coward whose fears are remarkably droll. The central comic scene, in which he hides from the Williamite soldiers in a barrel, had already been used in a short play in Irish by Douglas Hyde, *Rig Seumas*. Hyde's fine little sketch had appeared in the Christmas 1903 number of *The Weekly Freeman*, along with a translation into English by Lady Gregory. Amusing as Hyde's sketch is, it pales in comparison with Lady Gregory's full-dress treatment. Her biographer ranks it as one of her two best history plays, and by Lady Gregory's account, 'When my *White Cockade* was first produced I was pleased to hear that J. M. Synge had said my method had made the writing of historical drama again possible.'[37]

The first production of the play on 9 December called forth the following comment from *The Freeman's Journal*:

The character of the old lady is strikingly pathetic. The great dignity of the sorrow-laden lady who has lost her estates, her ever-buoyant hopes expressed in stirring and poetic pathos, are magnificent features of the play, which raise it to a high level in the dramatic art. . . . As to the cast, it was well chosen. Foremost in it stands Miss Máire Nic Shiubhlaigh, who took the part of the Old Lady. There was a ring of pathos in her voice, and she treated the part with much grace and dignity. Mr. Arthur Sinclair was allotted the part of James. It is a difficult role to fill, but it was fully done justice to. The comical gestures expressing fear, and the undignified attitude in the barrel scene, were admirable.[38]

The Dublin Evening Mail agreed: 'Mr. Arthur Sinclair was worth coming a long way to gaze at, for his resemblance to the portraits of the Stuart King is quite startling, while his changes of expression from terror to relief, and his assumption of dignity while uttering the most ridiculous bombast could scarcely have been better.'[39] *The Daily Express* added: 'The critics of King James II have been numerous, and they have also been bitter, and it must be confessed that Lady Gregory's presentation of that monarch on the stage does not possess any feature of attractiveness.'[40] Perhaps the only telling criticism of the play was written years later by its original producer, W. G. Fay:

It is not as good a play as *Kincora*, for it lacks dramatic movement and the character of James is not well conceived, being neither fish, fowl, nor good red herring. Moreover, when a play is a mixture of fact and fiction the actors are likely to suffer from having to play a series of short scenes none of which has enough emotional scope for anyone to show his quality. In spite of his poor part, the success of the evening was Arthur Sinclair, who played King James in a make-up that was a triumph in its resemblance to the original, if we may judge by the portraits.[41]

*   *   *

Probably the most significant change for the Abbey in 1905 was the vote to dissolve the Irish National Theatre Society, and to found in its stead the National Theatre Society, Limited. This change had both immediate and lasting consequences. Immediately, it caused many petty dissatisfactions to coalesce and was a principal cause of many players resigning from the society. More importantly, it signalled the end of a democratic society of amateur

34

players by concentrating the governing responsibilities in the hands of a board of directors which consisted of Yeats, Synge, and Lady Gregory. As Gerard Fay put it, 'the first change in relationship was that the players and the small stage staff, who had been fellow-members in a society, became, overnight, employees.' [42]

One Abbey Theatre commentator, Peter Kavanagh, asserts that it was Miss Horniman who, in return for her guarantee of £600 annually for the players' salaries, 'asked that the Society assure her of its good faith by becoming a limited liability society, thereby protecting her against any serious financial loss.' [43] However, this assertion seems contradicted by the following letter which Miss Horniman wrote from the Standard Hotel, Dublin, on 26 September:

> Dear Mr. Yeats,
>
> I have already spent nearly £4000 in the Abbey Theatre and it is now proposed that I should aid in making the society into a Limited Company. I am most willing to do this but I consider that the value of the shares should bear an exact proportion to the voting power. I have always been accustomed to this in the Companies in which I already hold shares and in these Companies I obviously hold a position with a very small voting power.
>
> Yours sincerely,
> A. E. F. HORNIMAN. [44]

There are two letters of Yeats — one to John Quinn on 16 September, and one to Florence Farr in October — which make it clear that Yeats was the Machiavelli behind the change. He wrote, for instance, to Quinn:

> I think we have seen the end of the democracy in the Theatre, which was Russell's doing, [45] for I go to Dublin at the end of the week to preside at a meeting summoned to abolish it. If all goes well, Synge and Lady Gregory and I will have everything in our hands. [46]

This change was a traumatic one which was discussed for several months and which occasioned much opposition. Earlier in the year, W. G. Fay had written to Yeats:

> Our friends the enemy are saying the wildest nonsense. I met Colm today. My God, the samee gamee. Said he was coming to interview me or be interviewed. Said you were on the wrong track; I said How? [He said you were] not with the popular voice of the country. I said what is the popular

voice — Griffith, Moran, or the *Nationalist* or *Claidheamh Soluis*? . . . I asked if you were on the wrong track was he on the right one? He said he didn't know. I asked him if he was ever introduced to the Popular Voice or would know him if he met him; no reply. Says he is awaiting more evidence and will come round and see me again. Great Lord, they are beyond anything. I would as soon teach metaphysics to babies in arms as try to talk common sense with these people.[47]

In June, Colum, still disturbed, wrote to Yeats:

> As you are aware I voted for the establishment of a limited liability Company in order to save the Society from a disastrous split. I come back to Dublin and I find the Society hopelessly shattered. The one thing to be done is to re-unite the Society. Until this is done the dramatic movement is hung up. I appeal to you — I earnestly appeal to you to take steps to re-unite the groups.[48]

Despite his basic lack of interest in the theatre, Æ was regarded by many of the actors as more their natural leader than Yeats, and so he found himself their spokesman. Willie Fay's reaction to democracy in the theatre was predictably impatient, and he wrote to Yeats:

> I have just read your letter and I do not feel the slightest inclination to help Russell with his rules. They were introduced first of all by him under protest from me, for I knew quite well that in a business like this there can be no democracy. But at the time I thought it would tide things over.
>
> But now this further tinkering with them will be only temporary, and I don't feel any anxiety to dabble in them. About the voting of my position, I have stated my position which is strictly in accordance with theatrical usage. If I don't suit, a fortnight's notice concludes my engagement at any time, and as for this voting Russell may be reliable on creameries, but he hasn't the Ghost of an idea about the managing of any business as far as I can see. Would he suggest electing the Secretary of the Department by vote of the officials, or is a man put into the position because a capable person to do the work?
>
> Without my brother and myself there would never have existed any acting society to produce these plays, and if these people that we have made don't think we are competent we are both ready to leave them to do as they like when they can

elect and vote and play rough till further notice. I am just
telling you my own private feeling on these matters. I am just
fed up with this crowd of incompetent gas bags that we have
here, and they have had all the rope I intend to give them.
I've put up with more insolence and impertinence from them
than I ever put up with from anyone breathing before, and
life is too short and the world too wide to go on with it.
I am either fit to do this work or not. If I am not, well then,
the sooner I am got rid of the better for the place. If I am
supposed to be capable, then I demand as a right some respect
from these people for my position and for what work I've
done. A man can do no work that is useful if he's treated
like a dog by every boy in the place. Russell's rule pre-
supposes there is someone else in the society to do my work;
if there be in his opinion and in that of his followers, let them
bring him forward, and I will cheerfully give him my sweet
little job and depart on my travels once more. If Russell had
from the start impressed these friends of his that there is
nothing to be got in this world without plenty of hard work,
instead of listening to all their little squabbles it would have
helped us more materially than all his drafting of rules.
I feel very much upset about the desertion of the cause by
these people who signed their names and pledged their honour
to Miss Horniman and you to go on with this work to the
end, and now when the time comes to take it on in earnest
want to draw back and keep playing at it for God knows how
many years. I had no idea of this place as a place of amusement and have never from the start of it said anything but
that it was going to be real stiff work, and it seems to me now
that Russell's whole contention is that the people are being
overworked or made to do things they had never undertaken.
I will guarantee that if the present position of the Society is
placed before any competent theatrical person they will say
as Lady Gregory, yourself, Miss Horniman and any one that
has common sense, that there is only one way to go on with
it, and that is on strict businesslike lines; and as for asking
people to risk their livelihood with a society carried on in the
present slack style, it's absurd. I have no objection to do
anything in the place or obey orders when I can feel some
confidence the people who give them know what they are
talking about, but it's childish to expect me to take the
opinion of people like Starkey or Roberts on matters theatrical, when all they know about it they have heard from my
brother or myself. I expect that the Walkers won't accept the

guarantee. Máire has suddenly developed an extraordinary interest in her brother and thinks he ought to be offered more money. I said I have no objection to him getting more, and that I stated the sum as a starting basis to see how he would get on. I don't know of course whether he would settle down to work or not. . . . The brother [Frank] says he feels very shaky about them all seeing how they have shown up under present crisis, but of course he is always extra pessimistic, but still I think it will want very gentle handling to prevent a bad rupture. I feel very angry myself with them but want to do what's best for the place. It's very tough work, but I've no doubt we'll weather it some way or another.[49]

Frank Fay, of course, supported his brother, and shortly before the crucial meeting he wrote to Synge:

I am glad you will be here for the meeting. My brother is greatly disgusted at a rule, which gives the *final decision* (in the case of a dispute between the stage manager and author, as to how a scene is to be acted) to a member of the Business Committee. Of course this is a rule drawn up by a person who has little practical experience but I hope people will be put on the Business Committee *because of their fitness for transacting business*, and not for deciding artistic questions. The whole thing it seems to me is simple. The desire to act and the desire to write plays, among a number of people, gave birth to this Society. Do these people desire, as keenly, to pursue their hobbies seriously, as one would go in for music or painting, to make a profession of them, or do they wish to go on *en amateur*? What is in danger of disabling the Society, if not smashing it up, is just this and nothing else. . . . A thing that amuses me is when I hear some of our members complaining of the small audiences. How do they expect the public to take them seriously when they don't take themselves *seriously enough*? The real trouble is the lack of strong desire, except among the authors, and people must get it into their heads that this is going to be our *life work*![50]

A principal argument for changing the Society into a Limited Liability Company was that the actor-shareholders could now be paid a salary, and so the Directors sent out letters to the actors formally. For instance, Yeats wrote to Máire Garvey:

My dear Miss Garvey,
I want to remind you that there is a paid-up share in the new company awaiting your acceptance. I hope you will still

38

continue one of our players; but the share is for you whether you do or not, if you care to accept it. If you will come on with us as a player, we shall be able to find parts for you that you can do better than anybody else. I have just put three women into *Baile's Strand* and there is *Deirdre* coming on, and I hope we will have the chance of casting you for verse parts again, as well, of course, as for prose. Please let me know in a day or two.

Yours,

W. B. YEATS.[51]

The highest salary was naturally Willie Fay's two pounds a week, for his labours as director of the plays, principal actor, scene painter, and business manager. The Directors, however, probably made a tactical error in offering salaries to the others based on their importance to the theatre. Thus, Frank Fay, Arthur Sinclair, and Mary Walker were offered thirty shillings, but Frank Walker was initially offered only ten. Willie Fay discussed the matter of salary with Mary Walker and then wrote to Yeats:

> I had an interview with Moyra Walker last night and she is willing to take the moneyed engagement, but reckoned that her brother was worth more than 10s. and of course I think they are all worth more but we are too hard up to give it. But as she seemed very anxious that he should be along with her I said that I am sure we could promise him the 15s. the same as the others.[52]

On 19 December Holloway wrote:

> Had a chat with F. Walker, McDonnell [Arthur Sinclair], and Tunney on my way home. Walker told me that he intended severing his connection with the National Theatre Society, and we tried to persuade him not to. He showed us a letter he had received, signed W. B. Yeats, asking him to decide to-day as to his becoming a salaried member (15s. a week was the sum proposed to give him for his services), and he had not replied to it. McDonnell was offered £1/0/0 per week for his services. The new Company seems to have given general dissatisfaction to the members of the troupe, other than those at the head of affairs, viz — Presidents, W. B. Yeats, J. M. Synge, and Lady Gregory, Stage Manager W. G. Fay, and Secretary, F. J. Fay. And I fear there will be a smash-up of the company as at present arranged. Of course, the National Theatre Society will manage to pull itself together all right

after a time by the procuring of new blood, but the seceders are likely to drop out of the movement altogether, which would be a pity. Eternal bickering and jealousies are the curse of any movement, artistic or otherwise, in this country.[53]

There was, as Holloway predicted, a smash-up of the old company. The members who remained were Yeats, Synge, Lady Gregory, the Fays, Sara Allgood, Emma Vernon, and Udolphus Wright. Some of the players stayed on to help with the English tour and with the production of *The White Cockade* on 9 December. But the task now was to build up a new company.

* * *

Late in November and early in December, the Abbey went on tour, visiting Oxford, Cambridge, and London, and was everywhere received with respect and even enthusiasm. A commentator in *The Oxford Chronicle*, for instance, remarked that 'the main attraction in the acting of the Abbey Theatre Company is not found in its individual parts, but in the general high level attained.' Arthur Symons, in a letter to *The Sunday Times*, wrote, 'They do not seem to me clever at all; it is we who have clever actors; but one of these men [F. J. Fay] can bring beauty upon the stage and the other [W. G. Fay] can bring life.' The exposure to foreign criticism had undoubtedly a salutary effect, for that criticism was not always without some healthy reservations. For instance, the London critic 'L', writing in *The Sunday Sun*, thought:

> In Mr. Yeats's heroic play, *On Baile's Strand*, Mr. F. J. Fay, who filled the part of Cuchullain, appeared in a wig of black hair and a black gaolbird costume that made him look, as someone remarked, like a cross between a villainous James II, and Hamlet — a ridiculous and most unheroic figure. The yellow hangings, too, I found very unpleasant to the eye; and in *Kathleen Ni Houlihan*, Mr. Yeats's dramatic utterance of all that is finest in Irish patriotism, Miss Máire Nic Shiubhlaigh, as the principal figure, had her charming face wrapped in a mass of whiskerish tow that took away sadly from the dignity of her appearance. . . . Both in the literary and the dramatic point of view, *The Well of the Saints* is an affair of European importance.[54]

The arrangements for the tour had been made by Miss Horniman who booked the halls and handled the publicity. On 19 December, writing to Holloway about a slight renovation in the theatre, she mentioned the recent Abbey tour:

Mr. Fay wants something done in regard to bringing the musicians into the theatre from behind the scenes. Please try and manage this somehow. I know that you will be glad that there is to be music between the acts now. . . . I find that the net profit of the tour was £135; it was fruit of much hard work by many people. I wonder if Dublin believes that an Oxford don sold sixpenny programmes in his enthusiasm and imitated Cuchullain's "little mutterer" speech to the sword, walking home along the street in broad daylight? In London I hear from all directions of people who would have gone to see the plays if the time had been extended.[55]

The favourable reception in England did not go unnoted or uncriticized at home. For instance, an anonymous writer in *The Nationalist* remarked:

The visit of the National Theatre Company, Ltd., to Oxford, Cambridge, and London, has been, we believe, a commercial success. According to the promoters it was undertaken in order to raise money which would enable the Company to tour the provinces of Ireland. We should be written down quixotic to object to this arrangement, since the Abbey Theatre, in which the Irish National Theatre Company has been located and, we may add, lost, owes its establishment to British money.[56]

Then, after objecting that Colum's *The Land* was performed at only one matinee, whereas Yeats's *On Baile's Strand* was performed every night, the writer went on to wonder:

What is the next move of the National Theatre Company, Ltd.? It is now, of course, a commercial company, and, therefore, very properly, the actors are to be paid. It would be well if we could receive information on some points, as, for instance, what connection, if any, has the new company with the old *Irish* National Theatre Company? Are there any of the old company's funds on hand, and if so, who holds them? . . . We ask these questions that we may know how far this new venture is a National Theatre and how far it is a speculation run for the aesthetic benefit of some members who have plays to produce.

*   *   *

41

What makes the Abbey Theatre's history so interesting is partly that its critics numbered not only ardent Nationalists and narrow Philistines, but also eminent intellectuals. For instance, plays about Irish history and legend, such as *Kincora and* On *Baile's Strand*, were generally admired by patriots and well-wishers of the literary revival, but there was a small, vocal, dissenting opinion over the years which thought that such dramatizations made the subjects seem trivial. Many people had thought that the Moore-Yeats Grania was too like the modern woman with a past from a Pinero play. Standish O'Grady had said that it was definitely a mistake to dramatize the legends, and now in a newspaper article Oliver St. John Gogarty made the same point:

> I cannot help feeling that experiments like *Baile's Strand* tend to lilliputianise our legends. . . . The actors, too, by their apparent theory that the audience should be constantly reminded that each actor is to maintain, as an actor, an individuality apart from that of the character represented, when on the stage, encourages one to wish for the literary excellence of the pieces being again made the authors' only aim, regardless of misunderstanding, or present lack of appreciation. This actors' affectation of tradition, with its elocutionising and attitudinising put in place of passionate interpretation, is quite in keeping with an age which even by the very way in which we furnish our houses betrays a craving for exhumation, a craving to get out of the present and revive the life of an hundred years ago; and it is this that makes fictitious and unreal any character, no matter how forcibly it may have been portrayed by the author; it is this that made ridiculous and insignificant the definitely-drawn character of Cuchullain of *Baile's Strand*, and transformed him into a trivial, peckish, and wavering old man. The fact of the unpretentious farces being so successful and excellently acted makes the turgidity of the more serious pieces less excusable and more absurd.[57]

A distinguishing characteristic of the Irish Literary Revival is that there always, at any given time, seemed to be more writers outside it than in it. Although the criticism of the intellectual outsider has often been mere choleric indignation and denigration, it has sometimes been thoughtfully evaluative. The following selections from a long critique by Maurice Joy, a promising young poet, reflect a balanced view and are still worth consideration:

> Again, while I admire the splendid friendship which has impelled him [Yeats] into his petulant defences of Mr. Synge,

I am entitled to smile at his prophecies. Not at prophecy — it
is the only godlike virtue the lowest of us is still permitted to
exercise — but at the retributions which time is to thunder on
Mr. Synge's critics. I hope that Mr. Synge is to have a
European reputation, but I still await the evidences of it. So
do many others. Are we too sceptical? Perhaps — but then
Mr. Synge has been spoken of with Shakespeare, Aeschylus,
and Heine, and it may be we have sought in his work some
suspicion of an impossible synthesis. Then again, in a theatre
which was to be art first, art second, and art third, we have
heard heroic speeches very similar to the orations of the
modern platform, and bagpipes between the acts to console
us, I am certain, for the want of straw. We have seen a comedy
(veritably a triumph of the obvious) [probably a reference to
Boyle's *The Building Fund*] belonging to that earlier tradition
of Irish comedy which, we had supposed, the Abbey Theatre
came to abolish. However, we do not wish to press these
points, for we recognise the difficulties attendant on a young
movement; and we are by this time accustomed to the strange
ways of "circles" in all countries. They have, not seldom, the
unique power of dividing the world into two violent factions,
one which is as proud of their personal idiosyncrasies as of
their genius, and one which condemns both in the same
category. Ireland seems to be at present so divided on the
merits of Mr. Yeats and his companions — if indeed the
opponents do not believe that indifference is a greater weapon
than violence. There is room for a third party, yet, which shall
welcome with a sane admiration all good literature. . . . It
could admire Mr. Synge's pulsing, beautiful dialogue, full of
strange wandering lyricism, without thereby accepting Mr.
Synge' dramatic ventriloquism as the pure speech of the
peasant. . . . We do not ask our artists to change but we
reserve our right to accept or reject them as they are. If they
despise their audiences, they should not whine when the
compliment is returned in kind. Sometimes they make unnecessary troubles for themselves. For instance, the substi-
tution of the name, Abbey Theatre Company for Irish
National Theatre Company (which is absurd), would make
plain the way of drama here. To put the matter tersely: I do
not understand what conception of honesty justifies Mr. Yeats
in assuming the greatest Irish name it could bear for a theatre
which is, at present, obnoxious to all but a handful of the Irish
people. . . . The Abbey Theatre, at present, is doing something
to stifle the dramatic impulse which a short time ago was

apparent. . . . In a country where self-conscious literature is a new arrival it has, as it were, to prove its right to citizenship; it must show that it is sincerely a part of the authentic business of life. Its own life depending on the intense inner life of the people, it should keep for that a seemly reverence and respect. . . . There is, I am aware, too much aspersion cast on the work of Mr. Yeats and his colleagues without allowing to them their share of glory. Mr. Yeats, himself, has shown the importance of a people, and whatever be the fate of the Abbey Theatre, it will not be hard to establish his relationship with the coming literature in Ireland. Certainly, without him, literature in Gaelic would of necessity have been driven to the folk.[53]

A less tolerant criticism of Yeats and Synge was made by Daniel Corkery, who was to become an influential critic and teacher as well as a short story writer and an occasional playwright. Writing under the pseudonym of 'Lee', he made the following observations upon a lecture Yeats gave in Cork to the local theatre society:

There is no necessity to follow the lecture. We all now pretty well know the ideas of the National Theatre (too big a name, we are afraid for the Abbey Street Theatre, but handy as a label). . . .
He concluded by asking for questions from those who didn't understand. . . . a young man not, we should say, a member of the society, then got up, and rather severely and justly, we think, criticised Mr. Yeats's crowd for identifying themselves with some plays of Mr. Synge. His objection was — that those plays were not Irish plays inasmuch as they misrepresented the Irish peasant. Now, in answering, we think Mr. Yeats juggled, and fell into literary heresy. He gave a brief account of the plot of Mr. Synge's play, *The Well of the Saints.* . . . Think, said Mr. Yeats, commenting on the play, of the splendid dream these peasants had while blind — the splendid dream of each other's beauty, the splendid dream of life. Think, say we, answering, of the very sensual dream of life they must have had, if their dream was a matter of bodily beauty. Were not the minds of the two peasants known to each other by all the senses except one? — they spoke to each other day after day, they touched and kissed and yet they knew each other so ill that the appearance of their countenances, not being regular, turned love to hate. Our idea is that the dramatist stayed his hand before he had got to his matter. Give the peasants their sight; grant the shock; then

44

let God do His work; let the past years, with their loves and their trials, let these speak as undoubtedly they would; let the mere physical world fade before the memory of the love of the darkened years, and the knowledge that, in spite of the physical, such things could again be, until the peasants welcomed blindness once more lest the bodily infirmities should ever, as in the first shock, overthrow their love again. Here was a dream! — how did the man stay his hand?

Excusing this play, Mr. Yeats said that the peasants were not typical peasants — that there was no necessity why a dramatist should select typical peasants. We think this heresy. Now, there are average peasants and typical peasants. Mr. MacManus gives us the average peasant; Mr. Colum gives us the typical peasant. The shallow writer of short stories gives us the mind of the average peasant, the mind that speaks in the barber's shop, and in the current language of the day; the poet, because of his imagination, gives you the mind that sits silent in the barber's shop (though the man may speak), and that will seldom talk in the language of the hour; his characteristic quality, rusticity, having seldom occasion to speak at all. His rusticity is from age to age, seldom changing. We accordingly believe that the poet does write down the typical peasant. To take it as a guide that is not necessary to do so, what is it but to change Shakespeare's saying — "Hold the mirror up to nature," into "Hold the mirror, not up to nature, but up to nature's freaks!" This, we believe, is what Mr. Synge has done.[59]

*   *   *

The chief rivals of the Abbey Theatre in Dublin were patriotic players connected with the Gaelic League. The Keating Branch of the League was particularly active, but the players in the League's main branch organized themselves during the year into the National Players' Society, with Maud Gonne MacBride as President, Seumas MacManus, Edward Martyn, and Arthur Griffith as Vice-Presidents, J. O'Reilly as Treasurer, and Brian Callender as Secretary.

On 27 and 28 October the Keating Branch of the Gaelic League presented Thomas Hayes's *Seaghan na Scuab* and Father Dinneen's *Creideamh agus Gorta* at the Abbey. Also featured in the evening's entertainment were harps, pipes, traditional dances, and violin selections. Holloway was at the second evening and reported:

In the evening I attended the Irish concert and dramatic performance given by the Keating Branch of the Gaelic League at the Abbey Theatre and spent a delightful evening there. The pit was full, but the balcony and stalls were only fairly so. So much for all the talk about the need for plays, etc., in the Irish tongue. The people who clamour for theatre, and abuse all other artistic efforts in the English language, never attend when the opportunity arises like tonight or last night.[60]

The Gaelic League's Samhain Festival, which commenced on the following Monday in the Molesworth Hall, was billed as 'A Great Week of National Plays,' and presented an ambitious programme. On 30 October, Douglas Hyde's *An Posadh*, Lady Gilbert's *Boycotting*, and Seumas MacManus's *The Lad from Largymore* were presented. On 31 October, Hyde's *Teach na mBocht* was paired with Edward Martyn's *The Tale of a Town*. On 1 November, *An Posadh* was repeated with two more of MacManus's plays, *The Woman of Seven Sorrows* and *The Leadin' Road to Donegal*. Some of the same plays were repeated on 2, 3, and 4 November.

Arthur Griffith wrote about the Festival in two successive weeks, and his second notice was interestingly critical. His first review, however, said in part:

> The opening performances of the Samhain festival were given in the Molesworth Hall, Dublin, on Monday night. The plays produced were Dr. Hyde's *An Posadh*, Seumas Mac-Manus's *Lad from Largymore*, and Lady Gilbert's *Boycotting*. The first two have been frequently performed in Dublin, and age does not wither their attractions. Lady Gilbert's play was produced for the first time. It was written apparently in the height of the Land League agitation, and some pregnant references which occur in the text are lost on the audience of to-day, but this detracts little from the merit of a piece which has the distinction of being farcical and yet graceful. The play was enthusiastically received by the audience, and given a stage which permits of a quick change of scene, *Boycotting*, we prophesy will be one of the most popular plays Cumann na nGaedheal has yet produced. . . .
>
> *Teach na mBocht* and *The Tale of a Town* were produced before a large audience on Tuesday night. Dr. Hyde's little piece has been performed, and it sustains the reputation he has made in the dramatic field. Mr. Edward Martyn's play *The Tale of a Town* was performed for the first time, and

46

we hope to see it performed often in the future. An Irish play which brings home to us, as this does, the secret of the endurance of foreign government in this country is a national asset.[61]

However, the second notice might have convinced Yeats that Griffith did not save all of his barbs for the Abbey:

> The plays produced at the Molesworth Hall last week, with the exception of Mr. Martyn's *Tale of a Town*, are all slight pieces, which will serve a good purpose, however, by supplying the needs of local amateur dramatic societies, whose resources are not equal to producing lengthy plays. . . . The presentation of most of the pieces was unsatisfactory owing to the smallness of the stage, which prevented anything like grouping, and necessitated ringing down the curtain for a considerable interval between each scene. In such circumstances, even skilled professional actors could not do justice to a play, and the sympathy and insight of the audience was needed and given in the Molesworth Hall to make pieces of intrinsic merit go. The moral is an obvious one. . . . There are three regular theatres in Dublin, and the next Samhain dramatic festival ought to be celebrated in one or other of them. Until the stage of the regular theatre in the metropolis of Dublin is at least introduced to real Irish drama, the foundation of the National dramatic movement is insecure. The production of Irish drama as an annual event in small and difficult halls was a progressive step in 1901 and 1902 and 1903 and 1904, and perhaps even in 1905 — but it will spell retrogression in 1906.[62]

Seumas MacManus, a Vice-President of the National Players' Society, was born in County Donegal in 1861 and died almost a century later, in 1960, in New York. He was a prolific and popular writer best remembered for his humorous short stories, but he did write short plays, one of them *The Townland of Tamney* being done by Yeats's group in 1904. He was too broad a writer for great merit, and his plays are among his less remarkable works. Still, several of them were often played by amateur societies, and it is worth noting that *The Woman of Seven Sorrows* was on this occasion enthusiastically—doubtless over-enthusiastically—received:

> Mr. Seumas MacManus has given a play of great merit to the Irish dramatic stage. It is a powerful allegory, and in its production last night in the Molesworth Hall its full effect was brought out. . . . Sheila, the figurative Erin, stricken sore, full of sad memories, deserted by her children — even the

poet flying from her to seek fame and fortune in another's service, and her sons and daughters rushing off to America for gold — is upheld by Hope through all.

When she is betrayed for thirty pieces to Might, the Britannia of the allegory, she raises a cry for help, and in response to her call there throng in her faithful children of the Gaelic League, the workers in the Industrial and Language revival, and by them she is rescued from her thraldom. The climax is one of real enthusiasm and inspiration.[63]

*   *   *

The strongest rival of the Abbey was the Ulster Literary Theatre in Belfast. The second number of the theatre's journal, *Uladh* came out in February, and J. W. Good offered in it some thoughtful, qualified praise for the movement:

> The Ulster Theatre may never produce an epoch-making play, or evolve a distinctive school of acting; but if it aids, even a little, in breaking down the barrier that has so long divided the North from the South, its work will not have been in vain.
>
> But it would be wrong to imagine that its members have sacrificed art to propaganda. . . . In their plays you will find propaganda — all writers in new movements cannot hope for Mr. Yeats's serene detachment from sublunary things — but it is so handled as not to obscure the main object of the pieces as studies of character.

Of Lewis Purcell's *Reformers*, produced in 1904, he wrote:

> The theme offers open arms to vulgarity and insincerity; but if Mr. Purcell has not achieved all he aimed at, he has at least succeeded in avoiding these pitfalls. . . . I do not say his comedy is perfect; some of its developments jarred on me, and with some of its sentiments I find it impossible to agree; but a lack of subtlety is inevitable in the work of almost every young writer of promise.

And of Bulmer Hobson's *Brian of Banba*:

> Like Mr. Purcell, he has a fine eye for a dramatic situation; but he hardly succeeds as well in his presentation of the conflict of character. . . . His work is hampered by the fact that it suggests, inevitably, a contrast with the plays of Mr. Yeats; and there are few living poets who can bear the

comparison unscathed. If in *Brian of Banba* the words do not "sing and shine" as in *The Countess Cathleen* or *The King's Threshold*, if Mr. Hobson's figures have not the austere simplicity and magic appeal of Mr. Yeats's creations, yet he has drawn his inspiration from the same wells, and there is in his work something at once elemental and significant, "beauty touched with strangeness."

Of the acting he remarked:

> As yet it has not the spontaneity or the ripeness that distinguishes the Dublin Theatre, but the performances . . . proved once and for all that there is no real ground for the fears . . . that the Ulster temperament would prove an insuperable bar to success on the stage. . . . *Deirdre* showed that as far as acting went the movement was yet in its infancy; but it also proved that in the no less important art of staging and dressing the Ulster Literary Theatre need fear no comparison with its more famous rivals. Even Mr. Yeats, who in this respect will not tolerate anything that falls far short of perfection, would, I think, have been pleased with Mr. Jack Morrow's dressing and preference for convention in place of a sham naturalism, the severe simplicity of the costumes, and the skill with which they composed their colour scheme. In *Brian of Banba* they were even more successful than in *Deirdre*. It was a poetic play staged as one had often dreamt that poetic plays should be staged. The women, and the vague figures looming up against the dull-coloured draperies of the background, had in it the spirit of tragedy, and touched one as with a new revelation. To Mr. Fred Morrow in particular the members of the society wish to record their indebtedness, for they recognise that it is to him, in the first instance, that they owe whatever measure of success has been gained.[64]

The Ulster Literary Theatre feared trouble with what one might call the spirit of Ulster, and Good commented on the problem in an essay in the May issue of *Uladh*:

> That a nation should strive after industrial success need not be disputed, least of all in Ireland, which has suffered so sadly for lack of it; but that success is always worth the price the Ulsterman pays for it is not so obvious. Energy, tenacity, and thrift are considerable qualities in the making of a people; but they are not the only qualities. . . . Ulster holds by one side in this dispute, while those who have organised the new theatre urge the other. . . . All are good in themselves; but

49

when thrift verges on meanness, when tenacity becomes obstinacy, and energy finds its only outlet in a frantic struggle for wealth, it is time for those who care for life and the beauty and graciousness of life to protest. And, because the Ulster Literary Theatre seeks, before the comfortable things of the body, the more comfortable things of the spirit, and is passionately interested, not in barren abstractions, but in men and women and the expression of vital emotions, it will make that protest even if by doing so it should forfeit popular favour. We may not achieve popularity, but if our authors labour with that sincerity and devotion that the ideal they aim at demands, I do not think that an audience will be wanting. . . . To-day, as in ancient times, when young men see visions, and old men dream dreams, all things become possible.[65]

On 5 May Forrest Reid wrote an appreciative letter about the Ulster Literary Theatre to *The Northern Whig*:

> I should like to draw the attention of your readers to the two plays which are being produced this week by the Ulster Literary Theatre in the Clarence Place Hall — *The Little Cowherd of Slainge*, by Mr. MacCathmhaoil, and *The Enthusiast*, by Mr. Lewis Purcell; and I should particularly like to draw attention to Mr. Purcell's comedy, because in it he has given us a play which, in construction, in unity of effect, in dramatic power and insight, in humour, in freshness, in originality, is infinitely superior to any modern play that I have ever seen performed in Belfast, with the exception of two or three comedies by Oscar Wilde and Mr. Bernard Shaw. *The Enthusiast* is, in short, a little work of art, and worth a hundred of the productions of the Pineros and Joneses we are so frequently asked to applaud to-day. The acting and staging of both pieces are, too, quite admirable, so that to neglect this opportunity of being present at performances in every respect so praiseworthy, so sincerely artistic, is to be guilty of a lamentable indifference to the art of the drama at a time when that art is most in need of support and encouragement.[66]

Arthur Griffith saw the May productions of the Ulster Literary Theatre in Belfast, and gave them the following short notice:

> The play *The Enthusiast*, as befits a comedy of life, is not complex in conception. Each character is drawn with simplicity and strength, without over-elaboration of detail. The construction also is of a very high excellence. The dialogue and action are brisk, and full of dour, dry Northern humour.

50

From start to end, *The Enthusiast* is a piece of fine work of high artistic finish, admirably staged and acted. If Mr. Purcell, as we expect, develops along the line of his *Reformers* and *The Enthusiast*, he will have reason to deserve well of Ulster.

> *The Little Cowherd of Slainge*, by Seosamh MacCathmhaoil, which was published in the Samhain number of *Uladh*, was the second dramatic item on the programme. It is best described in the author's words as "a dramatic legend," for of dramatic development and climax there is, strictly, too little for our satisfaction. . . . Dramatically the play is weak, but the acting of Miss Josephine Campbell (Fionnghuala) in the first scene was admirable. Given such a part as Gormleith in *Kincora*, Miss Campbell would have opportunity to show her power. . . .[67]

In the fourth, and unfortunately, the last issue of *Uladh*, which appeared in September, there appeared the following unsigned note about the production of *Brian of Banba* and *The Enthusiast*:

> *Brian* quite carried away the audience in all parts of the hall. The heroic play, therefore, with actors like Messrs. John Campbell and Gordon in the leading parts, is a sure popular success in the country. In *The Enthusiast* the effect on the audience was curiously instructive. It was of a mixed kind. They entered into the fun and the homely touches of type, local idiom and situation generally with the greatest enthusiasm. But it is very doubtful if the tragedy, the point of the play, reached more than a very small number of those present. This was due to the over-subtlety of the shortened final scene; the significance of the sound of the drum was not made plain enough. This, and other points of a similar nature in works of the kind, will in the future require to be made unmistakeable for the country audience; quite blunt and plain in fact.[68]

In the same issue, Seosamh de Paor gave a trenchant resumé of the work of the theatre thus far. He opened by answering a criticism of provincialism:

> It seems to me that if Ulster be true to its instincts it must of necessity have a somewhat different point of view from the rest of Ireland. . . . North is North, and South is South, irrevocably, and though the line of demarcation be not so firmly drawn as between the Occident and the Orient, it nevertheless demands recognition. Ulster *has* "its own way of things"; Belfast differs as widely from Dublin as Madrid from

51

Seville; and for it to ape the South, East or West were every whit as reprehensible as that the people of those districts should continue in slavish imitation of things English. . . .

The Northern Theatre is, of course, too young as yet for any real comparison with that of the Irish metropolis. There seems, however, to be this initial distinction that whereas Mr. Yeats, Mr. Martyn, and Mr. George Moore set out to create an Irish stage, whilst obsessed by Ibsen and Maeterlinck, our Northern playwrights appear to have written of their own spontaneity, without consciously imitating anyone. . . . For my part, I think if Mr. Purcell had studied the Norwegian dramatist's treatment of the subject, *The Enthusiast* would have profited considerably. As it is he has by no means realised the possibilities of the situation; he has dealt too curtly with it. The same method applied to Iben's play would mean confining it to acts one and four — in the first the doctor launches his discovery, in the other it is rejected by the community, and he is proclaimed an enemy of the people.

Of *The Little Cowherd of Slainge*, he wrote quite justly:

That Seosamh MacCathmhaoil can produce good work is indisputable; that he has not done so in this little picture of ancient Ireland is equally so. It is not adapted for dramatic presentation.

And finally he concluded:

The Ulster Literary Theatre Society may not yet have reached the level of Dublin so far as acting is concerned — I do not concede the fact — but if they have not they certainly must be admitted to be very little behind. If they have not Mr. W. G. Fay, they have Mr. Fred. Morrow, than whom a better stage-manager for their purpose could not be desired. Under his care each successive performance has marked a distinct improvement. With regard to the plays themselves, Mr. Purcell's are the only ones which show a difference from the ideals of the metropolis, and of them it may safely be said that they go far to justify Ulster's claim to have a personality of its own. There are other Ulstermen now a-writing, and I think it will not be found that their productions will further support that claim. I could wish, however, that at least a few of the plays were in Gaelic, for if we are ever to have a distinctively National Theatre, its performances must be in the native language. Some of the Dublin men have journeyed Northwards to see the productions of the Ulster Theatre;

52

perhaps some day soon the Ultonians may return the visit. Certainly they need now fear to face neither an audience of the Irish nor of the English capital.[69]

'John O'Loughlin' was the pseudonym of J. J. Horgan, who wrote, so far as we can discover, no other plays. And, indeed, the Cork National Theatre Society, despite its auspicious beginning, mounted no further productions; and there were no more stirrings of the dramatic movement in Cork until the formation of the Cork Dramatic Society in 1908.

*   *   *

On 25 March Griffith gave a short notice to a recent programme of the Cork National Theatre Society:

> The Cork National Theatre produced recently before a large and appreciative audience in the Assembly Rooms three plays, *The Last of the Desmonds*, by Miss Alice Milligan; *Kathleen Ni Houlihan*; and *The Nation Builders*, by "John O'Loughlin", of Cork. The plays were, on the whole, well-performed. *The Last of the Desmonds*, which was published in *The United Irishman* some months ago, deals with Irish life in the days of Hugh O'Neill. The costumes, which were designed by Miss Milligan, were pretty, and gave a romantic touch of colour to the stage. The parts were acted realistically; indeed, in one instance, perhaps too realistically. *Kathleen Ni Houlihan* suffered from the failure of the audience to apprehend its symbolic character. Mairghead Ni Chronin performed the part of Kathleen Ni Houlihan, with grace and sympathy. The third play, *The Nation Builders*, dealt with the language and industrial movements. In the strict sense of the word, *The Nation Builders* can scarcely be called a drama, but it was undoubtedly a successful and very effective way of preaching the National ideals.[70]

Arthur Clery, in *The Leader*, gave a further short description of *The Nation Builders*, which was one of the first social dramas since Fred Ryan's *The Laying of the Foundations*:

> *The Nation Builders* was a most original play. Evidently propagandist in character, it was intended as an expression of the Irish Ireland movement on its industrial side. It dealt with the fortunes not of a man but of a company. . . . The moral of the piece is that Irish industry should depend on Irish capital.[71]

*   *   *

53

The offerings of the commercial theatres were little changed from previous years. Among the notable attractions at the Gaiety were Edmund Tearle and his Company in a repertoire of melodramas and Shakespearean tragedies; Laurence Irving, whose brilliant father died during the year; the Compton Comedy Company; the Representative Irish Players, including the 'famous Irish Actor' Mr. E. C. Matthews in Boucicault; the D'Oyly Carte; Marie Tempest in a light comedy; and Harry Lauder and his Recital Party. Of the latter, Holloway remarked disgustedly, 'This week for the first time in the history of the Gaiety Theatre was its stage given over to a variety entertainment pure and simple, and I sincerely hope that the experiment won't be repeated.'

The year's most remarkable commercial productions were probably Beerbohm Tree and his Company in *The Tempest* at the Theatre Royal, and Sarah Bernhardt and Mrs. Patrick Campbell at the Gaiety in Maeterlinck's *Pelléas and Mélisande*. Holloway thought that Tree's *Tempest* 'with all its noise, music and scenic splendour . . . turned out nothing more or less than a rotten pantomime — with the fun omitted.' Despite the Divine Sarah and Mrs. Pat, Holloway thought *Pelléas and Mélisande* too static for the stage, and it reminded him of Yeats's *Shadowy Waters*: 'Dream folk, in a dream atmosphere of dim light and shade — all wailing — all gloom — all sorrow!' [72]

The Queen's also continued its usual programming policy, but there was one curious exception — the revival by Osmond Tearle's Shakespearean and Old Comedy Company of Gerald Griffin's *Gisippus*, which had first been presented by Macready at Drury Lane in the mid-nineteenth century. It retained little power to please.

Another commercial development which was a significant symptom of the growth of interest in Irish drama (and, naturally, in Irish literature in general) was the publication on 18 November of the first book by a new Dublin firm, Maunsel & Co. The leading spirit was George Roberts, who had been a member of the Irish National Theatre Society, and the firm was to number among its publications of new Irish works many plays, particularly in the first fifteen volumes of its distinguished Abbey Theatre series.

*   *   *

With the exception of Synge's play, all of the new pieces at the Abbey were greeted with respect and even admiration. The plays of William Boyle and Lady Gregory became relatively popular. The case of Boyle's *The Building Fund* is particularly interesting, because it was a hard and caustic comedy which amused audiences at the same time as it presented the Irish character in a distinctly unflattering light. Yet all of the commentators, save Griffith, went out of their way to make a distinction between Boyle's work, which made to them a valid criticism, and Synge's, which seemed to them simply insulting misrepresentation. The reason for this distinction may have been that Boyle's easily apprehensible realistic dialogue aroused laughter, and that the rich embroidery of Synge's difficult dialogue did not so much arouse laughter as demand admiration. At any rate, it was Synge, rather than Lady Gregory or Boyle or Padraic Colum, who seemed to typify in the minds of Dubliners the Abbey Theatre.

Interestingly enough, the suspicion and animosity directed towards Synge was phrased in the same terms as that which, four and five years earlier, had been levelled at George Moore. They were both described as morbid, sensual, decadent, un-Irish, and influenced by the highly suspect French. It is particularly fitting that Moore should from time to time express his admiration for Synge, upon whom to an extent his own mantle had fallen. The following valedictory interview with Moore seems, then, an appropriate conclusion to 1905:

Mr. Moore has decided to live in Dublin no longer. Not that "all those charms have fled." Its beauties, he admits, remain. But Dublin is becoming nowadays "no sort of place to live in."

"It is," he said, "growing more and more provincial every day. There is no life, intellectual or artistic, or social, in any true sense of the word. I stayed until I found myself the one solitary person who was in Dublin for any other reason than that of having to be. Then I gave it up. The only people who live there are officials. Even they are getting into the habit of living out of the town. The place is emptying, house by house. Frankly, I think they will soon have to bring in a Bill just to compel officials to take houses in Merrion Square and St. Stephen's Green!" . . .

I suggested, in a final gasp, the literary revival. "There is no literary revival," replied Mr. Moore crushingly. "There is only one man, Mr. Synge, and he has written only one really beautiful play, *The Well of the Wise* [sic]." [73]

1906

In his memoir, *The Fays of the Abbey Theatre*, W. G. Fay summed up 1906 by remarking:

> . . . taking it all round, we had put in a creditable year's work. We had produced seven new plays and toured for more than ten weeks, securing future dates at eight theatres where we reckoned on doing better business every time we visited them. At the end of October I managed to dash over to Glasgow for a week-end, and in Shamrock Street of happy omen was married to Brigit O'Dempsey. For me, at any rate, 1906 was a successful year, the most successful of my life hitherto.[1]

But if 1906 was a year of growing popularity, it was also a time of increasing internal tensions which threatened to split the Abbey Theatre hopelessly apart. First, there was the secession of Máire and Frank Walker, George Roberts, Máire Garvey, and Padraic Colum who were during the year to found the Abbey's most formidable rival, the Theatre of Ireland. But even more important was the growing irritation of Miss Horniman with Willie Fay. Slights and fancied slights finally culminated in her insistence on hiring an English manager who would replace Fay as producer of all but the peasant plays.

*   *   *

On 9 January Miss Horniman wrote a formal letter to Yeats:

Official
To the President of the Irish National Theatre Society.
Dear Mr. Yeats,

I am informed that various of the members of the Irish National Theatre Society, yourself amongst them, have formed a Limited Company called the National Theatre Society, Ltd. I highly approve of this for, as I have spent so much time and money on my side, I consider it to be fair that every precaution should be taken by the members towards carrying out the objects as announced by you. I hereby transfer my gift of the free use of the Abbey Theatre (on the same conditions as before) to the National Theatre Society, Ltd., as I consider that the Limited Company will honestly carry out my intentions. Those members who have not followed you have completely ignored me, and so I have no reason to believe that they wish for my further help in any way. They have never formally protested to me against your new plan, and so under whatever name they may choose to call themselves, I can have nothing to do with them. The theatre is a means for carrying out a certain theatrical scheme, and as long as you continue in the same path, the theatre is at the disposal of you and your friends under whatever title you may choose to use.[2]

The dissatisfaction which the Walkers, Roberts, Máire Garvey and others had felt with the Irish National Theatre Society and with the change into a Limited Company resulted, early in 1906, in the second major secession of the Society's actors. Yeats's reaction to the new secession appears in this letter of 6 January, which he wrote to Synge from London:

I have had a wire from Fay: "Enemy rehearsing *Land* author present letter tonight Fay." I am delighted. This is far better than a vague feeling of irritation. Everything they do would only reveal the superiority of our work. *The Land* without the two Fays will be a miserable thing. If you see Colum be firm with him, he is with them now for all his works, and if he comes back to us he comes with all his work. They will either collapse after a performance or two or they will become more and more crudely propagandist playing up to that element in the country. This too will be a gain for it will show the division that underlies all the petty disputes, the division between those who want good play-writing, and those who do not. We will lose none of our people in that battle, for the few hundreds of supporters — four or five hundred at the most, three hundred to the worse, I am judging by sale of programmes — are from the general public and they care no more for clubs than we do.[3]

Miss Horniman felt that the seceders were impelled merely by political motives, and she wrote to Synge from Paris on 7 January:

We must know where we stand quite clearly. My personal position is this — I gave a theatre for a certain scheme — changes were made in the government for the benefit of the scheme — I approved of it — the objectors completely ignored me and their own signatures to a letter of 1904 — they have never lodged any complaints with me nor have they given me any reason for their actions — I have sent the original of the enclosed to Mr. Yeats — maybe it will not be sufficient but it will do to let people know my intentions.

I never made the slightest pretensions to any political sympathies and the objectors knew this quite well when they accepted the use of the theatre. If they had asked me before signing the letter it would have been much better. I only had time to send you a postcard yesterday to catch the post. I will carefully follow any advice sent to me so that our position may be made quite clear.

I wrote on Sunday to Colum and told him that he could not have the theatre. If anyone thinks that "Irish" or "National" are anything to me beyond mere empty words used to distinguish a Society, merely a title for convenience, they are much mistaken. I have a copy of my letter here as well as the original signed answer. The theatre was given for the carrying out of Mr. Yeats's artistic dramatic schemes and for no other reasons. These patriots are all jealous of *Art*, they want to keep the standard down so as to shine themselves. "In the Kingdom of the Blind, the one-eyed man is King."

This row will perhaps even further diminish our audiences; but we must have patience and show a bold front. It is possible that if the fuss becomes public it will eventually do some good as shewing that we are *not* a "political side-show." [4]

On 7 January Lady Gregory wrote to Colum:

Dear Mr. Colum,

I have heard on what seems to be good authority that *The Land* is being put in rehearsal by a section of the old Society which has not so far joined the new one. I can hardly believe this, especially as Mr. Yeats sent me a letter he had received from you on the subject of the Theatre a few days ago, in which you did not make any mention of this performance, and I feel sure you would not act in an underhand way.

My first thought was "It cannot be true"; my second, "If true, so much the better; it was resentment about the cast of *The Land* that led in some measure to the break-up of the Society. William Fay will be justified now; and both the Fays who are being attacked here and there, will justify our belief in them when it is seen how heavily the play loses by their absence. Let it be acted by all means." My third thought, after a day of quiet consideration, is that if it is true, you are thoughtlessly committing a folly which you will probably be afterwards sorry for. You may spare a few hours before making a decision that will, I think, affect your work and your life. I want you to sit down and read Mr. Yeats's notes in the two last numbers of *Samhain* and to ask yourself if the work

59

he is doing is worth helping or hindering. Remember, he has been for eight years working with his whole heart for the creation, the furtherance, the perfecting, of what he believes will be a great dramatic movement in Ireland. I am proud to think I have helped him all through, but we have lost many helpers on the way. Mr. Lecky, who had served us well in getting the law passed that made all these dramatic experiments possible, publicly repudiates us because of Mr. Yeats's letter on the Queen's visit. Edward Martyn withdrew when we had to refuse the *Tale of a Town* which did not as we thought come up to the required standard. George Moore from a friend became an enemy. Then after he had become President of the Irish National Theatre, which has done such good work, others were lost for different reasons, Kelly and Digges, and Miss Quinn and Mrs. MacBride, all of whom had been helpful in their time. Now others are dropping off. It is always sad to lose fellow workers, but the work must go on all the same. "No man putting his hand to the plough and looking back is fit for the Kingdom of God." He is going on with it, I am going on with it as long as life and strength are left to me. You, who being younger, ought to take some of the burden off our shoulders, will not, I think, intentionally make it heavier. There are two special reasons why you will not think it right to even consent to this performance of *The Land*. One is that your doing so at this moment would be looked upon as a corroboration of the most unjust and unworthy insinuations made in some papers that it had been intentionally given the worst place in the London programme. The other is that you cannot have forgotten the most generous and wholehearted help Mr. Yeats gave you on this very play, taking his best thought, his time and energy from his own work to do so. He has never alluded to this himself, and would not like you to feel under any debt, but I feel sure that you would not like to show lesser generosity than his. I am sure you are having a good deal of worry. It is hard to hold one's own against those one is living amongst. I have found that, and I have found that peace comes not from trying to please one's neighbours, but in making up one's own mind what is the right path and in then keeping to it. And so, God save Ireland and you, and believe me your sincere friend,

A. G.[5]

Two days later, Lady Gregory wrote to Colum again:

60

You ask me to urge Mr. Yeats to take steps towards re-union. I thought I might find in your letter what the complaint against us is, but I only find that we are becoming less and less a theatre of the people. I don't agree with you, I think we are nearer being one, because of the plays we now have in stock. . . . I was always against a 1/- pit, but it was decided to let Miss Horniman have her way about it for a year or so. I think we shall very soon be able to change it for a 6d one. . . . I have heard very little of the other side except from Mr. Roberts, and his only complaints were against William Fay as stage manager, and we certainly do not intend to give him up or to give him less authority than is given to other stage-managers. . . . We refused and must still refuse the "one man, one vote" (an English Radical cry); it gave too much power to lookers-on. Authors were given the chief power as directors. I told the others that I hoped to resign in your favour after a time (the sooner that could be, the better I should be pleased) but for your own sake as well as our own, we decided it was better I should share the responsibility for the present.[6]

On 10 January Lady Gregory wrote to Synge:

Russell is responsible for a great deal, for he undertook to settle the whole matter in the summer; he proposed to do so himself and left us worse than before. Yeats wrote to him the other day, and only received a letter full of all the disagreeable things and personalities he found possible to say, and the real cause comes at the end: "you went about sneering at *Deirdre* and saying it was a bad and popular play"! I am sure he never said it was popular![7]

Eventually the Abbey group made a settlement with the seceders, allowing them some use of the theatre, some of the costumes, and a portion of the theatre's surplus funds. Still, there were difficulties and omens of future difficulties. On 20 February Lady Gregory wrote to Synge that Miss Horniman:

. . . demands to see a list of all plays proposed to be played in the Theatre, and will refuse its use if she disapproves of plays, that is, if there are propagandist ones. She has, no doubt, a right to do this but her exercising it just after we had "agreed" to the opposition playing in the Theatre might put us in a very uncomfortable position. She would, Yeats said, object to *The Saxon Shillin'*, and this would quite possibly be on the first or second programme. It seems as if honesty calls on us to warn the other side about this, but if we do, it may make them refuse any arrangements, for they would get backing if they could say an English woman was exercising censorship, and that they refused while we submitted to it. Of course we should not submit to it, but if we said that, they would say they were being treated unfairly in being expected to do so. All that matters to us is that we should have our conscience quite clear in the negotiations, and I am inclined to think Russell ought to be told of this new and exasperating move of Miss Horniman. . . . I myself think a propagandist theatre would be very useful, but it is not what she spent her money for. But I wish she would let them act what they will, and show their weakness, and fizzle themselves out.[8]

By now, there had been so much dissension that inevitably there was a lingering bitterness between the two groups. For instance, in *The United Irishman* for 10 March Arthur Griffith reported:

We have received the following letter from one of the members of the Irish National Theatre Society. As some of our readers are aware, the attempt to convert the Abbey Theatre into "a Theatre of Commerce", has led to the strenuous opposition on the part of the bulk of the members. However, the commercial minority has secured possession of the theatre, and is now about to proceed on a tour through the country, arrayed in the plumes of their opponents. It is this last injustice which has impelled our correspondent to place the position of affairs with regard to the Abbey Theatre before the public. He writes: — "A dramatic society calling itself 'The National Theatre Company from the Abbey Theatre' gave performances in Wexford last week. It might be interesting to your readers to know exactly what pretensions this body has to lay claim to the title 'National'. From the official lists I find that they were registered under the Friendly and Industrial Societies' Acts on October 24th, 1905. The signatories requesting the registration are Lady Gregory, Mr. W. B. Yeats, Miss Vera Esposito, Mr. Udolphus Wright, Mr. John Synge, and Messrs. Fay. It would be well for the general public to know that they in no wise represent the Irish National Theatre Society which was registered on the 30th December, 1903, for the purpose of producing dramatic work which would have a definite bearing upon the national aspirations of this country. The company which performed in Wexford is a secession from the original society, representing those members who had definitely abandoned the possibility of producing good dramatic performances on broadly-defined national lines. In confirmation of this I would adduce the following fact. One of the rules of the parent society is as follows:

Section 6 (d) — No play shall be accepted or rejected on political grounds solely, and the literary, dramatic, and acting merits of the play shall primarily be considered, and no objection raised to a play on the ground that its performance would antagonise any political party shall be valid unless it should be considered that there is any degradation of National ideals in the work submitted.

This rule, which no one can accuse of being intemperately worded was deliberately repudiated by Mr. W. B. Yeats in his capacity of President of the original Irish National Theatre Society at one of their meetings. Mr. Yeats is now the leading spirit in the seceding members who, having abandoned the fundamental principle of the original society, nevertheless keep on appearing before the public without a word of explanation as carrying on the objects for which the parent body was formed. Any person who attended the performances in Wexford in the hope that he was encouraging the development of a national drama will be sadly mistaken. The National Theatre Society, Limited, is a body run in the interest of one person, Mr. W. B. Yeats, who has proved himself capable of absorbing for his own personal ends the disinterested work of a large number of people given on the understanding that they were aiding in a work which was devoted primarily to the development of the highest interests of nationality in this country. If any further proof of this is required I have only to point to the fact that in the formation of the new society Mr. Yeats deliberately dropped the names of those — such as Douglas Hyde and Padraic Colum — who were committed to definitely Nationalist or political beliefs. His own opinions in this direction have vacillated so considerably of late that it would be impossible at this moment for any sane man to say what they are. A man's opinions can, however, be very fairly gauged by the company he keeps, and when we remember that the two names Mr. Yeats has deliberately chosen to assist him in his undertaking are Mr. John Synge and Lady Gregory the objects he has in view will become much clearer, for both his fellow-directors have distinctly stated that their interest in the movement is purely a literary one. The plain fact then remains that Mr. Yeats is trying to foist a purely literary movement upon the people of Ireland as a national one. If this were distinctly stated, I for one would have much sympathy with it, but coming in this way, as a wolf clothed in sheep's skins, I can only raise a note of warning, and point out clearly that in spite of imprimatur from John Redmond and the like (founded chiefly upon ignorance of the actual state of affairs) anyone supporting the performances of the National Theatre Society, Limited, under the impression that he is thereby supporting the cause of nationalism, is labouring under a grievous misapprehension. Mr. Yeats took particular pains when founding the new society, by numerous consultations with his lawyers, to ensure that his power in the society would be predominant. This he has secured by having it registered as an industrial society, in which every member has a vote for every share he holds. No one member can hold more than 200 shares of £1 each, and it is a matter of public knowledge that this amount has been, or is to be, put into the society by friends of Mr. Yeats, either in his name or in that of one or more nominees, to ensure his control being predominant."

The letter reveals a very regrettable condition of affairs which could not have arisen if Mr. Yeats had followed the advice we gave a few years ago in these columns. Everybody will be sorry for the conversion of our best lyric poet into a limited liability company.[9]

*   *   *

Although the Abbey produced some of its more memorable and popular plays in 1906, the newspaper accounts of the productions are disappointingly unilluminating. The brilliant short plays of Lady Gregory tended to be dismissed in a terse paragraph of vague praise, while Yeats's work, if praised for its poetry, was usually damned for its lack of theatricality. In short, the year's journalism sheds little light on either the quality of the plays or the nature of their playing.

When *Hyacinth Halvey*, Lady Gregory's classic comedy, was first produced on 19 February, *The Irish Times* could only generalize that it was 'very amusing' and that Lady Gregory displayed 'a keen appreciation of true humour'. *The Irish Independent* thought that it was 'extremely amusing' and that Lady Gregory had skilfully introduced 'a good deal of quiet and characteristic humour'. *The Freeman's Journal* more impressively noted that 'the risible faculties' of a 'large, cultured and fashionable audience' were kept employed.

On 16 April the Abbey produced Lady Gregory's translation from Molière, *The Doctor in Spite of Himself*, and a much-revised

64

version of Yeats's *On Baile's Strand*. *The Irish Times* noted that Lady Gregory 'presented a dialogue which is easily acted, while all the humour of the original is faithfully preserved.' None of the papers made any more discerning remark, but they all agreed that the audience was amused. As *The Freeman's Journal* somewhat typically put it: 'Continuous peals of laughter testified to the risibility of the farce.'

In this instance, the poetry of Yeats's play was admired, but the theatrical effectiveness was also admitted by *The Irish Times* and *The Daily Express*. *The Freeman's Journal* was somewhat more specific and critical:

Like nearly all reconstructed dramatic works, it did not reach the high anticipations which the very fact of remodelling engendered. Nevertheless, it must not be thought that it does not attain to a considerable height of excellence. It would not, however, have suffered if some of the speeches had been curtailed or so broken up by interjected dialogue as to deprive them of the character of lengthy monologues. Mr. F. J. Fay's portrayal of the erstwhile unbending and ill-fated Cuchullain was cast in an undeniably heroic mould. Deeply effective was his frenzied declamation on learning that the youth who had so stoutly confronted him in mortal combat, and whom he had slain, was his own son. Mr. W. G. Fay did some excellent fooling in his depiction of Barach, whilst as Fintain, the blind half-seer and burly mendicant, Mr. A. Power added considerably to the success of the drama. Mr. U. Wright was rather stiff in his delineation of Cuchullain's son, but his make-up, so as to convey the idea of femininity, by which his father discovered in him a likeness to his mother, was unimpeachable. The piece was admirably mounted, the oath scene being weirdly grand. The play was enthusiastically applauded.[10]

On 19 October the Abbey opened its winter season with Lady Gregory's short tragedy, *The Gaol Gate*, and William Boyle's new comedy, *The Mineral Workers*. Of Boyle's play, Yeats wrote in the theatre's new magazine, *The Arrow*:

Mr. Boyle has used the struggles of an Irish-American engineer who is trying to smelt ore in Ireland, as a symbol to represent the difficulties of any enthusiast who attempts, in a country demoralized by failure, to change anything or establish anything that would mean a break with settled habits and interests. He knows the country well — or rather the country-side where he was born and bred, and no man knows more of the world than that, if the knowledge one means is that instinctive kind that goes to making plays of character. His people are individuals, but they are also types, and there is something of the national tragedy in the play. Every man is ready, in Mr. O'Grady's phrase, to break ranks and go hunting hares, because no man believes that the marching is going to bring him to anything better than a night's sleep. But if you have no mind for meanings, you can take the play, and I hope any play we produce, as a story, and be content.[11]

The Irish Times described the piece more specifically:

It deals with the discouragements and trials of a smart Irish-American engineer, who is trying to smelt ore in a purely pastoral district in Ireland. The break on the part of the peasantry with settled habits and interests, the change from farming to industrial enterprise, and the reluctance of the people to accept the new order of things are intensified by the mischievous activity of the local agitator, but in the end the young engineer triumphs.[12]

The play was a hint of the direction which the Abbey was to take, and actually rather resembles some of the comedies that George Shiels was to write in the 1920s and 1930s. Much simpler and more conventional than the work of Yeats, Synge, and Lady Gregory, Boyle's plays tended to be overpraised. In this case, *The Irish Independent* thought it 'an exceedingly clever and pleasant comedy'. *The Irish Times* considered it 'splendidly written . . . with many a sparkling epigram on the rooted inconsistencies of Irish life.' *The Freeman's Journal* saw it as the best of Boyle's plays, 'instinct with mirth-provoking humour, incisive repartee, telling situations, and far and away and above all, lifelike presentations of certain types of Irish character.'

In contrast, Lady Gregory's masterly short tragedy, *The Gaol Gate*, was dismissed by *The Daily Express* as 'a work of mournful type' and by *The Irish Times* as 'a rather unconventional, not to say unconvincing, piece of work'. Only *The Freeman's Journal* remarked, 'into that one act is thrown an all but infinity of the deepest pathos.'

The criticism of acting tended to be just as imperceptive and peremptory. When a player was liked, he either 'gave a display of high histrionic powers' or 'delivered a capital interpretation' or 'was a decided acquisition to the play'. *The Gaol Gate* gave both Sara Allgood, as the suffering mother, and Máire O'Neill, as the young wife, one of their finest roles. However, *The Freeman's Journal* could only remark that they 'artistically sustained the parts', while *The Irish Times* even thought that their portrayal of grief 'lacked convincing power'.

Yeats's *Deirdre* was first produced on 24 November.[13] The most sympathetic notice that this short verse tragedy received was from *The Freeman's Journal* which considered it 'powerful' and, somewhat bafflingly, 'racy of the soil'. *The Daily Express, The Irish Independent,* and *The Irish Times* all thought it beautiful but undramatic. 'It is,' wrote *The Express,* 'too heavily weighted with grandiloquent melancholy.' 'It lacks,' according to *The Independent,* 'certain of the essentials of a successful stage production.' 'It is charged with poetic feeling, and enlivened with all the charming fancies of a highly cultivated imagination,' wrote *The Irish Times,* 'but these admirable qualities, even when they are welded into smooth-flowing verse, do not compensate for the absence of . . . dramatic elements. . . .' 'It is,' wrote Mícheál O Conaire in *Sinn Féin,* 'of course, no nearer to being a play than any of his previous attempts. The devices and general shifts of his stagecraft (or want of it) are as palpable and futile as ever, but the lyric sung by the three musicians at the entrance of Deirdre is a superb thing. . . .'

For this production, Yeats had brought in an actress who used the stage name of Miss Darragh,[14] and who had recently had several successes in London. Although admired by the Press, she was resented by both the Abbey actors and the Nationalists. Again, as Mícheál O Conaire wrote in *Sinn Féin*:

> The acting on Saturday night does not call for much notice. We were informed on the posters and in the papers, for weeks before the performance, that the leading part would be played by the famous Irish actress (*from London*) who had played in (of all plays in the world) *The Walls of Jericho,* and we got exactly what we might have, if we had been wise, expected. Miss Darragh is thoroughly competent. She has almost everything that the modern players' art can teach her. No trick is missing from her repertoire. Her exit was as fine as gesture and facial expression and the superficial art of the player could make it; but — wanting is what? Well, that I leave to those who remember (and who that has seen it once could forget?) the splendid and sorrowful beauty of the Deirdre of Máire Nic Shiubhlaigh in Æ's play. A performance which stands out as the play itself does, absolutely alone. Mr. Fay in his interpretation of the rather insignificant figure

of Naisi did all that he could with such a knock-kneed part.
. . . "A word of praise" is due to Miss Sara Allgood, the
music of whose voice was some compensation for the total
want of it in the lady who played the leading part.[15]

Years later, W. G. Fay analyzed Miss Darragh's acting also:

The public and the Press voted her magnificent. She was
manifestly a highly trained professional, the like of which was
not among us. But in my eyes it was just this manifestness
that ruined the show. It did not fit with our technique, which,
for all its lack of obviousness, had been slyly planned so as to
get a special effect out of special material. It was like putting
a Rolls Royce to run in a race with a lot of hill ponies up the
Mountains of Mourne, bogs and all. The ponies, knowing
each inch of the way, could outpace the Rolls every time. On
the one hand, Miss Darragh made our company look young
and simple, and, on the other hand, their youth and simplicity
made her look as if she were over-acting.[16]

On 8 December the Abbey produced Lady Gregory's *The
Canavans* and a revised version of Yeats's *The Shadowy Waters*.
For Yeats's play, Robert Gregory designed the set and supervised
the lighting effects, and Arthur Darley composed some special
music. A preliminary notice in *The Freeman's Journal* noted that
the play's enchanted sea and strange birds made it reminiscent of
Coleridge's 'Ancient Mariner'. Yeats himself wrote in *The Arrow*:

I began *The Shadowy Waters* when I was a boy, and when
I published a version of it six or seven years ago, the plot
had been so often rearranged and was so overgrown with
symbolical ideas that the poem was obscure and vague. It
found its way on to the stage more or less by accident, for
our people had taken it as an exercise in the speaking of
verse, and it pleased a few friends, though it must have
bewildered and bored the greater portion of the audience.
The present version is practically a new poem, and is, I
believe, sufficiently simple, appealing to no knowledge more
esoteric than is necessary for the understanding of any of the
more characteristic love-poems of Shelley or of Petrarch. If
the audience will understand it as a fairy-tale, and not look
too anxiously for a meaning, all will be well.[17]

The reviews all said the same thing. *The Daily Express* said it
bluntly: 'The composition has great literary merit, but for stage
representation it lacks dramatic body and strength.' *Sinn Féin*
said it caustically:

. . . *The Shadowy Waters* by Mr. W. B. Yeats, and *The Canavans* by Lady Gregory. The first-named is described as "a play in verse," and the second as "a comedy in three acts." It was, however, somewhat difficult at times to discover the "play" in the first item, or the "comedy" in the second. . . .[18]

And *The Freeman's Journal* said it fulsomely:

. . . Mr. Yeats plays his fancy with exquisite delicacy. The contrast of the sceptic crew and the trustful dreamer, the apparition of the woman yearning for the past, and mystically even for the unending future, constitute a picture painted in colours ethereal, yet intense, pervaded with a cool warmth which cannot stir the blood, but must heat the imagination. The picturesqueness of the situation . . . the uncommon imagery, the harmony of expression, the deep sway of emotion, make one wish to read the ideal love poem alone; but it is devoid of that kind of action and exhibition of character we seek upon the boards, and thus performed it is, at best, a costume recital. As such the programme had high merits.[19]

Of *The Canavans*, *Sinn Féin* remarked, 'Mr. W. G. Fay frolicked about the stage in his usual entertaining whimsical fashion . . . and provoked roars of laughter from the audience. But no amount of good acting can make up for fundamental dramatic ideas. . . .' *The Canavans* is certainly not one of Lady Gregory's best plays, and it received a more just criticism from *The Freeman's Journal* than her better pieces usually did:

Here, on the other hand, we have a piece that is a play, and was very nearly being an exceptionally good play. It is clever enough; the dialogue is admirably vivacious; the char-acters are foiled against one another with real dramatic skill; the humour is spontaneous and wholesome; the caricature restrained and effective, and the sarcasm mordant, yet genial. The only fault is that the story does not bear the expansion of three acts, and the almost dazzling promise of the opening is disappointed in the weakness of the climax. . . . With such a gift of dialogue, Lady Gregory ought to be able to present some notable work in comedy before very long. As it is, one is very loath to find any fault whatever with a piece which created so much amusement from first to last. Mr. W. G. Fay is a comedian native to the manner. He emits his drolleries in the quaintest fashion, and enters into the fun of his work

69

with a spirit which will never fail to tickle the spirits of an audience. The only criticism that need be suggested is that he is so "sure of his laugh" as W. G. Fay that he sometimes forgets he is Canavan the miller. Mr. J. A. O'Rourke is a little too mechanical in demeanour and monotonous in expression, which is a pity, for he evidently has a keen sense of humour.[20]

* * *

Much of the internal dissension in the Abbey may be seen developing in the following batch of letters, mainly from Miss Horniman. The difficulties overtly started on the year's second English tour which began on 27 May at the Theatre Royal, Cardiff. From there, the company played in Glasgow, Aberdeen, Newcastle-upon-Tyne, Edinburgh, and Hull. Miss Horniman, who accompanied the players, found much to distress her. For instance, at the Trevelyan Hotel in Leeds, she had been scolded by the proprietress who could not sleep until after two o'clock because of the noise of the company whose members kept running from room to room, and because one of them was blowing a tin trumpet. The trumpet would have been played through the streets of Leeds, but for Miss Horniman's objection. She also thought that the girls in the company misbehaved on railway journeys. They would sit with their hair down their backs on platforms when waiting for trains, and they also conversed with a drunken man from one of the train windows. As Miss Horniman wrote:

> Miss Gilden tells of Mr. Bell's behaviour at Edinburgh on the way from Aberdeen to Newcastle. The company hung out of the carriage windows and shouted to the people on the platform — Miss O'Dempsey shaking the window bar like a lunatic the while.[21]

She also noted that during the night journey from Cardiff Brigit O'Dempsey spent much of the time playing the tin trumpet in the train corridor. Arthur Sinclair was drunk at Cardiff Station and wanted to travel with Miss O'Dempsey. Alfred Wareing, an English theatrical agent hired for the tour, objected and put Sinclair in a compartment at one end and the girls in a compartment at the other. Miss Horniman also had many reservations about the acting and staging of the plays:

> Stage management!
> Lights. On Monday curtain went up on *Riders to the Sea* with footlights full up white. I hurried round and checked

70

them down to half and the local Stage Manager arranged to put ambers in the next morning.

The light outside the cottage in *Kathleen ni Houlihan* was not strong enough — at Hull it was a dense blue. Only one or two rehearsals were called on tour, while to properly present the pieces rehearsals should have been called constantly.[22]

From Glasgow, Synge wrote to Lady Gregory:

We are distinctly a success in Glasgow; we had £38 in the house on Wednesday and Thursday, and £41 last night.

Things however are not going very smoothly. Mr. Wareing as I suppose you heard went off to London and they got down a Mr. Bell to replace him, a profoundly self-satisfied and vulgar commercial man, that none of us can abide. He got Miss Horniman more or less into his hands, and at last she sailed round to Fay one evening just before the show to suggest that Bell should "make up" the company. Fay broke out forthwith and she describes her exit as that of "a stage cat driven out of a kitchen with a broomstick." She complains pathetically to me that everyone knows in Glasgow that she is paying for our show and that she feels in a rather foolish position when she has to confess that she has no authority over it! We will have to be very careful indeed about our next step. I am not writing much to Yeats while he is with Miss Horniman; he is so careless about his letters. . . .

My address next week will be Her Majesty's Theatre, Aberdeen. I have got out of the advance work and let Wareing go on ahead this time. It is all very well to go round with him if he wants, but I objected strongly to doing the hack advance work alone, fagging round with the little books to reporters and booksellers. I told Miss Horniman it was a mistake from a business point of view to set one of the authors and directors to such work, so I got off. I am far more use in the town where the plays are running.[23]

On 12 June Miss Horniman wrote to Yeats from Edinburgh:

I have written to Lady Gregory to say that the £50 for the fit-up is ready at the Bank, that I told Mr. Gregory about it and have waited for the bills. But I refuse to send it to Fay to be dribbled away without any account being rendered to me. I do not ask Fay for detailed accounts, only the bare fact that he wants more and how much is left and an acknowledgment of what I send. I don't get anything from him, he looks on me as "commercial" doubtless because I have self-respect.

71

. . . You know how anxious I am to have all artistically right. It may be commercial to want Frank Fay to have his wig on right, if so I glory in being commercial.[24]

There was a whole further series of letters in June from Miss Horniman, complaining about Fay's mishandling of bills and accounts. For instance, on 21 June she wrote from Edinburgh:

My dear Demon,
This last is too much — Fay gave the the account to Mr. Bell who gave it to Mrs. Wareing, who posted it to her husband here. It was purely a matter for me to pay out of the Abbey Theatre account, *not* the tour. Fay said he wanted it to be paid at once because the people are poor; but he did his best to keep them from getting their money soon. This has annoyed me very much indeed. . . .
If what you disapprove of as "commercialism" is a desire to pay accounts at once and to get acknowledgments for money and to know how money is spent — I don't agree with you. It is that using of big terms and philosophical phrases by Fay which is his means of blarneying you. . . . When the tour is over we must make some clear arrangements as to the future so as not to be worn out by these petty intrigues and annoyances. You authors must not waste your time and strength fighting the wind and waves and being made too tired and weary to work. As I have always said it is for the whole movement, not individuals that we must act and if Fay insists on overdoing the part of the old-fashioned Prima Donna, he *must* be brought to his senses.[25]

On 23 June she complained:

Fay tells you one thing and other people another thing so as to get his own way. The only possible course of action for me now is to resign all connection with the theatre except that I shall hand over to the Directors the money to carry it on. I have been virtually dismissed by Fay and as the performances are absolutely under his control, the only way I can practically help the Directors is by putting the power of the purse into their hands.[26]

On 2 July Synge wrote to Yeats from Hull:

I do not quite know how the company are acting, everything is done accurately but I sometimes fancy they are getting a little mechanical from so much playing of the same pieces to poor audiences. In Dublin the continual change of programme

72

keeps them up to the mark. However a number of people in Edinburgh, — Mrs. Maguire, if that is how you spell her, Paterson, and others were so entirely carried away by our shows that there is no doubt our people are doing well, if not always at their best. W. G. Fay by the way is not good just now as he is too much occupied with his love affairs. *The Hour Glass* is to be rehearsed here this week, and the Longford programmes are in hand. . . . Poor Frank is in terrible despair wondering what he will do with himself when the tour is over! [27]

Miss Horniman had a different view of the acting, and wrote on 4 July:

At Edinburgh the slovenly appearance of the performance had not improved and, with the exception of Miss Allgood, no one took the trouble to act at all. . . . I have come to the conclusion that I cannot ask the paying public to come to see performances which are liable to become at any moment like those I saw at Edinburgh. . . .[28]

On 13 July Miss Horniman wrote to Yeats:

You have a hard struggle before you, but hold tight to the remembrance that you can always claim my help. By the time that these new arrangements have had a fair trial and you have got together a trained reliable company, fit for self-respecting exertions, I shall have got enough money together for experiments, in other directions most likely. But if your efforts are in vain and you cannot get anything but what will be practically rehearsals in the Abbey Theatre, you will have many good plays ready and much experience and a little band of earnest practised dramatists. I do not now feel that things will go as we hoped until lately and this letter is just to give you confidence in the future. None of these set-backs have shaken my determination to bring great things in the future before the public. . . .

What distresses me is the want of loyalty in Mr. Synge and Fay, the not-caring about our status when entering on professional life. It is so easy to sneer at "details" but *we* ought to have striven to be beyond reproach in every tiny matter which we could by any means control. I shall not tell Boyle anything more than is absolutely necessary about our troubles, but he must be informed that I am not "backing out" and that if Dublin efforts lead to nothing, if he goes on writing suitable plays and has them rehearsed there, I'll help when

73

the right time comes. . . . If by Christmas you tell me that £800 a year is not enough I'll send more and at any time in case of emergency apply to me at once. But this must not be known to anyone except you. Shew this letter to Lady Gregory if you like, I know that she will sympathise with my attitude, though hers is different. Fay must not suspect that there could ever be further sums to come from me. Get these things arranged and then set to your own work.[29]

On 16 July she also wrote:

My dear Demon,
I have tried to make Miss Darragh understand that there is now complete Home Rule and a subsidy from London for the Abbey Theatre and that I will in no way interfere any more. I have told her that as soon as I found that you and I did not agree about "decorative treatment" I never interfered with the *mise en scène* again and that I do not approve of the sacrifice of the dramatic interest by decorative treatment. I told her that time, money and labour had been expended by me . . . over details — that as soon as my back was turned they were omitted or reversed. I've told her that if she can bear the burden which was too heavy for me, that it would be well. But it must be made perfectly clear to your Directors that under the present "regime" I cannot interfere in any way. I have not got what you admire as "Pride", I have what is dearer to me, "Self-respect", and any further interference with the theatre affairs would hurt that. I have completely lost all confidence in the future of the company as at present constituted. . . . If you and Lady Gregory can prove that my forebodings are false, all the better. But you must not reckon on Mr. Synge. He feels that Fay's nerves and fads and fancies are of more importance than our status in the eyes of the public. He can't help it; I scarcely blame him. You told me that he allowed me to speak in Ireland in a way that he did not like and yet made no demur, and I called it cowardice. Every bitter thing I have said about Ireland has been put into my mind by my experiences among your people; am I to blame for that? [30]

By now, Miss Horniman's objections had definitely focussed upon W. G. Fay, and on 17 July she wrote to Yeats:

My own personal unbiased opinion is that Fay is absolutely unsuited to the part of Stage Manager. Your ideas against faults of what you call the "commercial" drama have been played upon by him, so that he should be free to indulge in all slovenliness. He does not know about make-up except for the characters he plays himself and he will *not* learn, and his proposals as to fines are blarney of an obvious sort. Grease paint is *not* washed off but first removed by the use of clarified lard. Chemises do not go up so high in the neck as to ·be in the way; that is a *lie*. Ask Marian to tell you as the servants at Coole are likely to wear the same undergarments as those girls. The clean boots and tidy aprons of the peasants are purely Gaelic League vanity. This is part of how you told me that they objected to cottages looking poor and shabby. Fay cannot expect to be able to discipline MacDonnell [Sinclair] or anybody else; he talks of Mr. Synge leading him astray by a bad example, but no one accuses Mr. Synge of rowdy conduct out of a railway-carriage window. Fay hates the honest hard-working professional life and wilfully misleads you when he joins in your words against the "commercial drama". He wants an excuse to be lazy and slovenly whilst you want an even great care and greater loyalty to Art. His disgust at Mr. Bell's suggestion of a gag is absurd — he speaks the American bit in *Hyacinth* exactly as if it were a gag and so vulgarises the little play. The clowning of his snores in *Shadow of the Glen* is quite different from the real sleepiness and fatigue which he represented so well when the play was first put on. As to the little dog — your nose will give you the final information when you return to Dublin unexpectedly; a surprise visit will be necessary.[31]

On 22 July she wrote to Yeats from London:

What does Mr. Synge mean by telling you that Fay "has fallen off in his acting" and yet he objected to my presumption in seeing it for myself. I'm one of the *educated* public who mar or make, and whose verdict is the final one. It is an impertinence of Mr. Synge to write about me to you as he did; now it is *impudence* to avow an opinion as his own which he had not the courage to express until he found that I had support. Perhaps cowardice is the root of what I call impudence. . . . The Mollie Allgood affair is not as serious in one way as the influence of Fay; if he marries her and she gives up acting, he will be free from Fay; yet on the other hand he may keep close to Fay so that she shall have good parts and have in time a larger salary.[32]

On 13 August Yeats wrote to W. G. Fay from Coole Park:

My dear Fay,

Lady Gregory has read me your letter. I can't understand it, as you first tell us that you are very glad that Miss Darragh should play *Shadowy Waters*, but do not like the idea of her playing *Deirdre*, and then go on to argue against her playing *Shadowy Waters*. I think I recognise your brother's voice as well as your own. I know of course that it was *Shadowy Waters* that we discussed when you were here, but I got such strong remonstrances from your brother about the waste not only of Miss Allgood's time but his, that I saw the matter in a different light, especially as *Deirdre* contains an excellent part for a woman as well as the title part. I think this is the fairest way to put it. If I decide to give Deirdre to Mrs. Campbell, about which I am very doubtful, then Miss Darragh will play Dectora on its first production, and Miss Allgood Deirdre in Dublin. If on the other hand I keep the play for the Abbey Theatre, Miss Darragh must play Deirdre and Miss Allgood will play Dectora. Since you were here the part of Deirdre has grown so complex, so full of continually changing emotion, that nobody could play it adequately except an emotional actress of great experience. If I got a fine London performance an inadequate Dublin performance would not matter so much.

I feel however that I cannot establish my reputation as a poetical dramatist with quite the same cast as is sufficient for a peasant play. Your brother is of course more delightful to my ears than any player I could get in England and your performance in *Baile's Strand* was of course a masterpiece. But you can see yourself as well as I do or better, that the performances of my verse work have imperfections that one does not find in the peasant work. Neither Synge nor Lady Gregory could ever get anything like so good a performance in any other theatre, but the training that perfects an actor or actress for peasant work does not perfect them for tragedy in verse. Miss Darragh is a tragedian and nothing else, born to it as you are born to comedy, as Miss Allgood is born to certain kinds of character work. The moment I thought of her for Deirdre I began to write better. I thought of moments of her Salome, and ventured and discovered subtleties of emotion I have never attempted before. Miss Allgood may discover a tragic personality for verse, but she has to be tested, and no one is denying her that test. She will not lose but gain from understudying a fine tragedian, and if I am wrong and she prove herself the better, no one will suffer in

76

the long run. Miss Darragh is not likely to play more than occasionally for us, at least not unless we were to make a great success. If she gets another engagement she might not play for us this winter at all. This is the issue. Can we get sufficiently good performances of my work from the National Theatre to refuse it to all other English speaking companies? Lady Gregory and myself have been inclining more and more to the opinion of a London manager (not Wareing) that we should keep all plays in the hands of the theatre. This is especially important with a view of our ultimately going to America, our one chance of making a large sum of money. It is also very probable that if we can hold to our whole mass of plays and give adequate performances of them we may get very good offers for London shows. When we go to America, one quarter let us say, of the work or one third, would be romantic and poetical. We will have to do that work not only finely but finely enough to compete with emotional acting of players of very great reputation. By emotional acting I mean acting which arises out of the expression and definition of passion as distinguished from character. It will be of enormous service to us to have got a powerful actress who is Irish, used to our method. The choice before us is the choice that comes before every sort of movement. We have all to choose between a narrow view of the interests of our little community, a generous and far seeing view. Every player in the company though he may get slightly less to play increases his chances of a big reputation and a decent income with every new player who increases the efficiency of the company. Miss Allgood is a most admirable actress, powerful, moving and sincere, one of the best actresses within her limits that I have ever seen, a great possession to the Theatre, but remember the finer the artist the more definite the limits. You cannot do everything though you have been years upon the stage, and she cannot do everything. Besides I long to see her measured against an equal, whose limits will just because she is a good artist be as precise and narrow.

I have a few slight alterations in the text of *Shadowy Waters*, but you will have them in good time.[33]

An undated letter of Willie Fay, apparently written in reply to the one above by Yeats, suggests some of the harassed manager's difficulties:

I am sorry my bad composition made my letter hard to understand, but I will try again. You asked me in Longford to get Miss Allgood to let Miss Darragh have Dectora. Act 2. Lady Gregory wrote me in Enniscorthy that you wished Miss Allgood to have her choice of Deirdre or Dectora. Act III. You write this morning and say Miss Darragh must have Deirdre. Now what am I to make of it? I don't care a red cent which of them plays either part, but is Dectora now finally to be rehearsed by Miss Allgood? I've got to keep down rows here but I can't if we change about week by week. I don't see any means of comparing Miss Darragh with Miss Allgood but they are certainly not equal in experience. I don't know a bit how much of Miss Darragh you want; it's no affair of mine, but it will be no use losing any of what we have for something we might possibly get in the future.

The bridge across the stage is finished. Is O'Rourke to go on the pay list at 10/- a week? Will you let me have Boyle as soon as possible? Are we to have 6d. seats this Autumn, for we could spend it a bit if we are? The window cleaning people want 8 or 9 shillings a month for keeping the place clean. Will I close with them? [34]

On 30 August Miss Horniman summed up her feelings about the tour in a letter to Yeats:

I have tried to make Miss Darragh understand that I have really nothing more to do with the show personally. This is final in the present state of things. A stage manager engaged for the job if you wanted to tour in England or America would be quite useless. You did not see those Edinburgh performances, but *I* did. . . . O'Rourke always speaks as if he had a very bad cold; unless this can be cured either medically or surgically I can't see the use of keeping him. . . . You must keep in mind (please impress this on Lady Gregory), that Henderson can have *no* power or influence behind the scenes. . . . Mr. Synge let *Shadow of the Glen* go to pieces; he toadies Fay and had got completely under his thumb. He owned this to me when he said that he only got his own way by "humouring" Fay. You told me that he was angry at some remarks that I made about the Irish and I said that he was a *coward* not to speak to me at the time, and you made some remark about "feeling a certain obligation". I've come to the conclusion that he wanted to serve me out and did so by supporting Fay's behaviour on tour so as to give me as much annoyance as he could. Biting off his nose to spite his face perhaps — but I've seen plenty of that.

I want you to believe thoroughly that I feel that I've done

78

what I could and that the personal help I gave to your scheme had to cease as soon as I saw that it was an impediment. . . . Everything was made as hard and unpleasant as possible in ways that to you seemed to be of no importance and I am *thankful* to feel that it is over. I hope that it will be a long long time before I am obliged to go to Dublin again, to be snubbed and affronted by snarlers and sulkers and always fearing the insult of being forced into George Moore's presence.[35]

On 3 September she wrote to Yeats from Dresden:

My poor dear old demonical Director,
Before you get this £200 will be in the National Bank, so you can pay the people all right. The next £200 shall go in on December 1st unless something very extraordinary happens. What must be faced is that these people are paid for doing nothing for three weeks out of each month and that this is ruinously extravagant if they don't tour. Having nothing to do for so long they ought to be able to learn bits of impossible plays for practice, etc., and to *dance*. . . .
If ever solid Art work is to be done at the Abbey Theatre it must be done on a firm basis of solid effort. It's of no good to only use people's *natural ways* for big work, that teaches them nothing and when the first freshness has gone, there is only a dull uninterested amateur left. As to Mr. Synge — he too has proved himself to be of no good. Any holiday can be put off for a few days when necessary. Has he had the courage to take Mollie Allgood with him? Or has he gone to escape from her? Is the man content with what he has done already or does he think that he can get along without the help of the theatre? . . .
I don't think that one or two appearances by Miss Darragh can have much effect on the company; she won't have long experience of them to be able to manage or impress them. They will despise her as being "commercial" and "made in London".
Steel cigarette-cases are not the most valuable ones now but I have got one as I know that you like them better than silver. . . .
Poor old Henderson, he does not know what is before him. Sympathy to Lady Gregory.

Yours,

Annie[36]

On 22 September Miss Darragh wrote to Yeats from England:

I'm so glad *Deirdre* has risen and is in full flight and that everything your side is so smooth. Now as to Miss Horniman — she lunched with me on Tuesday and in her own words burst into song from 1.30 till 5. So I listened and said about six sentences which resulted in her asking me to see her on Monday to meet a Miss Spencer who would tell me more grievances, etc. She is dining here on Thursday, so you see I am paying her all those ridiculous little attentions which she values so much and which she has firmly fixed in her mind none of the Irish Theatre have paid. . . . Of course she is in a state of seething fury about the whole thing and says she hates everything and nearly everyone apparently connected with the Irish Theatre. However through it all she has a tenacious hankering after it, partly hatred and partly to prove herself right in her judgment of art and acting. Her views are perfectly sound and in the main she is right. My common-sense tells me that. Fay is of course her obsession and one that will remain too — till he is put in the position of a paid leading actor and producer *only* of peasant plays I doubt her doing anything more for the Company.[37]

That Miss Horniman had more loyalty to the company than Miss Darragh would allow may be seen in a letter to Yeats written on 26 October: 'I think that the real reason of our refusal of *John Bull* should be made known as the play is referred to in the paper you sent me. I hate the thought that we should be considered cowardly.'[38] On 14 November she wrote to Yeats from Blois:

I'm extremely glad that Saturday night was such a success. You must not on any account "kow-tow" to the "patriots" by dropping Mr. Synge. The 6d seats are quite enough of a climb-down to their desires. I am sorry that what I expected to be the case has been confirmed professionally about Molière. Edward Martyn's opinion on such a subject is valueless, he would only know what words were said and "business" done, not the way they were carried out. . . . What you say of O'Rourke (whose nasal voice must be cured if he is ever to be of any good) as the policeman fits in with my great objection to the Fay system, which is to use messily the material already in the *amateurs* not to increase and broaden them into *professionals* and learn to act not merely to be as life has taught them only. *That is not Art* at all.

I wish you were not going to risk *Antigone* so soon, who will teach the men not to look foolish in the costumes? And their make-up will look far worse than in modern plays. But these things are not my business now — *thank goodness*. The bored audiences won't be very happy but they will feel "superior".[39]

Less than two weeks later, however, Miss Horniman had begun to proceed more actively against Fay. On 26 November she wrote to Yeats from London:

No one with any sense could doubt Fay's capacity as an actor when he takes the trouble to act nor his real power when he cares to let the audience hear what he is saying. . . . I hope that Mr. Synge is well again now and that *The Playboy* will act successfully. Molly Allgood won't be such a source of trouble in the future as I fear you will find Mrs. Willie Fay. . . . If *The Canavans* was not ready you were most wise to withdraw it. Lady Gregory's work must be well treated — she is the best "draw" of the lot of you. I am so proud of her because she makes the people laugh in a witty manner, and I felt murderous when her work was treated as wickedly as at Edinburgh. . . .

I will on no account employ Fay again — he could not expect it; if for no other reason than that he never acknowledged the £10 I sent to him by Mr. Synge at Glasgow. . . . I've made some more money on Hudson's Bay shares but it will go into capital this time.[40]

Sometime early in December, Lady Gregory wrote to Synge describing the difficulties of working with Miss Darragh: she was not quite what they expected, either as an actress or as a co-worker; she has now been 'allowed to leave' and has proposed to Miss Horniman putting Hermann Vezin in charge. Apparently the dismissal of Miss Darragh forced the Directors to send new proposals to Miss Horniman for the future of the theatre, and Yeats then wrote the following memorandum, dated 2 December, for his fellow Directors:

The National Theatre Society has reached a stage in its development which makes some change necessary. This has partly come from increasing work making it more and more hard for two or three people to do all the work of management and teaching, but to a still greater extent from the necessity of enlarging the capacities of the Company and increasing the number and types of plays available for per-

81

formances, and of training our audience to accept many different forms of art. At the present moment the theatre is extremely accomplished in the performance of Irish peasant comedy and in nothing else. It cannot run indefinitely on peasant comedy for to do that will be to tire its audience out and to come to an end for lack of plays. The popularity of the Theatre at this moment depends on two writers, Mr. Boyle and Lady Gregory; I do not say that individual plays by other writers have not assisted them but these are the only two writers who can be counted upon to draw audiences. There is no indication of their creating successors and in all probability the next dramatic imagination will be a complete contrast, for the imagination works far more by reaction than imitation. If they produce imitators the imitators will be bad. Ireland is not sufficiently large, sufficiently well educated to supply a theatre of one specialized activity with plays or an audience for them. On the other hand my work will hardly draw large audiences for a considerable time, . . . though verse drama might well create a school of very varied temperaments, and multiply its chances of creating writers. The natural means for it to do this is to perform selections from foreign masterpieces chosen as much for a means of training as for anything else, and to add to its players and if necessary to its teachers as opportunity offers. We should keep before our minds the final object which is to create in this country a National Theatre something after the Continental pattern. This Theatre should be capable of showing its audience examples of all great schools of drama. It was of a theatre of this kind that I was thinking when I said in the first number of *The Arrow* that we could not accomplish our work under ten years. Such a National Theatre would perforce keep in mind its educational as well as its artistic side. To be artistically noble it will have to be the acknowledged centre for some kind of art which no other Theatre in the world has in the same perfection. This art would necessarily be the representation of plays full of Irish characteristics, of plays that cannot be performed except by players who are constantly observing Irish people and things. It might very well happen also that a beautiful representation of plays in verse would be an art it had the mastery of, but this must depend on individuals, there is nothing in the conditions to bring it about of necessity. Such a Theatre must however if it is to do the educational work of a National Theatre be prepared to perform, even though others can perform them better, representative plays of all great schools. It would necessarily look to a national endowment to supply it with resources before its work could be in any way completed upon all sides. If however we are working towards this end we must keep it in mind and see that our activities lead towards it however slowly.

I now come to the immediate future, to the next step, or steps. The whole Theatre at this moment depends upon its executive side upon one overworked man, and upon a group of players who are necessarily and must necessarily so long as the Theatre remains as it is be chosen for their capacity in a single highly specialized form of work. Every course I should suggest will be founded therefore upon the necessity of adding other forms of personality and activity.

(1) The natural course as it will occur to the mind of any ordinary business man is to get more capital and to engage some actor or actors whose imaginations will express themselves in other forms of work with the same ease and abundance with which W. Fay's imagination expresses itself in comedy. He is not a romantic actor, he is not a tragic actor, he is a very clever man and can do not badly many things that are not his natural work, but the other side of the Theatre — I am trying to speak as the hypothetical business man — requires the entire time and thought of a different sort of actor or teacher. We might say to this business man should he come, or to Miss Horniman let us say if she were to find him, "We can only understand the Irish comedy; there we can have no interference; Mr. Yeats must of course retain the rights natural to the only verse writer in the Theatre over the production of his work. As to these things we want the principles of *Samhain* 1904, but as to the rest we are ready to accept any efficient professional help that can be found. We are ready to employ any efficient teachers you can find us; our comedy people must be properly paid, for if you want to develop the Theatre on the other side and we can agree to some scheme of work that is educational or sufficiently educational not to sink us below a Continental or Municipal Theatre, why you are our benefactor and we do what you like. Our interest is to preserve the Irish base, and that is our whole interest." I don't know whether Miss Horniman would be willing or able to supply this capital but if she were or if she would be willing to supply it at some future time, I can imagine that she would engage some old actor, if Hermann Vezin were a little younger he would serve her turn, and put him in charge of the non Irish work or of some portion of the non Irish work, legendary

plays for which one does not require Irish knowledge. She would then select, or rather that man would select, one or two young actors and would set to train these and such of our own people as did not desire to specialize in comedy of Irish life only for the production of representative masterpieces. Both William Fay and this hypothetical man would have their time entirely occupied without interfering with each other for such a Theatre would of course play continuously. I do not pretend that this scheme is practical in its details. I give the details to define the scheme not to show its working. The scheme in essence simply would be more capital, new actors, selected from the professional Theatre to stiffen our own company with non-comedy elements, and some mind in control to which romance and tragedy is a natural means of expression. It is hardly necessary to add that such a theatre would probably require a paid managing director to correlate all its activities. It would be expensive but not too expensive if Miss Horniman would be ready for a scheme of this kind at the present moment. I can see William Fay's face as he reads this sentence. It will brighten like the face of a certain old Fenian when Mrs. MacBride's Italian revolutionist wound up a detailed project for a rising in Connaught with the sentence, "I see no chance of success before this course." I think however that this scheme will come of itself in the course of time. We will want more capital, we will get it from some quarter, it is obviously artificial to confine our non-Irish work to actors of Irish birth. It will grow more absurd as time passes; as it becomes possible to pay at ordinary rates we shall be more inclined to take the best available talent; it will be more and more important for one man to do all the teaching.

(2) This larger scheme is certainly impossible for the present and the consideration of it is not vital at the moment. But a smaller scheme which is a gradual development towards it in all probability is pressing. William Fay must be freed from all work except his artistic work, that the comedies must be as fine as possible, instead of consciously enlarging our work which we cannot do without capital, we must perfect what we have and that is principally comedy, and be content to add other elements very slowly. We must see that William Fay's own work which should be the chief attraction of all our comedies, is given the opportunity to develop. If he has to do the work of an Assistant Stage Manager as well as that of a producer and actor, in a few years people will begin to talk of the monotony of his acting. He will be satisfied to express

his personality instead of creating self consistent personalities. He will have less and less time for teaching. The business side of the Theatre and the non artistic side of the stage work must be put into other hands. This will ensure the efficiency of the comedy. I must ask for certain measures to ensure the efficiency of the other side of the work. Frank Fay is a born teacher of elocution up to a certain point, but people come from his hands certainly with great clearness of elocution, with a fine feeling for both line and passage as units of sound, with a sufficient no less infallible sense of accent, but without passion, without expression, either in voice or gesture. William Fay has in comedy a most admirable understanding of gesture and of course of acting, but his ear for verse is very defective; only experiment can say whether the two together can teach verse speaking. I am doubtful, for verse expression is essentially different from prose expression. Something can be done I know; if William Fay were to take in hand let us say Miss Allgood he would certainly make her a useful speaker of verse, but I doubt if any combination of the two contrary talents can be relied upon to create fine speakers of verse. I hope that it may be possible by some such plan as the suggested elocution classes to make an annual visit of Mrs. Emery to Dublin for teaching purposes, self supporting. I am most anxious that my work shall not cost the Theatre more than it is worth to them in the long run. I must however ask more than this. The verse speaking at the Theatre through the exclusive development of the comedy side has not improved. Máire Walker had not passion or power of characterization in verse, but she had considerable rather delicate expressiveness. She also alone among the women who have played for us in verse had the tragic note. Miss Garvey was a verse speaker of more feeling, even with some slight touch of passion, though a very narrow range. Since they have gone there has been no good speaking of verse among the women of the company. I do not regret Starkey [Seumas O'Sullivan] though he could get through a quiet passage creditably but what is more serious is that MacDonnell [Sinclair] has not advanced upon his performance at the opening of the Theatre. I got Power to speak a few lines to me the other day, and I saw that he could not be relied on to speak a passage with force and simplicity. Frank Fay is always beautiful to listen to, but he is not improving, I am not quite sure he is as good as he was. I do not want to add acting in the sense of movement as he thinks, but I have always asked for a degree of expressiveness in voice, not less but more than that required for prose drama. From the first day of the Theatre I have known that it is almost impossible for us to find a passionate woman actress in Catholic Ireland. I remember saying that to somebody when we were playing in Molesworth Hall. I must however have the right to bring in a player or players from without when I can do so without burdening the finances of the Company more than my work is worth. To do this it will be necessary that he or she sometimes play in work other than mine. I mean that my work in its present immaturity and in the immaturity of our audience be able to be self supporting. For instance we might find at some future time that *The Vikings of Heligoland* [sic], I merely give it as an illustration, might succeed with our audience, and make it profitable to bring in a player who would enable me to get a competent performance of some play of mine. The company would not lose by this as the other work chosen would necessarily be chosen from its possible popularity or from some other definite value to the company. In this scheme everything remains as at present except that some experienced man is engaged to take non artistic work off Fay's shoulders, and Miss Darragh or Mrs. Emery or some equivalent is brought in occasionally and some foreign masterpiece chosen. Some re-arrangement of dressing rooms is implied.[41]

The following memorandum of Yeats to his fellow Directors was probably also written on 2 December:

PRIVATE I have made number 1 proposal with the following private knowledge.

Miss Horniman I know has always had before her the German Municipal Theatre as an ideal. She has stated to one or two people and almost in so many words to myself, that she has £25,000 for the development of the Company under certain circumstances. She has also stated to one or two people that if the company goes on in its present lines she will not continue the subsidy longer than the patent period. In four years and a half we shall therefore very possibly find ourselves face to face with the necessity of a new application very possibly seriously opposed for a renewal of the patent, and with neither Subsidy or Theatre. In fact I don't see how we can apply for a renewal of the Patent without her cooperation. It is possible that she might agree, though stopping the subsidy, to allow us free use of the Theatre. It would be her interest to do so or at any rate her interest if we did not

86

require a too constant use of the Theatre, as the value of her property depends on the Patent to some extent. But considering how little she thinks of her interest in comparison to her feelings the position is one of the greatest possible peril. We might hire the Theatre but I know no Theatre in any English speaking country which is able to consistently perform intellectual work. Every English and American critic of standing has claimed that a conditional subsidy is necessary to keep intellectual work on the stage. But subsidy or no subsidy I cannot at this moment think of a Patent which depends upon friendly working as in other than extreme danger if we permanently quarrel with her. The scheme marked number 2 will I believe keep her for a time friendly for the appointment of a stage manager of the kind I suggest has been her one condition. I believe that I have it in writing that she would use the £25,000 for our English and presumably our American tours if we had a permanent Stage Manager, and I know that I have it in writing that she is prepared to leave William Fay producer (we owe this to Miss Darragh's friendliness as she has insisted in talking to Miss Horniman on Fay's paramount importance). It possesses the disadvantage that it will leave the National Theatre Society many opportunities for Miss Horniman to quarrel with it; every tour would be an opportunity. She is now very anti-Irish.[42]

The following undated comments by Synge appear to be his thoughts after reading Yeats's memorandum:

A dramatic movement is either (a) a creation of a new dramatic literature in which the interest is in the novelty and power of the new work rather than the quality of the execution. (b) a highly organized executive undertaking in which the interest lies in the final and careful interpretation of works that are already received as classics.

I think that this secondary executive movement can only come (naturally) in a country where there has been a long creative movement. So far our movement has been entirely a creative movement — the only one of its kind now existing and that is why we have attracted so much notice. To turn this now — for what are largely extreme reasons into an executive movement — would be a disaster for us and a disaster for Ireland. I am prepared to stake everything on a Creative movement even if we all go to the work house at the end of the four years. None of us are suited for the working of the Executive movement — it will be done in good time in

Ireland — by a dramatic Hugh Lane — if Ireland is ripe for it. Yeats speaks of making our theatre a copy of continental [theatres]. That is exactly what for the ten years at the least we should avoid. National dramas have never been created by such theatres. Goethe at the end of his life said that he and Schiller had failed to make a German drama at Weimar because they had confused their audiences with, one day, Shakespeare, one day Calderon, one day Sophocles and another Racine. If we do the same we are doomed. An occasional foreign play that illustrates our own work should be done, as we have played *The Doctor*, and are going to play *Oedipus*. Beyond that I do not think we should go, and for that reason I opposed Yeats's suggestion as to continuous playing. Our supply of native plays is very small and we must keep our company very small so that this little store of native work will keep it occupied. A larger and more expensive company with more expensive people in it, and the consequently necessary raising of the salary list all round, (otherwise we should lose our present people) would force us to play a great deal of foreign matter and destroy the distinctive note of our movement. There is another objection. All Miss Horniman's money together would not pay for a big theatre. Bohemian subsidy is £12,000 as year and all scenery found. The interest on Miss Horniman's £25,000 would be about £800, I suppose, which would hardly do more than pay our own company adequately. I am perfectly convinced that if we embark on a big scheme we shall collapse in six months as Phillip Carr collapsed and so many other attempts of the kind have done also. If we are to get a grant from the Government in Ireland it will [be] a small one only, and we shall never get it if we become too English. I object to giving Miss Horniman any control over the company whatever. If she is given power it ceases to be an Irish movement worked by Irish people to carry out their ideas so that if any such arrangement becomes necessary I shall withdraw, — my plays of course might remain if they were wanted. I object to Miss Horniman's control not because she is English, but because I have no confidence in her ideals.[43]

On 3 December Miss Horniman wrote to Yeats from London:

I gather from your typed letter which arrived on Saturday night that there had been no open "row" and that you personally were quite hopeful about everything. The whole of your new schemes for development and a stage manager and everything else depend on one thing alone — who runs the show? Miss Allgood I know learned much on the tour, none of the rest condescended to do the same. Fay will use her to get rid of Miss Darragh if he can. In *Kincora* some at least of the servants, if none of the Kings, ought to have some vitality; the girl who wears too much jewellery in day-light should shows signs of life, and Gormleith should be a perfect terror— but Fay does not permit anything of this. He knows the trick of one of the vulgarest forms of commercial drama (American farce) and he has the genius to reverse. There everyone and everything but star is made as noisy as possible; Fay keeps everyone and everything *dead* so as to show himself off, and he tells you that it is noble and practical and everything else that he wants you to believe, whilst really he tries to keep them like fish who have been dead for some time, to show himself off. I'm sorry if you put on *Heather Field* — it is dull, immoral and false to human facts of life, and besides needs some actors who can look like gentlefolk. Where would you get the little boy? . . .

Your father's sentiments are much stronger than his critical faculty — he taught me this when he struck me dumb by his admiration for Moira Walker's (non-existent) figure, especially her (invisible) shoulders. If he liked Miss Darragh he would see no faults. I daresay that she has modified her performance, let it ripen in fact, and would do it perfectly in a fortnight. But by that time the rest would be weary of their parts and are not artists enough to care to hide the fact. Maybe that want of life and vitality is naturalistic and true to Irish life but it ought to come from the *art* not the natural slothfulness of the players; to me it shews clearly why the young people who have some individuality and don't care to become Gaelic League helots long for America.[44]

On 10 December she wrote again:

Boyle has a certain virility (I don't know what else to call it, it has nothing to do with the quality of his work) which is missing in Yeats and Synge work; Lady Gregory has it too. It makes a barrier which has a very good side — it forces the actor into a certain character and keeps him there. I don't believe that O'Rourke will ever be of much good even if he does learn to use his nose properly and it is a great pity that *The Canavans* had to suffer. When you revive the play I hope that you will be able to put in someone else. . . . When you get back I must have a number of questions answered. I'll remove all reading matter from within reach, and you will have to give me your full attention, to abstract yourself from life, as I'm not at all cross and trying not to be sad, and I certainly will not worry you, for I have my own dignity to consider.[45]

On 12 December she wrote:

I'm so "out" with you for a traditional reason; our interests are like Tweedledee and Tweedledum, and they fought a renowned battle. The time seems to have passed away when my active help was needed, but I thought of floating skirts the other day and told Henderson to get a fire-guard for the tea-room. My wishes, as everyone must know, have all pointed to the larger interests of the whole scheme. I cannot comprehend how people did not understand from the very beginning that my idea was to make a great theatre in the future if possible. Everything which could help to enlarge and solidify the foundations seems to arouse new opposition.

As to any touring, I cannot prevent it, but I will have nothing to do with it until I feel assured that it will not damage us. I have done all I could to urge that Mrs. Pat Campbell should have *Deirdre* and even now I consider that if she would still take the play that any conditions she might offer should be accepted. My point of view being that the sacrifice of one play of yours would be an enormous gain to the whole scheme. Now don't mistake the real cause of the out-cry against Miss Darragh's dress. This is touching loyalty on the part of Moira Walker's admirers — her skinny chest and shoulders are impossible for exhibition and so they want to cover up everyone else's!

Miss Darragh had doubtless London (or those of any other city where there are recognised theatres) stage traditions which would annoy the Columbines. To learn a part thoroughly, to make-up decently, to try to *act* a character, to try to keep up for a run, or number of performances as the case may be, to the action arranged at the first are all things quite apart from talent or country or class of work. Laurence [possibly W. J. Lawrence] is evidently jealous of you and your efforts, and I am delighted that he was hissed.

I have never hesitated in my opinion that Fay has a genius for acting, but his carelessness I remarked on to you when I saw him for the first time, and did not hear enough of what he said in *Twenty-five* to gather the meaning although I sat in the second row. You say that there are already "complaints" so I suppose that things are beginning to be noticed more carefully. What would be passed over and forgiven in beginners cannot be excused now.[46]

In a letter dated only 'Saturday', Lady Gregory expressed her feelings to Synge about the proposal for an English manager:

> I enclose Miss Horniman's letter and Yeats's explanation of it. Thanks for yours today. It was very needful, for though I had a very long letter from Fay, he is so bad at expressing himself I could not make out if he meant resignation or not. I have wired to Yeats "Fay refuses, Synge relieved, my instincts with them but most unwilling to go against you." That really expresses my feelings. I would not for a moment think of accepting this "fancy man" but that I think Yeats wants a new excitement, a new impetus, or will tire of the theatre, and I feel myself very much bound to him; besides personal friendship, because we are the only survivors of the beginning of the movement. I think his work more important than any other (you must not be offended at this) and I think it our chief distinction. I think on the other hand it will suffer rather than gain by the new element, but he must have experiments, and it would be a very great pity if he had to go to England for them. . . . I don't think any compromise is possible with Miss Horniman but that wouldn't matter if we could arrive at an understanding with Yeats. My chief difficulty is that he is pressing Miss Darragh for Fand and I will not consent to having her for any work outside his, which we can't help. I think her Deirdre was a degradation of our stage, and that she has been the cause of Miss Horniman's new arrogance. The reason Yeats is suggesting a vote of the company is that Miss Darragh was forming or thought she was a "party". Yeats thought they would have voted for her management against Fay's before she left. Mac and Miss Molly and Kerrigan are supposed to be her warm supporters, I and the Fays the only impregnable ones. I would not mind putting it to a company vote, only that I think Yeats would be badly beaten, and would feel it, and I want to keep him and his work to Ireland.[47]

Synge included some further reflections in a letter to Lady Gregory dated 15 December:

> W. Fay must be freed, that I think is urgently necessary if he is to keep up the quality of his acting. An assistant stage manager as we agreed will do this if we can find the right man.

91

For the verse plays — Yeats's plays — I am ready to agree to almost any experiment that he thinks desirable in order to ensure good performances. Mrs. Emery [Florence Farr], as you suggest, might be of great use. At the same time I think he is possibly mistaken in looking on the English stage for people that are needed. . . . I greatly dislike the impression that *Deirdre* or rather Miss Darragh has left on me. Emotion — if it cannot be given with some trace of distinction or nobility — is best left to the imagination of the audience. Did not Cleopatra, and Lady Macbeth, and Miranda make more impression when they were played by small boys than when they are done by Mrs. P. Campbell? I wonder how one of Dunn's kids would be in *Dectora*?!

I would rather go on trying our own people for ten years than bring in this ready made style that is so likely to destroy the sort of distinction everyone recognizes in our own company. Still that is only my personal feeling and as I said, I think it essential that Yeats should be able to try anything that seems at all likely to help on his work, which requires so much skill.[48]

A further undated memorandum from this time in Synge's handwriting reads:

There are two important points about which we owe it as much to Miss Horniman as to ourselves that there should be no misunderstanding:

First we must be quite free to maintain our own stage tradition as it is laid down in *Samhain*.

1. Fay must continue to produce — in the sense that he directs actors as to their speaking, movements, and gestures, and positions — all *dialect* plays, whether peasant or not.

2. For other plays the producing and stage management must be left to the discretion of the directors in so far at least that it must not be a part of our agreement that say Irish verse-plays like *Fand* are to be handed over to the Managing Director till we are quite sure that he will produce them according to the *spirit* of the *Samhain* principles. This is very important, as no amount of recommendation from stage authorities in London gives any real assurance of this point. Some of the most aggressive, vulgar stage management I have even seen was in Irving's production of *The Merchant of Venice*. All the talk I had with Wareing and others connected with the London stage gave me the same impression. That is a vital point on which I — as far as my vote counts — will

not give *in* — it would be better for us to come to find ourselves gradually driven into the sort of stage management that George Moore urged on us in his article in *Dana*, which is after all the efficient stage management of the recognized London authority. There could be no better evidence that we have a sort of method of our own than George Moore's attack on Fay.

3. As to Fay's position I feel that his feelings on the subject must to some extent be consulted partly because he has had such a large share in building up the movement. . . .[49]

On 17 December Miss Horniman wrote formally to Yeats:

Dear Mr. Yeats,

As I am leaving England on the 27th for a month I now give you formal directions as to the engagement of a Managing Director for the company. Someone of known theatrical position will I feel certain be willing to introduce you to a suitable person and to advise you as to the exact amount of his salary. He should be fairly young, of good manners and such a temper as will make the position possible for him. He must have practical stage experience as well as experience in stage management of all classes of plays. He would need to be able to stage-manage anything and be competent to produce all plays except those treating of Irish peasant life. I should like this engagement to be made as soon as possible and this letter is to be taken as pledging me to guarantee the money.

Yours sincerely,
A. E. F. HORNIMAN.[50]

On 19 December Miss Horniman wrote to Lady Gregory:

I have given much careful thought to the present state of affairs; it should not continue. The following proposition has not been suggested by Mr. Yeats, and it is for all or a majority of the Directors to accept or refuse it.

I propose that they should engage a Managing Director at a good salary (say £400 or £500 a year) who would be able to stage manage all the plays and produce such as would be performed, except when the Directors wished to do them themselves or to leave them in the hands of an artist; Fay to retain the production of all Irish peasant plays and to have nothing to do with the rest except his own parts. This would free him from much wear and tear and allow him to perfect himself in his own lines.

The engagement of this Managing Director would of course

be under the control of the Directors and he must be recommended by someone of known theatrical position. This would remove my objection to touring under the present state of affairs and would I believe be extremely advantageous to all concerned.

I should not engage him and he would be responsible to the Directors and I would pay the money for his salary to you. I leave this offer open until my return on January 21 but as time is of value, if you accept it Mr. Yeats holds a formal letter authorising such an engagement immediately. Will you kindly communicate this to Mr. Synge as I should like all the directors to accept this; but as in the case of the subsidy a majority is sufficient, Mr. Synge never having accepted it.[51]

On 20 December Lady Gregory sent Miss Horniman's 'very generous' offer to Synge, remarking, '. . . the letter is not quite clear as to whether Fay is to give up stage-managing the peasant plays. I don't think she can mean that he is to do so, yet she says the new man is to stage-manage "all plays".' Later in December, Lady Gregory wrote again to Synge, still uncertain about what the new stage manager would do and what Fay would do:

> . . . what I hold to is that the Fays should not be shoved out either by force or gentler means. . . . I think as Yeats and Fay represent the extreme right and left, we who are the moderate centre are best out of it, leaving the arrangement to them. I am inclined to think Fay will agree, if the responsibility of refusing is thrown upon him and if he does so I am not afraid of the experiment. But if he feels that he could not accept the new arrangement with self respect and the respect of the company, then I think we must just work on as best we can and without Miss Horniman's further help, or goodwill.[52]

On Boxing Day, Miss Horniman wrote to Lady Gregory from Algiers:

> My formal letter making that offer to pay a Managing Director only put the matter very boldly so that you and Mr. Synge might see it clearly. Now that you understand what I mean I want to put it from my point of view. As you know well *I* am extrinsic to *your* scheme not intrinsic; I mean that the fact of the theatre being in Dublin and the limitations of Patent, etc. are impediments to me and my ideas. The local circumstances and people which to you are intrinsic, are extrinsic to me. I have never dwelt on this before or made any point of it, but I have never tried to hide it, and I believe that

many of our difficulties which arose through Mr. Russell and his lambs came from his instinctive feeling of deeply felt opposition to *my* aim — the Art to be for its own sake, and to be done as well as possible. During all my long time of diplomatic sulking I was as you know most carefully watching events. I did my best out of my income to aid you to conquer a Dublin audience, knowing quite well that success in this would be *to me* a side-issue. I gave Fay his chance to carry out what he could and now, to me, his absolute incapacity has been proved and his present acting capacity is being endangered. If my offer to you looks like spite against him I cannot help it; but I must try to protect what has already been done, not sacrifice it to any individual. My Synge's letter made me really angry; it carried this to my mind — let us have a theatre where foreign classics and other plays may be used to train actors to play Synge, let the other authors go hang! The lessee has no vote, she is bound by her Saxon sense of honour. It is "absurd" that her views or desires should be regarded except when she admires and pushes Synge's plays. If he thinks honestly that Dublin was anything to me but a mere geographical detail when I made my original offer he is making a great mistake. Fay is necessary to Synge himself but neither are anything but extrinsic to my root idea. Now when I found that the audiences were increasing in quality and numbers, and *plays* were getting ready for touring, I saw that my wise and necessary objection to touring would soon become unfair to the authors; yet the scandalous carelessness of the stage-management remained an immoveable hindrance. So I thought the matter over and came to the conclusion that I was justified in offering to pay this salary from the income of the legacy which is to be used for *really* public objects. I put the conditions in my letter as clearly and simply and fairly as I could, but they are in distinct opposition to Mr. Synge and as presumably you have the casting vote, the whole depends on you. It is so much to Mr. Yeats's advantage that you should accept it (and promptly too) that his sense of delicacy may prevent him from urging it as strongly as he feels it. He was most indignant when I put it in the light that I would not pay a man who could not dismiss Fay or anyone else for just reasons of course, under the Directors. But when he saw that I meant an educated man who would lift a great burden off his and your shoulders, and who would be able to help his plays to worthy representation he was much relieved in mind. I reminded him that I have never asked anything for myself nor for any friend and that in the matters in which I have interfered it has always been as I imagined for the sake of the whole scheme. At present in the public eye, I have spent large sums on an Irish *toy* — I am willing to spend more to try to raise it to the dignity of an Art Institution. I decline to pretend to approve of allowing Fay to try experiments with plays he is not sufficiently educated to produce, in any theatre, making me ridiculous in the eyes of cultivated strangers. Great classics must be treated with respect, poverty of means can be forgiven; but carelessness and ignorance and playing games with them cannot be forgiven. Those Greek plays bore me, but that is a personal detail of no importance at all. What is the use of Mr. Gregory's artistic help if as soon as his back is turned he is to be insulted? *I* resent this as having happened to an artist in an institution for which I am at any rate somewhat responsible in the public eye.

If you can come to a decision soon, Mr. Yeats can busy himself at once about finding a suitable man. I am anxious for him to see some at least of the rehearsals of *Playboy* so as to keep it up to the mark during the performances and to be on the spot when you are putting on translations.[53]

The following undated, unsigned, typed memorandum was probably written by Yeats. Proposal A seems to reflect Yeats's reaction to Miss Horniman's offer, and Proposal B seems to reflect Synge's.

Proposal A: We agree to work with the new man for six months as cordially as possible. Whatever foreign masterpieces our own people are thought fit for can be put on. Mr. Yeats can bring in anyone he likes for his own plays, according to compromise, and in the case of *Phèdre* can bring in Miss Darragh as he had promised it to her.

At the end of the six months if any of the Directors are dissatisfied with the new methods, a meeting to be called. If any of the actors wish to leave they are naturally free to do so; if any of the authors wish to leave they must be allowed to take their plays with them, their agreement to leave them with the Society for the term of the Patent being cancelled.

Proposal B: We cannot with self respect, and looking at the list of plays produced and the notices of them, accept Miss Horniman's statement that we are "in the public eye an Irish toy." We cannot accept her statement that our stage manager having had "his chance to carry out what he could" had "proved his absolute incapacity." To accept the new man would be to accept these statements.

We claim six months in which to work in our own way. We claim the right of taking our work to London and elsewhere before the end of that time, that "the public eye" may judge what we can do, while still working by ourselves.

At the end of six months, should Miss Horniman renew her offer, we should hold a meeting of authors and actors and make our decision.

If this proposal is accepted I would ask leave to reorganize at once, engaging a new man at say £2 a week to help business side, and I would give all possible time to the theatre for the next few months.[54]

On 28 December Yeats wrote to Synge from London:

. . . What I said to her was this: "it is necessary for our sake and for Fay's sake that all work except acting and production be taken out of his hands. He is an artist not a business man and should not be made to do things which anybody else or somebody else could do as well or better. He should produce but the work should go from his hands to a stage manager." These were not my exact words but they were the sense of them. I expected that she would give us a stage manager at two or three pounds a week. Wareing who was there made difficulties of a practical kind about the divided control. I refused to hear of any authority of any important kind being given to the kind of man we would get at this price. Next day she proposed getting a first rate man and paying him four or five hundred a year and making him Managing Director in my stead. . . . I tried to get her to give to this new director only so much right over the artistic side of the work as we would have given to the two pound a week man. I said something like this — "It is obvious that there is no other man whatever who could produce the peasant work besides Fay. I am not yet certain that he has any special faculty for verse work but considering what he has done for the theatre he should be tried in this. He should be given a definite period during which he could show what capacity he had when freed from other bothers in the production of verse plays." I held out for several hours on this point though I made no secret of the fact that he had not yet shown remarkable capacity that way. I pointed out that various failings of various verse plays were failings of stage management not production. Finding I could not carry my point with her (I imagine that she has had very decided reports about Fay in that capacity, not I think from Miss Darragh) I proposed the new man should be engaged for a time — a year let us say — with the object of his teaching our people and training some less expensive man to do the work. This she refused on the very reasonable ground that we could not get a thoroughly good man unless he had an opportunity sufficiently great to attract him. . . . If I had had a more innate conviction of Fay's capacity for verse work I might have carried the point — though I doubt it very much. . . . When I am talking to you and to Lady Gregory I put Fay's limitations (when I have a point to carry) but I assure you I put even more strongly his genius when talking to Miss Horniman. . . . I do not think Fay need fear for his position; indeed I believe he need only fear for it if he shrinks from this change and tries to go on in the old way. . . . The liberation from other worries will give Fay the opportunity to become in reality a great actor instead of a great actor in promise. . . . Fay is thoroughly unfitted for the management of people. Two or three years ago Fred Ryan came to me privately and said this — That if somebody else could be put into control there would be no trouble (this was at the time of the first split). He said the same to me when we came back from the tour. Miss Walker's various reasons for not rejoining us always in the end got down to Fay's management. For obvious reasons he awakens suspicions in all directions. . . . You and I and Lady Gregory have the same excitability though in very different ways. None of us are fit to manage a theatre of this kind and do our own work as well. Lady Gregory's work this autumn would have been twice as good if she had not the practical matters of the theatre on her mind. Several times in the last two or three years the enormous theatrical correspondence has been the chief event both of her day and mine. Many and many a time we have had to go to the typewriter the first thing after breakfast with the result that our imaginations were exhausted before we got to our play-writing.[55]

On 31 December Miss Horniman wrote to Yeats from Algiers:

My letter to Lady Gregory may cause her to be willing to take her right position in the matter; whether for or against acceptance of the scheme. I cannot alter my offer in any way, it was carefully considered at the time and no new evidence has been laid before me. Any modification on Mr. Synge's lines would simply be the undoing of my intentions. I will make some remarks on Mr. Synge's letter and you can dispose of this as you may think fit.

1. The right of voting on your board is not a matter in which I can interfere.

2. He must be free to engage or dismiss actors; if not supported by the board (or a majority) he must go. In this *I* should have to decide whether I should authorise you to engage a new man. If he were unsuitable we could try another; but if otherwise suitable and yet not supported by the directors, things would return to their present position.

3. I carefully left it open for a play, *at the wish of the author*, to be put in the hands of any Director or artist instead of the new man; if an author chooses Fay, let him take the risk. But only the author can choose the producer; where the author is not at hand it must be done by the new man. If the "Samhain Principles" are to be stretched into an intention to go in every way against the rules of the ordinary stage *where these rules are right and necessary*, I have been under a serious delusion. At present my position is "false and absurd" in the eyes of the public and I naturally object.

I leave the Directors free to carry out their own ideas as long as they are in harmony with the "Samhain Principles". I consider the decorative staging of plays anti-dramatic but I put no obstacles in the way of your experiments. Any consultation with Fay or modifications to please him are not in my province. He is amply represented at present on your board.

I never saw anything in the old Lyceum stage-management as common and vulgar as Fay's behaviour in *Hyacinth Halvey* at Edinburgh when he deliberately turned to the audience and spoke certain sentences as if they were vulgar gags.

The offer must be accepted or refused finally by January 21st.[56]

On 31 December Miss Horniman also wrote to Yeats a letter marked 'Private':

My dear Demon,

Mr. Synge wants Fay to run the show, he is too lazy to care about anything except his own plays and too cowardly to fight for the whole. Unless Lady Gregory will decide you will be obliged to give in and Fay will only permit a cheap man whom *he* can virtually dismiss to be engaged. Over and over again the road has forked before you; at this moment Fay, in the form of Mr. Synge, points one way, and I and your interests point in the other. The remark about the *amount* of future touring is quite beside the point. I cannot and will not

99

strengthen the present state of things; it would be most foolish of me to do so, it would (to put it baldly) be sheer waste of money. If the offer be accepted the only honest advice I can give you is to resume your literary and practical work, go on writing plays, get them produced wherever you can and only trouble about the Abbey Theatre when it is to your own advantage; and to discontinue this great expenditure of time and labour over a scheme which must practically fizzle out if run to please the vanity of one man. Your work is too valuable to the World, my dear friend, for me to allow any loyalty to the theatre on *my* behalf to cramp it. So if my last effort to help you to carry out your old ideas comes to naught you must not think that you can make things right by giving up your energies any longer. Life is short and you are only just coming into your full powers, you must work for a larger world than that in which something run under Fay can reign. That you are the head and real source of the whole movement is clear to all except those who should be most grateful to you. *Don't* telegraph here now at all or to Tunis, but either put my offer out of your mind as being refused or else engage the man. Yet, I allow you to remember it as being an effort made by me on your behalf and that of your work. . . .

A Happy New Year to you,

Yours,
Annie.[57]

*   *   *

A helpful glimpse into conditions backstage at the Abbey during this period is from Willie Fay:

It was about this same time that we got a valuable addition to our back-stage accommodation. Thanks once more to Miss Horniman's generosity, we acquired a house that adjoined the theatre on the right and which, after being converted by Mr. Holloway, gave us a passage leading from the stage to a scene dock and property room, a comfortable green-room on the ground floor, a manager's office, a wardrobe room and, what we needed very badly, a rehearsal room for use when the stage was occupied by the staff. The green-room was, of course, an ideal place for holding a party whenever Lady Gregory arrived from Gort with one of the famous barm bracks. Many a one of these was devoured there after a dress rehearsal, for there is nothing that can arouse so fine an appetite as three or four hours of rehearsing. After the first

100

night of a play a tidy number of visitors used to find their way there for a cup of tea and a chat about the show.

Whenever we produced a period play the costumes, except when Miss Horniman had been good enough to give them to us, were made of hessian and dyed in a zinc bath on the green-room gas stove. It was a stiff job and a dirty one, especially when there was a lot of material to be dealt with. In those days hessian was 6d. a yard and two yards wide, so that at a cheap rate we could cover a multitude of sins. Once Mrs. Patrick Campbell, seeing one of our girls in an outsize costume of this material, murmured to her gently, "At first sight, darling, you looked as if you were about to give birth to a grand piano." Our peasant clothes were real, and by the time we got our wardrobe room, there was a fair collection gathered from all parts of the country to put into it. One place where we got some really valuable old clothes was a pawnshop in Galway. We had them cleaned and stoved before putting them into stock. One old body-coat I used was over ninety years old, and we had some linen shirts with the very high collar attached that had rows of tucks all down the front. The members of the company, too, helped to stock our wardrobe by cadging suitable pieces from their friends and relations.

Our scenery had so accumulated that latterly, before we got our store-room, we could hardly move on to the stage. We had started with only a little for ourselves and a set of stock scenery that I had made for hiring out to lessees — the traditional kind of thing, an oak chamber, a kitchen set and a wood scene. It would have been useless to offer lessees any of our own stuff, which they did not think was scenery at all, and indeed from their point of view it was not. In the earliest days I had to make it and paint it myself, but presently I got a clever young mechanic to come to us and learn to be a stage carpenter. It would have been easy to get an experienced one — indeed several called on me to ask for the job — but I wanted someone that would grow up with the players and learn to work in our way without having to forget a lot of previous knowledge. Shaun Barlow was very quick and smart with tools, and soon learned not only to make and paint scenery but to take complete charge of every department of the stage. He was one of the best stage carpenters I have ever had to work with, and I have had to work with a few in forty years.[58]

*   *   *

101

The situation which had led to the second major secession of players from the Abbey and to the formation of the Theatre of Ireland company is reflected in an entry Holloway made in his journal for 15 May:

> Had a chat with Fred Ryan re theatrical matters, and he was disgusted with the whole thing. Said he had enough of it and did not intend to join any company. The bickering was awful when he was secretary. Kettle summed the situation up when he said that W. B. Yeats did more than anyone to get a theatre for Irish plays and now he does more than anyone to keep people away from it.[59]

On 16 May Holloway received the following letter, however, from the seceders' camp:

> A sum of money being available for the formation of a Society to further dramatic work in Ireland, it has been considered advisable to call a meeting of those interested in this object for the inauguration of such a Society. We would be very glad therefore, if you could be present at Meeting to be held at 28 Clare Street (Irish Art Companions' Rooms), at 8 p.m. on Friday next (the 18th inst.).
>
> In the event of such a society being formed, Mr. Edward Martyn has kindly consented to act as president.
>
> Thomas Keohler, Trustee
Padraic Colum[60]

On 18 May that first organizational meeting was held, with Stephen Gwynn in the Chair. It was proposed 'That a new Society be formed to carry on national dramatic work in Ireland, to produce plays in English and Irish, and the masterpieces of foreign dramatic authors.' [61] The members of the provisional committee were Nellie O'Brien, Helen Laird, Constance Markievicz, James H. Cousins, T. M. Kettle, Thomas Keohler, Edward Martyn, John MacNeill, George Nesbitt, Padraic Pearse, George Roberts, Dermot Trench, J. S. Starkey ('Seumas O'Sullivan'), Maurice Joy, and Padraic Colum, who was elected secretary. A deputation from the National Players stated that their group would cooperate with the new society.

At another meeting on 25 May, it was decided to call the group Cluithchéoirí na h-Eireann, and, at the next meeting, to call it also the Theatre of Ireland. At a meeting on 6 June officers were elected. Edward Martyn was the President, Nesbitt the Stage

Manager, Keohler the Honorary Treasurer, and Colum the Honorary Secretary.

The group started with some money, for as Colum told Holloway on 17 May, 'the seceders from the Abbey Theatre got £50 of the fund in hand when the severance came.'

Nationalist approval was given to the new group by, of course, Arthur Griffith:

> . . . *Samhain* was once the recognised journal of the dramatic movement and a record of progress; it is to-day a personal and arbitrary statement, and may be styled, without much stretching of the imagination, the gazette of Mr. Yeats's dissolution; for it is a faithful record of that dreadful progress which must end in the loss of a poet. . . . We have before us a few programmes of the early performances of the Irish National Theatre Society, and a glance over the names of the various casts is not without interest. . . . It will be seen that of the names here mentioned *only one*, that of Mr. Fay, still remains on the programme of the present Abbey Theatre. Now it is perfectly fair to ask where are the others? And what was the reason of their deserting the Society? It is quite obvious that in this number are at least five of the best players the movement has yet produced. The Lavarcam, Delia Cahil, the Angel, and Dectora of Máire Nic Shiubhlaigh; the Naisi, Wise Man, and Michael Gillan of Dudley Digges; the Sibby of Máire Quinn; the Michael Ford of P. J. Kelly; and Honor Lavelle's magnificent portrayal of the Old Woman in *Riders to the Sea*, are still the high-water mark of Irish acting. But still more significant is the fact, with which these old programmes bring us face to face, that amongst these names are all the Nationalist element of the original Society, and moreover that the gradual secession of these members is almost proportionate to the denationalising process which has undoubtedly been taking place in the Society for the past few years. . . . From the National point of view, the 'National' Theatre Society is, we fear, as dead as a coffin nail, and assuredly the centre of the future Theatre movement in Ireland must be looked for elsewhere. The Theatre of Ireland must be bi-lingual and National, National in more than name.[62]

A good many of the difficulties of the Abbey's chief rival may be inferred from the following letter which Máire Garvey wrote to James Cousins:

Dear Mr. Cousins,

Thank you very much for the offer of "Nancy". I regret I had not the pleasure of seeing *The Racing Lug* on the stage, but my recollection of it is very keen from reading it in *The United Irishman* and I take this opportunity of congratulating you upon such a splendid little piece of work. The congratulations are late but nevertheless they are sincere.

I have no intention of troubling you *personally* with a list of my grievances against the "Theatre of Ireland", yet I fear you may not understand my position if I do not enter a little into one or two points which, as a member of the Committee of the "Theatre" you may be able to explain.

From the first I had intended working unsparingly in the new Society and to that end would have played anything and everything they desired, but the conditions under which it is evident that they desire me to work have made it impossible for me to continue. The Committee, (perhaps I should say the "Theatre") rent a hall in High Street for rehearsals at the rate, I believe, of 7/- a week. On hearing of the situation of the hall I objected to go there constantly, as the locality is very much overcrowded and it is not quite the atmosphere one would like to look forward to after being shut up in an office all the rest of the day. I spoke of this to the Secretary and he said it was not so bad and Miss Laird, Colm and myself went down to rehearse in it; we found, however, that it was what Miss Laird described as "corpsey" and we came away, as we could not bear it. Colm promised to look out for some other place and asked me if I knew of one to let him know. I heard no more about the new hall and after about a fortnight I spoke of it to him again and told him of a room he could get for 2/6 per week. After about another fortnight he informed me that Mr. Martyn had objected to the size of the room I suggested. I asked him if he had taken the trouble to find out on what space he was going to play *An Talamh*, as I had already played in the Round Room in the Rotunda and was well aware that the rehearsals were being carried on over much too large a space. To this he paid no attention as Mr. Martyn's objection seemed a weightier argument, but I am quite certain that if Mr. Martyn went to that hall for three nights and remained in it for 3 to $3\frac{1}{2}$ hours at a time he would not go there on the 4th night, and I am also certain that Mr. Martyn would have seen the advantage of a saving of 4/6 per week in the rent of the hall. I was told that there was no place to suit the "Theatre" except one where they could store scenery. As a matter of fact there was no scenery for *An Talamh*. Then again, there were very objectionable incidents in connection with the opening of this hall; on three occasions at 8:30 rehearsal I had to go to Walker's shop and then to their house looking for the key. . . .

Then the Blackrock incident. I have been told outside that certain members of the "Theatre" say I am most disagreeable to get on with, and I presume it is in connection with *The Last Feast* they say this. Colm came to see me one night in High Street, and, first warning me that he was speaking quite unofficially, he asked me if I thought the "Theatre" ought to produce *The Last Feast* in Blackrock. He could not give me any particulars as to for whom the play would be produced, except that he believed that it was the Gaelic League. I do not believe in the Gaelic League producing plays in English at present. There are numerous little plays in Irish suitable for the open air and very easily got up, and to produce a play in English under the Gaelic League auspices during Oireachtas week seemed to me to be very bad policy, both for the League and for any Society professing to take any serious interest in the language. I expressed these views to Colm and he agreed, and went away from me without the least doubt as to whether I would play Grainne. Then several days afterwards Miss Laird came to me and asked if I would play Grainne at Blackrock. I asked her who was getting up the play and she told me it was not the Gaelic League, but that the proceeds would go towards the children's feast in a League class. I told her I had too much to do with Ellen to dream of taking up Grainne and that I could not possibly do what she wished, i.e., play Grainne without a rehearsal. Afterwards Colm came and asked me again, and I continued to say no. I do not think I have been otherwise than straightforward with the Society or "Theatre", and I must say that I was surprised to be told they considered me very disagreeable.

There is yet another matter, probably occasioned by all these. I am not quite satisfied with my place in the "Theatre". I do not seem to have any voice in its work, and I find it hard, placed as I am in the position of a "disagreeable" actor, to continue to have much enthusiasm in me for the welfare of the Society, or Theatre. Several people asked me last Saturday evening when were we starting to work and if we were having any meetings to arrange our programme. I said I did not know; they then asked me if I was not a member; I said yes, but I knew nothing of the work of the "Theatre". What they

105

intended to do or say was a sealed book to me. . . .

Believe me, I am sorry to refuse you, but what else can I do? Try to forgive me for inflicting all this on you. It was because I wished you to clearly understand my difficulties over accepting the part you were so kind as to offer that I wrote at such length.[63]

The Theatre of Ireland produced *Casadh an tSugáin, The Racing Lug*, and an episode from Ibsen's *Brand* at the Molesworth Hall on 7 and 8 December, and was given a generally affirmative review by *Sinn Féin*:

The hall was well filled upon both occasions, and the plays were received with great interest by a sympathetic and interested audience. . . . *The Racing Lug* is a simple little piece, but it afforded a splendid opportunity for Mr. George Nesbitt's fine character study of the old fisherman. He was ably supported by Miss Máire Nic Shiubhlaigh as "Bell", Mr. Proinsias Mac Siubhlaigh as "Rob", the young fisherman, and Miss Honor Lavelle [Helen Laird] did excellent work as the old woman. Indeed it is likely that this little play was never produced before by so strong and capable a cast. And yet one realises very clearly that the dramatic movement has out-stepped work of this class. Both audiences and actors demand a more comprehensive organism through which to give expression to the dramatic life that is surging all around.[64]

By 1906 there were many other amateur groups which played for several days or a week in the Molesworth Hall or the Rotunda or the Abbey or the Queen's.[65] One such group was the National Players Society, which on St. Patrick's day gave a matinee and evening performance at the Queen's, doing *Liudaide óg na Leargagh Móire*, an Irish translation of Seumas MacManus's *The Lad from Largymore*, as well as MacManus's *The Hard-Hearted Man* and Lover's *The White Horse of the Peppers*. On 26 December the company appeared at the Molesworth Hall in *The White Horse of the Peppers* and Alice Milligan's *The Deliverance of Red Hugh*. On the next night, the Lover play was followed by Felix Partridge's *An tAthrughadh Mór*. The plays were produced by Brian Callender, but reports suggest that the quality of this group's production was never high. On 23 September, for instance, Holloway attended their open-air performance of Cousins' *The Sword of Dermot*, and wrote:

The whole thing was a farce, as none of the performers had the most elementary idea of acting a serious dramatic piece

106

in English. The National Players seem to become worse and worse each time I see them. . . . It is well to keep such performances in the dark.[66]

The National Players Society depended mainly on revivals, but the Oireachtas each year produced one or two new plays. In 1906, the festival took place during the second week in August at the Rotunda. 8 August saw the premiere of *Seabhac na Ceathramha Caoile, or The Hawk of Carrowkeel* by Thomas Hayes. This was a four-act drama which, as *The Freeman's Journal* remarked, 'depicts the exciting exploits of "The Hawk", a famous traditional character in County Clare in the eighteenth century.' On 9 August there was the first production of *An tAthrughadh Mór*, Felix Partridge's comedy about the speaking of Irish, which was performed by one of the branches of the Gaelic League. On the same evening, the Theatre of Ireland produced *An Talamh*, a translation by 'Torna' of Colum's *The Land*.

The Gaelic League's Samhain celebration occurred in the first week of November at the Abbey. On 3 November a revised version of Connell's *Robert Emmet* was produced, and on 5 November there were three plays — Cousins' *The Sword of Dermot*, Partridge's *An tAthrughadh Mór*, and MacManus's *Orange and Green*.

Worth noting also are a production of Edmund Leamy's *Cupid in Kerry*, a three-act comedy done at the Queen's on Easter Monday, 16 April, and a production of John Dever's *Rosaleen Dhu* done on 3, 4, and 5 May at the Rotunda by the Drapers' Dramatic Club. Leamy, who had recently died, was an M.P. and a friend of Griffith. His play was presented under 'the Patronage and Presence of John Redmond, Esq., M.P. and the Irish Parliamentary Party.' It was reviewed in these doubtless extravagant terms:

> The comedy coruscates with true Hibernian wit, while the humorous and intensely laughable situations which abound in the piece will keep the audience in an incessant, not to say painful, state of hilarity from the rise to the fall of the curtain.[67]

John Dever's, also unpublished, play sounds somewhat strange. The opening scene was in Connemara, but the second act was in the quarters of the French army in Algiers. Nevertheless, *The Freeman's Journal* assured its readers that 'Irish dances are danced, and Irish songs are frequently introduced', and that the play was 'thoroughly Irish in tone'.

* * *

A columnist in *The Freeman's Journal* remarked on Thursday 6 December that:

> The Ulster Literary Theatre produced two admirable new plays at the Examination Hall of Belfast's Queen's College on Tuesday night. *The Turn of the Road*, by R. Mayne, follows somewhat on the lines of Padraic Colum's peasant dramas, but has a strong Northern distinctiveness and rugged humour. *The Pagan*, by Lewis Purcell, introduces a decidedly new note into the dramatic revival movement. It had all the appearance, as regards stage-mounting and costume, of being a Yeats-like mystic antique production, but amazed its audience by being a strong piece of character painting. . . . The costumes were superb, erring on the side of showiness, but then the piece was a comedy, and exaggeration in everything was in keeping with its spirit.[68]

The Northern Whig wrote more fully:

> The Ulster Literary Theatre is undoubtedly going ahead. Last night, under the auspices and in aid of the funds of the Queen's College Literary and Scientific Society, it presented in the Examination Hall of the College a couple of new plays to a larger and perhaps a more critical audience than it has ever been favoured with. It is something of a feat to open a season with two new pieces written, staged, dressed, and acted entirely by members, and the fact would excuse many shortcomings in details. Fortunately the Ulster Literary Theatre does not need to have many allowances made for it; the keenness and earnestness of those belonging to it have helped them to surmount difficulties and avoid pitfalls that are fatal to so many amateurs.
>
> The plays call first for consideration. *The Turn of the Road* is Rutherford Mayne's first dramatic essay, and in its setting and the characters resembles somewhat Lewis Purcell's *Enthusiast*, produced by this company last season. As in *The Enthusiast*, we have a typical Ulster family, one son of which for the love of music — as the enthusiast, with the desire to reform the world — rebels against a narrow routine of life on a County Down farm. The resemblance, however, is merely superficial, for Rutherford Mayne has plenty of originality of his own; his types are the result of personal observation in that unexplored artistic field, Ulster peasant life. He knows how to tell a story, too, and to endow with dramatic appeal everyday incidents in an Ulster farmhouse — the return from

108

market, the crack round the turf fire, a courtship, a marriage bargain, and the petty squabbles that colour what to an outsider is a very monotonous existence.

The struggles of an artistic temperament in such an environment are painted with truth and insight, and, best of all, with humour that rarely flags from curtain to curtain. There are weak moments in the play, and the author has some difficulties with his exits, though this is a problem that a little experience will enable him to avoid. The epilogue is well written, but, good as the grandfather's speech is, it seems superfluous, for the play logically came to an end when Robbie John with his fiddle goes out into the night, or if it is necessary to emphasise the father's repentance, it should be done without a new scene being added.

It is the use that the author makes of dialogue that will probably impress Ulstermen most. We are accustomed to think of Northern speech as harsh and unmusical, a patois of no value in art, but Rutherford Mayne shows how admirably it has been moulded by successive generations to express the character of the race, and he fairly revels in its raciness, its tang of the soil, its fine, vivid phrases. The dialogue is written with a gusto that proves how fully his heart was in the task, and to that gusto the actors last night did full justice. They put the best of themselves in the piece, and the characters really lived. One of the finest studies was that of Mrs. Granahan, the sharp-tongued, busy housewife, a portrait of rare artistic merit, and the audience appreciated, as well they might, the part of Samuel James, that strange mixture of stolidness and cunning, which was played — it is not giving secrets away — by the author. Of equal merit was the hard-hearted, narrow-minded William John Granahan, and Robbie John was remarkably clever. Thomas Granahan, the grandfather, had comparatively little to do, but did it well, and John Graeme was effective. . . . The staging was on a level with the best that the Ulster Literary Theatre has done, and the costumes and setting in *The Pagan* need fear no comparison with those of any amateur and few professional companies.[69]

The Irish News and Belfast Morning News thought that Mayne's piece was clever but not of an uncommon type, while Purcell's marked an entirely new departure:

We have had historical and quasi-historical plays go leor in Gaelic and English; we have had Mr. Yeats's poems in dramatic form which he called drama; we have had several

Deirdres (including Æ's beautiful play of that name); we have had King Charles in a barrel, the French on the sea, and similar works by enthusiastic Gaedhilgeoiri — but not until now has anybody had the temerity to adventure on comedy of ancient Ireland. This is what "Lewis Purcell" has done in *The Pagan*. The scene is laid within the enclosure of Crimall Ruadh, a free ceile of the tribe of Ui Nial, on the slope of the Cave Hill, and the period is the sixth century. Furthermore, the comedy is remarkable for the fact that there are no royal personages nor great chieftains in it. Cormac MacRuairi, the hero, is but a petty chieftain of the MacUilin tribe, and none of the other characters are of higher social standing.

Despite the comedy element, the play is a conscientious attempt to delineate some phases of the struggle between Paganism and Christianity at a time when the gospel of peace and goodwill to men was new in the land. Some of the characters are professing Christians, but in their hearts the old gods still reign, and the fierce spirit of the olden days breaks out from beneath the thin assumption of meek Christianity at the first hint of strife. Nuala, the heroine, though conforming to the new faith, yet despises its teaching of humility — almost unknown to herself. All her sympathies are with the brave days of old — the days when a strong arm never yielded, save to a stronger. And so when Gorman MacRory, who lies to recuperate from wounds in her father's dun, demands her for his wife and will not take no for an answer, but sends a message home to prepare for the bridal feast, she is overcome by his masterfulness. At first terrified by his curt, overbearing method of love-making she comes in the end to say "Here is a *man*, self-confident, resolute, imperious, as a man should be." And so, Christian though she is her Pagan heart turns to warrior Pagan, turns reluctantly, fearfully, yet with a timorous joy that she should be wooed, however roughly, by such a being.

Around these characters there cluster some half-dozen others, all well-drawn and requiring careful acting. . . .

The author has made a distinct advance in playwriting since he essayed *The Reformers*, and in the present piece displays a knowledge of stagecraft which could only have been gained by careful study of the best models. He has, too, a keen eye for a picture, and the tableau at the end of each scene is exceedingly well-devised. Indeed, so far as stagecraft goes the question frequently suggested itself last night — "Where is now the boasted superiority of the metropolitan

110

companies." Of course, in some things the Abbey Theatre Co. and the National Players are still ahead of the Ultonians, but the latter are gaining upon them with marvellous rapidity, as was predicted in these columns last year and the year before. In many things, too, the Ulster players seem to have a nicer discretion than their Dublin confreres; their sense of the artistic is not bizarre, and they certainly would never have allowed a Deirdre, in a modern low-cut green evening dress, to disfigure their stage. And their acting has gained by their cohesion throughout the years since the Ulster Literary Theatre has come into existence.

The acting last night was very good, even for the Ulster Literary Theatre players. But then, in each play they had congenial flesh and blood characters to enact, not merely shadows mouthing platitudes in prose, or reciting long poems. . . . All the costumes have been designed by the members of the Theatre, and are, so far as possible, correct historically.[70]

*   *   *

The dramatic movement was a continuing occasion of critical speculation. The following speeches, interviews, and essays were particularly notable in 1906.

On 5 February Dr. George Sigerson read to the National Literary Society a paper entitled 'The Irish Peasantry and the Stage', and the following lively discussion ensued:

Dr. Sigerson, who was warmly applauded, in the course of his paper, said: — ". . . Of course, we have heard the doctrine of Art for Art; it was known even in the days of George Sand, who thought it should be altered to Art for Truth. . . . It certainly should not mean that Art may isolate itself, thus cutting itself off from life. Still less can this be spoken as regards dramatic art, concerning which an old and experienced master directed that the mirror should be held up to Nature. This is a counsel which may be commended to the new schools of Irish dramatists, whose enterprise, originality, and genius we are glad to applaud, in order that, being more true to nature they shall be more in touch with their nation. There need be no limit to their study except what is drawn by truth and taste. . . .

Mr. J. B. Yeats, in proposing a vote of thanks to Dr. Sigerson, said there ran all through his lecture a subdued affection and enthusiasm for the Irish nature with which everyone sympathised. Mr. Synge represented the Irish peasants as a strong, vigorous sensible kind of people. A man like Carleton seemed to him to be a perfect curse to the Irish nation, to the Irish character. He had fixed on the Irish character, on the Irish peasant, an indelible stain; he had painted him as a man with a shifty look, a poor servile creature waiting for the signal until his master called upon him. That unfortunate example of Carleton had been followed by Miss Barlow. In Ireland they had still a peasant life, and Mr. Synge and Mr. Colm had taken it up, and he hoped it would go on.

Mr. Joy seconded the vote of thanks. He thought that Mr. Synge could stand as a great artist apart from any question of objective truth. But he found practically nothing in *The Shadow of the Glen* or in *The Well of the Saints* that he could say was objectively true of Irish life as he knew it.

Mr. Holloway continued the debate.

Mr. Colm maintained that all art was subjective art, and that Mr. Synge's plays should be criticised from that point of view.

Mr. W. B. Yeats said Ireland had for centuries been in two attitudes of mind, both of which were destructive of literature and the habit that created literature—Ireland had been forced into continued attack and on the other side into continued defence. If they wanted a law passed by the English Government they got the law passed not by reasoning over it, but by attack. The Ireland of the present day, in its relation to literature, was the most abjectly material nation in the world because of its absorption in history, owing to its tendency to be always apologising, always believing itself in the dock, always calling up its virtues from the past, always looking upon history as the brief handed to it for its defence. It endeavoured to enslave the artistic mind and to lay down that he should not try to express what was in himself, the thing that came from eternity and was going to eternity, but that his business was to express accidental forms taken by life under the cover of material circumstances.

Mr. T. M. Kettle said he was afraid Mr. W. B. Yeats had constructed his own views of Irish life. Mr. Yeats had done more than anybody else in Ireland to create an Irish Theatre, and he had also done more than anybody else to prevent anybody going there (laughter). He thought the fundamental mistake into which Mr. Yeats had fallen was that he had mistaken life for literature. Inside the seas of Ireland there were roughly two millions of Irish peasants; and amongst these they would find every virtue and every vice. And if

112

anybody called up a type to which everybody must conform under pain of blasphemy against the national idea then he (Mr. Kettle) did not think anybody could profess to understand him. He did not know why the Irish peasant should monopolise the stage. The city was infinitely more interesting than the peasant.[71]

In June, Padraic Colum contributed an article on 'Ibsen and National Drama' to Griffith's *Sinn Féin*, and in it he took this sunny view of the present state of Irish drama:

> The Ireland of to-day is far more advanced dramatically than the Norway of Ole Bull and his colleagues. The theatre with which Mr. Yeats is associated has not achieved popularity, but it has attained astonishing maturity; its mere educative effect must be reckoned on as a powerful asset. The more spontaneous drama which we see at the Oireachtas is probably far in advance of the first performances of "Norway's Theatre". There are effective dramatic societies not only in Dublin, but in Belfast and Cork. The plays in Irish and English which have grown up around the Gaelic League and kindred societies show that there is a real dramatic movement in the country.

Colum went on to discuss his view of the responsibility of audience and of playwright. His view is characteristically middle-of-the-road, but interesting in the light of the *Playboy* rows which were only a few months in the future: 'As an audience we should be tolerant, condemning no man for a point of view that is his own; as authors we should be sincere and serious, giving no wanton provocation.' [72]

When the Abbey opened its winter season on 13 October, the highlight of the evening was an address by Yeats:

> Mr. W. B. Yeats said that in speaking to them that night he felt that for the first time he was able to say that the theatre was about to show some of the characteristics which had marked national theatres elsewhere. It had been a very slow development, but he hoped he would be able to explain why that development was necessarily slow. One thing, he thought, they might look back upon with pleasure was that for the first time they were really going to play tolerably constantly. That winter they would play every Saturday, and for the first three months there would practically be a different bill every Saturday. When one realised that not one of those plays, apart from the foreign classics, had been in existence five or six

113

years ago, when they talked on the creation of a National Theatre one would see that their work had been a little fruitful. At these performances they hoped to be able to draw a better audience to the more popular parts of the house than hitherto; they had for the first time sixpenny seats (applause). He saw by their applause that they knew there had been a very constant demand for these seats in the theatre. Before that winter they could not have played continuously, or even once a week. They had not enough plays; they had not sufficient actors. It was a very long business to create dramatic tradition and to create a skilful company. They were working under conditions that no actor or manager was working under in any English-speaking country. For the great part of their work they could not take any actor from the existing theatres. They had to train their actors from the beginning, because they wished to set on the stage Irish life. They had tried to get plays on Irish life produced by English actors, but it was always a failure — their mere accent made it a failure. Neither had they the necessary knowledge or thought or feeling of the country. They had, therefore, to create Irish actors. There were a few Irish actors on the English stage when the Irish theatre movement began, but they had all learned the traditions of an alien theatre, and of an alien habit of thought, and they were at their very worst when they tried to play Irish characters. The Irishman of the theatre of commerce had a very slight relation to life. When he was first imagined, he represented one type out of hundreds that went to build up a nation, and he had become gradually to appear the type of all Irishmen; he had now ceased to represent accurately the solitary type of whiskey-drinking, shillelagh-whirling man who once did exist in this country. They had the usual number of peasant plays; he imagined they had rather more peasant plays than their regular frequenters would like. They had more or less to deliberately choose to found their theatrical art on some phase of Irish life which was full of Irish characteristics. Looking into the history of national theatres and national dramatic movements, they would find they always began by founding themselves on the history and legends of their country, or on the peasant life of the country. If a national theatre were to try and draw a greater portion of its subjects from the drawing-room, it would be as impossible as to develop national feeling by contemplating a building in some French boulevard or in Stephen's Green or in Kensington. As there was a kind of cosmopolitan archi-

114

tecture that went all over the world, and was . . . the same everywhere, so there was a phase of life that went all over the world, and that was very much the same everywhere. In order that they might test their peasant work by high standards, they had begun to adopt the custom of translating certain foreign masterpieces which, in feeling, seemed close to the peasant life of this country. They had already played and would repeat Molière's *The Doctor in Spite of Himself*. But side by side with perfecting, so far as they could, the skill of their company in the performance of peasant work they were beginning to seriously build up what they might hope would be equal skill in the performance of romantic and historical work. So that they might test their work and judge that they were working in the spirit of sincerity, they were putting on a great foreign and romantic work. A little after Christmas they would do *The Antigone* of Sophocles. Mr. Wilfrid Scawen Blunt had written an Irish play, *Fand*, dealing with Cuchullain's adventures, and it would be produced at the end of January. They would also perform Racine's *The Pleaders*. He thought that looking ahead they would create a National Theatre not unworthy to stand beside some of the Continental theatres in ten years' time; it would take that time fully. When they started the movement they were fully prepared for a long wait. They would not allow themselves to be led away by any little breath or any contemporary feeling. They would not allow their weather-cocks to veer too much into the Norwegian or French wind, but to represent equally all sides of the great dramatic literature of the world. They would require the support of the reader of books and the ordinary people who went to be amused and excited. The ordinary theatre had driven away from it the people who read books and who looked at pictures, so that playwrights and managers had to produce their plays for an audience that had not fine taste. He thought that they were going to get the support of the plain man and the readers of books in Ireland. In this country there was not only real capacity for acting, but there was a real interest in the drama. In conclusion, Mr. Yeats said that their business was in the course of a few years to create a genuine and new art for the theatre (loud applause).[73]

Part of Yeats's address drew forth a lengthy critique of the Abbey and its practices from Frank Dalton, an Irishman and a professional actor who was old enough to have worked with Boucicault and whose son, Louis D'Alton, was in later years to be one of the Abbey's most successful playwrights. Dalton's chief criticisms were that the Abbey staging and acting were unprofessional, and that it was a great error to ignore such traditional Irish playwrights as Boucicault and Lover, as well as Sheridan and Goldsmith. He said in part:

I saw Abbey street in London. Of course, it was clearly given out that no one was to shout, as they were only amateurs doing their best. Still the atmosphere would be Irish. It will be home again. And it was. I felt as if back in the old Rotunda looking at one of those performances which used to reflect so much credit on the young men of the drapery establishments. Very nice, indeed. But the alien actor would, I am sure, do at least equal justice to his author, nor would he need to be apologised for. Sufferance need not be the badge of an Irish National Theatre. When its actors have the courage of their ability, let them test it. When they stake their worldly existence on it as a profession they will begin to learn, and know more than the first dimensions of a play, that it has more than length, that there is form and substance in it. They will soon be told that straggling the stage in wandering ineptitude may be farcical enough, but is not farce; that the spirit of Celtic tragedy need not be reduced to droning bass or the feeble and plaintive whining of a baby play; that to be ineffective is not always artistic, no more than dulness is profundity. These things they have yet to learn. But, under present conditions, they never will. They don't advance; they move in circles like the firmament, or a lost trapper on a trackless prairie — they just go round.

Some of their plays are full of excellence, but short and sketchy — single phases. Not one of sustained interest capable of testing the resourcefulness, construction, or power of analysis in author or player. Still, better than Boucicault! Yes — in spots.

Charles Dickens once described *The Colleen Bawn* as *"The Vicar of Wakefield* of the stage." He may be wrong, but could the Irish National Theatre provide us with another such, many would be quite content to let them shelve a very large proportion of their present stock. . . .

In my admiration for Mr. Yeats there is a flaw; he is far beyond my praise in the work he has done. What he will do may be greater still, but he will never arrive at the full inheritance till he succeeds in lifting the Irish National Theatre to a much higher plane; till he dominates more effectually;

till he gives us plays fit to challenge comparison, long enough and strong enough to fight their way the world around, and as a step in that direction retains a few capable artists — "Saxon or Italians", if need be — anything that will give cohesion to his tyro units, mould them out of their crudeness. Instead of chantings teach them with readers' skill to expound their authors. Let him run his theatre as an academy, even if he has to charge fees, or get a Corporation grant to do it on (Dublin might even lead with the Municipal Theatre).

Keep the house going during regular periods; keep the company busy at any good work that is likely to enlarge their views and methods. In the meantime prepare and develop the literary work. Produce good native plays wherever he can get them.

Let him and Douglas Hyde give us a spacious work, not drastic fragments. No more patchwork programmes, and not so much of the petty playwrights. A theatre calling itself Irish and National should, in its work, stand comparison with any. A select circle of nice little playwrights, making pretty little plays, for good little amateurs, and all in the name of a nation, would be grotesque. If I may be excused saying so, any common coterie of log-rolling back-scratchers could do as much. Mr. Yeats is far above that sort of thing; his genius and resources should have helped him to a higher aim. If there is not a great change, I fear and regret that the Irish National Theatre has not come to stay — and its only too appropriate cradle was the Morgue.[74]

On 17 October Holloway was at the Abbey in the morning, and Henderson told him of the society's new journal, *The Arrow,* 'which they intended posting to some thousand people. The nature of the journal would be a description of the plays, etc. Yeats to be editor and probably sole writer.' Yeats was not the sole writer. In the first issue, Lady Gregory amusingly catalogued some of the criticisms of the theatre:

Some time ago at a debate in Dublin a speaker complained that the Irish peasantry were slandered in *Spreading the News,* because no where in Ireland would so improbable a story grow out of so little; and in the same speech he said our Theatre was not worthy of support, because we "had given our first performance at the Castle". Another speaker pointed to this fiction as a very Spreading of the News. Since that day it has been said to us that we never play but in Irish, that our Theatre is "something done for the Roman Catholics," that it has been "got up by the Irish Parliamentary Party with Mr. Healy at the head of them," that we have a special fee of fifty pounds a performance for anybody from Trinity College who wishes to hire the Theatre, that our "attitude to the Irish peasant arises out of class prejudice which keeps us from seeing anything that is good in him," that we encourage agrarian outrage by the performance of *Cathleen ni Houlihan*, that through fear of offending the English we will not play anything founded upon events that happened since their arrival under Strongbow, that we are neglecting Dublin for England, that we are "a Fenian lot," and that we give ourselves airs. Some at least of these accusations must be founded on evidence as airy as that given in the case of the murder of Jack Smith.[75]

In the following article entitled 'The Value of Criticism', Stephen Gwynn discussed the significant difference in the reception of Synge's plays and in the reception of William Boyle's.

Irish public opinion, or public feeling rather, is in an odd state at present. The mere hint of "stage Irishman" will banish all tolerance from the minds of most of our acquaintance. . . .

It comes to this, that if any Irish personage or incident is presented in a spirit of irresponsible gaiety, half of us would sooner die than laugh, because we are afraid of laughing at the wrong thing — afraid of our own propensity to laughter. And yet, concurrently with this, there is a most surprising latitude given to any man who applies ridicule to things and persons in Ireland. So long as we are clear that he means more than to raise a laugh, he may caricature as he pleases. These reflections arise in my mind after looking at Mr. Boyle's astonishingly clever play, *The Mineral Workers*, the third of his comedies, in all of which the purpose of satire has been increasingly evident. No one ever presented more disagreeable Irish types than the whole family in *The Building Fund*, *The Eloquent Dempsy* in the play to which he gives his name, or that Mr. O'Fogarty and his ally the Poor Law Guardian in "this new piece." Perhaps we hardly realise how disagreeable they would be if played by an actor without Mr. W. G. Fay's marvellous gift. We can forgive anything to his O'Fogarty, his Dempsy, and the other worm (whose name I have forgotten) in *The Building Fund*, because of the extraordinary vivacity of their wrigglings. Exuberant life is always attractive. In the case of explicitly propagandist plays, like those by Seumas MacManus, there is less need for tolerance of the

118

hard hitting at Irish vices, because the satirised persons generally undergo conversion: and in the cleverest of all this class, *An tAthrughadh Mór*, the man who sets his back up against the Irish language, is loveable in his perversity. A more notable example of my point is afforded by *The Seething Pot* and *Hyacinth*. Much has been forgiven, and rightly forgiven, to the author of these books even by those who were most sharply attacked, for the sake of that earnest love of Ireland which is evident in every line of them.[76]

It is no bad trait of contemporary Irishmen that they will stand almost anything in the way of criticism from men of whose honest intention they are convinced. The constructive value of criticism depends essentially upon two things: First, that the critic shall endeavour to understand thoroughly the motives of those to whom he applies his scalpel; and, secondly, that he shall not use the knife without a hope of a cure. But it is curious to note how thin-skinned we still are when confronted with a presentation of Irish life when no purpose is apparent. Dispassionate art finds it hard to secure a footing; and Mr. Synge gets little of the tolerance so freely extended to Mr. Boyle. We are in danger of insisting that all our authors be preachers, and that would be destruction to literature. The most valuable criticism of life is that upon which — as upon Shakespeare — every man will place his own interpretation.[77]

The constant and continuing criticism of Yeats was evolving into an identification of the National Theatre Society as the embodiment solely of Yeats and his work. For instance, 'Scrutator', in a review of Yeats's *Poems 1899–1905*, wrote:

Viewing the work of the National Theatre Society in the light of, and as expounded by this book, one stands well-nigh aghast at its almost hopeless aloofness from humanity. . . . Whether Mr. Yeats sees it or not, if he really has the interests of the movement at heart, the proper thing for him to do would be to add one more renunciation to that one mentioned in his preface, and expunge his plays for the time being from the Programmes of his Society. . . . Coming to the plays themselves, a little examination of them will, I think, show that Mr. Yeats's ideas about drama are of the most superficial and trivial nature possible. . . . He cannot — at any rate he does not — conceive things and think them out naturally after the manner of drama.[78]

Alice Milligan, however, defended both Yeats and the Abbey:

> This is a subject that never tires. In effect I agree with your last criticism that Yeats is not essentially a dramatist, but a strayed lyrical songster. All the same let us be just. He did right and well to stimulate the present literary dramatic movement, and but for him would it be as far as it is or would it exist at all? I think, moreover, the dramatic impulse brought our poet back from a region of mysticism and moonshine to solid earth. His *Kathleen ni Houlihan* is worth an infinity of such volumes as *The Wind among the Reeds* and in *Countess Cathleen* the tragedy of the famine era finds ample expression. Then leaving aside what he has written himself, is he not to be credited with having turned Lady Gregory from the pathos of magazine literature and essay writing and of having commanded her to be a comedian? I must say that nothing I have read in recent years seems so wholesome and good for national propaganda as some of her writing, notably *The White Cockade*. I have only one complaint to make about the Abbey Theatre, namely, that it has not an acting-school attached to it, and a varied troupe of actors to draw on. Mr. F. J. Fay would make an excellent instructor, and should be led to school people for the parts instead of filling some of them in an absolutely unimpressive manner.
>
> There is one of Lady Gregory's pieces that has not yet been staged. Is it because the players cannot sing traditionally? I allude to *The Rising of the Moon*. The day that it is acted first I will be there to see, though I should travel from Cahir Daniel, or Malin or Slyne Head. I think, moreover, on that night the gallery will be quite full, and the Abbey Theatre will ever after be popular.[79]

In December, Colum, although overestimating the importance of drama in Irish, made some significant predictions about the drama of the future:

> Our own national movement gathers force, and one sign of its growth is the desire for dramatic expression. Dublin is certainly interested in the effort to create a national drama. Since the Abbey Theatre made a practical appeal for support, there have been audiences for the National Theatre Society's plays. Interest in ideas, eagerness about problems, are part of the intellectual vigour necessary for the creation of drama, and these interests grow with the national movement.
>
> The Irish dramatist dealing with his own country, his own

people, and their traditions, has great and unused material before him. The myths of our heroic age have hardly been touched. Our history has not been touched at all, and if it may not be taught in the school, it should be taught with greater effect in the theatre.

Our social drama has scarce been hinted at. There are the peasantry, with their powerful individualities and their long tradition, meeting the impact of a national and constructive movement. There are our middle classes coming into contact with the problems and ideas of modern Europe. Norway, during a period of national reconstruction, produced a dramatist, who, out of her life, and traditions, created a great modern drama. So far, Ibsen remains a great dramatic influence. The Germans followed Ibsen in subject and method. They failed, because Ibsen had perfected that particular form, and there could be no developments.

The Scandinavian drama, with its rigid form, and economic dialogue, is bound to break up. Already we are relieved when we come to an abundant passage in a prose play. It is not suggested that there will be a reaction towards loose construction and aimless dialogue; but there ought to be a return of the elements that the Scandinavian dramatist had shut out; ample character and large action. A fullness of life expressing itself in abundant and coloured speech. These the Irish might bring back to the European drama. If our dramatist deals with heroic myth he has this ample character and this large action. If he deals with peasant life, and the powerful individualities in peasant life, he has the ample character again. Both in Irish and English we have abundant and vigorous speech. We might bring back that eloquence which has been so long out of European literature.[80]

On 10 December the National Literary Society had a notable meeting. After a lecture by Colum:

Mr. F. Ryan said he thought they would have heard something on the subject of the drama, national or otherwise, but he had not been able to discover anything of that nature. He had hoped that the lecturer would have given them something in his paper in the way of criticism of some of the works in the new forms of national drama in which so many curious theories are developed, and where people "walk out of their own skins" (laugh.) Let them apply themselves to the lives they led every day. It was not possible to deal within such limitations and to give human interest to the problems of kings and warriors in the form of Irish drama of mythical times.

Mr. W. J. Lawrence said that he had been at the Abbey Theatre on Saturday, and had there seen what, after all, might by some be not unnaturally termed the first pantomime of the season (laughter). It was a mistake to attempt to gerrymander national drama, and there was no reason why a country like Ireland could not yet rise to the dignity of having a national drama. They could not force it or do it by breathing poetics like Aristotle. They had, of course, with them Mr. W. B. Yeats (a laugh), and tried by any test could he be found wanting? (Cries of "No.") The speaker concluded by rather severely criticising one of the recent Abbey Theatre plays. . . .

Mr. W. B. Yeats, who was received with applause, said he was under the disadvantage of not having heard the lecture nor much of what followed. His belief was that the shock of the new subject was the source of the greatest interest and intensity, and so long as their plays dealt with Ireland they would be better acted by Irishmen and in Ireland than anywhere else (hear, hear). That was to say that being done by actors who know the people and can represent them as they are. No one could represent the Irish peasant as they could, and he believed the end would be the creation in Dublin of a large municipal theatre as in Germany, which would go on bit by bit as the playwright arises until the thing expands gradually and greatly (applause). As they got their seed, they must leave it to grow spontaneously (applause). . . .[81]

1907

By the beginning of 1907, the Irish theatrical revival may be said to have reached full force; good new plays were appearing regularly, and the National Theatre Society had attracted the attention and respect of the public. But the most memorable theatrical event of 1907 was to change the course of its history, for early in the year riots broke out in the Abbey Theatre during the opening performances of J. M. Synge's *The Playboy of the Western World*.

There was reason to expect trouble at the première of Synge's new play. His earlier *In the Shadow of the Glen* had been criticized as un-Irish and, indeed, offensive to Irish womanhood. The label 'French decadent' had been attached to him, owing to his earlier residence in Paris. In the weeks before the opening performances of *The Playboy*, unusual secrecy was maintained about the new play. Joseph Holloway was for once barred from rehearsals, but he reported the rumour passed on by one of the actors, Harry Young, that there was an organized opposition present to hiss *In the Shadow of the Glen* when that play was performed just a week before *The Playboy* opening. He also, three days before the première, recorded the following rumour:

> Mr. Henderson was looking gloomy at the Council Meeting of the National Literary Society and I knew something was wrong at the Abbey. I soon learned that Yeats had withdrawn *The Pot of Broth* from the bills on Saturday next — he refused to let it be played in conjunction with Synge's new play, *The Playboy*. He sent his refusal by telegram when all the printing had been done. *Riders to the Sea* has been substituted.[1]

All along, Yeats and Lady Gregory had misgivings about the language of the play, and Lady Gregory reported:

> There were too many violent oaths, and the play itself was marred by this. I did not think it was fit to be put on the stage without cutting. It was agreed that it should be cut in rehearsal. A fortnight before its production, Mr. Yeats, thinking I had seen a rehearsal, wrote, "I would like to know how you thought *The Playboy* acted. . . . Have they cleared many of the objectionable sentences out of it?" I did not, however, see a rehearsal and did not hear the play again until the night of its production, and then I told Synge that the cuts were not enough, that many more should be made.[2]

123

To forestall criticism of the language, Synge wrote a programme note defending the authenticity of the phrases used in the play, and the factual basis of the plot:

> In writing *The Playboy of the Western World*, as in my other plays, I have used very few words that I have not heard among the country people, or spoken in my own childhood before I could read the newspapers. A certain number of the phrases I employ I have heard also among the fishermen of Kerry and Mayo, or from beggars nearer Dublin, and I am glad to acknowledge how much I owe, directly and indirectly, to the folk-imagination of these people. Nearly always when some friendly or angry critic tells me that such or such a phrase could not have been spoken by a peasant, he singles out some expression that I have heard, word for word, from some old woman or child, and the same is true also, to some extent, of the actions and incidents I work with. The central incident of *The Playboy* was suggested by an actual occurrence in the west.[3]

It was at those very points that the most vehement critical attacks on the play were levelled. The *Daily Express* review is representative, in that it praises the acting and parts of the play, but baulks at the language:

> Expectation was raised to a high pitch in anticipation of the production of another new play by an Irish writer, one who has made his mark in the repertoire of the National Theatre Society. Accordingly there was a large audience at the Abbey Theatre on Saturday evening, when *The Playboy of the Western World*, a three act comedy, by Mr. J. M. Synge, was presented for the first time to the public. The characters in the play are drawn from the people of the West of Ireland, and their language and methods of expression are as simple, unadorned, and direct as those of the type which they purport to represent. The comedy is in three acts, which are neither long nor heavy, and the dialogue is in many parts sparkling and witty. It would, perhaps, be the better for some slight revision here and there, particularly in the third act in which there is a sentence spoken by the hero, which gave rise to an emphatic expression of dissent from the gallery, and which nobody could say was not justified. . . . Mr. W. G. Fay invests the part of Christy Mahon with that touch of humour which he knows so well how to impart to it. The part of Margaret Flaherty is quite a good one, and Miss Mary O'Neill displayed

her undoubted power in impersonating the publican's good-looking daughter. Mr. Arthur Sinclair's make-up, as the bucolic publican, was admirable, as his return home next morning from the "wake" somewhat "under the influence" was suitable to the occasion. The Widow Quin plays a prominent part in the story of this playboy, Christy. She is his most persistent suitor, and her role is probably the most comical in the whole piece. Miss Sara Allgood, shawled and coiffed in the manner of the Western peasant women, fulfilled the part to perfection. . . . The first act is brilliant and witty in dialogue and it made an excellent impression on the audience. The two following acts did not, however, quite maintain the standard thus set up, and the final curtain descended leaving many persons dissatisfied with the denouement. The incident already referred to — the howl set up at the objectionable phrase given to Christy to speak — spoiled everyone's chance of appreciating the finish of what is, on the whole, a clever piece of writing, cleverly acted and appropriately staged.[4]

The Freeman's Journal, however, called the new play an 'unmitigated, protracted libel upon Irish peasant men and, worse still, upon Irish peasant girlhood,' and added, 'It is quite plain that there is need for a censor at the Abbey Theatre.' 'Jacques', writing in *The Independent*, objected to the lurid dialogue and the inaccurate characterization, and reported that some of the first night audience shared his dissatisfaction. Speaking of the central character, he commented, 'His language, his garb, and his actions may excite laughter in some, but it was a tribute to the good taste and common sense of the audience that hissing and booing mingled with the cheers which greeted the final development of the character that, let us hope, exists only in the lively imagination of the author.' *The Evening Mail* review was entitled 'A Dramatic Freak', and criticized the plot as 'absurd and un-Irish . . . [it] smacks of the decadent ideas of the literary flaneurs of Paris rather than of simple Connaught. . . .' And even *The Irish Times*, which later printed a favourable review by 'Pat' Kenny, concluded its first review by saying, 'Mr. Synge, we are afraid, must to some extent sacrifice the "remorseless truth" if his play is to be made acceptable to healthy public opinion.' A letter to *The Freeman's Journal* signed 'A Western Girl' objected in particular to Pegeen's mention of the word 'shifts' in the second act — 'a word indicating an essential item of female attire, which the lady would probably never utter in ordinary circumstances, even to herself.' That phrase, as well as Christy's reference to 'drifts of chosen females standing in their shifts' provoked hissing from the first night audience, and caused Synge and Lady Gregory to send a telegram to Yeats, who was then in Scotland: 'Audience broke up in disorder at the word shift.'

But, unfavourable though the first reviews generally were, they do not seem sufficient to provoke the riots which occurred during the next performances. On Monday night, hissing gave way to almost continual shouting. Throughout the week, the opening piece, Synge's *Riders to the Sea*, was attentively followed and applauded. But, starting on Monday, the main presentation brought trouble. *The Daily Express* reported:

> As soon as the curtain was raised on *The Playboy* it at once became evident that a large section of the audience were intent on expressing their disapprobation of the piece. . . . Indeed, the disturbance became so loud that it was impossible for those in the front seats to hear a word said on the stage, the mingled boohs, groans, and hisses turning the play into a dumb show. Mr. W. G. Fay, who took the part of the parricide . . . made several attempts to address the audience but was shouted down. He was understood to say that, as a Mayo man himself, he could not understand the objections of a certain section of those present. The play was then continued, but the row became worse than ever, and six constables had to be called in, whose presence, however, had no effect in checking the disorder, and they left the building at the request of Lady Gregory and Mr. Synge. The falling of the curtain at the end was the signal for a renewal of the demonstration, besides the groans and shouting there also being loud applause from those who seemed to wish to disassociate themselves from the disorder. Calls were made for the author, but he did not appear. Mr. Fay came before the footlights and said, "Those who hissed to-night will go away and say they saw the play." This was greeted by a retort from the gallery, "We saw it on Saturday," and loud cheering followed. The audience would not disperse until the lights had been lowered. It is understood that the management have decided to make no alteration in their arrangements, and *The Playboy of the Western World* will again be staged tonight, and every night during the remainder of the week.[5]

The management's determination to continue the scheduled performances aggravated the situation, and the next night's performance brought even greater turmoil in the theatre:

Last night the performance at the Abbey Theatre was accompanied by disturbances more remarkable than those of the previous night. The hostility then shown towards Mr. Synge's new play, *The Playboy of the Western World* was again displayed in a marked manner, and the confusion was increased by the presence of a number of young men, who noisily championed the author's cause, not by trying to maintain order, but by replying to the hostile remarks by counterblasts of shouting. The performance is timed to commence at 8:15. By eight o'clock the pit was well filled, and a few minutes later there trooped into the stalls about fifty young fellows, who subsequently expressed their sympathies with the author. One of the most high-spirited — Mr. Yeats said later that he was intoxicated — rose up and made what he declared to be a speech, which he wound up by shouting, "I don't care a d—— for the lot of you." The rest of the audience took this very good humouredly, and the amusement caused by the opening episodes gave no indication of the fierce scenes which were to follow. The same young fellow confessed that he was "a little bit drunk." He next went to the piano and commenced playing a piece called "Valse Bleu," but on being requested by the attendant to desist he resumed his seat with a remark to the audience that "You are no lovers of music." *Riders to the Sea* was first given, and passed off very well.

Immediately the curtain fell on this, Mr. W. B. Yeats appeared on the stage, and was kindly received. He said:

"A difference of opinion has arisen between the management of this theatre and some of the audience as to the value of the play which we are now to produce, and as to our policy in producing it. If any of you wish to discuss the merits of the play or our rightness in producing it, I shall be delighted to discuss it with you, and do my best to answer your arguments. I will endeavour to get an audience, and invite any who wish to speak to come on the stage and do so."

At this point a gentleman in the audience rose and said, "I have one thing to say, and —" (cries of "Order").

Mr. Yeats — "On Monday evening I shall be pleased to hear you. We have put this play before you to be heard and to be judged, as every play should be heard and judged. Every man has a right to hear it and condemn it if he pleases, but no man has a right to interfere with another man hearing a play and judging for himself (hear, hear). The country that condescends either to bully or to permit itself to be bullied soon ceases to have any fine qualities, and I promise you that

127

if there is any small section in this theatre that wish to deny the right of others to hear what they themselves don't want to hear — (a voice: "We will put them out") — we will play on, and our patience shall last longer than their patience" (general applause).

The curtain then rang up on *The Playboy of the Western World*. All went well for some minutes, but when one of the characters reached a point in the dialogue in which he says he doesn't like to do something because he "didn't know what Father O'Reilly would say," someone shouted out, "You terrible priest-ridden fellow." The "intoxicated" young man yelled "Shut up." Amidst the shouting Mr. Yeats came forward, and after a time secured quietness, as the result of calls from the audience for "Order" and "The play." Mr. Yeats said: "I ask you to remain seated in your places, and to listen to a play by a most distinguished countryman of yours (cheers and a few hisses). It deserves your hearing. If it is a play that is bad it will die without your help (hear, hear). If the play is good your hindrance cannot mar it. What you can mar very greatly is the reputation of the country for fair play" (boohs and hear, hear).

The play was then proceeded with, but gradually a din arose, created by tin trumpets and stamping in the gallery, and soon it was impossible to hear the dialogue. One of the disturbers was ultimately removed. The scuffle in the attempt to put the young fellow out had put the whole place in disorder, and Lady Gregory, therefore, asked that the police, who were behind the scenes all the time, should be brought in. Seven constables then filed in, and in the period of quietness which ensued a gentleman in the stalls mounted his seat, and said — "Just one word, as a member of the public —"

A Voice — "Who are you?"

"It doesn't matter who I am. I am a member of the public. The management are responsible to me for having brought me here." (A Voice — "And to us also.") "They are responsible for giving me something, and they are not allowed to do so. You also have made a contract, and want something for your money, to see this play. Have you seen the play?" (Loud shouts of "Yes.") "I say you have not, and you have no right to judge it until you have."

The attention of the audience was diverted to the movements of the police. They seemed doubtful as to whether they had a right to remove anyone, but Mr. Hugh Lane, who was sitting in the stalls, pointed to two men and said he would charge them, and he demanded their arrest.

The constables still seemed doubtful, and intended only to warn the men pointed to, who seemed disposed to be quiet. At this point Inspector Flynn entered, and on Mr. Lane's demand he had one of the men removed. When the curtain rang up for Act II, a large number of constables had been drafted into the building. A few minutes afterwards Mr. Lane demanded the removal of another man, who was accordingly hustled out by the police. There was not much noise until the point in the play where Peggy asks Christy Mahon was he the man who killed his father. On his replying in the affirmative Peggy exclaims, "Then a thousand welcomes to you." This drew forth a perfect Bedlam of yells, and various cries, such as "That is not the West; I defy you to prove it," "Travesty," etc. From this point a steady drumming of feet was sustained, through which the play could only just be followed. By direction of Mr. Yeats another man was removed. Mr. Yeats and the police were loudly boohed.

The next point of offence in the play is where one of the characters refers to an undergarment in a way which it is unusual to reproduce on the stage. There were loud boohs, and cries of "Oh, oh." Following upon this uproar there were some verbal exchanges amongst the audience which was not in complimentary terms. The dialogue of the play then proceeded to where one of the characters says to the parricide, "I give you my blessing, and no doubt Father O'Leary will do the same." At this there was a further demonstration, one of the remarks that could be distinguished being "The little travesty should be beaten off the stage." At every hiss and booh the young fellows in the stalls clapped and cheered, which called forth the remark, "The boys all got a free seat to come and clap." In spite of the fact that some of the most offensive expressions had been expunged, the audience found frequent occasions for demonstrations of disapproval, and throughout there was the constant drumming of heels which made it very difficult to hear the play. Almost as often occasion was found by the police to remove members of the audience. They were all taken from the pit. The point which caused most offence was where Peggy finds that Christy has only wounded and not killed his father, and exclaims, "You let on you had him slitted, and now you are nothing at all." The most frequent exclamation was "That's not the West." When the curtain finally came down, at 10:30, the members of the company were loudly boohed, though there was a shout,

129

"It's the play, not the actors." Those in the stalls sang the National Anthem, and the others replied with "A Nation Once Again" and "God Save Ireland."

At length the police cleared the building. Outside the students formed up, and marched off singing the National Anthem. A crowd gathered round them singing "God Save Ireland." In this way they went along Eden quay and into Westmoreland street, where the crowd rapidly increased, and the scene became so disorderly that the police, after a sharp scuffle, arrested one of the leaders, and he was taken to College Street Station and charged. The rest of the crowd was dispersed by a body of police under Superintendent Byrne and Inspector Flynn.[6]

Synge did not appear on stage during any of the performances, and was clearly upset at the violent reaction to his play. His comments made to an *Evening Mail* reporter after one of the performances were uttered in a fit of pique, but they were often thrown back at him in the days following. In answer to repeated questions of why he wrote the play, he blurted out, 'It does not matter a rap. I wrote the play because it pleased me, and it just happens that I know Irish life best, so I made my methods Irish. . . . It is a comedy, an extravaganza, made to amuse.'[7]

On the issue of continuing the run of the play, the Directors and the company were united. In an interview with a *Freeman's Journal* reporter, Lady Gregory said:

We have already declared publicly this winter that, in the opinion of those conducting this theatre, it is the fiddler who chooses the tune. The public are quite at liberty to stay away, but if they come in they must take what is provided for them.[8]

The most severe critics disagreed, claiming that once the dissatisfaction of the audience, or at least a large part of it, was seen, the theatre, as a National Theatre, should bow to their wishes. Yeats's persistence in continuing the play until it got a 'fair hearing' brought to the surface the long-smouldering resentment of the extreme nationalists against the Abbey generally and against Yeats in particular.

However, after two nights of violence, most of the newspapers called for peace in the theatre. The *Daily Express* Wednesday editorial found fault with both sides of the dispute:

The Irish National Theatre has awakened to find itself famous, or, as some of its critics would prefer to say, infamous. For some years it has flourished quietly, if not obscurely, in the little Abbey Street Theatre, triumphantly living down the associations of the building, which was once the Morgue of the Coroner's court. Mr. W. B. Yeats, Lady Gregory, Mr. Edward Martyn, and Mr. J. M. Synge are the leading spirits in this movement for a National Theatre which aims, as we were led to understand, at establishing a drama that shall be national in form, scope, and subject. Quite a number of clever little plays have been produced under these auspices, but they made no great sensation in the world of the playgoer. A small and enthusiastic public made the little theatre on the quay its intellectual centre; but the man in the street passed by on the other side, where, it is to be supposed, he found matter more attractive. But on Saturday night a new play, described as a comedy, by Mr. J. M. Synge, was presented, and it received a very unfavourable verdict at the hands of the critics. . . .

Mr. Synge has since been interviewed and has explained that his comedy was merely an extravaganza, based on an idea which appealed to him, at least, and which he worked out accordingly. He simply tells the public that he doesn't care whether they like it or not. As to the probability of the incident, he has his own opinion. And, he adds, he actually knew of a case in the Aran Islands where a man murdered his father, and was protected and befriended by the islanders, and ultimately assisted to escape to America. And then, he says, there was the Lynchehaun case, where a man, known to have brutally murdered a poor woman, was aided by Irish peasant women to conceal himself and to escape from the arms of the law. Candidly, we think Mr. Synge's illustrations beside the point. In his comedy the peasant women not only assist the worst form of murderer — a parricide — but fall in love with him at first sight. Of course when he explains that it is an extravaganza, there is nothing more to be said. Everyone to his taste is a very good maxim. But nothing can excuse the rowdy behaviour of that section of the audience which deliberately prevented the rest from hearing the play. Because one man dislikes a thing, that is no reason why he should prevent another man from getting a full and free opportunity of judging it for himself. This organised intolerance is quite as objectionable as the false dramatic conceptions of the playwright, and much more dangerous. It is quite intolerable that people should be prevented from hearing what they have a mind to hear by the antics of a few spoiled hobbledehoys. When this is said, however, it must also be said that it is a matter of doubtful wisdom on the part of the management to continue to present a play in spite of the public. There is nothing in the play to justify a heroic attitude; no dramatic principle at stake. The right of freedom of judgment is a very important thing indeed, and nowhere is it more important than in Ireland. We could wish, however, that those who are making this a test case were on safer ground. A play so stupid evokes no enthusiasm; and so, even if the theatre wins, the gain must appear trivial, if it illustrates nothing but the right to stage what nobody wants.[9]

During the week, the trials of those arrested at the theatre were held. The published accounts reveal the tenor of public opinion about the play and also how the whole Irish theatrical movement, and even this production, were identified by the public with Yeats. On Wednesday, Patrick Columb, the father of the young playwright, and Piaras Beaslai, who later became a dramatist and historian, were tried for offensive behaviour in the theatre — 'shouting, hissing and booing and stamping his feet; and with (when spoken to by a constable) using obscene language to the annoyance of the audience.' A newspaper account of the trial reported:

> Police Constable 47C deposed that he was on duty in the Abbey Theatre last night, when a disturbance occurred, commencing between 10 and 11 o'clock. He saw defendant stamping his feet and booing and hissing. This caused disturbance and annoyance to the audience, some of whom called "Hush." A number of others also caused disturbance, defendant said, when witness put his hand on him, and asked him to stop, "Who are you, you ———." He refused to stop creating a noise.
>
> Cross-examined by Mr. Lidwell — I went into the theatre at about twenty minutes to ten. There was great noise in the place. We were called in to quell the disturbance. Some of the audience wanted to hear the play and some did not.
>
> Did you hear anything offensive on the stage?
>
> I heard one offensive word used.
>
> Police Constable 87C said he was called to the Abbey Theatre about twenty to ten. He heard defendant hissing and boohing, and saw him stamp his feet. Some of the audience asked to have defendant put out. Witness and Constable 47C cautioned defendant, and defendant used an offensive expression loudly in the hearing of the audience.

Constable 113D, who was also at the theatre, deposed to there being a great deal of noise. The majority of the people in the pit were hissing and booing, whistling and stamping the floor. The people in the stalls were calling for order. Defendant was in the pit. Witness corroborated the statements of the previous witness as to the offensive expression used to Constable 47C.

Cross-examined by Mr. Lidwell — There was a general tumult. I could not hear anything on the stage, owing to the noise.

Mr. Wm. Yeats, examined, said he was the Managing Director of the Abbey Theatre, and was there last night when *The Playboy of the Western World* was being performed. From the first rising of the curtain there was an obviously organised attempt to prevent the play being heard. That was from a section of the pit. The stalls and balcony were anxious to hear the play. The noise consisted of shouting, booing, and the stamping of feet. He did not hear six consecutive lines of the play last night owing to the noise. The section that caused the disturbance was not part of their regular audience. The conduct of this section was riotous and offensive, and disturbed and annoyed the audience.

Cross-examined by Mr. Lidwell — We have a patent for this theatre. I read this play and passed it. The play is no more a caricature of the people of Ireland than *Macbeth* is a caricature of the people of Scotland, or Falstaff of the gentlemen of England. The play is an example of the exaggeration of art. I have not the slightest doubt but that we shall have more of these disturbances.

Mr. Mahony said he was satisfied that the defendant had been guilty of disorderly behaviour. He imposed a fine of 40s, and costs or a month, and ordered him to find sureties in £10 for his good behaviour.

A SECOND CASE

Piaras Beaslai, aged 25, was charged . . . with a similar offence. . . . Mr. Wm. B. Yeats deposed that he saw the defendant at the performance in the Abbey Theatre last night. There was an organised disturbance by a section of the pit to prevent the play being heard. Witness saw defendant arrested and saw him before arrest rise up and yell at the top of his voice.

Mr. Mahony — Did he say anything?

Witness — He addressed some words to me in Irish.

133

Mr. Mahony — Were they complimentary or the reverse?

Witness — I am sorry to say I understand no Irish.

Mr. Mahony — Well I know some Irish, and one can say some very scathing things in Irish.

Defendant — If your Worship had been present you would have heard nothing unedifying from me.

Mr. Mahony — Now Mr. Beaslai, what have you to say?

Mr. Beaslai stated that he was no member of any organised gang who went to the theatre to object. He went with two friends, and did not know the other objectors, and his blood boiled at the attempt to coerce public opinion. The men in the stalls standing up and shaking their sticks. Mr. Yeats stood over him, and said he would give in charge the next man who booed. Just then a particularly objectionable expression was used on the stage, and he (the defendant) in common with a number of others booed. Mr. Yeats then pointed him out to the constable, and he was taken in charge. He was satisfied with the result, and no threats or penalties would deter him from objecting to what he considered an outrage on the Irish people. Previous to this he had been an admirer of the Abbey Theatre, and a regular supporter.

Mr. Mahony said this was a different case from the last.

Defendant — I have made my protest. I consider every true Irishman would act in the same way.

Mr. Mahony — You are entitled to indulge in legitimate criticism, and also in a reasonable form of disapproval, but you are not entitled to be guilty of such behaviour as would be offensive to the persons in the play and prevent their performance.

Mr. Mahony (continuing) said he understood the defendant to be an enthusiast with regard to the thing. He did not want to be hard on him if he would give an undertaking that he would not take any part in these disturbances in the theatre again.

Mr. Yeats said he would be satisfied with such an undertaking.

Defendant said he would make no appeal to Mr. Yeats, but wished him rather to push the matter to the utmost extremity. They would then have the spectacle of a man brought into the police court for making a protest against an outrage on Irish Nationality.

Mr. Mahony — A protest which the law does not permit. Surely you can make a protest without breaking the law.

Defendant — Mr. Yeats pointed me out to the police, and

134

is responsible for this prosecution.

Mr. Mahony — You were determined to stop the play.

Defendant—I was not your worship. I particularly objected to a thing I heard.

Mr. Mahony — I must fine you 40s or in default you must go to prison for a month, and I will take your own sureties for good behaviour.[10]

The trials on the subsequent days were held before a different magistrate, and the widespread resentment toward the Abbey Theatre is reflected in the court proceedings:

Yesterday, in the Northern Police Court, before Mr. Wall, K.C., James Delaney, student, was charged by Constable 144C, Inspector Flynn, and Constable 126C with having been guilty of offensive behaviour in the pit of the Abbey Theatre, between 10 and 11 o'clock, last night, on the occasion of the production of the piece *The Playboy of the Western World*, by shouting and booing to the annoyance of other persons there, and refusing to desist when cautioned.

Mr. Tobias, who prosecuted, said this was a case in connection with the disturbances at the Abbey Theatre. The case was brought under the Summary Jurisdiction Act of 1871.

Inspector Flynn examined said he was on duty at the Abbey Theatre.

Mr. Wall — What do you mean by on duty? Where were you?

Inside in the pit, your worship.

Mr. Tobias — Did you observe this young man there (pointing to defendant)?

Yes.

Mr. Wall — What time was this?

Between 10 and 11 o'clock.

Mr. Wall — The play was going on then?

Yes.

Mr. Wall — All this will advertise it well in London. The vile Irish will be well exposed up there.

Continuing, the witness said he saw the defendant and several others in the pit close beside him.

Mr. Wall — Sitting or standing?

Standing, your worship.

Standing on what?

Standing on the floor at the right-hand side of the pit.

Was there a seat for him to sit in?

There was. He had been sitting down before that.

135

Continuing, witness said he heard defendant shouting and booing.

Mr. Wall — What did you hear him shout?

"Oh, oh, oh," or something like that (laughter). I spoke to him to desist.

Mr. Wall — Was the play going on at the time?

It was.

Did you hear what was going on at the time — the words used on the stage?

I could not, your worship.

Witness said there were others booing.

Mr. Wall — But they were not isolated?

Yes, they were here and there.

Continuing, witness said he spoke to the defendant and asked him to desist, but he would not and said he had a right to protest.

Witness said he would arrest him if he did not desist. The defendant refused to desist, and witness took him into custody on the charge of causing annoyance to other parties in the theatre who were calling for order, and calling on all who were standing up on the forms to sit down. He would not suggest that the defendant obstructed the view of any person in the theatre. He only arrested him for causing a disturbance.

Mr. Wall — Where did the cries of "Order" and "Sit down" come from?

Witness — From the stalls, your worship. There was a kind of opposition between the occupants of the stalls and the pit. I understand he was protesting against the play.

Mr. Wall — Did you understand why he protested?

Witness — He did not say why, your worship. But I heard a number of young men, who were near the defendant, say that the play did not represent Western Irish life as they understood it. Some of them said that they were from the West of Ireland themselves.

Mr. Wall — Was he the only one who boohed?

He was the only one I could identify. If I could have identified any others they would be here to-day.

Mr. Wall — Who were on the stage at the time?

Witness — I could not say, your worship. I did not take any particular interest in the play.

Mr. Wall — Could you hear, at the time, what was going on upon the stage?

Sometimes, your worship, and sometimes not.

Mr. Wall — Was there a riot going on?

Witness — It is riot, according to law, but there was no violence.

Mr. Wall — Did you make any other arrest?

Witness — No, your worship.

Mr. Tobias — That is my case, your worship.

Mr. Wall — Very well, Mr. Tobias. What do you ask me to do in this case?

Mr. Tobias — I understand that Lady Gregory, one of the parties concerned in the promotion of this theatre —

Mr. Wall — Have you any other witnesses?

No, your worship.

Mr. Wall — I don't know anything about Lady Gregory or anybody else. I am administering my duty on oath.

Mr. Tobias — Well, it is my duty to point out that this man has rendered himself liable to a fine not exceeding 40s. or a month under section —

Mr. Wall — Oh, I know all about the section. Why is there not a prosecution for riot in this case and in all these cases?

Mr. Tobias said this was an offence specifically provided for in the statute, and the defendant had been brought there charged with it.

Mr. Wall said as he understood it the people in the pit were of one way of thinking and the people in the stalls of another, and there was so much shouting going on that the audience could not hear the play. Was not that a riot?

Mr. Tobias — Offensive behaviour is what we charge him with here.

Mr. Wall said some people were shouting one way and some another, and those who did not belong to either side were not allowed to hear the play.

Mr. Tobias — That is exactly it.

Mr. Wall said that when people combined and took sides to "booh" in a theatre, and spoil the hearing of a play, that constituted riot, and what right had he to deal with the case? In a case of riot a magistrate could not convict on any of the minor offences which composed the riot. Had Mr. Tobias considered that point?

Mr. Tobias said he had. The section was expressly passed to give a magistrate in the position of Mr. Wall power to deal with isolated cases.

Mr. Wall — How do you make this an isolated case?

Mr. Tobias — The officer arrested this man.

Mr. Wall — Those people were protesting. This man says he has a right to protest, and I understand that by law a man

137

has a right to protest; and how this man's conduct was riotous is what I want you to show. What is riotous behaviour?

Mr. Tobias — He was shouting.

Mr. Wall — How is he to protest?

Mr. Tobias — By getting up and saying that he protested.

Mr. Wall — He is to whisper, "I protest."

Mr. Tobias — He was roaring and booing.

Mr. Wall — Well, how is he to protest?

Mr. Tobias — Well, your worship, I can say no more about it.

Mr. Wall, proceeding to deal with the case, quoted a decision given by a former Lord Chief Justice Bushe in a similar case which came before him, a judge as to whose worth all creeds and sections of the people of his time agreed. That judge had said that the rights of an audience in a theatre were very well defined. They might cry down a play which they disliked, or hiss and booh the actors who depended for their positions on the good will of the audiences. But they must not act in such a manner as had a tendency to excite uproar or disturbance. Their censure or approbation, though they might be noisy in expressing it, must not be riotous, and must be the expression of the feeling of the moment. If premeditated by a number of persons combined beforehand to cry down a performance of an actor, it became criminal. That was the opinion of one of the most respected lights of the legal bench.

Mr. Wall next referred to a judgment of Lord Justice Vanston, giving effect to a similar view as to the rights of theatre audiences. So far as he knew no such privilege as was attached to a theatre was recognized in regard to other places of amusement. A theatre was on different grounds. The theatre in Ireland had always been supposed to be in olden times the resort of people who sought interest and culture and instruction, and expected to get these, and not to have their people lampooned and reviled. If this young man had been guilty of any special individual misconduct it would, of course, be a proper case for summary jurisdiction, but in this case the young man appeared to have been exercising his privilege, although the Inspector had acted perfectly right in the discharge of his duty in trying to put down the row which was going on. It was lamentable that the parties who were responsible for this most regrettable condition of affairs were not brought to book. On the other hand, it might be well to consider on the part of the Crown whether those who persisted in bringing forward theatrical procedure of such a character as to excite popular odium and opposition, and which could not be tolerated, at all events, in Ireland, where, practically, there were two worlds, one wishing to be at the throat of the other, and one wishing to avoid what the other wished to intrude — whether those who were responsible for that should not themselves be brought forward. He did not think the defendant's conduct was any worse than the conduct of the others, who differed from him. Why the case was not tried as a riot he did not know. It was a melancholy thing, Mr. Wall went on to say, that in an institution which he understood was for the popular view of the Irish drama there should have been caused all that appeared to have happened during the past week, and that matters should have been put forward on the stage that great numbers of the Irish people resented. That, he said, was a strange complication of theatrical matter for the amusement of the Irish people. However, this was only by the way. On the whole, he must convict the defendant, although he did not consider it a case for serious punishment (To Mr. Tobias) — What penalty do you ask for?

Mr. Tobias — Half the penalty.

Mr. Wall — I fine him 10s.

Defendant paid the fine.[11]

The next day's trial, that of Patrick Hughes and John Duane, ended with the following exchange:

Mr. Byrne [legal counsel for the Abbey Theatre] said Mr. Wall had said hard things about this play, and he would like to state that the only people who took offence were the few such as the men in the dock, who sought to be more Irish than the Irish themselves.

Mr. Wall — I cannot hear you; you are not in Court. I know nothing about the play. If it is an offensive play —

Mr. Yeats — It is not.

Mr. Byrne said the play was a good one, and was neither religious nor political. He extended a hearty invitation to his Worship to come and see it.[12]

And the report of the final trial of the week concluded with an exchange which shows the magistrate's impatience with the whole affair:

Mr. Wall — Have you prosecuted any of the people who applauded?

Mr. Tobias — No.

Why?

Because —

If one is as bad as another —

Will you allow me to answer you?

I asked you a question.

And I was answering you.

You were not.

I was.

What is your answer?

That the people who were applauding were not interfering with or obstructing other people. This defendant says he was brought there for a purpose. That purpose was to obstruct.

I must take the whole of what he says. Why do you omit part of it?

What he is said to have said was, "I was brought here for a purpose. I came to protest against the play."

Mr. Wall (to defendant) — Have you anything to say?

I went to see the play, and there were portions of it I objected to, and I hissed them.

Mr. Wall said he had heard this case, which he considered a most extraordinary one, to bring up a man for hissing, when he is the only one arrested, the house being in a state of tumult, one side hissing and another applauding, one party was expressing approval of what did not seem to him to deserve approbation. There was nothing very extraordinary in people hissing such incidents as have been here narrated. That people should have approved of it appears to have been more extraordinary than that they should have hissed it. He thought there was in this case rather a straining of words in the charge "offensive behaviour" when it was said that it applied to hissing. It seemed a strange thing that this man was singled out and arrested, while the people all around were either booing or hissing. "I think it," Mr. Wall continued, "an extraordinary way of administering the law. I am afraid, however, that the defendant went to the theatre with a preconceived intention, and the fact that others were not charged cannot prevent me from dealing with his case. I will say 10s." [13]

As the week progressed, the newspapers came to agree that, bad though the play seemed, the riots were unconscionable. On Thursday, the *Independent* printed the following editorial:

The author of the play which has created such commotion in Dublin during the past few days could hardly have foreseen

140

that his efforts would have obtained, unsolicited, such a huge advertisement. We are certain he did not seek it or desire it on the terms, for Mr. Synge is still, we would fain believe, a child in these matters. He is undeniably an artist who can detach himself from all other interests for the sake of his work. Therein lies his strength and his weakness. As a dramatist, he is a discovery for which that rather tiresome chatterer and poseur, Mr. William Butler Yeats, takes credit. We make bold to say that Mr. Synge, were he to do himself and his art justice, would not need the sponsorship of the Managing Director of the Abbey Theatre. It would not require twenty years of resolute booming to gain him a European fame. For the sake of Irish dramatic art and of the National Theatre which we had hoped to see flourishing in our midst, we regret that the road to notoriety has been shortened by the presentation before any audience of *The Playboy of the Western World*. Mr. Synge is an Irishman, whose early upbringing, if we mistake not, would scarcely permit of his making too close a study of peasant life; the years of his student life abroad certainly did not add to his opportunities; but the knowledge acquired during the protracted exile in the West, which, in his devotion to his art, he endured, should have saved him from the perpetration of this gross offence against Art and Truth.

Those who had the opportunity of seeing, and hearing, the play on its first production, with few exceptions, left the Abbey Theatre with a sense of having been fooled. They went to see a comedy by a writer of recognised power and distinguished promise. The first act they passed in expectancy of the pleasure to come; the second was wearisome where it was not worse, and many left before the curtain fell; the third act was insufferable. The critics who denounced the play said nothing that was too severe. The staging of the piece was an act of inexplicable stupidity on the part of the management, on whom the heaviest censure should fall. Mr. Yeats's vapid heroics notwithstanding, we think that the verdict of the first-night audience — as sympathetic a house as actors ever played to — should have been accepted, and the play withdrawn. Last night many of the offensive phrases were cut, but the pruning did not make the play one whit more presentable. It was not for the purpose of lessening Ireland's self-respect and holding her people up to the ridicule of the world that the "National Theatre" was established — at least, that was not the avowed intention of its founders. If they have changed their minds, they should change the name to suit the altered circumstances.

To condemn the management of the Abbey Theatre for producing Mr. Synge's play does not, however, impose on anyone the obligation to condone the conduct of the opposition. If Lady Gregory, Mr. W. B. Yeats, and Mr. Synge chose to defy the opinion of impartial critics, and a large section of the faithful patrons of their theatre, that was their affair. The Abbey Theatre is not a portable property, and former patrons could quietly resolve to seek amusement anywhere in the future. To give way to hysterics and threaten vengeance on play and players was folly as unpardonable as the offence of the management in producing the play at all. To go night after night paying for the privilege of howling at a meaningless pantomime on the stage may be a testimony to zeal, but certainly not to discretion. Moreover, the peace and good name of the city are alike set at naught by the disturbers, whether in the stalls or in the pit. Senseless clamour will not carry the day; intelligent public opinion must and will, in the end, decide the point at issue, and that without reference to the judgement of a Police Magistrate. An expression of sympathy, in which all could join, might well be offered to the talented players of the Abbey Theatre Company. They have been placed in a false position, and, through a sense of loyalty which has something admirable in it, they have stood courageously by the management who have done them so ill a turn. They are fit for better things.[14]

At the week's end, the weekly papers renewed the assault on the play. *Sinn Féin* called it 'a vile and inhuman story told in the foulest language we have ever listened to from a public platform.' And *The Leader* stressed the irony of the whole situation:

We have written much against the imported stage; on Monday night we were seated in the theatre established as an antidote to imported buffoonery and smut. Is there not comedy in the fact of a cure being attacked with far more vigour than the disease? In so far as "crime" is condoned by the Irish people, the attitude of mind is to be explained by plain historical causes. A large amount of the "crime" of Ireland has been associated with the endeavours of Ireland to combat the tyranny and injustice of England, and the officers and trappings of "justice" have got inextricably mixed up with English tyranny and injustice in this country. Everybody who knows Ireland from the inside understands this attitude of the mind.

Mr. Synge comes along, and whether from malice, stupidity or desire for cheap notoriety, he puts up a common parricide, a man who believes he has committed the awful and unnatural crime of murdering his father, into a position that might be occupied by, say, one who had participated in the rescue of James Stephens, and who was being hunted down by the police; and when some of the people who hate crime probably more than any people in Europe, and certainly much more than do the English or the Scotch, protest — it may be not wisely, but too well — the authorities of one of the antidotes to the imported theatre call in the police! Is not that suggesting that parricide, and a low, sordid order of parricide at that, is a cause of great popularity in Mayo, and when an outraged people protest, Mr. Synge calls in the police. Truly, we witnessed rare comedy on Monday night! [15]

But by the time these reviews appeared, the disturbances in the theatre had almost ceased. In fact, by the end of the run, the determination of the management had clearly succeeded:

The closing performances on Saturday of *The Playboy*, which excited much vigorous comment and attention during the past week, were characterised by an extraordinary change of feeling on the part of the audience. Indeed, the opposition, who demonstrated their resentment in such a marked way at the beginning of the week and maintained it with a spirit worthy of a better cause, would seem to have had all the courage taken out of them by the determined front displayed by the management, as well as of the players themselves. At the matinee the piece was patronised by a fairly good house, and was listened to with attention and order. It was naturally anticipated that there would be a renewal of the disturbance on Saturday night, and accordingly the police arrangements were again carried out in a manner calculated to put a stop to any further unseemly scenes. Both inside and outside the building there was a strong contingent of police, and quite a large crowd of people assembled in Abbey street and Marlborough street in the expectation of witnessing more lively incidents. Both police and people were doomed to disappointment. The house was well filled in all parts, but as *The Playboy* proceeded on his career it became evident that he had achieved a certain amount of popularity. True it is that now and again cries of disapproval and dissent were indulged in, but they were delivered in a legitimate way, and did not interfere either with the work of the performers or the comfort of those who had come to listen to Mr. Synge's latest effort. The only incident worthy of note is that early in the performance three men were ejected, but their exit was so expeditiously effected that scarcely any comment was excited. At the close of the performance there was a hearty round of applause, mingled with some hisses, and the author was called on, but he did not respond. The audience then quietly dispersed. It was intimated by means of a poster in the entrance to the stalls, headed "Freedom of Speech," that a debate will take place this evening in the Theatre on the subject of the play and "The freedom of the theatre." Mr. W. B. Yeats is announced to lead off, and should the debate take place an interesting discussion may be confidently looked forward to.[16]

There is one significant point which has never been made about *The Playboy* riots, and that is that they were caused by a rather small number of people. When the theatre was full (a rare occurrence), it held 562 people, and a full house represented about £32 in box office receipts. Here follows a list of the receipts for each performance during *Playboy* week:

26 January (Saturday)	£32. 14. 10
28 January (Monday)	5. 2. 6
29 January (Tuesday)	12. 10. 1
30 January (Wednesday)	24. 13. 6
31 January (Thursday)	19. 8. 1
1 February (Friday)	22. 18. 9
2 February (Saturday matinee)	13. 7. 3
2 February (Saturday evening)	29. 15. 0 [17]

From these figures it can be seen that on Monday night there were only about 80 people in the theatre, on Tuesday night only about 210 people, and on Wednesday night, a fairly good house, about 420 people. And, of course, it should be remembered that a certain, fairly significant proportion of the audience did not engage in the disturbances. From these figures one might, then, conclude that small numbers can make a loud noise.

The open discussion about the play was held in the theatre on Monday, 4 February. The theatre charged half its usual admission for entrance, was packed to capacity, and brought in receipts of £16 9. 0.[18]

The occasion was a unique one, and seldom, if ever, have proceedings of such a character taken place in a Dublin theatre before. The excitement aroused by the demonstrations in the theatre, the expulsions and arrests, and the prosecutions

144

and convictions which followed, was still manifest in the audience which eagerly sought admission when the doors were opened. The fact that there was an entrance charge did not apparently affect the attendance, which was fully equal to the capacity of the building. The principal persons concerned in the opposition to the play were early arrivals, and their supporters were also present in full strength. The clientele who supported Mr. Yeats were hardly represented in the same relative degree, but their lack of numbers, especially when it came to a question of making a demonstration, was compensated for by an apparently irresponsible section, who seemed to have come with the sole object of enjoying the prospective fun, and of making a little on their own account if the entertainment did not come up to expectation. Portions of the audience looked grimly in earnest, notably the group of long-haired young men, between whom and other little knots of serious youths who affected broad-leafed hats, there appeared to be no love lost. Another section were evidently abroad for frolic and hilarity, and scattered promiscuously throughout the audience. Principally in the stalls and gallery were a number of ladies and young girls. The proceedings, which were announced to begin at a quarter past eight, were far from being punctual, but the early arrivals amused themselves with whistling, and a song of many verses, having pungent references to "The man who killed his Da," was sung, and applauded with great gusto. At length, after a somewhat weary wait,

The chair was taken by Mr. P. D. Kenny, better known under his literary soubriquet of "Pat." His appearance in such a position did not seem acceptable to a large section of the audience, who hurled quite a miscellaneous variety of cries at his head, chief amongst which were references to the whereabouts of the police, who, as a fact, were not in evidence in the interior of the theatre at all. As soon as an opportunity presented itself of making his voice heard he proceeded with his speech. He said he had been asked to take the chair, and he was very glad to do so. A few interchanges in Irish followed between a group in the pit and the chairman, who answered back in the same dialect, and then went on to say that he was not going to be put off his purpose by interruption, and if order was not going to be kept he would take care it was not his fault. He then outlined the course of debate, which would be divided into two heads — first the liberty of the theatre, and next the play itself. An equal amount of time would be allowed, as far as possible, to the discussion of each. That

145

discussion would be as wide and full and free as possible. (A Voice — "The police are at the back.") That theatre was not a political institution. (Another Voice — "It should be a national one"). If it were a national institution, rejoined the Chairman, it should be protected by the police against rowdyism (groans and hisses and shouts of "No, no"). It seemed to him extremely courteous on the part of the directors of the theatre to set an evening apart for the public discussion of these matters which had arisen. (A Voice — "At so much per head"). He did not believe a Dublin audience would refuse Mr. Yeats an opportunity of letting them know what in his conception the freedom of the theatre was and ought to be. (A Voice — "Will he justify the play?"). He asked them in conclusion to put aside the warmth of the past week and consider that they were on new ground with a new subject and met for a new purpose.

Mr. Yeats, who then came forward on the stage, received a very mixed reception. His friends cheered him with their utmost might, but the hissing and groaning predominated, and for a time the air was thick with rival and conflicting cries. At last having obtained a comparative silence, he began by saying that as he thought over the events of the past week he was reminded of a previous period when he had a difference with the public over one of his own plays, *The Countess Cathleen*. Then he had been attacked with great violence, and a newspaper then his friend was now his enemy, but no man should be cast down by the enmity of an Irish newspaper, or elated by its friendship. He was freer to-day than he was then, and he stood now as the representative of an artistic institution (laughter). On the former occasion his position was complicated. He was president of the Wolfe Tone Association (renewed laughter); and also upon that occasion he had called in the police (hear, hear, and groans). He was there that night to justify himself for having done the same thing. His position was prouder that night, being a greater one in being simply an artist, but otherwise the situation was not different. Yes, he did notice one difference. He remembered during the time of the row in '98 the audience did not rise during the performance of the play to make speeches. Last week they did (laughter). It was having noticed these signs of increased animation on the part of the Irish public that he had invited them there that night, and given them the proper opportunity for making the speeches they were prevented from making a week ago (cries of "Shame"). He had seen it stated again and

146

again that they had prevented the audience from the reasonable expression of dislike. He (Mr. Yeats) would certainly never like to set plays before a theatrical audience that was not free to approve or disapprove even very loudly, for there was no author that did not desire a live audience. But last week they had to face something quite different from reasonable expression of dissent. On Tuesday and Monday night it was not possible to hear six consecutive lines of the play, and this deafening outcry was not raised by the whole theatre, but almost entirely by about forty persons in the pit, who acted together, and even sat together. It was an attempt to prevent the play from being heard and judged. They were under contract with the audiences. They received money on the understanding that the play should be heard and seen, and they consider it was their duty to carry out their contract (groans). Mr. D. J. O'Donoghue had declared that the forty dissentients in the pit were doing their duty because there was no Government censor in Ireland. The public, he said, was the censor where there was no other appointed to the task. But were those forty — they had them counted up on Monday night, and they were not more — alone the public and the censor? What right had they to prevent the far greater number who wished to hear from hearing and judging? They themselves were preventing judgment (applause and groans). There was not a Sinn Féin man who would not call in the police if he found a burglar fiddling with his strong box; and the burglar, after all, represented merely an active minority pressing its claim at the expense of the majority (laughter and applause). They had appealed to the fundamental civil rights of a man (A Voice: "To protect a demoralising play."). When he spoke two or three years ago to 4,000 of the Clan-na-Gael in America he told them of the evidence he had that the Irish were an imaginative and animated people in the passionate way they received drama, and when he went back again next autumn he would describe how he had to call in the police so as to give them a proof of the vitality and intense life of the Irish people with the drama which touched the things in which the people were interested. Mr. Yeats, in conclusion, referred to the financial success of last week at the Abbey Theatre and, amidst cheers and groans, announced that the takings had been nearly £100 better than any previous week. Before he finished the Chairman had to appeal once or twice for order, and the confusion and noise was general over the house.

The Chairman then invited discussion.

Mr. W. J. Lawrence, who was the first speaker to accept the chairman's invitation, ascended the platform amidst cheers. His appearance was not familiar to the majority of the audience, and there were loud demands for his name. When it was announced and recognized as that of a well known writer on dramatic subjects he commanded a ready hearing. He went straight to his subject with commendable directness. He was not, he said, a member of any league or society in Ireland. He came on the platform as an Irish Nationalist, and as one entirely unbiassed, and entitled to speak as a representative Irish playgoer. In some of his recent writings Mr. Yeats had said that praise, except it came from an equal, was an insult. "I am not going to praise Mr. Yeats tonight," declared Mr. Lawrence, amidst laughter and cheers, "— I came to bury Caesar, not to praise him." The speaker, going on, said he stood in a sort of unique position. He had heard four performances of last week's play. (A Voice — "It's a wonder you're alive," and loud laughter.) He was present on the first occasion when Mr. Yeats himself was not, and he was therefore in a position to speak in regard to the reception it got on its first night. He had twenty-five years' continuous experience as a playgoer, and he had never seen a more thoroughly intellectual audience than filled the theatre on the Saturday night when the play was first submitted. The play got a fair and honest hearing. (A Voice — "It didn't on Monday night.") When the curtain fell on the first act there was certainly some applause, due, in his mind, to the good acting. Throughout the second act there was no audible dissent, but anyone who like himself was accustomed to feel the temperament of an audience could observe that there was discontent at the indecent verbiage and blasphemy and Billingsgate that was indulged in (applause). When it came to the third act, within ten minutes of the dropping of the curtain the occupants of almost the entire first row of the stalls walked out, and immediately afterwards a rather flagrant allusion by one of the actors was made, and almost instantaneously from all parts of the house, except the stalls, there arose a deadly fusillade of hisses. Following that there was a round of applause, which was drowned by a torrent of booing. In the whole house there was not one single call for "author." That was a righteous condemnation of the play, and that condemnation was emphasised by the Press on Monday morning. He therefore believed, after viewing the reception the play got on Saturday night, and the verdict of the Press, the National

Theatre Society would have been well advised if they had, in deference to public opinion, taken the play off the boards (loud applause). Mr. Yeats had won a Pyrrhic victory. (A Voice — "He will be sorry for it.") It was not the first time that a wrongly administered British law had violated Irish freedom. Mr. Yeats demanded a free theatre, and he (Mr. Lawrence) had no hesitation in telling him that he had struck one of the strongest blows of modern times against the freedom of the theatre. There was a movement in other countries for the suppression of theatre censorship. Mr. Yeats's attitude was not only an argument in favour of the retention of the censorship, but the creation of a censorship in Ireland (applause).

The Chairman at this stage suggested that it would be well if they had speakers on each side alternately, and they would confine themselves to debating the point whether if one man in a theatre objected to a play he had a right to prevent another man from hearing it who did not object to it and wished to hear it.

Mr. F. Sheehy-Skeffington was the next to take possession of the stage. He said he divided the subject into three parts — the play, the disturbance, and the methods employed to quell the disturbance — and summarising his opinion he declared that the play in his opinion was bad; the organised disturbance was worse (uproar), and the methods employed to quell the disturbance were worst of all. Mr. Yeats had alienated from the National Theatre the great mass of Dublin playgoers and had deprived himself of their support. Even if the opposition to the introduction of the police was entirely fantastic, Mr. Yeats, as a director of the theatre, should have known better than to bring them in and alienate the public. This introduction of the police to crush the freedom of the theatre was, said the speaker, the worst feature of the whole business, and had led to such extravagant conduct as that of the Western Board of Guardians which, without having seen or heard the play, had condemned it by resolution (loud laughter).

Mr. Cruise O'Brien, who followed, also lost no time in letting his opinion be known as anti-Yeats. The audiences towards the conclusion of the week had been quoted as justifying the play. His contention was that the first audience was the best test. The supporters of the theatre were fully represented, and the people were there who had come to the theatre since its inception, and supported it loyally all through. There were no rival mobs of boohers on the one hand, or of

149

claque on the other. They came to discriminate and to judge, and having judged and found the play wanting, it should then have been withdrawn at once. In face of the enormous disturbance which took place on the next night it then most certainly should have been taken off the stage to prevent the theatre being turned from a place of art into a bear garden.

A young man whose name was not announced distinctly, the Chairman explaining that it had been handed to him in Irish, and that he could not pronounce it correctly, introduced himself by saying he was not a speaker, he was not an artist, and he did not pretend to be cultured (laughter). He had seen enough of the play to justify his attitude in protesting against any such production being placed before an audience of the men and women of Dublin. He also protested against the bringing in of the forces of British law to put down the right of the people to protest against insult offered to the Irish people.

A Voice — I would ask the gentleman, for his own sake, to remember that there are a number of G men in the background (interruption, and cries of "Put them out").

Mr. Yeats, coming forward, declared that so far as he knew there were no police in the building.

Mr. Richard Sheehy said if Mr. Synge slandered an individual he would be amenable to the law. When he slandered a nation, was he to be allowed to go scot free? (Loud cheers.) The audiences of last week were perfectly within their rights in proceeding to the lengths they did to quash this play and put it off the boards (renewed cheers).

The discussion was continued by Messrs. P. J. Nevin and Pierce Beazley, the latter of whom taunted Mr. Yeats with having cut a sorry figure in the police courts when he had to confess that he, a Connaught man, did not know a word of Irish, and yet professed to be the leader of an Irish literary movement.

The Chairman at this stage said they would now discuss the play. Up to this the speeches had been most discursive, and wandered generally over the debatable ground. The audience had apparently lost any seriousness it had, and the proceedings were fast developing into hilarious farce, the speakers without exception being made the butt of all kinds of jocose remarks and shouts having no particular reference to the subject in hand.

Mr. J. B. Yeats, who stood up to defend the play, was practically shouted down, his words being audible only at intervals. He said he had not read the play. He had been at the theatre two nights with the strange result that he had seen the play but did not hear it (laughter). But he did know Mr. Synge (a voice, "So do we"), and he knew that the man had an affection for the Irish people which would make it impossible for him to disparage them. He had lived among the peasantry, and had been made an intimate member of their households. (A voice — "They should put him out"). He (Mr. Yeats) did not forget that this was an island of saints — plaster saints. He himself was not very proud of saints, and he rather enjoyed the thought that this was an island of sinners (fierce hissing and groaning). At any rate, he would prefer Synge's sinners to the types that had been left them by Carleton. Even if Mr. Synge went beyond the border, still the man was honest. Several voices — "Bring him out," "Let us see him," and uproar, during which Mr. Yeats retired.

An eccentric young individual, who gave no name, and who asked for a hearing because in the first place he was a peasant, in the second place because he knew peasants, and in the third place, because he was a medical student, next entertained the audience with some quaint observations.

Dr. Mark Ryan, London, next spoke, and was followed to the stage by a young gentleman in an advanced stage of inebriety, who, while apparently anxious to say a few words, seemed to have lost the power of speech. A key to his condition was found when, after being gently removed down to the stalls, he made a second attempt to mount to the stage, and a large bottle fell from his pocket and crashed to the floor. With this incident his oratorical ambition disappeared.

Two or three other speakers continued the debate, and

Mr. Yeats then replied with difficulty on account of the disorder. He was unable to make himself heard for a considerable time, and then only with constant interruption. He began by speaking of the wear and tear of nerve to which the players were subjected as a reason for deciding to take strong measures to quell the opposition instead of wearing it down by patience. His business was to obtain a hearing for both author and actors (groans), and to do that as quickly as possible. He had to charge respectable young men instead of leaving it to the police, and [to go] to the police courts to give evidence against them. The reason he did that was this, that having called in the police he thought the manly thing was to go the full length. He chose men he could respect, knowing the dispute that lay between them was one of prin-

151

ciple, and he went to the police court because he felt it right to go the whole length. No one could say that he had flinched from his fight (cheers and continued hissing and groaning). He did not regard himself as a mere entertainer of the public. He was there as a deliberate artist, setting before the public what he believed to be fine works of art, and insisting that they should receive a quiet and respectful attention. (A Voice: "They don't deserve it.") He had been charged with catering for the "garrison," but he reminded his audience that when many so-called Nationalists had their heads bowed in the dust at the time of the Royal visit, it was the author of *The Countess Cathleen* who spoke out against it when their patriots were silent. He refused to give up the work of a man of genius because the mob cried out against it. Some novelists represented the Irish peasant as a cherub with wings and no body. Mr. Synge represented him with a body, but without wings, and he was sure that even "the man who had killed his father" was a more acceptable figure in a woman's eyes than the timid, cowering creature who was afraid to stay in the house with his lover for fear of "what Father O'Reilly would say" (great groaning and hissing).

It was now bordering upon half-past eleven, the audience were tired of the speeches and their own noisy demonstrations, and it was a relief to everybody when "Pat" left the chair and declared the debate was over.

The audience separated good humouredly, after a night not so much tinged with rowdyism as with boisterous foolery.[19]

As would be expected, the critical reactions to the play by other Irish writers were divided. Padraic Colum wrote to Synge during the first week's performances:

I've been to *The Playboy* again. I disliked the third act the first time I saw it, and though it is still far from satisfying me, I did not dislike it so much last night. There are several things wrong in it, I think. The crowd standing by and apparently watching a man being beaten with a loy, the girl putting a red hot coal on Christy. The latter was cut last night and the other thing was so swiftly done that one did not realise it. Peggy is a creation distinctly acted splendidly. Still I think she would have stood by her man when he was attacked by a crowd. The play does not satisfy me.[20]

And George Moore wrote, giving the reasons for his dissatisfaction:

152

Oscar Wilde or somebody before him said, "the majority is always wrong." I wish he had added as a corollary "but the majority is never wholly wrong." If what I hear is true that the audience accepted your play gleefully up to the last five minutes of the third act, I confess to sympathising with the audience. Your play does not end, to my thinking, satisfactorily. Your end is not comedy, it ends on a disagreeable note, and that is always a danger, especially when one chooses parricide as a subject of a jest. The comedy end and the end which would make it acceptable to an audience seems to me to be that at some moment the old man Mahon discovers that his son is about to marry a very rich girl; the peasant's instinct for money overtakes him, causes him to forget his wounds, and he begins to boast like his son: "no one has ever overthrown him in this world, and no man ever will except his own son." To the peasant anything is preferable rather than money should pass out of the family; and with his boasting about himself and his son he induces Pegeen's father to accept Christy as his son-in-law. This end would be in keeping with the facts. Your end is not only not the comedy end but it is a little out of keeping with the facts. Christy has distinguished himself in the "lepping" and by his horsemanship in the mule race (forgive the bull); he is clearly not such a dolt as his father represents him. I suppose you want the play revived, and I am sure that the last few pages will always prejudice it whether the audience be an Irish, an English or a French one. Forgive me for speaking so candidly; I do so because I sincerely admire the play.[21]

Synge thought Moore's suggestion for revising the play unacceptable and commented to Frank Fay that it was an idea he himself had considered and rejected as "too commonplace."

In March 1907, when *The Playboy* was published by Maunsel and Company, T. W. Rolleston contributed an article to *The Irish Independent* praising it, and George Roberts, of Maunsel and Company, published an article in *Shanachie*, in which he argued convincingly that Synge is truly a national dramatist:

One cannot but regret that the demand in Ireland for National Drama should have become associated with a demand for Irish soap, and tweeds, and so on. That this association has been responsible for an enormous waste of time on the part of those well-meaning persons who strive to manufacture native plays need not concern us; but that it has created a false standard, and atrophied the judgment of audiences in Dublin, is a most undesirable result.

If it had been recognized that the best plays could not fail to be the most national, the desire of the "Irish Ireland" public would have been simply a wish for good plays; some sort of standard would have been formed, and praise or blame accorded for the right reasons. Let us by all means persist in condemning a play which does not truthfully represent the national life; but let our reason be that such a play must be bad art, for the drama bears such a close relationship to life that the degree of truthfulness of the representation may almost be said to coincide with the degree of excellence of the drama. Truthfulness is not to be interpreted as meaning a stenographic accuracy of speech, or a mere reflection of obvious and common characteristics; but truthfulness to the tendencies, qualities, and impulses that lie hidden in the heart of the race. A good play reflects life in the same way that a well-cut diamond reflects and reveals the many colours in a ray of light; it makes apparent more than we have seen in life itself, and hence it can only be written by a man possessing great depth of insight and capable of sensitive apprehension of currents of thought and emotion. It is obvious that a dramatist cannot have any very profound insight into the life of any other country but his own; so that if he go deep enough into life to write a good play, he cannot, even if he would, be other than national. . . . The Irish dramatist of to-day, representing but a ragged remnant of a race, in a country where alien influences predominate, has, indeed, a restricted field. He will find but little of the necessary depth of emotion or clash of will in the actual life of the peasant; for he is dealing with a race which has never realized its aspirations, and yet never lost them; which has never mastered life; which has never achieved coherent nation-hood, and which, because of the strength of its unfulfilled desire, finds its most joyous moods, its most poignant griefs, in the life just a little beyond the actual, the life of the imagination— which indeed at times becomes the more real life of the two.

It does not affect the subject under consideration whether this unrealized desire resulting in a continual retreat from the actual, in the maintaining of an ever accessible point of escape, is the cause or effect of the present condition of the Gael, but it cannot be denied that it is at the basis of his nature, at once his strength and his weakness, and often the mainspring of his action; and it is because Mr. Synge has discovered and revealed this so supremely that his plays are as typical and representative of Irish life as it is possible for drama to be. This desire for life, foiled by circumstance or circumscribed by isolation, and its consequent effect on the actions and development of his characters, is the theme of all Mr. Synge's dramatic work. . . . The lovers in *The Playboy*, in the exquisite love scene in the third act, spend their passion not in making love, but in talking of the delightful conditions under which they will make love in the future, all the time half-humorously, half-pathetically conscious that it is the imagined personality love has given that inspires their passion. This love scene, indeed, is a marvellous piece of writing, and can be compared with nothing hitherto seen on the stage; so characteristically Gaelic is it in thought, feeling, and expression, that we must go to *The Love Songs of Connaught* for a parallel. The same intermingling of the wildest untrammelled fancy with homely details, the same passionate longing characterize equally this piece of purely Irish drama and the best example we know of Gaelic lyrical poetry. To have written this scene, proves Mr. Synge to be, like all dramatists who have achieved greatness, a poet. But to have concluded it with Christy's reference to "bloody fools," and the subsequent interruption by the return of the drunken publican and his companions, puts him among that very small class of supreme poets who can mingle their poetry so cunningly with actual conditions that it becomes a living thing, fully realized, and a part of life itself. . . .

It is not this scene only that makes *The Playboy* his finest and consequently his most national piece of work: the theme, the setting, the characterization, the rendering through the actual speech of the peasant of all his innate fierceness and brutality, his extravagant humour and wistful tenderness, are all the outcome of a most profound insight into the depths of Gaelic personality. The comedy of a man imagining himself a hero, through his readiness to accept the appreciation of the crowd . . . and his subsequent belief in his own story, has its root in a very common tendency in Ireland. The characters of the drunken publican and his companion, the priest-fearing Shawneen, the widow Quin and old Mahon, contrasted with Pegeen and Christy, make the play an extraordinarily complex and complete representation of Irish life.

Another quality which marks Mr. Synge's work as intensely national is its relation to Gaelic literature. Just as the people he depicts still tell the stories of the Sagas, and consequently still feel the influence of their native literature, still shape some of their ideals from a delight in strong, courageous men, an appreciation of bodily perfection and of youth; so throughout these plays this influence is everywhere apparent. The feeling for youth, and horror of uncomely age, for instance, is surely a survival of that which prompted the imagining of a tir-nan-oge — a paradise where there was no growing old. His method, too, of mingling the wildest incidents, the most exceptional occurrences, with incidents of every-day life reminds one of the extravagant realism of the folk-tale. And by his intense love and exquisitely sensitive rendering of natural appearances and effects; the marvellous way that by a few touches, a phrase here and there, he can re-create the feeling of a hillside, a country road at night, or still more subtle and undefinable effects, he accomplishes with a more perfect art what so many of the Gaelic poets attempted.

It is not to be wondered that an art so unusual, so untouched by alien influence, which has gone deep into life and to the only native literature we possess for inspiration, should not be popular. It is too complex, too unfamiliar to be understood at present. But when Irishmen cultivate a higher standard of judgment, and at the same time acquire some self-knowledge, there is no doubt it will receive a portion of that appreciation it deserves.[22]

There were often-repeated claims that W. G. Fay and others did not follow Synge's script, and that their language was more offensive than that which appeared in print. In the next issue of *The Arrow*, Lady Gregory admitted that changes had been made in softening the language, but she was eloquent in defending the integrity of the play, and all the offerings of the Theatre Society:

I may say that the play was never acted as it is printed. I know, though I was not present, that it was considerably cut in rehearsal; and after the first public performance, we, the players and I, went through it and struck out any expressions that had given offence, and which were not necessary to the idea. It was so played during its Dublin week, and so it will be played in England. We did nothing, however, to soften or to hide the central idea; we felt that would be an insincerity. This idea may be taken very seriously if taken as a yet to be fulfilled prophecy, and is it not said that every work of art is either a memory or a prophecy? It is a foreshadowing of what will happen if emigration goes on carrying off, year by year, the strongest, the most healthy, the most energetic. . . . The old are always left to us, and the very young, the weakly in body or in mind. Some day it may be not a prophecy but a commonplace that a man coming with a name for strength and daring even in crime may take the mastery of a feeble countryside. Can anyone say that such a tragedy is impossible? And if the idea be a mere fantasy, who is so thin-skinned as to take offence? There are some critics, town dwellers for the most part, who would be "more royalist than the king," and cry out if the Irish peasant is represented with the lack of any virtue — no, if he be even called a peasant. And what then about other classes? The first play produced by our Irish Literary Theatre was Mr. Edward Martyn's *Heather Field*, the subject of which is the driving of a husband from idealism to madness, by the narrow and vulgar conventionality of a woman of my own class. *The Bending of the Bough* founded on his *Tale of a Town* had the same idea differently treated. Protestant friends of mine have been able to admire, as I do, the spiritual beauty of Father Dinneen's *Faith and Famine*, though we believe its picture of Protestant bigotry to be not only a caricature but an impossibility. A Unionist paper made an attack upon *The Rising of the Moon*, on the ground of its belittling the Royal Irish Constabulary, and yet I have been told that there was "never such great laughing" as when the little comedy was read in a Belfast Police Barrack. The plays we have produced must be taken as a whole; there are types of nobility in them as well as of greed or folly. Scanchan's high pride stands against Dempsy's ignoble bendings.

I am sorry Mr. Synge laid the scene of his play in Mayo if Mayo people are offended. He might have mentioned some undiscoverable Irish district. Yet if Mayo has cause to complain it may remember that Mr. Yeats has made his young bridegroom, who gives up love, home and all to follow Cathleen ni Houlihan, a Mayo man. I am not sure there are not counties which would adopt the "Playboy" and his whimsical admirers into their baronies, if they might also claim Michael Gillane as of their kin. I do not think it will be very long before Mayo, while thanking Clare and Galway for well meant resolutions of denunciation and of patronage, will say that in such questions it will prefer taking its soul upon its own shoulders, and judging not by hearsay but for itself.[23]

The extreme nationalists could not be dissuaded by any such claims. *An Claidheamh Soluis*, the organ of the nationalists, made it clear that they had washed their hands of the Irish National Theatre Society:

> We cannot congratulate either the Theatre or its critics on the way in which they have acted in face of a crisis. . . . We do not believe that Mr. Synge intended his play either as a picture or as a caricature of Irish life. The charge which we bring against him is graver. Whether deliberately or undeliberately, he is using the stage for the propagation of a monstrous gospel of animalism, of revolt against sane and sweet ideals, of bitter contempt for all that is fine and worthy, not merely in Christian morality, but in human nature itself. . . . The Anglo-Irish dramatic movement has now been in existence for ten years. Its net result has been the spoiling of a noble poet in Mr. W. B. Yeats, and the generation of a sort of Evil Spirit in the shape of Mr. J. M. Synge. . . . Mr. Yeats triumphs for the moment; but he has lost more than he has gained. As for Anglo-Irish drama — it is the beginning of the end.[24]

The effect of the rejection by the nationalists was evident in the Abbey's small audiences during the following months.

Another serious result of the protests was the decision by William Boyle to withdraw his plays from the repertoire. He wrote to Yeats on 31 January:

> I regret to be obliged to withdraw my three plays — *The Building Fund*, *The Eloquent Dempsy* and *The Mineral Workers* — from the repertoire of the National Theatre Company as a protest against your action in attempting to force, at the head of a riot, a play on the Dublin public, against their protests of its being a gross misinterpretation of the character of our Western Peasantry.[25]

A few weeks later, Yeats wrote in *The Arrow*:

> I have reprinted in the present *Arrow* my speech at the Debate in the Abbey Theatre on the 4th February upon *The Playboy*, and the measures taken to preserve order, and certain extracts from the *Samhain* of 1905, and from patriotic papers of various dates. These quotations show how old is the attack and how old the defence, and that no satirical writer of the Theatre—certainly not Mr. Boyle, who has left us because we fought Mr. Synge's battle — has escaped a misunderstanding unavoidable where certain crude general ideas and propagandist emotions have taken the place of every kind of

thought. If we had withdrawn the play those that hissed or cried "stage Irishman" at the next performance of *The Mineral Workers* would have tried to drown the next play of Mr. Boyle's, that they objected to, by the stamping of their feet and the blowing of tin trumpets. We have claimed for our writers the freedom to find in their land every expression of good and evil necessary to their art, for Irish life contains, like all vigorous life, the seeds of all good and evil, and a writer must be free here as elsewhere to ripen weed or flower, as the fancy takes him.[26]

Boyle's action was unmistakably a protest against theatre policy, for he withdrew his plays without having seen or even read *The Playboy*. His action received a good deal of publicity, and even a few months later he was explaining his motivation:

When I read in the Irish papers lately accounts of the disturbances created over *The Playboy of the Western World*, I felt there must be something unusually offensive in the piece. I read the Dublin papers of various shades, and found absolute unanimity in their condemnation of the play as the grossest libel on the Irish peasantry ever put upon the stage. I read of how the police were called in to suppress all voiced expression of dislike, of proceedings in the Police Courts, where the magistrate, who had listened to sworn testimony as to the nature of the play, hinted plainly that, in his opinion, those responsible for its production were the real offenders. I saw from this that the disapproval of *The Playboy* was not the act of any clique or section, but a sincere expression of sincere dislike, and that the efforts made to stifle this objection and to force the play, at any cost, upon the public were the latest form of the old attacks upon the conscience of the nation. I know that attached to the licenses in London are conditions which forbid profane language on the stage or anything "calculated to produce riot or a breach of the peace." I do not know whether there are similar conditions attached to the licenses for Dublin theatres, but, if there are, I know that Dublin Castle would be slow to enforce them on behalf of popular rights. I felt these rights to be of more importance than any Abbey Theatre production, and withdrew my own work as a protest against the play itself and against the attempt to dragoon public opinion into its acceptance. Whether I acted precipitantly or not, my instincts appear to have guided me aright. *The Playboy* is now published, and anyone sufficiently interested can read it for himself. In my opinion, it is

159

gross in conception, coarse beyond possibility of quotation, and false to the verge of absurdity. It shows its author absolutely ignorant of the life he assumes to portray. . . . As in the older calumnies, the Irish peasants are portrayed as lustful, idiotic, drunken, murderous, admiring the torture of defenceless animals, devoid of reverence for religion, and sunk in the lowest depths of savagery.[27]

Sincere though those objections were, Boyle did not reveal the full reason for withdrawing his plays. He was on bad terms with the Directors of the Abbey before the riots occurred, and welcomed the excuse for removing his works. In a letter to D. J. O'Donoghue a few weeks before Synge's play opened, he mentioned some of the difficulties:

Many thanks for your letter and cuttings. They are very interesting. How well that writer in *The Leader* burlesques W. B. Y's style and views. Strange to say he seems put out with me because all sorts of people like *The Mineral Workers*. I expect they'll soon have another burst-up at the Abbey.

I'm glad you think *Dempsy* worth printing. I haven't yet quite decided whether I shall restore some scenes W. B. cut out. He told me they would spoil the play, but I am beginning to think he doesn't want any play of mine long enough to fill an evening's bill by itself. I have sent *Dempsy* and *The Mineral Workers* to an American agent who undertakes to place them for me. I have stated on *Dempsy* that some scenes have been omitted which I would like to restore if desired. All the people I have shown this play to complain of its being too short. Now until I see whether these scenes are to go in or not I can't print it. After it once went into print I would not alter it, as such a proceeding advertises oneself as lacking in will and judgment. That is my only reason for delay. I'll soon find out, however, if it is wanted as it is at the Abbey or longer, and then let you have the manuscript. Maunsel and Co. have given me nothing and won't answer my letters even. All this is between ourselves. I don't want those folk in Dublin to know I am trying to get the plays on in America without them. The thing may not come off and if so better say nothing about it.

I am rewriting *Shane O'Neill* in prose and it is turning out a much stronger and more natural production altogether. I am *not* going to offer it to Yeats you may be sure.

I had a visit from W. G. Fay lately. He told me a lot of W. B. Y's tricks I don't care to write about. He is evidently a crooked person — the shadowy one.[28]

Although the relations of the Directors with Miss Horniman were strained, she stood by them on the issue of *The Playboy*. Immediately on hearing of Boyle's withdrawing his plays, she wrote to Lady Gregory:

> As Mr. Boyle has apparently neither read nor seen *The Playboy* I shall not answer his letter at all unless circumstances change. *The Tribune* this morning says that the magistrate wants the Crown to intervene. That I suppose is what the Gaelic League and Sinn Féin desire.
>
> You may count on me to stand firmly by you. Owing to some delay in changing investments I have a large sum of ready money at hand in case of necessity. If the Crown intervenes we must give way but I don't think that it will if we are legal in all our doings. The abuse of Griffith will do us no harm except amongst his ignorant readers.[29]

At the same time, she wrote to the Directors protesting that she had heard that the actors were contributing to the riotous behaviour in the theatre. She had always insisted that the theatre be non-political, a place solely for artistic endeavour, and so this report of hissing from the stage infuriated her:

> I am informed by Mr. Hugh Lane that low behaviour (I mean hissing) took place *from* the stage and that this hissing was political. Now I am of course aware that everyone was in a great state of excitement that night and maybe got carried away. But it must be clearly understood that I will not allow my theatre to be used for political purposes and the actors must be informed that hissing the drunken vulgarity of the stalls is just as bad as the patriotic vulgarity of the pit. I am fighting for us to stand above all low political spite on either side. I make this protest at once, it is a matter of honour that the directors should do their best to prevent conduct in the actors which would justify my closing the theatre. From the very first and ceaselessly I have held firm to the position that *I will have no politics*. I should despise the idea of buying peace by bowing low to the Castle, you know that by my suggesting *Kathleen* for next week.[30]

When she read the play, she was prompt in complimenting Synge on it: 'I've just read *The Playboy* — it is splendid. Those silly people who made a noise were jealous at heart, none of them can do anything that counts and so they boo and hiss.'[31] She then made her position clear by writing to the Dublin newspapers:

During the excitement caused by the performance of Mr. Synge's *The Playboy of the Western World* at the Abbey Theatre, Dublin, it seemed wiser for me to be silent. Now that all is calmer will you kindly give me a little space in your paper to explain my connection with the affair?

It is well known that I gave the free use of the building to the Irish National Theatre Society, and I went to great expense in petitioning the Government for a patent. The directors are in a position of trust in regard to my property, and when there was a threat to pull down the curtain it became their duty to call in the police. They knew that I have no prejudices on that subject, because I approved of their action when the police were called in to put a stop to low behaviour after a performance last October. I heartily applaud the strong measures taken on behalf of the paying public who wished to hear Mr. Synge's play.

I have read the prompt copy of *The Playboy of the Western World*, and I do not understand on what grounds such a clamour has been raised. I hope to see and hear it some day, so as to judge it fairly. The language is not that of the drawingroom, but that is a dramatic necessity.

The accusation of the too light and frequent use of sacred names is out of place from people who hoot and hiss "God Save Ireland" or "God Save the King." I do not care which anthem may be preferred, but both should be treated respectfully.

An audience who calls out, "Kill the author," is ridiculous when it takes exception to imaginary culpable homicide. No jury would bring in a verdict of wilful murder against Christy Mahon under the circumstances.

The title of the Irish National Theatre Society was settled long before I gave my help. I would subsidize either a Nationalist or a Unionist theatre. It should be clearly understood that I aided the Society solely from my desire to assist thereby dramatic art. I intend to continue my present arrangements at the Abbey Theatre until Christmas, 1910, when the patent will lapse. By that time either the theatre-going population of Dublin will have given us such support that it will be worth while for me to apply for a renewal of the patent, or else I shall see that further efforts would be a waste of time and money. A fair amount of encouragement would soon improve the performances in every way, and a great art centre might be made in Dublin which would be the envy of other cities.[32]

*   *   *

On other issues confronting the National Theatre Society, such accord with Miss Horniman was not always secured. She had insisted on bringing in a new manager from outside, to take over some of W. G. Fay's duties, and by the beginning of 1907 such an arrangement was nearly completed. Yeats worked with Miss Horniman to secure the new man, while the other Directors were apprehensive about further upsetting relations within the company. Before the opening of *The Playboy*, Synge wrote to Yeats:

> It will be well — I think — to impress on the new man that he is to cooperate with — and help Fay in the friendliest way. A house divided against itself cannot stand up, and if they do not get on I don't know where we shall be landed. I would take time, if I were you, and make sure you get the right man, it would be much better to wait a few months than to bring over a man who would make a mess of it.[33]

He outlined the arrangement which he would consider equitable:

> We accept the new man at the following terms —
>
> 1. £100 a year added to W. G. Fay's present wages.
>
> 2. We — the authors — to be free to withdraw all our plays at the end of six months — in other words that the agreement we signed as to the Irish rights to be cancelled at the end of six months.
>
> 3. You are if possible to talk out scheme of duties for new man with some one who knows and submit same to us.
>
> 4. We take it for granted that my suggestions have been agreed to — if not let us hear.
>
> 5. Fay must have a written contract defining his duties and giving him control of dialect work.
>
> 6. It is evident that new man will have more business than Stage Management and it is essential that he should be a thorough theatrical *business* man, if possible an Irishman.[34]

Lady Gregory had similar misgivings about Fay's position in the new management:

> I don't know the different meanings of "stage manage" and "produce" very well, you and Fay would know that. And I don't know if the Molière plays come under the head of "Irish Peasant Plays." You will probably have heard this from Miss Horniman.
>
> At present I don't feel that I can give a definite opinion. The one thing I hold to is that the Fays should not be put out

163

either by forcible or gradual means. I don't know by the wording of the letter if the proposal is one that we ought to advise Fay to accept. But you will see him and can talk the whole matter over and learn his views. I am not writing to him because I don't know enough. He might be inclined to accept a man of high position in the theatrical world (and we should get one at that wage) rather than someone to take the mechanical side only such as we should have to get from our own resources. Indeed I feel the question is more for Fay than for us. I suppose we should be shut out from London etc. if we refuse this offer, at least that we should have to go against Miss Horniman's wish. This would prevent us from making the money we look to outside Ireland. On the other hand £500 a year is a very heavy extra obligation to be under, unless we think the increased efficiency and the better arrangement of tours would justify it.

Would the Managing Director have a vote equal to Synge's and mine? And there are questions as to division of office etc. you would have to talk over with Fay.[35]

By the time of the production of *The Playboy*, it had been decided to hire Ben Iden Payne, who came from F. R. Benson's company and had broad experience in the theatre. Apparently it was Yeats who chose Payne, under conditions specified by Miss Horniman. She wrote to Yeats:

In the case of your engaging Mr. Payne or any other person as paid Managing Director, will you consider the question of Mr. Fay's being paid for the production of the Irish Peasant Plays? I should propose that he should be offered the choice of £100 a year for this or else the sum of £15 for each one act play and £20 for those of two or more acts. This to be in force as long only as Mr. Payne is employed — if for any reason he were to leave, the payment to Mr. Fay to cease and all to return to the present state of things unless I see cause to renew the present proposed arrangement or to offer some other. . . . It must be clearly understood by all concerned that I have had nothing to do with the choice of Mr. Payne except that I asked Mr. Vedrenne to advise Mr. Yeats. In the case of his leaving I must be considered perfectly free to refuse any further aid to the scheme beyond the free use of the theatre, the subsidy and the payment of half the cost of such things as are used by my tenants.[36]

By 11 February she submitted to Yeats a month's salary, £28/6/8, of which £20 was for Payne and the remainder for Fay. The

164

unsettled question of producing adaptations of Molière by Lady Gregory was a point of dissension on which Miss Horniman was vehement:

> I've made my protest against *adapting* Molière instead of using a good translation, so I have no more to say on the matter. I never saw a programme until Saturday when *The Playboy* came wrapped in an old one. The absurdity of people with French names talking with a brogue reminds me of the plays I saw in the "seventies." You may trust me to remain silent on the point — I'm not likely to tell people unnecessarily that the Directors approve of making Molière into a sham Irishman. But I will not countenance it being brought to England on any pretence; I consider it to be most undignified from the literary point of view however many such adaptions may have been made, turning Red Indians and their ways into Welshmen or Spaniards into Scandinavians, etc. etc.[37]

Miss Horniman expected trouble when the new Managing Director took over, but for a while the arrangement was amicable, and Holloway passed on this report from the Abbey's business manager, W. A. Henderson:

> Payne was getting on well at the Abbey. Frank J. Fay and he were at one with regard to acting and actors. Payne had the selecting of plays just now — how long his power in this direction would last was another matter. There was over £10 in the house on Saturday. It was to be feared that the natural playing of the actors would suffer by the set principles of the usual stage type proposed by Payne from his training with the Benson Co.[38]

In March, Miss Horniman cautioned Yeats against allowing Payne to play Oedipus in his own production, on the grounds that others would claim that she was replacing Frank Fay with an Englishman for a lead role. When the company decided to let W. G. Fay direct *The King's Threshold*, even though the provision was for him to handle only peasant plays, she objected. And when she received a piece of stationery with Fay's name listed as manager, she was furious and even threatened action:

> Let the Directors please face the question simply — a majority of them only formally accepted my offer; if a majority now come to the conclusion that it was un-wise to accept the offer they must let me know and tell me that Mr. Payne has been given notice, that Fay is to lose his £100 a year as

165

producer and that I am to cancel all arrangements for the tour. But it is only fair to tell me this clearly; not to force me into a most disagreeable position, that of ceaselessly making a row to get our bargains carried out. If Fay insists on some office or post being given to him beyond his acting parts and his producing, why was I not told? Why am I to be always the person who has to be put into difficult places? [39]

Yeats replied with an angry formality:

Dear Miss Horniman:

Your letter has made me extremely angry. If you had thought a moment you would have seen that the letter heading was a clerical error of Henderson or Payne's (I never saw it or heard of it till I got your letter) and yet you write a letter assuming that those you have been associated with for years are liars and rogues. It is intolerable.

Yours,
W. B. YEATS.[40]

Apparently the arrangement made between Yeats and Payne was clear to no one else. Frank Fay wrote to Synge late in April, expressing his uncertainty over who was responsible for what plays on tour. Early in June, Miss Horniman wrote impatiently to Yeats:

I wish that you had told me a little more explicitly that our verbal arrangement that Fay should have £100 a year to pay him for the production of Irish peasant plays *and to give up stage management* has proved impracticable. I was not surprised because of a remark made on Tuesday . . . night by Lady Gregory in my presence which led up to what you said yesterday. I am very disappointed that your works should not get the fair chance I have tried my best to give them. Mr. Synge's plays would gain immensely if they were properly stage-managed and so would Lady Gregory's, and it is sad that they will not allow yours to have the advantage they object to for themselves.[41]

One actor, Ambrose Power, complained about salary. W. G. Fay thought he wanted too much, but Power 'told him he had nothing to do with the matter, that it rested with Payne.' As a result, Fay cut him out of the plays he controlled, although Power continued playing for Payne.[42] Internal relations in the company seem to have been disintegrating.

Controversies continued, with everyone dissatisfied in some way, until Payne resigned on 21 June 1907. Then Miss Horniman appointed him general manager of her new theatre project, the Gaiety Theatre in Manchester. She advised Yeats to leave the Abbey as a hopeless cause, and expressed her great disappointment with what had happened.

But, for all her disgust with the society, her payments continued, and the Abbey company did tour England, playing Cambridge, Birmingham, Oxford and London, with *The Playboy* on the programme. Of the plays, Yeats remarked:

> The Plays we bring to London are a selection from a considerable number which has been produced at the Abbey Theatre, and sometimes we have had to choose some particular one, not because it is the best, but because it suits our players or as many as can travel. I would myself sooner have been represented by *Deirdre* or *The King's Threshold*, than by *The Shadowy Waters*, which may not seem a play to any but the lovers of lyric poetry, or *On Baile's Strand*, which is part of a cycle of plays on the life of the ancient hero Cuchulain. The training of verse speakers has become the most laborious part of our work, for a player may be excellent in all else and yet have all to learn in verse or be altogether unfitted for it. In the first state of our theatre it proved to be impossible, no matter how great the enthusiasm of individuals to keep to work so arduous and prolonged players who had to earn their living in some workshop or office. Even yet we have only made a beginning, and with the exception of one or two speakers, cannot claim more than the rightness of our methods. Good speech of some kind has always, whatever the play, been our principal pre-occupation — for only when there is musical, finely articulated, delicate, varied, deliberate speech, can style, whether the play be in verse, or as the greater number of ours, in dialect have any effect upon the fortunes of a play, and as St. Beuve has said, style is the only thing that is immortal in literature. It is to set arbitrary limits to the office of player, to grant it gesture and facial expression, but to deny it, as some do, a fine speaking of fine things, or to think that the stage has become more really the stage, more consistent with itself, in forgetting the feeling for fine oratory that made possible the rogues and clowns of Ben Jonson and the Princes of Corneille and of Shakespeare.[43]

Miss Horniman, incidentally, insisted on bringing *The Playboy* to London, on the curious grounds that refraining from presenting it would constitute a political act. After the tour, Henderson told Holloway that 'the players had been very well treated, getting bonuses at Easter, extra pay for *The Playboy*, and six weeks vacation with salary unstopped.' [44]

Clearly, Miss Horniman's sole interest in the Irish National Theatre Society was to further artistic drama, especially that of Yeats. In her dealings with the society, she was remarkably generous; it was not too much to expect some degree of control over the management of the theatre, or at least proper information about about its activities and organization. Her discouragement made her suspect W. G. Fay of taking on too much authority, and eventually she suspected Synge and Lady Gregory of plotting against her interests. But she still maintained an unshakable faith in Yeats's importance as a playwright:

> Lady Gregory and Synge grovel at Fay's feet. They sacrifice your work and keep you a bond-slave to them because you are "touched" by that vampire Kathleen ni Houlihan. If they had wanted the theatre to become an Art Theatre, they would have behaved very differently. But they only care to show themselves off to a small set in Dublin *at any expense*, without caring for anything beyond their own vanity. . . . You are ceaselessly victimized by Lady Gregory on the score of your gratitude for her kindness. You are being made a slave, your genius is put under a net in that precious "garden" and you are only let out when you are wanted to get something out of *me*. Then you are staked down again — not allowed to have your plays properly performed nor to be treated personally with decent respect by the company. . . . I know that I am being very cruel to you and you will be angry with me. But that does not matter — your name and fame are dear to me and I am willing to defy your anger because I see your slavery. [45]

Reinstated as manager of the society, W. G. Fay found it no easier to maintain control of the actors. Yeats wrote to Synge that summer that he thought Fay unsuitable as a manager, although fine as an actor:

> You know of old that I don't believe that Fay is a very competent man to run a theatre, that in fact I think him particularly unfitted for it, but Miss Horniman has definitely announced that she will do nothing more for us at the end of the two years. In all probability Fay may survive us, and at the end of that time may carry on some sort of touring company with our good will and what he wants of our plays. I wanted somebody in control over Fay but now that that

plan has failed and that we have lost Miss Horniman I think we must give Fay every opportunity to acquire experience and amend his faults. . . . I need hardly say that if anybody gave us some thousands of pounds I should for one insist upon Fay giving up everything but acting and such parts of stage management as he is competent for. I am very doubtful of his being able to hold the company together, considering his queer temper, but I don't see what else we can do. We want him to work for us as enthusiastically as possible with a view to his ultimately making his living out of the thing and helping others to make theirs.[46]

Some indication of Fay's difficulties around this same time appears in the following letter he wrote to Yeats:

More trouble in Ireland. The man I had playing Carter struck yesterday for money he wanted to be paid he said. I pointed out the fact that he could not speak English and didn't know how to act and asked him to think it over. So this morning he came in and said he couldn't go on as he had a job to go to. That's Carter off. The genius I had playing the Soldier hasn't turned up either so there's no chance of getting *White Cockade* to Galway by the 17th September. I don't know where the Dickens to look for people. You see it's got round town we are paying people and that we did well on tour, so that every sundowner that turns up expects to be paid and it's perfectly absurd the cheek they have. They can't speak King's English, walk or do a thing. One has to begin at the very beginning with each of them and waste the time of our own people. I'm short even for *Spreading the News*. I've no Tim Casey the part Wright used to play. I suppose O'Rourke's money covers the last sole cash we had. What is to be done? . . . You see we are at present depending on men that can't get a job at anything else; that's where the trouble comes in.[47]

By 1 December Fay's situation was so bad that he wrote to the Directors, making the following proposals:

1. That the Directors put up a notice shortly that all contracts with the National Theatre Society terminate on such a day. That people wishing to re-engage write in to W. G. Fay.
2. That all engagements be for a season only and terminable by a fortnight's action on either side.
3. That where the Directors require special actors or actresses for their performances I should engage them on terms to be

decided between the Directors and myself and for such parts or performances as the Directors shall decide.

4. That the power of dismissing those under my contracts shall rest with me after due consultation with the Directors in the case of principals.

5. That there shall be no appeal to any other authority than mine by the people engaged by me on all matters dealt with in their contracts.[48]

The Directors met on 4 December to consider Fay's proposals, and decided:

1. That we could not agree to his proposal about dismissal of the Company and re-engagement by him personally.

2. That we cannot enlarge the powers already given under contract.

3. We cannot abrogate the right of appeal to the Directors already possessed by the Company.

4. That an improvement in discipline is necessary, and that rules with this object be drawn up in consultation with the Company. That the Company be asked to elect, say, three members to consult with the Stage Manager and Directors as to the rules of discipline. That the rules so drawn up be put to the Company as a whole for their decision.

5. That it be explained to the Company that this Theatre must go on as a theatre for intellectual drama, whatever unpopularity that may involve. That no compromise can be accepted on this subject, but that if any member find himself unable to go on with us under the circumstances, we will not look upon it as unfriendly on his part if he go elsewhere, on the contrary we will help him all we can.

6. That henceforth a Director must always go with the Company upon the more important tours.[49]

Denied any new authority, Fay felt that he had less control than ever, and wrote to Yeats:

I wish to bring to your notice that out of seven rehearsals on tour, Miss M. Allgood was only in time for one and on one occasion was an hour late. A rehearsal is called for this evening and her sister Miss Sara Allgood told me that she . . . could not come to rehearsal as she had an appointment. I asked her what the appointment was and she said it didn't matter. Owing to the fact that I have no direct control over

170

these people, and consequently have no power to make them obey my orders, I must refuse to accept any responsibility as to the date of productions arranged. My agreement with the Directors on taking over the management of this theatre again, at a reduced salary, was that there was to be no communication between any of the employees of the theatre and the Directors, except through me as Manager. This agreement has been repeatedly broken through during the last season, the inevitable result being that the members of the company think that if they don't like to obey my orders, they can appeal to the Directors. If you and Mr. Synge have a plan for getting into better working order, the sooner it is put into operation, the better.[50]

On hearing this, Yeats wrote to Synge, 'The whole situation is perilous, and all the more so, because it is quite obvious that Fay hasn't the least intention of resigning. I mean that we must have a change somehow, or we shall all be worn out, and that change must be more than good resolutions on everybody's part.'[51] And so he planned a formal investigation of Fay's management, in which the players' complaints of his violent language, erratic attitudes towards punctuality at rehearsals, and the charge of substituting Brigit O'Dempsey for Sara Allgood in the Glasgow performance, would all be discussed. That Yeats was trying to ease Fay out of the company seems now obvious. Yeats wrote to Synge at the end of the year, giving details of the coming meeting and recognizing hazards ahead:

Lady Gregory is afraid and I think rightly so, that Fay and Vaughan are looking for a cause of quarrel and that the cause they will try for is that we are suppressing, or are trying to suppress, popular work like *The Dressmaker* in the interests of our own unpopular work. This is an issue very difficult to fight, for we will never make the ordinary man of the pit with *The Leader* and *Sinn Féin* taking up the case against us, believe that we are not suppressing young talent. How can we make them understand that *The Playboy* which they hate is fine art and that *The Dressmaker* which they like is nothing?[52]

*   *   *

In addition to *The Playboy of the Western World*, 1907 saw first performances of more than a dozen plays worthy of attention. The strong reaction against Synge's play resulted in a partial boycott of the Abbey Theatre, which was particularly unfortunate because it diverted attention from a number of important pieces presented in the months following the riots.

On 23 February Lady Gregory's one-act comedy, *The Jackdaw*, was introduced. In a programme note, the author commented on its genesis:

> Before I belonged to the Irish National Theatre Society I sent in a little play, *Twenty-five*, and it was refused, one of the grounds being that some of the members "did not approve of money being won at cards." Things have marched since then, and *Twenty-five* has been acted, and it was especially liked in England "because it is so sentimental." I have myself a leaning towards sentimentality, and to convey it have written a parody of the old play, letting loose *The Jackdaw* to croak upon its grave.[53]

The Freeman's Journal recorded a good house for the first night and praised the leading actress:

> It is a trifle such as will be found useful in triple bills at the Abbey, especially when the audience is in good humour, as it was on Saturday night, and prepared to laugh on the slightest provocation. Everything that Miss Sara Allgood does she does excellently. She has a rare talent for the boards. Already her repertoire of characters is unique of its kind, and it has now a splendid addition in Mrs. Broderick, the general store dealer. Nothing could be more lifelike and genially humorous. It is complete, as finished a study as could possibly be conceived, perfect in voice, gesture, expression, deportment. Surely the *ars celare artem* could scarcely be carried to greater success. Who could forget the enraptured, beaming astonishment with which she turns to old Nestor suspecting a proposal. The delight in the voice, in the pose of the figure, in the eyes shooting out of their sockets, is irresistible.[54]

The Evening Mail thought the play excellent fun, but *The Irish Times* commented:

> There was a small, but an appreciative audience, and the amusing situation which the piece develops appeared to meet with much approval. The comedy, however, is somewhat unconvincing. At any rate that was the impression conveyed, but this view may have resulted to some extent from the difficulty of following out the various ideas contained in it, owing to the unnecessarily rapid rate at which some members of the cast delivered their lines.[55]

The Irish Independent also complained that some of the players spoke too rapidly and that the play was 'somewhat unconvincing':

> The dialogue — or what could be heard of it — is bright and mirthful, but the plot is hardly what one might expect a writer of Lady Gregory's abilities to work upon. The scene is laid in the interior of a small general shop at Cloon, and the play deals with a most unusual — if not, indeed, extraordinary — incident in the life of the Irish peasantry.[56]

On 9 March the Abbey presented Lady Gregory's little classic of wry comedy, *The Rising of the Moon*, which, however, *The Irish Times* condemned because of its subject:

> The first impression which the enactment of this latest production suggests is that the management of the theatre have in the selection of their plays been by no means successful in suiting the popular taste. The scenes which occurred in connection with the presentation of *The Playboy of the Western World* are quite fresh in the public recollection, and the protests which some previous ventures called forth are by no means quite forgotten. *The Rising of the Moon*, it may be safely predicted, will also come in for a good deal of hostile criticism, and the possibility that such a development was unforeseen reflects very little credit on the intelligence of those to whom the destinies of the Abbey Theatre are entrusted. If there is one body in this country which more than another Irishmen of all classes feel a just pride in it is the Royal Irish Constabulary, and any attempt to hold up its members as cowards and traitors is certain to be bitterly resented. . . . The metamorphosis effected in the case of this worthy officer of the law, in the course of a few minutes, is quite remarkable. From being a man burning with zeal to do his duty, and faithfully fulfil his oath, he becomes first a rank coward in face of danger, and secondly a man whose sense of duty is undermined by the recital of a few songs. . . . With all due respect to Lady Gregory this is not a fair portrait of the typical Irish constable, and the Irish public will be most reluctant to accept it as such. The artists — Mr. W. G. Fay, Mr. J. A. O'Rourke, Mr. J. M. Kerrigan, and Mr. Arthur Sinclair — proved most efficient in their respective parts, but even their high artistic attainments were unable to redeem a piece essentially false to experience, and having as its hero a treacherous poltroon.[57]

173

The Irish Times, of course, reflected the views of the Anglo-Irish establishment, and none of the other papers regarded it as unpatriotic. *The Freeman's Journal* thought it:

> An excellent little curtain-raiser, depending, of course, almost entirely on the chat — spirited, pointed, witty — between the ballad-singer and the policeman, while the situation — two of them puffing and singing on the barrel — is extremely funny. There isn't a word wasted, and interest, excitement, and uncertainty are worked into a climax which is exceptionally clever and telling. There is not much scope for acting.[58]

The Dublin Evening Mail, however, particularly complimented the acting of W. G. Fay, who played the ballad singer:

> Mr. Fay is capable of the widest range from farce to perfectly conceived passion and tragic force. The part was an undoubted triumph. We can hardly say as much for Mr. Sinclair's policeman. He did not look his part, and so his acting was spoiled. His wig was incongruous, his uniform was hopelessly ill-fitting, and he did not look elderly as Policeman X should. And he seemed to find it hard not to smile while saying what was meant to be serious in his mouth, though amusing to the audience.[59]

On 23 March the first foreign play not 'adapted' into Irish dialect was presented; it was Maurice Maeterlinck's one-act play, *Interior*. It was on the same bill as *On Baile's Strand*, and was preferred to Yeats's play, at least by *The Freeman's Journal* reviewer, because 'the pathetic little play gripped the attention of the audience from start to finish.' This was the first of the performances under the management of Ben Iden Payne.

A week later, on Easter Monday, 1 April, another new play was presented — Winifred Letts's *The Eyes of the Blind*. In this simple piece a murderer is discovered by a blind man and goes out, remorseful, to confess his crime. *The Freeman's Journal*, which had been one of the papers most opposed to *The Playboy*, found praise for this play, as it did for so many of those performed later in the year. But *Sinn Féin* vehemently attacked it as being too close to Synge's *In the Shadow of the Glen*. The similarities seem tenuous, except for the similar settings in a Wicklow cottage, but it was a production of *Riders to the Sea* that inspired Miss Letts to write her play. As she reminisced years later:

> This was not a play, it was life: it was the eternal battle of man with the sea, the sea as they know it in the western

coast, not our polite sea that let us bathe so safely at Black-rock Baths. This was tragedy as the Greeks knew it. I cannot remember any applause, only that hush which falls on supreme art. The small audience (how woefully small in those days) had a discretion, a sense of tragedy, that purges through pity and through fear. . . .

I went home, still dazed, still entranced, to the suburban placidity of Blackrock (we always went back to a punctual supper). But the spell of Synge's speech and tragedy lay upon me. I was eager to write something in the same medium. Of course it was a poor little play, something that could be parodied and torn to pieces. I called it *The Eyes of the Blind*; it concerned a murder on a Wicklow bog. I must concede myself one dramatic moment when my blind beggar saw the ghost of the murdered man behind the murderer's chair. Frank Fay told me later that his own part as the blind man had meant something significant to him. . . .

The manager at that time was Iden Payne. I recall him as a rather harrassed young man with pockets bulging with papers. Better I remember the two Fays, Frank and Willie. They looked then just as they do in their pictures by J. B. Yeats in the Dublin National Gallery. . . . On the first night there were no shouts for author, no bouquets on the last night. Indeed my verdict came from an old woman in the pit. I sat behind her at the matinee, anxious to test reactions there. She wore a black bonnet with bugles and they shook as she turned to her companion: "I don't think much of that" she said. But, woman of the bugles, you did get a thrill when the blind man saw the ghost, for the bugles were frozen for that moment.[60]

The Poorhouse by Douglas Hyde and Lady Gregory was first produced on 3 April, but received very little critical attention. *The Irish Times* dismissed it as 'a mere trifle'.

On 20 April Wilfrid Scawen Blunt's play, *Fand*, was presented. *Sinn Féin* damned it by associating it with Synge's plays, but the attack was directed more at the Abbey style of acting than at the play:

The Abbey Theatre is growing duller and duller. Soon even its Merrion Square audience — whom the inanities of the Castle season cannot tire — must inevitably begin to be bored. There was a new play on Saturday night. They are very prolific in what they call new "plays." The daily newspaper preliminary puffs informed us that this was the ninth new play performed this season. If this were so, it would be a very remarkable performance. But it is not so. Most of them were not plays, but playlets. They are probably called plays because the authors spend as much time on them as would suffice for writing a real play — if only they knew how. The new play on Saturday night was by an author who is outside the Abbey set, namely, Wilfrid Scawen Blunt. It is called *Fand*, and deals with the well-known incident in Cuchulain's career, connected with the goddess. It was difficult to get any definite idea of the play itself. The acting was so prominent that the play was obscured. What I intend to convey is that the eccentricities of some of the actors were so marked as to distract one's attention from following the unfolding of the plot. And even if one wished to do so, it was rendered vrey difficult by an indistinctness of pronunciation which was particularly noticeable in Mr. Arthur Sinclair and Miss Máire Ní Gharbhaigh. This was due to some extraordinary affectation in speaking which made them almost unintelligible. It is puzzling to understand why this peculiar intonation was adopted. Such mouthing has never been heard at the Abbey before, not even when Mr. Yeats defended *The Playboy*. . . . I have mentioned the distracting eccentricities of the actors. Mr. Arthur Sinclair as Conchubhar was the first to develop along these lines. He seemed perturbed by his very long beard, which was very much out of proportion to his height. This would not have mattered much if he had not persisted in trying to swallow his words in it. They rolled and gurgled and chortled in the act of elocutionary deglutition, and almost petrified the audience with astonishment. But there was more to come. Miss Máire O'Neill (the most unsuitable member in the company to play the part) came on as Fand. She was restrained at first, so long as she posed as the ancient crone who was going to cure Cuchulain. But when she flung aside her outer garment, and revealed herself, arrayed in delicate blue, as the goddess herself — then was the very spirit of melodrama rampant. She could not keep quiet for a moment. She ranted and raved and waved her hands, the very incarnation of the wronged and injured heroine of the amateur theatrical society. Why, Mr. Stage-Manager, did you not tone this down a little? Is your conception of a Celtic goddess, the English parlour-maid in a fit of heroics? The music set to the songs was also most inappropriate. It was the most ludicrous thing imaginable to see the goddess Fand sitting beside the bedside of the bewitched Cuchulain trying to awaken him with an air for all the world like one taken from a musical medley such as the "Shop Girl." But when, at the beginning of the second act, Fand and Cuchulain come on the stage arm-in-arm, Fand again singing one of her musical comedy melodies, the height of amateurish sentimentalism for the evening was reached. It was 'Arry and 'Arriet at 'Ampstead for Bank Holiday to life. . . . Some of the speeches, no doubt intended by the stage-manager to be taken seriously, failed utterly in their intention, and were received with cheers of ridicule from the audience. Mr. Blunt's play is not, so far as I could gather it, a particularly good one. But it is a sincere work, and it is a pity that it should be treated to the indignity of a burlesque performance, particularly in Ireland. The one redeeming feature of the whole production was Miss Sara Allgood's beautiful and dignified acting as Emer. She never once stooped to the level of private theatricals. Mr. F. J. Fay was also good. But there was too much attitudizing. One could almost see him trying to recall the positions studied so diligently beforehand in his looking-glass.[61]

Although less biased, *The Freeman's Journal* also criticized the speech of the players:

There is . . . a mannerism in monotone and a tremolo in declaration developing amongst the artistes at the Abbey which tends to become fatiguing, and some of them let their voices fall constantly so as to make it irksome to strain after a sentence. The pleasure of listening is thus seriously impaired. To make every word distinctly and easily heard is the first essential in good playing.

It praised the acting of the rest of the cast, particularly Máire O'Neill who 'made a charmingly poetical figure, and sang with great delicacy of feeling the delightful lyric "Beautiful Eyes, Awake".' But the fact that the play was written in Alexandrines made it a curiosity piece, rather than an effective play: 'It was apparent that the poet had exhausted upon the urgencies of rhyming strength requisite for essentials in a drama of passion.'[62]

In the autumn, a new and important playwright appeared, the Kerryman George Fitzmaurice who had been working as a civil servant in Dublin and writing short stories for various weekly papers. Now, when his *The Country Dressmaker* was performed on 3–5 October, it was so well received that another weekend's performances were added. However, *The Dublin Evening Mail*, after noting the play's good reception, went on to remark that:

. . . it displays the Irish peasant of Kerry in a light scarcely less loveable than Mr. Synge's "Parricide." Yet, no murmur of dissent impedes its easy flow. In *The Playboy* the Irish girls were debased enough to fall in love with a parricide. In *The Country Dressmaker* everybody seems to be a bad lot, save Julia. Julia, it seems, had been in love ten years ago with Pat Connor, who had gone to America to make his fortune. Tired at waiting for his return, Julia is at last persuaded by her mother and by the village match-maker to marry a strong farmer in the neighbourhood. They are no sooner engaged than the Yank returns. Then the sordid scheming begins. Everybody in the neighbourhood wants to get the Yank, with his dollars, into their clutches. Clohesy, the social lion of the neighbourhood, makes tremendous efforts to isolate him from others, but in vain. Ultimately he marries Julia, after several preliminary misunderstandings have been cleared up.

The merit of the play is that it gives Miss Allgood an opportunity of a good study of Julia, the country dressmaker, with her ways superior to her class, and her corresponding difficulties in life. Mr. W. G. Fay is an amusing village busybody, but his lines are in many places very thin. Mr. J. M. Kerrigan made a very fair effort at the returned American, though a little slow, and not quite cock-sure enough to convince. The play is a promising effort, but rather hurried in the dialogue. And the repetition of the same phrases is very tiresome. "In the heel," for example, seems to recur at every other sentence.[63]

The Irish Times thought the play 'an exceedingly clever elaboration of a flimsy theme' and Sara Allgood's elocution 'somewhat monotonous'. *The Evening Telegraph* also liked the play, but, in tones which echo the criticism of Synge, questioned its realism:

The author has most unquestionably, in his dramatis personae, given us some remarkably true types of Irish character, and has drawn an accurate, though incomplete, picture of Irish country life. Much though Irishmen, filled with a genuine patriotic spirit, would wish to see their countrymen and countrywomen without serious blemish, it cannot be denied that such a type as "Michael Clohesy," crafty, and treacherous and lying, finds his prototype in the flesh. It must be admitted that his scheming wife and quarrelsome daughters are not pure creations of the imagination. But there is the consoling reflection that they are the almost inevitable products of the twin degrading influences of Irish landlordism and centuries of foreign rule. . . . The whole picture which the author presents is incomplete. He might, without straining beyond the borders of accuracy, have introduced a few more lofty and more Irish types than appear in his conception. The scene is laid in North Kerry. But it is to a very much Anglicised community that the author introduces us. It even appears that it is from a cheap English periodical, and a sensational English weekly paper that the locality receives its literary sustenance. . . . There is no breath of the Gaelic League in the whole play, and no suggestion of the new National spirit which is sweeping over the country.[64]

Even Yeats had reservations about the play, and claimed it gave a worse view of the Irish than did *The Playboy*.[65]

The growing reputation of the theatre is attested to by a special professional matinee on 13 October, for two prominent theatrical companies then playing in Dublin. Beerbohm Tree's and Forbes Robertson's troupes saw plays by the three Directors, and this was such a success that a special performance was later given for Mrs. Patrick Campbell's Company, and yet another for the companies of Martin Harvey and F. R. Benson. After the last performance, Benson said, 'These plays are beautiful, are art, and are true, and I feel humiliated in listening to them when I think of the ordinary drama of the day.' [66]

On 31 October Lady Gregory's new play, *Dervorgilla*, was produced, with Sara Allgood in the title role. *The Freeman's Journal* said:

Now the play itself is far the best that Lady Gregory has yet accomplished. It is interesting not alone by reason of its subject and the method by which it is dealt with, but there is in it a really wonderful contrast of character that deeply interests the sympathetic spectator and listener. It is a one-part play, no doubt, because the Queen of Breffney, of course, and most naturally, dominates it. And here is the most appropriate place to speak of Miss Sara Allgood's really marvellously striking performance as Queen Dervorgilla. It is questionable whether any actress on the stage of whom we have any knowledge could have made so singularly effective this part. Her perfect intonation, her apparently intuitive power of expressing worlds of pathos and impressiveness seem to be all her own, for one can recall no actress of our day who possesses quite the same power. Her performance, upon which the entire play may be said to have leant, was as

179

nearly perfect as could well be imagined, even by the most hypercritical.[67]

'Jacques', writing in *The Irish Independent*, playfully criticized the plot:

> Last night at the Abbey we had half-an-hour of sadness followed by nearly two hours of laughter. The gloomy half-hour was because of Dervorgilla. Lady Gregory puts her sitting in a chair, and makes her deliver long, prosy, high-falutin' speeches to old doddering servants, young men and girls (who talk about sport and needle-work), and a wandering song-maker. 'Tisn't likely they understood her big talk, at least they didn't look as if they did.[68]

On 21 November the Abbey presented Lady Gregory's and Yeats's reworking of his earlier play, *Where There is Nothing*, now entitled *The Unicorn from the Stars*. Yeats called this play 'almost altogether Lady Gregory's writing', although, he added, it contained more of his spirit than the earlier play, which was written by him, Lady Gregory and Douglas Hyde.[69] *Sinn Féin* thought little of the new piece:

> *Where There is Nothing* was no more dramatic in its construction and development than any of Mr. Yeats's stage failures. Nevertheless it contained the rudiments of a play, and there were in it many of those purple and magnificent (if now tattered) glories, which hung around him till recently, like old vestiges of royalty about some King in exile. But *Where There is Less* — I mean *The Unicorn from the Stars* — well, if it is not the end it is at least the peroration! Before such a hopeless conglomeration of unmeaning phrases and wild speech and "folk" inanities the critic is silent.
>
> Even the actors of the "Abbey," who God knows by this time ought to be adepts in the portrayal of nothingness, even they seemed to be unable to cope with this ultimate monstrosity. It would be a sheer unkindness to criticise their good-humoured attempts to make the thing act. Mr. Frank Fay, as the dreamer, spoke his lines with all his old and heavy distinction. Mr. W. G. Fay lent the production a touch of delicate comedy by wearing a soft hat (such as the Dublin jarvies wear) amidst the eighteenth century costumes of the other actors, and the "human interest" was added by the firing of a gun![70]

Other reviews were mixed. *The Daily Express* criticized the central intention of the play:

> The play reminds one of those books written for children, which the Beaconsfieldian reviewer says "will prove equally attractive to grown-up children." It does please, because of the light and fanciful writing displayed throughout, but the central idea is unworthy of the serious treatment accorded to the play. The actors did all they could for it. . . . But it is unlikely that the efforts of the players will save a play which has for its action nothing more — when regarded with a mind cleared of elaborate nonsense about visionaries and saints — than the ravings of a maniac. This is a re-cast of another writing; if Mr. Yeats wishes to try again let him go in honestly for "screaming farces." [71]

The Evening Herald called it 'one of the most striking plays yet produced by the I.N.T.S.' But 'F.M.A.' in *The Evening Mail* was firm in denouncing it:

> The collaboration is not fortunate, the work of the two writers is hopelessly incongruous and never fits together, you can separate one from the other with a clean cleavage, there is no organic unity, nor even dramatic cement to keep them together. . . . There is neither incident nor character in the play. Not a vestige of drama. "Where there is nothing, there is" — Mr. Yeats! . . . No wonder the audience was bewildered and frozen. They tried occasionally to be interested, once or twice they laughed feebly at nothing, for it was all dreariness set forth in the dreariest way. [72]

Historians of the Abbey Theatre have usually discussed the exciting events of 1907 with much portentousness. Here, after all, was a small band of brave, dedicated and enlightened artists staunchly defending the bastions of Art against the narrow Nationalists and crass Philistines. A solemn and significant time, indeed, in the annals of the Irish stage. But lest it seem too solemn, here is an anecdote of these early years from Sally Allgood:

> Another time we were in Sligo, playing a charity performance for the Church to get funds. This happened in the very early days when we were all buoyed up with the thought of the great literary movement we were in. It was a small "fit up" stage in the school house, with curtains on each side to close off our entrances and exits. I looked through a hole in the curtain and out at the audience, and I said to the man

who was deputized to pull the curtain up and down, "The audience seems to be enjoying the play."

"Well," he replied, "Ye see, last week we had *The Streets of London*; the week before we had the *Tale of Two Cities*; an' the week before that we had the *Girl Who Took the Wrong Turning*. Ye see, they [the audience] are tired of the high-class stuff; yez are a great relief to them." [73]

*　　*　　*

Other Irish theatre groups were thriving. The Ulster Literary Theatre brought to Dublin on 30 March two plays which had been first performed in Belfast at the end of 1906, Lewis Purcell's *The Pagan* and Rutherford Mayne's *The Turn of the Road*. *Sinn Féin* was enthusiastic:

> There has been no better demonstration of the artificiality of the school of Dublin writers who are endeavouring to establish a National drama in Ireland, than the visit of the Ulster Literary Theatre. This company, from Belfast, put on the boards of the Abbey Theatre, on Saturday night, two plays, one dealing with heroic life, and the other with contemporary peasant life. But the outstanding fact, and the predominating merit of both plays, as compared with those produced by our Dublin dramatists, is their essential humanity. They were crude and raw in many respects. The acting was slovenly at times, and sometimes even showed signs of coarseness. But always the spectator felt the one great redeeming fact — so wanting as a rule in the Abbey Street playwrights — that here, whatever their defects, one was at least face to face with humanity, and with the facts of life. The first play, entitled *The Pagan*, a comedy in two scenes by Lewis Purcell, is placed in the sixth century, and the scene is the Cave Hill, Belfast. . . . We have not here, of course, the polished verse, or the decadent sophistries of men like W. B. Yeats. We have the portrayal, in awkward dialogue, and haphazard incident, of the very real love of a charmingly natural maiden. . . .
>
> There are no theories here. There is no feeling of the ultra-modern literary school. . . . Their excellence is their fidelity to reality. For this we forgive many blemishes! And in this lies the chief deficiency of the Abbey Street dramatists.[74]

The Freeman's Journal also reported that the performances were popular and had general praise for the company. *The Irish Times* called Mayne's play 'beyond question one of the most sterling products of the Irish literary revival ever seen at the Abbey

Theatre.' W. J. Lawrence, writing in *The Lady of the House*, concurred in preferring Mayne's play to Synge's:

> With the possible exception of *The Mineral Workers*, no play produced by Mr. W. B. Yeats's organisation has gripped the intelligence and worked upon the emotions with the surety and force of *The Turn of the Road*. Mr. Rutherford Mayne has shown the decadents of Dublin that in the drama of rural life, artistic realism may be attained without preaching the gospel of hopelessness and despair or overstepping the bounds of good taste. The dominant note of the Ulster dramatic movement is undoubtedly its sanity. Neither Mr. Lewis Purcell nor Mr. Mayne has been obsessed by those cobwebs of the brain that make (especially in Mr. Synge's case) for morbidity. Not for them is that Swift-like horror of humanity that renders so much of the work of the Irish National Theatre Society repulsive.[75]

On 26 December the Ulster group presented in Belfast its most popular production, *Suzanne and the Sovereigns*. *The Irish News and Belfast Morning News* reported:

> *Suzanne and the Sovereigns*, an extravaganza by Lewis Purcell and Gerald M'Namara, is the most ambitious venture the Ulster Literary Theatre have yet made, and the success of the first performance, which was given last night in the Exhibition Hall, quite justifies the construction and presentation of the piece by this energetic band of playwrights and players who have, it will be freely conceded, already accomplished a great amount of finished and excellent work. *Suzanne* marks a departure from the lines previously pursued by the Theatre in their productions, being written wholly in the lighter vein, and leaving out altogether any attempt either to seriously present an ideal or to delineate types and phases in the life around us. The authors in calling their work an extravaganza have used the word in its proper sense; throwing aside all responsibility, they have constructed a play of purely fantastic turn, dealing with that epoch in Irish history which lies in the latter end of the seventeenth century. Anything savouring of an attempt to seriously achieve historical accuracy or realism has been carefully avoided by them; they have made it their aim to create as many laughable situations as possible by a bizarre conjunction of up-to-date localisms with certain revered historical episodes, and they have been thoroughly successful in doing so, without violating any canons

of artistic taste, with a marked degree of discrimination and judgment. The characters include King James II and King William III (heroes), Lundy (a traitor), Wilhelm Van Tootil (Court banner painter to William III), Sir Joseph Jackson, William John M'Auley, and Francy M'Cann (members of a Belfast deputation); Admiral Ginkel, Duke Schomberg, Robert Hamlet M'Bride (an inn-keeper), and several others, in addition to Suzanne, described as a beauteous maid, who, according to the authors' idea, is the cause of all the trouble.

We are introduced to the Stadhuis at Amsterdam to the strains of "By the side of the Zuyder Zee"; the Belfast deputation appears to beg the Prince of Orange's attendance in Ulster, where King James, they represent, has not given entire satisfaction; he at first refuses, but consents on learning that the mysterious Suzanne (whom he has admired, when she visited Holland as one of an excursion party) dwells there, and is the adored of James. So the story runs through a mad and merry maze of grotesque happenings, with mock melodrama interspersed, the Siege of Derry and the Battle of the Boyne being "worked in" as incidental items, and the whole proves a delightfully irresponsible, but none the less amusing, production. The Theatre may be congratulated on having made a decided success of this initial excursion into the realms of extravaganza, which in modern times has either been set apart and docketed as "Gilbertian," or has degenerated into the inanities of pantomime — the simple application of satirical wit to presumedly serious incidents and events, the possibilities of which form of dramatic art the authors of Suzanne have endeavoured, and not without success, to indicate. As a play for holiday amusement, it is both novel and entertaining, and in this, as in other respects, the Ulster Literary Theatre may, without assuming too much, take credit to itself for giving a lead, and presenting the public with a wholly original and well-manipulated idea.

Of the merits of the performance itself, one can speak highly, allowing for the disadvantage of a first public presentation, though such defects as are usually observable on an occasion of the kind, were noticeably few. Many little devices from the details of stage management to the form of the printed programme with which the audience was supplied, indicated the fact that the Theatre have departed entirely from the much-worn grooves wherein the amateur company usually moves, and are giving expression to quite distinctive ideas. The acting was very good indeed, and, though the members of the cast, as usual, remained anonymous, it may not be out of place to single out the two Sovereigns, Lundy and Francy M'Cann, as being particularly well enacted, the spirit of the piece being remarkably well sustained in these parts. The mounting is very handsome, and the costumes excellent, whilst the lighting arrangements and the stage management proved faultless. It was satisfactory to find the audience a large one, and still more so to observe the fact that the play "went well" from start to finish, and never failed in its object of amusing by its extravagancies, whilst sustaining a connected interest, and the only thing that we might venture to suggest in connection with such a successful performance is a little condensation to bring the main "hits" somewhat more closely into conjunction.[76]

To produce a play dealing in any fashion with the religious tensions of Ulster is even now a decidedly brave undertaking. However, *Suzanne and the Sovereigns* was done with such light-hearted good spirits that it delighted all sections of its audience, and was revived in the following year.

The Theatre of Ireland presented several new plays and some revivals. Padraic Colum's *The Fiddler's House*, which was a revision of his earlier *Broken Soil*, was produced for the first time on 21 March at the Rotunda, on the same programme as Alice Milligan's *The Last Feast of the Fianna*. This group stood to profit from the reaction against the Abbey, and audiences for their shows were large. The *Sinn Féin* reviewer, 'Scrutator', reported:

I am not going to say that the performance was perfect. As I saw it on Thursday night the third act requires a lot more pulling together. But on the whole it was excellently done, and the amount of extraordinarily fine and careful work in the first two acts amply atoned for the blemishes in the third. I don't think that a play more difficult to be effectively performed than *The Fiddler's House* has yet been produced amongst the numerous tribe of modern dramatists. Mr. Colum has had very little regard for the exigencies of the theatre. The clue to a whole scene is sometimes contained in a single sentence. Important information, absolutely necessary for the proper understanding of the plot is also frequently conveyed in the same inadequate way. . . . There is not much dramatic development in *The Fiddler's House*. It is essentially pictorial, and the scenes are concerned more with the elucidation of the central character of Conn Hourican, the fiddler, than with the progression of the action. . . . The dialogue of the play,

185

apart from the tendency towards compression, is astonishingly good. . . . Mr. Colum was exceedingly fortunate in his cast, and no amateur organisation anywhere else in Ireland could boast of such a combination of talent.[77]

The Evening Mail added that the third act of the opening night performance was 'much spoiled by the voice of the prompter which was loud in the land'.

Internal problems and lack of experience hampered the group. It had planned to hire the Abbey Theatre for performances early in February, but had to postpone them for a month and move to the Rotunda. George Nesbitt resigned as Stage Manager and was replaced by Fred Morrow. Máire Nic Shiubhlaigh, one of the founding members and a leading actress, cited the coming of Morrow as providential. He had met the members of the Theatre of Ireland at a reception given for the Ulster Literary Theatre during their visit to Dublin in the spring of 1907. When he left Belfast and moved to Dublin to set up his interior decorating business, he offered to become stage manager and was welcomed. The Morrow brothers contributed enormously to the Irish theatre. With Fred Morrow came his brother, Jack, who designed scenery, while the third brother, Harry, under the pseudonym of Gerald MacNamara, was the author of *Thompson in Tir-na-nOg* and other amusing plays, and co-author of *Suzanne and the Sovereigns*. Fred Morrow brought experience and imagination to the new company, but again during 1907 the minutes of their meetings show the Theatre of Ireland planning performances which never occurred and postponing productions of plays. A letter of Padraic Colum to W. G. Fay indicates that Colum, at least, did not see the Theatre of Ireland as replacing the Abbey, and that he still had hopes for the I.N.T.S. becoming a truly national theatre:

My dear W.G. I am sincerely glad that you are going to make an effort to work up an audience in Dublin. Would it be possible for you to make a reconciliation with Miss Walker and Starkey? I think it is a great loss on Miss Walker's part to be out of the Abbey Theatre. With us she will get few shows and little practice. Starkey is a man of the utmost sincerity and you cannot leave him out of account. Another thing, . . . *Be National*. Put yourself in the way of that great wave that is certainly breaking across the country. If we are not with it, we will be of no account. I have been living in the country and I feel that Ireland is full of life. We have achieved the nation and the Nation is about to become self-conscious.[78]

Finally, on 13 December, the Theatre of Ireland presented a new production of Æ's *Deirdre*, and the first production of Seumas O'Kelly's *The Matchmakers*. *Sinn Féin* reaffirmed its support of the Abbey's chief rival and praised the cast of *Deirdre*. It was quite a remarkable cast, including Russell himself, Padraic Colum, Seumas O'Sullivan, Seumas O'Connolly and the Countess Markievicz, with Máire Nic Shiubhlaigh playing the lead. *The Matchmakers* was the first of the comedies by the Loughrea playwright who was to become one of the most prolific and skilful of Irish writers. By 1907, his short stories were appearing regularly in the weekly papers, and he was soon to achieve a solid reputation for his popular play *The Shuiler's Child*.

The hypersensitivity of the Irish audience can hardly be over-estimated, for even O'Kelly's simple comedy was suspected of containing slurs on the Irish race. Máire Nic Shiubhlaigh reported:

> Oddly, despite its inoffensiveness and the cleverness of its construction, it annoyed some hasty members of our public who, because the story dealt with a "made marriage," came prepared to register their disapproval on the first night. Happily, however, the surprise of both the cast and the greater part of the audience itself was so apparent, that the objectors, a few of whom had begun a faint hissing, realised the folly of their attitude, and retired abashed. There were congratulations and apologies afterwards.[79]

The Freeman's Journal called it 'a distinct success', and reported that it kept the house in 'continuous outbursts of laughter', and *The Irish Times* agreed, terming it a 'brilliant success'. Clearly this was the sort of wholesome comedy preferred by the nationalists and those opposed to the literary theatre. The reviewer in *The Peasant and Irish Ireland*, for instance, wrote, 'Seumas has come to the rescue with a play free from the obscurations of sex problems and "typical" peasants singed with the heat of maudlin sentimentality.'

Dublin's third theatre group, the National Players, long associated with the Daughters of Erin, continued to offer occasional productions. To celebrate St. Patrick's Day, they presented a new play by Gerald O'Loughlin, entitled *The Rapparee* at the Queen's Theatre. The play dealt with the siege of Limerick, and from plot summaries seems packed with action:

> As a fitting accompaniment of that stormy epoch, clashing of swords and deadly encounters are some of its salient features. But the climax is reached when in order to save her lover, a

Jacobite officer, to whom she was to be wed the next day, and who is engaged in a duel with a Williamite colonel who has insulted her, the heroine rushes between the combatants, and receives a death-wound. As that winsome, artless daughter of Erin, Annie, Miss E. Moloney won well-merited plaudits.[80]

Also on the programme was James Cousins's *Sold*, which is also described as a first performance, but which had been presented at the end of the previous year in Cork. This was the play which Yeats had rejected for the Abbey, and which had been published in 1902 in *The United Irishman*. But reviews of this, too, were favourable. 'It scintillates with the true spirit of comedy, abounds in rapier-pointed dialogue, and is replete with attention-absorbing incidents,' said *The Freeman's Journal*. Joseph Holloway less generously reported, 'the staging of all three plays . . . was a disgrace to the theatre.' In his autobiography, Cousins recalled the performance:

"The first real comedy of Irish life," as Arthur Griffith had called the County Down play, *Sold*, when he printed it full-length in *The United Irishman*, brought down the final curtain on my dramatic episode in the land of my birth. The Queen's Theatre, on whose stage the young Henry Irving had mouthed some of his early lines, was to be demolished and rebuilt. Its last day in its old incarnation was given to new Irish drama. A new local company staged two plays, one a piece of political history and imagination, *Remy Dhu the Raparee*, the other *Sold*, "A Comedy of County Down Life." The company, being young and confident in inexperience, had rehearsed my play without reference to the author. At the matinee I learned the weird ways in which the meaning of a phrase can be made dead or half dead or half alive by the misplacing of a stress and the rising or falling of an inflection where it should fall or rise. Luckily the afternoon audience was small and un-important. No one laughed at the comedy, not even I. I got the cast together after the performance, and spent a hectic eternity chivvying the actors around to avoid various stage sins, and showing them where to bring down an accent like a paver's beater or where to avoid one like poison. By the time the theatre was crammed for the "night show" the cast was keyed up like "the harp that once . . ." or a fiddle-string for a country dance. My pink face had gone turkey-red. I stuck to the script; and after the political play had groused itself into thinly applauded silence, I took my place at "prompt" fiercely determined that the big crowd beyond the footlights

188

would miss no word or line, even if I had to bawl a "fluff" myself. The curtain fell on clean hearty applause, and I was hailed as the invoker of healthy laughter.[81]

For the Samhain festival in the autumn, the same group presented two new plays, Lily MacManus's *O'Donnell's Cross* and R. G. Walsh's *Before Clonmel*. As the titles indicate, both were historical dramas, and even *Sinn Féin*, which would have been anxious to find something to praise in this nationalist theatre group, admitted:

> As to the plays, though the appearance of two new authors is a hopeful sign, it can hardly be contended that the artistic level of former years has been excelled, if even attained. Both pieces were of a conventional type, and one did not carry away ideas. *O'Donnell's Cross* appealed too obviously, at times, to a Nationalist "gallery," and *Before Clonmel* was reminiscent of what, in unregenerate days, used to be called "the commercial theatre." [82]

The effect of the nationalist movement on the drama is evident in the advertisements for plays presented by amateur groups. The Bootle Branch of the Gaelic League presented *A West Briton's Romance*, and in the same week there was an advertisement for 'Denveer's Great 3 Act Drama: *Rosaleen Dhu* . . . Irish in conception and acting, in interest enthralling. Brilliant acting alternating with Music, Song and Dancing.' Amateur groups favoured such crowd-pleasers as H. C. Mangan's *Robert Emmet* and O'Gregan's *The Leprechaun*.

Early in March, the National Players Company met to consider forming a touring company to play in Irish, and Edward Martyn wrote a letter to *The Freeman's Journal* supporting such a plan:

> We have many little Irish plays and many who can play well in Irish. It ought not to be difficult to get together half a dozen players or so under the management of a reliable man. They might travel over the Irish-speaking districts and also the English-speaking, keeping chiefly to the small towns and villages. It seems to me there is nothing that could create so great a curiosity and interest in the language as this. The people have to be coaxed into learning and speaking Irish. It is not by being preached at and abused by an organiser, but by being amused that they will take up the study, and what is so amusing as the theatre? Every nation, especially ours, is fond of it. Irish players will be a delightful novelty to the Irish-speaking districts, teaching respect for the language,

189

as coming from a centre of prestige like Dublin. In the English-speaking districts the person who can understand the plays will be looked up to, while others will begin to learn the language, so that when the company comes around again they too may understand. These players might at first cost a little to the Gaelic League, but I think they would soon pay their expenses, and eventually make money. In any case, I fancy it would not be difficult to get subscribers to so promising a project.[83]

Martyn's interest in the project was clearly not based on its artistic effects, as he admitted to an interviewer for *The Irish Packet*. He had turned now to social concerns and set himself with the nationalists and against his former associates in the Irish National Theatre Society.

[Interviewer]: You believe, then, that an Irish theatre would save the language in the Irish-speaking districts?

[Martyn]: I am sure it would help to save it. It is certain that something must be done, and done at once. If anyone else can put forward a better idea, let him do so.

You think it would encourage Irish speakers to write, and thus develop Irish drama?

No. I do not believe it would do anything for the drama — at least not the drama from my point of view; but it would amuse the people, and bring a new life into the Irish-speaking towns and villages. The people want to be amused and coaxed into taking an interest in the language.

There have been some objections as to the possibility of always getting a hall for a performance?

But they could have a tent which might be pitched in a field. We do not want anything on an elaborate scale. About half a dozen actors, a piper, and a few fiddlers. The scenery and staging would be as simple as possible. . . .

You know the Irish peasant well, especially the Western peasant. Is that not so?

Yes. But I don't profess to know him as well as Mr. Synge. . . . I had a large property in the West, and knew my tenants very well.

I hope you had a good opinion of them?

I believe the peasant of the present day who has no Irish to be the greatest lout in Europe. His mind is a perfect blank. On the other hand, the Irish-speaking peasant is a perfect gentleman. He had that innate culture which comes from his wealth of tradition and story, and . . . if the Irish peasant lost the language this country will become a terrible wilderness.[84]

Padraic Colum wrote to *The Freeman's Journal* approving of Martyn's plan and suggesting plays to be performed, including translations into Irish of Yeats's *Kathleen ni Houlihan* and Lady Gregory's *The Rising of the Moon*.

Another play suggested by Colum was an original piece in Irish by Pierce Beasley, entitled *Cormac Na Coille*. It was first presented on 6 May at the Rotunda by the Keating Branch of the Gaelic League, and *The Freeman's Journal* reported that the performance was a great success:

> The Large Concert Hall was filled with a sympathetic and most appreciative audience, and at the outset it may be said that the reception of the piece was highly flattering both to the author and artistes. *Cormac na Coille* . . . is a romantic drama, constructed round historical personages, and associated with the historical episode of the appearance of O'Neill in Munster in the year 1660. The work deserves importance, if for no other reason than that it is the first of its kind which the Irish Literary and Dramatic Revival has produced.[85]

When it was repeated for the Oireachtas, it was again 'cheered tremendously' by the audience.

Reports of other plays in Irish outside of Dublin are frequently found in the newspapers of this time, and usually the performances are given by branches of the Gaelic League.

The patriotic protests against *The Playboy* were rather influential, and protests against stage Irishmen and alleged affronts to the Irish character became more common. Two of the most unlikely demonstrations were also reported in 1907. In February, while news of the *Playboy* riots was still current, a public meeting was held in Mullingar to protest the performance by the Hubert O'Grady Company of *The Wild Irish Boy*. The action was successful, and the play was withdrawn because it seemed to the towns-people 'calculated to throw ridicule on the Irish character'. In October in Liverpool, a man was arrested for protesting against a play which he considered indecent and offensive. The play, he claimed, introduced 'words of double meaning, suggestive of immodesty'. The man objected particularly to a scene in which a priest was depicted as drinking whiskey at a wake with the mother of a supposed dead man. The play so offensive to this exiled patriot was, of course, Dion Boucicault's *The Shaughraun*.[86]

191

1908

The domestic turmoils of the Abbey Theatre reached a climax early in 1908. First, some trivial dispute caused the temporary resignation of J. M. Kerrigan, and then the Fay brothers and Brigit O'Dempsey left for good. The departure of the Fays seemed to many the most telling blow that the theatre had yet sustained. But although the Abbey lost in the three Fays an amount of talent that would earlier have seemed irreplaceable, the situation was not quite the same in 1908. Arthur Sinclair and J. M. Kerrigan took over many of the brothers' parts and played them with great effect. Sinclair was to develop into a brilliant comic actor, and Kerrigan subsequently spent many busy years making films. The Allgood sisters had already laid the basis of their reputations and were considered, with Máire Nic Shiubhlaigh, probably the finest actresses the theatre had produced.

The three Directors took over much of the handling of the theatre's business, and delegated some of it to secretaries like W. A. Henderson. They also directed many of the plays, although from time to time they used the directorial talents of Norreys Connell and other authors. It is perhaps ungenerous to remark that the Fays' departure was, as George Moore said, a blessing in disguise. The Fays had done inestimably valuable work, but as long as W. G. Fay was stage manager, the control of the Directors would not have been absolute.

The reasons for the departure largely stemmed from clashes of personality. W. G. Fay was, for much of the time, hardly even on snarling terms with Miss Horniman, and he was often at odds with the company.[1] In his defence, it must be said that as the company's chief producer, chief comic actor, business manager and scene painter, he was monumentally overworked.

The parting was initially amicable. The Directors had been thinking of taking the company to America under the auspices of some commercial manager like Charles Frohman, and so, when Frohman sponsored the Fays' tour, Yeats apparently considered it a trial run for a later Abbey tour. However, despite good intentions, bitterness did arise which was difficult to dispel at a distance of three thousand miles. There was some misunderstanding between the Fays and Yeats's agent, John Quinn, over fees. One of Frohman's men irritated the Directors by initially billing the Fays as the Abbey Theatre Company. There were interviews with the Fays in the press that ruffled the feelings of those in Dublin. Finally, all of this suspicion and ill-feeling culminated in the Fays being formally expelled from membership of the Society which they had helped to create.

It is a complicated story and an unfortunate one, and we have attempted to present only its outlines.

*　　*　　*

On 3 January Holloway recorded:

> On visiting the Abbey re the painting this afternoon I met Mr. O'Rourke in the Gentlemen's Dressing room, and asked him if Kerrigan had left the Company or if he were ill, and he told me that he had left. I mentioned the fact to Mr. Lawrence who called in, and he said he had met Mr. Kerrigan in the National Library and got speaking to him, and he told him it was over the company wanting to play *The Playboy* on their recent tour, and he refusing to do so was the cause of his leaving. He was a bit reticent in speaking of the matter, but said things were at sixes and sevens with the company.[2]

The next day Holloway met W. A. Henderson at Eason's, the bookseller's:

> . . . we chatted about Kerrigan leaving the Abbey, and he said Kerrigan told him that he was late for rehearsal one day, and he was informed his services were no longer needed. Events led up to the sudden dismissal, of course, and may develop further as Miss Sara Allgood was very thick with Kerrigan. Willie Fay is very hard to get on with; his uneven temper was the cause of all the actors' troubles since the beginning of the Company. He lacks tact, and is too rough of tongue at times to be tolerated. Such is the general opinion of those who worked under him in the company.[3]

On 9 January Henderson dropped by Holloway's house for a chat:

> He spoke of Frank Fay as the importer of all the acting and elocution knowledge to the company — he is an admirable teacher. W. G. Fay can direct a rehearsal, but he can't impart like his brother. They are thoroughly disappointed with the present season. They thought with Vaughan to aid them (and he does nothing contrary to their will) things would be made trim; instead of that they have drifted from bad to worse. . . . Frank Fay had the gift of appreciation of a narrow groove of acting in others, but Willie had no appreciation for others whatsoever.[4]

194

Years later, Willie Fay summed up his reasons for leaving:

> Although I was nominally in full control again, the old spirit of camaraderie was gone and the company was thoroughly out of hand. Incidents of open insubordination were not infrequent. If I ordered anything that happened not to be to some member's liking, he (or she) would fling off to one or other of the directors with his (or her) grievance, and the chances were that I should be overruled. Now it is important to observe that up to this time not one of us, not even myself, had troubled about having a formal contract in writing with the National Theatre Company, Limited. Artists were engaged by me by word of mouth, and the matter was left at that — not a business-like procedure, I grant you, but one that worked well enough while we were all a happy family. But now that the old spirit was no more it was clear to me that the only way to restore discipline was to conform to strict business practice and to insist on written contracts of service clearly defining the conditions of employment. The contracts would, of course, be between each artist and the National Theatre Company, Limited; but I demanded that one of the conditions should be that no artist was permitted to approach individual members of the Board on any matter touching his work. If anyone had a grievance, let him submit it formally in writing to the Board, who could then take it up with me if they saw fit.[5]

Fay then went on to say:

> Unfortunately the lavish encomiums of the English Press had been too heady for our friends Yeats, Synge, and Augusta Gregory. They imagined we had arrived when we had no more than started. We had a company that could do peasant plays with an accomplishment and finish that have never been rivalled, much less excelled. But we should have to show much more than that before we could claim to be a real art theatre. We should have to create by degrees a company capable, both in numbers and experience, of performing any type of play, whether low life or high life, prose or verse. Frank and I reckoned that this would be a long and hard job — a matter of ten years at least, even with the excellent material we undoubtedly had.
>
> I put these considerations to the directors, pointing out that it would be idle for me to attempt such a task unless I were given the usual power of a manager and producer. . . . What

195

agitated confabulations the directors held I know not. All I know is that after a few days Lady Gregory came to me to say that they were not disposed to make any changes, and what was I going to do about it? I did the only thing that was left to me — I resigned on the spot.[6]

Actually, Fay had made his proposals in a letter on 1 December 1907, and the Directors met to consider his suggestions on 4 December. As the company was then on tour, almost a month and a half went by with nothing happening. It was not until 13 January that Fay wrote the following note to Yeats:

Dear Mr. Yeats,
    I regret that under present circumstances I do not see my way to continue my engagement with the National Theatre Society. I herewith give one month's notice. My engagement will terminate on Thursday 13th February 1908.
                I am, faithfully yours,
                      WILLIAM G. FAY.[7]

On the same day, Frank also wrote a note to Yeats:

Dear Mr. Yeats,
    I am resigning my engagement with the National Theatre Society, (Ltd.) and herewith give you the necessary month's notice. My engagement will terminate on 13th February.
I do not resign my membership of either the Irish National Theatre Society or the National Theatre Society, Ltd.
                Yours faithfully,
                      F. J. FAY.[8]

On the following day, Yeats included in a letter to *The Dublin Evening Mail* 'a paragraph written for a forthcoming number of *Samhain*':

We are about to lose our principal actor. William Fay has had enough of it, and we don't wonder, and is going to some other country where his exquisite gift of comedy and his brain teeming with fancy will bring him an audience, fame, and a little money. He has worked with us now since 1902, when he formed his company to carry on the work of the Irish Literary Theatre and feels that he must leave the younger men the long, laborious battle. We have his good wishes, and he will return to us if at all possible to play his old parts for some brief season, or seasons, and may possibly rejoin us for a London or an American tour. We believe that William Fay

196

is right to go, and he will have our good will and good wishes with him, though we have lost in losing him the finest comedian of his kind upon the English-speaking stage.[9]

On 14 January Holloway was at the Abbey and recorded:

I saw A. Power in the distance in the gallery and he came over to me full of the Abbey business. He wanted to know the inner meaning of it all. Of course, I could not tell him, as it is wrapt in mystery from me. He said he met Kerrigan. He is likely to play with them — the Theatre of Ireland — next show. The National Theatre Society threatened to leave him at Glasgow last tour until he appealed to Yeats and Lady Gregory and got a ticket back to Dublin. Power told me all about his interview with W. G. Fay at the Custom House over the salary asked for the trip to London in the summer, and it tallied in the main with the account I had already heard. Fay wanted him to accept £1.0.0 for a week in London, and Power told him he could scarcely live on dried fish for a week in the big city on that. They parted in high words, and Fay on his return told the company that Power said if they were used to live on dried fish he was not. This annoyed many of them and made it uncomfortable for him.[10]

For 15 January Holloway recorded:

Mr. D. J. O'Donoghue called, and told me he had a long chat with W. G. Fay, who told him he was going to London next week. He now agreed that William Boyle was right when he said that the theatre would come to grief within the year from *The Playboy*. They are starting an Irish theatrical club in connection with the Irish Literary Society in London, and probably that is what he is going to London to look after. He said he would call on Boyle, probably to soft soap him into giving him permission to play his pieces. Evidently he is as wily a customer as the great W.B. in his way, but Mr. Boyle is sure to see through his little game. As they were speaking, W. B. Yeats loomed in the distance, and W. G. Fay fled, and when he was gone Yeats was nowhere to be seen. Fay was of opinion it was time for the Abbey to burst up! This is a singularly egotistical opinion to hold, now that he is leaving. It is surprising how we all can be done without in this strange world of ours![11]

On 16 January Holloway had a chat with the Fays and Brigit O'Dempsey at the Abbey:

197

Frank said he was astonished to hear from Lawrence that Henderson and I were all for patching up the difference. I told him that was not so. What I thought was that it was a pity to resign before they had something else secured, which was quite a different thing. They were packing up to leave. . . . Frank remains on in Dublin and will probably start an Elocution Class. Vaughan also leaves the Abbey. Willie told me *The Piper* is not likely to be a success as it ridicules the peasantry of the '98 period. He found things becoming impossible when even the company refused to heed him.[12]

Two days later, Holloway recorded:

Had a long chat with W. A. Henderson, chiefly about the turn affairs have taken at the Abbey. Some twelve plays were sent in while he was connected with the Theatre. Vaughan it was that gave the Fays the notion of independence. Yeats did not pull with him lately, and so the Fays sided with him, with the result that they are now outside the theatre. Frank Fay told him that Synge and Yeats were in the office all day yesterday busy tearing up documents. Vaughan did the same when he arrived on the scene. Mr. and Mrs. W. G. Fay start for London tonight, full of high hopes. . . . Synge sticks to Yeats because he could get no one else to produce his plays for him. Miss Allgood is wavering in her allegiance to the theatre, but what will she do if she leaves? She had introductions to managers in London and tried to get their power, and nothing came of it. Miss Vera Esposito tried to get on in London some time ago and failed also. There is no open door to talent anywhere nowadays unless backed up by peculiar influence! It was the ending of McAlister's play *Nelly Lehane* that prevented the Fays presenting it. They thought the heroine should have returned to sin again and not resolve to lead a purer life as the author planned for her to do. Speaking of salaries to the Abbey actors, Henderson was surprised at the little Miss Darragh got per week — £2.10.0 he fixed it at.[13]

On 17 January Boyle wrote to O'Donoghue:

. . . I'm not sorry for Fay or the Abbey either. Still, if Fay calls I will be friendly to him. As a matter of business he may help to get my stuff forward here or in America, but, after his behaviour over *The Playboy* I can never think very highly of him. I'm afraid that "W" has allowed Yeats to sidetrack the issue. The main point was that the directorate of the Abbey "shelved plays that drew audiences and insisted upon

198

the performance of others towards which the public evince no great liking." Yeats can't deny that *The Eloquent Dempsy* was a play which drew audiences. Yet, on the British tour next after its production, he would not allow it to be played though Fay wanted it (he told me). Then in the visit which they paid to London two years ago they kept back *The Land* and *The Building Fund* till the day of a first performance of a Shaw play at the Stage Society knowing well the critics would be at Shaw's play and the newspaper space occupied with it. They also put off *The Building Fund* from the place they had assigned it on the programme to the very last item of their engagement — apparently for the same reason. Fortunately they did not succeed — the favourable notices it got probably preventing them from staging *Dempsy* on their next English, Welsh, and Scotch tour. Surely Yeats thinks the public have a short memory. Of course only the directors' own stuff was played at such high critical places as Oxford and Cambridge. I suggested that some press notices of the plays be printed in pamphlet form, and Miss Horniman promised me to have it done, but when the thing came out it was a "precious" production written by Yeats in which the reference to me was that it was my proud boast to have been born in a cabin, which happened to be a lie. I never made such a boast, and was born in perhaps as comfortable a house as himself and educated at much greater expense I'll swear. *Not that the thing matters a straw except to show that the fellow can't be truthful over anything.* . . . Norreys Connell's *Piper* is a horrid thing. He sent it to me two years ago and I told him then what I thought of it which vexed him. The dialect is pure English brogue of the worst sort, and the Wexford peasant of '98 represented by baboons and the English soldiers as heroes.[14]

The Fays' departure occasioned much comment and some far-fetched rumours. As one writer remarked:

We believe that Mr. Yeats is about to assume the duties of Stage Manager. It is even rumoured that he will replace Mr. W. Fay, in the latter's histrionic capacity; the experiment will be interesting. It is also suspected that the orchestra, always rather an eyesore to the fastidious poet, may be deleted. There are other rumours, but they seem to have little foundation, that the Theatre of Ireland will now join forces with the National Theatre Society, but this cannot be taken seriously.[15]

199

On 21 January Henderson and Frank Fay dropped by Holloway's house for a chat:

[Henderson] said he wrote to Mr. Connell re the producing of *The Piper*, saying it was just like Yeats to try the new company on outsider's work and not trust any of the Abbey trio's work to their tender mercies until he saw how it would shape. He recalled one evening when Willie Fay held forth to the company for a couple of hours on his experience with a travelling circus years ago. He also touched on Yeats's childish anxiety to know if the receipts each night for his *Deirdre* compared favourably with those of *The Mineral Workers* for correspondent nights. This incident illustrated the childish conceit of the man! He also thought Willie Fay was much to blame for many of the plays being refused; Fay would say to Yeats such and such a one would not act, and Yeats took him at his word, and the play was returned to its author in due course. Many of the plays sent in were hardly glanced at. Henderson said it was he pressed Willie Fay to put on *The Rising of the Moon*. Fay was of the opinion it wouldn't act well!

Frank Fay seemed very downhearted. He spoke of wishing to gain experience in Shakespearean work and would leave Dublin at any moment if he got a chance of a berth in a Shakespearean Company. They would not give anything for his teaching in Dublin if he had not the hallmark of such a training, he thought. We pooh-poohed the idea, but did not alter his opinion on the point. Since he had the influenza, he found his memory much improved; now he found no difficulty in memorizing; he could learn anything off by heart without trouble. He told us that Mr. Casey, an amateur actor, had been made stage manager at the Abbey. This Mr. Casey had written a play for the theatre also (*The Man Who Missed the Tide*). The caretaker in saying goodbye to Willie Fay said, "You'll be owner of this theatre yet." A prophecy I hope will come true.[16]

On 22 January D. J. O'Donoghue called in to Holloway 'full of the Abbey "break-up"'.

He had a long chat with W. B. Yeats in which he tried to defend his action in the matter in his usual egotistical way. Yeats spoke of "Wharton's" play as a terrible immoral one bringing in a priest, far stronger than *The Playboy*. No Irish audience would stand it. Yeats was on his way to ask Miss

Walker's younger sister to become a member of the Abbey when O'Donoghue met him. "Nobody but Willie Fay could keep Vaughan in his place — of course, we could not keep him. Fay's going gives McDonnell [Sinclair] and Kerrigan a chance of big parts." He wanted to know had I been speaking of the crises? O'Donoghue told him he had never heard me speak of internal troubles of the society, but that I freely expressed myself on the plays at all times. . . . Yeats said they would keep the manager's place open for Willie Fay for six months. O'Donoghue asked him were they going to shut up the Abbey, and Yeats answered, "Oh, no, only for a time until we have trained the new company!" The Theatre of Ireland are about producing *Maeve* by Edward Martyn shortly, and Starkey was in the hopes of getting Frank Fay to "coach" them. Rumour has it that Frank Fay intends starting a School for Acting in Dublin.[17]

On the same day, Boyle wrote to Holloway:

The interest that you have shown in sending me the Dublin papers containing particulars of the Fays' secession from the Abbey Theatre and the comments and challenges arising out of the affair deserves that I should tell you something of my own views on the matter.

Honestly I think it is the only thing Fay could have done if he wanted to retain his own powers as an actor. He's a man of temperament to whom an audience is essential. I haven't had the same opportunity of seeing him you had, but I noticed that he never played twice exactly in the same way. This shows the influence of his immediate environment on his work, and empty benches would I fancy quite destroy him in the end. Clearly he saw no signs of an improvement in the management which would draw an audience in, so he cut the painter.

As for Yeats and his challenges, etc. — we all know that his sole purpose is to keep before the public in one way or another. The outside public doesn't care about his work or his opinions, and those interested in him know well enough that the Abbey Theatre and every play produced in it were merely used to bolster up himself and Lady Gregory. They never draw up a programme with any other aim or issue a picture postcard or an *Arrow* or a *Samhain* without the object of puffing or explaining the importance of their own work. Naturally I observed this mainly in connection with my own things. They wouldn't give me a whole line on their bills

201

even after I requested it for the first production of *The Mineral Workers*, and they wouldn't play *The Eloquent Dempsy* on their English tour, for no other reason that I can see except that my *Building Fund* secured the best press notices on their previous visit. Then they shuffled their programmes, altered and manoeuvred the whole tour plans apparently with the same object. No doubt they did the same thing with Colum and to some extent with Synge though these writers may not have seen through the game as clearly as I did. Synge, however, had a powerful ally in Miss Horniman whose dislike of the Irish people his plays gratified. Probably you know all this already. But I want to let you see I know it too.

On the general aspect of Irish Drama, I am rather hopeless for this reason — the Irish public (or at least those who ought to lead in such matters) are indifferent. It's all very fine to blame the Abbey Directorate for the loss of Fay to Ireland. But what has Ireland done to keep him? The Abbey lords were playing for their own hands. Who has shown the same zeal — or half the same zeal for Irish drama? When the first secession took place, Colum and Russell tried to start a theatre of their own. No one with money — no body of importance — gave them any help. Then Mr. Mangan and some others had a try. No one of importance helped them. If Ireland, or rather Dublin, wants an Irish Drama, Ireland or Dublin generally must show they want it. I don't think any other country would show so great a lack of interest in a matter which concerns the characters of the nation quite as much as history, political or social. It's making far too much of Yeats to blame him entirely for the failure of the scheme to found an Irish Theatre. If a thousand men could be found to subscribe a pound each, Ireland wouldn't need the money of an Irish-hating English-woman to set up a drama of its own. Clearly, Dublin prefers the English Theatre it has. If a theatrical business man, like Gunn, say, saw money — in other words an audience — in it we wouldn't have to wait.

This is rather a formal sort of letter, but I want to formally express myself, and having an axe of my own to grind, can't rush into print in newspapers.[18]

On 26 January Holloway recorded:

I was with James Connolly who told me that the Abbey folk were trying to induce the members of the Theatre of Ireland to join the Abbey Company. A. Power had gone back. He was rehearsing pieces in both companies, a thing Connolly did not approve of at all. Annie Walker and Kerrigan were also rehearsing at the Abbey. . . . I showed Connolly *The Sunday Independent*, with the slashing article against Synge's new comedy, *The Tinker's Wedding*, just published.[19]

On 3 February Synge wrote to W. A. Henderson from the Abbey:

I dare say you have heard of the changes we have had here in the Abbey.

We are opening with two new plays next week and everything is going well.

I wonder if you are still disengaged and if you would care to come on with us in your old position and at former salary. For the moment I am looking after the money matters and I suppose between us we could get some system of book-keeping that we could work.

As you know, our arrangements are always liable to change from one reason or other, but if you come back we could offer you the post for certain till the autumn, if that would suit you. Excuse this line. I am very busy getting through [word illegible]. Please let me know what you think of what I propose, and when I could see you.[20]

By this time, W. G. Fay and Brigit O'Dempsey had gone to London where Miss Horniman, despite her difficulties with Fay, did attempt to help him. On 4 February she wrote to Yeats:

Mr. Chester Fox has just been here, sent by Frohman to enquire about the Fays. I impressed on him that you had lent them your rooms and that they would return to you for tours. I told him of their powers and how I believe that they are trying for engagements.[21]

On the next day, Holloway wrote:

D. J. O'Donoghue called in for a chat and told me that Frank Fay called in to him this morning for W. Boyle's address (W. G. and Mrs. Fay are staying with the latter) as he did not know when he would want to write as he was expecting to hear, at any moment, about an engagement from Frohman for America, and he might have to leave Dublin by Saturday. Fay was very indignant about Yeats's treatment of them, and said if he told what he knew about him and his doings at the Abbey, he would put a different complection on the matter of their leaving.[22]

On 6 February *The Irish Independent* carried an announcement that the Fays had been engaged by Charles Frohman to appear in some of their more successful parts in the United States and that they were to sail for New York almost immediately. A few days later, Yeats remarked to Holloway that:

> Things were going smoother since Willie Fay left with the general management of the theatre. Fay should never have been anything but stage manager and actor. The other duties irritated him. It was unfortunate that he fell out with the company. A beaten general always falls out with his men. Fay was disappointed that the company did not do better, and was irritated and discontented.[23]

On 19 February, shortly after the Fays arrived in New York, Frank sent a postcard to James Montgomery. Part of the card has been torn away, but Fay was discussing their opening. The critics were kind but not enthusiastic.

> Allan Dale, however, writes nicely about us and he is considered very important. We do *The Rising of the Moon* Monday with Digges in cast!! He has improved greatly and his wife (Miss Quinn that was) is ten years younger. We also met Kelly who is doing well with Sothern. The company that plays along with us were very kind and wished us success before the curtain rose and J. M. Barrie cabled it; but I don't think we have achieved it, and if *The Rising of the Moon* don't succeed, I dare say we shall go back. Barrie wrote Will in London saying that he hoped not only to see him playing alongside his piece but *in* one. He has a big opinion of Will, and I hope he will get a show. Our pieces are not strong enough I fear for here. I hope for Will's sake *The Rising of the Moon* will turn out a trump. Remember me to all. . . . I hope Will goes to London where he has a name: here we are mixed up with the Abbey Theatre.[24]

On the same day Fay also wrote to W. J. Lawrence:

> We are described on the bills as "the Irish National Theatre Company from Dublin, Ireland." They have used Yeats to boom the thing — all I needn't say against my wishes, but we can't interfere. We are not known, he seems to be very well known. *A Pot of Broth* is not strong enough for them, I think. Several of the morning papers belittle the thing because Frohman had boomed it beforehand. We got a good reception from the audience, and the people in the theatre say the notices are

204

very good. . . . Yeats must have made a great splash here when he was over as he is well known. His friend Quinn has not come near us, nor old J. B., nor Miss Yeats, and yesterday one of the papers let the cat out of the bag about our having left the Abbey Theatre.[25]

On 20 February Holloway noted:

I met and had a chat with Henderson in the vestibule before the plays. W. B. Yeats soon joined us. The latter looking very cut by a severe attack of "flu." . . . He mentioned he was pleased to hear of Willie Fay's luck re reported Barrie play engagement, and we got talking of the Barrie-Frohman visit last Easter to the Abbey, and how the celebrated pair came and went unrecognized by any in connection with the Theatre. Yeats added that the night of their visit Frank and Willie fought behind the scenes over *The Playboy*, and one of them had to be locked up in the dressing room. It was the first night of Miss Letts' play, *The Eyes of the Blind*, and all the company were in a very nervous state. Miss Letts' play got a very bad interpretation, but luckily Willie played in *The Rising of the Moon* excellently later on when the excitement had cooled down somewhat.[26]

In a letter of 21 February, Boyle wrote to Holloway about Yeats:

Did I tell you that he asked Fay to press Frohman to take the whole company. "I don't mind trying you," Frohman said, "but I won't have stuff forced on me." "Is Yeats the long, black fellow who was passing continually between the audience and the footlights?" Frohman enquired. Clearly, the American has formed his own opinion of the author of *Kathleen ni Houlihan*.[27]

On 2 March Holloway was at the Abbey,

. . . and had a chat with Henderson and some of the players, also a how-do-you-do from Yeats and Synge. Henderson told me Sara Allgood had a letter and paper from Frank Fay. The management intended putting a stop to the use of their name, National Theatre Society, being used to exploit the Fays in America. It was not fair to the company. It was taking a mean advantage. It was the paper containing Alan Dale's article that came. They showed me it in the Greenroom. Kerrigan told me that O'Donovan was a pupil of McHardy-Flint's. It was Frank Fay the company really missed. As a teacher he was great: get him sitting at the back of the stalls and you on the stage, and his instruction was most illuminating.[28]

On 7 March Holloway attended a Saturday matinee at the Abbey, and saw four of the short Abbey plays with new actors in the Fays' old parts.

"They never would be missed," sings Ko-Ko in *The Mikado*. . . . How true the refrain is received another proof at the Abbey, when new interpreters were found for The Tramp in *In the Shadow of the Glen*, the Ballad Singer in *The Rising of the Moon*, and the Wise Man and the Fool in *The Hour Glass*. . . . Frank Fay's creation of the Fool can never be bettered, nor W. G. Fay's Tramp either; therefore, their new impersonators, while doing remarkably well, I must say, did not give me the same artistic pleasure I always got from the Fays in those roles. O'Rourke's Fool had not the touch of poetry and distinction of Frank Fay and was merely a clever commonplace rendering of the part. Kerrigan as the Tramp did not suggest actuality as W. G. Fay always did, as Synge's poetic vagrant. . . . With the Wise Man it was different. For since Dudley Digges first played the part, none have made it so convincing as Arthur Sinclair did today. . . . W. B. Yeats asked my opinion of Sinclair, and I told him I thought him excellent, subdued and convincing. Kerrigan and O'Rourke as the Tramp and the Fool were not quite so good. In those parts the Fays were missed. He agreed with me and added, "Frank Fay's Fool was perfect." Again at the end as I was having a word with J. M. Synge, Yeats came over, and I said Kerrigan as the Ballad Singer was splendid.[29]

On 8 March Holloway picked up some gossip about the departure of the Fays:

. . . Kerrigan and Sara Allgood came out just then, and I walked as far as O'Connell Bridge with them. The Fays' departure from the Abbey and the cause was our topic. "It was all through a woman," said Kerrigan. "Mrs. Fay wanted to rule the roost at the Abbey and the company could not stand it." It was Willie Fay who called in the police on Monday night of *The Playboy*, and it was Lady Gregory who withdrew them from the auditorium. Willie's language in describing the audience was strong, to say the least of it. Miss Allgood said she took ill on the last tour in England and Scotland, and Willie accused her of trying to shirk work, and on their return, one day in the tea room . . . he set to at her in fishwife style, and she was nearly having to call a meeting of directors over the matter. . . . It was becoming impossible of late to work with W. G. If it suits him, later on he will cast off Frank without a qualm of conscience. It is Will's way. All the company are sorry for Frank; he was very moody of late, like he was a little touched at times. One of the American papers had an interview with Mrs. Fay giving her opinions on the drama. Fancy that. They also referred to the "row" behind the scenes on Easter Monday last — the night Barrie and Frohman visited the theatre — when Willie and Mrs. Fay fought, and Frank had to be held back by three members of the company. A woman is at the bottom of every trouble in this world since Eve came on the scene. Mrs. Fay it was who sent Willie, Frank and herself over to the land of the Free — the Ireland across the seas. "Playing to empty benches had little to do with it, and *The Playboy* rows nothing whatsoever." So says Kerrigan.[30]

On 9 March Holloway noted:

I had a chat with Henderson and W. B. Yeats . . . about the Fays' use of the name of the Abbey Company and Yeats's name. . . . The latest cablegram, Yeats added, says they are not going to take action, and that is the way matters stand. Yeats seems personally annoyed over the way his name has been used — as director, as actor, as author and whatnot. He has been freely written about in all three capacities. Fancy Yeats acting in his own farce *A Pot of Broth*, yet some of the papers I have seen say so. Yeats does not accuse Frank of doing anything, but what is right, but Willie always had a twist on him — never did things straight.[31]

On 17 March Frank Fay wrote to W. J. Lawrence from New York:

Talking of Boyle, Miss Marbury, his agent here, wants 25 dollars *a* performance for *The Building Fund*; in other words, more than our weekly salary!! Of course, I don't believe Boyle knows of this outrageous demand, but if we don't hear in a day or two from Quinn (Yeats's agent) allowing us to play *The Rising of the Moon* at Chicago, we shall probably return home, as there's no use our wasting the little we have saved. Pretty way to be treated in a strange country by our countrymen, isn't it? . . . It's bad enough to be robbed by Yeats and Lady Gregory of £8 a week; but to have one's friend's agent want all our money is funny, to say no more. . . .

We are still, *both of us*, members of the I.N.T.S. and the National Theatre Society, Ltd., and *I* at any rate don't intend to resign.[32]

On 30 March Boyle wrote to Holloway:

Thanks warmly for letter and papers. Well, knowing pretty well the facts of the case I don't think the Fays have any right to blame anyone for being left as they are. I doubt much that Frohman would have used the title "Irish National Theatre Company," without Fay's consent in the first instance. Afterwards no doubt they wanted him to alter this and he was too big a man to yield. He preferred dropping the show as he found it no good. To think that they have a claim for special consideration from me is absurd after having joined in the *suppressio veri* movement to keep my name from Frohman's eyes. Frank can comment unfavourably on old Yeats doing this in New York. But his brother did exactly the same thing while living "on the floor with me" as we say in Co. Louth. Apparently they think an author is a "Robber" if he asks payment for his work. "Yeats robbing us of £8 a week"!! Well £8 is what they pay him and if he *robs* them of £8, clearly they think he should get nothing at all. Will Fay proposed to pay him five shillings a performance. I told him that was certainly too little for America — if the piece was considered worth playing at all — of which I had doubts. Of course my agent asked too much. On the relative market value paid Yeats and Lady Gregory, however, it is quite fair. As a matter of fact, I told my agent *not* to ask high fees; and, by a letter which I had from Will on Friday evening last he had come to a satisfactory arrangement with my agent in New York but was doubtful if he could do *The Building Fund* owing to its length. Frohman, he said, would not give them over 20 minutes at his theatres, and he (Will) was trying to fix up another engagement at Chicago. Another point in Frank's letter reveals something. "If they had my piece they could be independent of Yeats & Co. *'till the latter came to their senses."* So, once more, I was to be the mere stop-gap in the old old Abbey Theatre way! It is odd they should want me to treat them on the lines of warm personal friendship while they treated me on strict commercial lines. But they are the victims — always the victims. The truth is, they are not half so clever in working dodges as they think. Even Yeats's training hasn't made them a match for a plain blunt man who knows his own mind and knows the world, the stage

208

and the devil thoroughly well. Yet, all the same, I'm sorry for their fix and now, having paid off my old scores am willing to treat them as if nothing unpleasant had occurred. I have sent Will a sketch for three — 20 minutes — and funny. I don't think he will use it. He can't unless he breaks entirely with the Art, Art, Art humbugs as ridiculous. This is the subject of the sketch. A tailor who wants to reform clothing on Art principles and a shoemaker who makes good plain brogues are the two male characters. It would convulse Dublin I'm certain. Don't mention it, however, as if Fay doesn't play it (or even if he does) I don't want to explain it. Keep this to yourself.

I'm working hard on plays — one a big one on the drink subject. I'm quite infected with it.[33]

On 10 April Frank Fay added a postscript to a letter he was writing W. J. Lawrence from New York:

The oracle has spoken. We received our suspension yesterday. "At a meeting of THE IRISH NATIONAL THEATRE SOCIETY held March 18th, 1908, present Messrs. W. B. Yeats, U. Wright, J. M. Synge, you were suspended from membership of the Society for breach of and under Rule V (R). Your breach of this rule might under different circumstances have been merely technical, but recent misrepresentations have made the step necessary in the interest of the Society. J. M. Synge (Sec.)." [34]

On 23 April Boyle wrote to Holloway:

Many thanks for letter and paper. They seem to be still trying to make stone broth at the "Abbey." Well, the sap is pretty well out of the old stones by this, and, if they want a scrap of mine to thicken up the broth they must apply to my agent — Miss Elizabeth Marbury, 20 Green St., Leicester Square, W.C.

At the same time I must say that I doubt very much that anything will ever bring an audience back to the "Abbey" under its present management. The rent they've got to pay their English proprietor is a periodical insult to Ireland and the Irish, and no sooner will an audience begin to gather than the tribute will become due again.

Anyhow I don't care. I have done enough to show my feelings to my friends in Ireland.

I've heard nothing further from the Fays. I suppose they open on the 27th at Chicago with *Building Fund*. I'm afraid that the Americans won't care for it as it is not romantic

209

enough for their notion of Ireland. My chief object in anything I have written is to show that my countrymen are not fools. According to the old drama they were sentimental idiots, according to the new — of the approved Abbey pattern — they are foul-mouthed idiots.[35]

On 19 May Boyle wrote again:

Again I have to thank you for keeping me supplied with the Dublin papers. My friends in Dublin are certainly rubbing in the lesson of the Fays' success in Chicago. Will Fay writes me that the "Immortals" have again become quite civil to him. They are coming "to their senses" again as Frank hoped they would when they found they could be done without.

In an "interview" with a Chicago paper Frank places Synge at the top of Irish dramatists, ranks me with Fitzmaurice & leaves out Colum altogether. He is evidently pining to perform in the putrid once more. Well, he's got a rude awakening before him if he tries it over there — poor chap. . . .

You'll be glad to hear that our friend Conroy [Pádraig O Conaire] has got the first prize for a little play for the Oireachtas. He is going to rehearse it here and bring his lads over to Dublin to perform it in August.

Colum seems wanting in energy. He made three appointments to come here and discuss his new play with me and broke them all. If he would drop the old woman and be guided by men he would do something. As it is, he's dawdling over little hack journalism of the "precious" school which is no earthly use. Though he is perfectly clean-minded himself, he too seems to have a sneaking admiration for the Abbey folks' putrescence. If such tastes fasten on him he'll find himself too old at thirty to do any life work. It's a pity.

At present I have suspended work. I am awaiting developments. Till I know exactly what is wanted and who wants it I'm too practical to go on writing. I can see that the Fays won't play my *Artistic-minded Tailor*. It would mean war on the "Abbey" lot and they're not ripe for that. For my own part I'm quite certain that nothing lasting can be done there under the present management. By the way, Miss Horniman told some one lately that she knows nothing about the Abbey now. "Mr. Yeats tells me nothing," she said. And he on being asked about her show declared, "Miss Horniman tells me nothing." Is this suggestive of a rift? Or an agreement?[36]

The growing bad feeling between the Fays and the Abbey Directorate was intensified when W. G. Fay gave an interview to the *Chicago Sunday Tribune*, in which he stated that the reason he had left the Abbey was that the Directors were discouraging young writers. This prompted Yeats to write a rebuttal for the press, remarking that the theatre, so far as he could remember, had refused only two plays suggested by Fay. Although Yeats did not name the plays, they were most certainly James Cousins' *Sold* and Anthony Wharton's *Nelly Lehane*. Then, for the first time, Yeats made public the real reason for the Fays' departure:

> Having quarrelled with the company on tour, he wrote to us that he would resign if we did not dismiss the company, and tell its members to re-engage personally with him. Our refusal was the reason of his resignation.[37]

At the same time, a letter appeared from four of the theatre's most prominent actors:

> With reference to the statements made by Mr. W. G. Fay in the *Chicago Sunday Tribune*, appearing in last night's *Mail*, the directors have for the first time acquainted us with the true facts concerning the resignation of Mr. W. G. Fay, and allowed us to see the proposals made by him on the occasion. The acceptance of the proposals of Mr. W. G. Fay by the directors would have led to the dissolution of the company, and we, the undersigned, take this opportunity to say that we certainly would not have rejoined under Mr. Fay's proposed conditions.

> SARA ALLGOOD
> ARTHUR SINCLAIR
> J. M. KERRIGAN
> MAIRE O'NEILL[38]

By 27 May the Fays were on their way home, and on that day Frank wrote to Máire Garvey:

> We did very well at Chicago with *The Building Fund*, but the Press rather belittled the *piece de resistance — Twenty Days in the Shade*, and so here we are homeward bound. If I am not wanted for anything else, I shall go to Allan Wilkie in July, and if I can do what satisfies him shall stay as long as possible to get a good knowledge of Shakespearean work. . . . My hope is when I am fifty to get to Dublin and start a Shakespearean Class and do Elizabethan staging. Of course, this is a dream but what would we be without our dreams? I am a good teacher, if little else, but Dublin would not accept me without the professional hallmark. . . . I hear Synge has had an

211

operation and am quite prepared to hear he is no more. Well, if he has gone, I envy him. It is not every one who leaves a *Riders to the Sea* behind. The rest of his work (except the Aran Islands) has been poisoned by his bad health. . . . You heard of course of Sara's great success as Isabella. She, Digges and Kelly have all played in Shakespeare, and here am I trembling lest I should not be fit even for small parts.[39]

On 2 July Boyle wrote to Holloway:

The return of the Fays took me by surprise. . . . Will and his wife are still in Essex and likely to remain there all the summer as he has no chance here at present. He has asked me to reduce the *B. F.* to half an hour's performance which I have done with great pleasure as I saw it was only a one act piece. I have restored it more to its *original* spirit. Sheila and the Collector love and marry (I've cut out one collector and made the one I keep a blend of both the old ones). Grogan is now the only nasty character in the piece. The old woman I left live. . . . It is really much better fun than the original version and truer to Irish character. Of course it is a version the Abbey folk would not have played as they like all Irish people to be shown bad or stupid. Practically this is all I have done for some time. . . . You will have heard from O'D. [D. J. O'Donoghue] about Yeats's visit to him and my reply. I dare say I'll hear no more on the subject. Colum was here last night. He returns to Dublin next week.[40]

The Fays after their return went separate ways. Frank for some years played with Allan Wilkie's Company, mostly in minor Shakespearean roles, and he also played with other companies in both Shakespeare and melodrama. Finally he did return to Dublin where he played occasionally with the Abbey company in small parts, taught elocution, and directed plays in local colleges. He died on 2 January 1931. Willie remained in England where he was active as an Irish character actor and as a producer. Once when he returned to Dublin on tour, he is said to have looked inside the front door of the Abbey, but he did not go in. He died in 1947. Their portraits by J. B. Yeats are prominently displayed in the new Abbey Theatre.

*   *   *

Despite the departure of the Fays, the Abbey produced eleven new plays in 1908: W. F. Casey's *The Man Who Missed the Tide* and Conal O'Riordan's *The Piper* on 13 February; George Fitz-

212

maurice's *The Pie-Dish*, Yeats's *The Golden Helmet* and Lady Gregory's translation of Sudermann's *Teja* on 19 March; Lady Gregory's adaptation of Molière, *The Rogueries of Scapin*, on 4 April; and her reworking of *The Poorhouse*, now called *The Workhouse Ward* on 20 April; Richard Brinsley Sheridan's *The Scheming Lieutenant* on 29 May; W. F. Casey's *The Suburban Groove* on 1 October; Lennox Robinson's *The Clancy Name* on 8 October; and Thomas MacDonagh's *When the Dawn is Come* on 15 October.

On 14 February *The Freeman's Journal* reviewed the first production of W. F. Casey's *The Man Who Missed the Tide* and of 'Norreys Connell's' (Conal O'Riordan's) *The Piper*:

A full house at the Abbey Theatre last night witnessed the performance of two new plays. First to be put on was a drama in three acts, written by Mr. W. F. Casey. The title is *The Man Who Missed the Tide*, and the story deals with the decadence of James Walsh, a young man, who having abandoned a clerical student's career after a couple of years, afterwards has to struggle sometimes against the taunt of "spoiled priest." On his return to his native town, the newly-married wife of Dr. Gerald Quinn takes up his cause. The frequency of his visits to her house gives rise to scandalous gossip at the local club. The husband hears it, and after a spell of suspicion, explains matters. The Quinns are happy ever after. Walsh has really been coming to see Mrs. Quinn because she is the go-between for him with his sweetheart, Sheila Kennedy; but Sheila also hears the false tale and dismisses him when he proposes. Finally he turns up in Dublin a gambler and tippler, a complete breakdown, whilst Sheila is in a convent. As Dr. Gerald Quinn, Mr. Arthur Sinclair gives a true-to-life study of a rather sentimental young Irish doctor. At the outset he is appalled by the dulness of the "provincial town in the North of Ireland," named Baragh. He is divided between drink and marriage as a means of relief. At the close of the first act he has a fine little scene in which he fills his glass, raises it to his lips, and, bethinking himself, says, "No, not that way." In the second act he plays the jealous husband with more feeling, and just avoids overdoing it. He has but little more to do. Miss Sarah Allgood is the maladroit wife, and she does her part throughout with a distinct appreciation of womanly dignity. . . . Mr. Fred O'Donovan's study of James Walsh is uncommonly good. He is weak and dependent from the first. His failures to get employment are attributed to the dead set against him, instead of to — what is evident — his own want of stamina. There is just a gleam of hope when he gets a position on the local paper, and is assured by Mrs. Quinn that his love affair prospers, despite his own backwardness and timidity. The dismissal, the reason for which remains untold to him throughout — this being the cleverest dramatic touch of the play — wrecks him absolutely. He goes to America as journalist, is tram-conductor and barman in turn, learns to drink and to back horses, and in four years is stranded in Dublin, a Bohemian, writing a little and imbibing much, and without a spark of self-respect. He meets his old chums in a hotel bar. They have prospered and are kind, but he has missed his chance, it is no use befriending him. This part of the story fills the last act, which is almost monopolised by Mr. O'Donovan. His acting here is perfect; he is shabby and devil-may-care, but not vulgar; he does not hurt the feelings, but arouses them to commiseration, and a slight trait here and there is reminiscent of the simple, good-natured boy he was when he came into the lives of these people at Baragh. Another notable success was Mr. J. M. Kerrigan as Martin Kelly. He is a shrewd, sensible Ulsterman, curt and plain of speech, and he has allotted to him much dry Northern wit which he delivers as if to the manner born. Miss Eileen O'Doherty doubles the parts of a pretty housemaid and a very polite barmaid.

The success of the play is almost wholly due to some good characterisation, brisk dialogue, and smart acting. Its construction is open to criticism. The first act is devoted to developing the peculiarities of the doctor, the Northern philosopher and the ex-student. The ladies appear only in the second act, and the philosopher drops out. The last act is practically a monologue. Still all went well, and the actors and the author were called before the curtain and warmly applauded. The drama is well worth a visit.

The second new piece is entitled *The Piper* — "An Unended Argument in One Act." It is by Mr. Norreys Connell. After a dreadful preparation of a darkened auditorium and slow music with the curtain down, some peasants, with guns and a green flag, and a British officer as prisoner are disclosed. The peasants jabber incessantly, their leader is absurdly eloquent, they are arguing whether they were "bate" or not. The half-witted piper sings the "Shan Van Vocht," the British prisoner explains that he is "no politician, though a professional cut-throat," and that he would "rather be an Irish rebel than a

214

yeoman." Finally the peasants, who have been meanwhile surrounded by the yeos, are surprised and shot down, and the poor piper is also shot whilst he waves the green flag. The British prisoner lays the green flag over him. It would seem that the piper is the hero, because his foolishness is natural, whilst with the others it is cultivated. Sara Allgood played the Piper. . . .

Some people walked away puzzled, some booed and hissed, others applauded. Perhaps a more idiotic picture of the Irish peasant than even *Punch* drew excited the applause, but to the great majority the thing was simply inane and beneath criticism. There have been characters on the Abbey stage that have been a challenge and have been resented, but this kind of fooling does not even arouse contempt.[41]

On the following evening, there was a mild disturbance in the theatre:

The attendance at "The Abbey" last night was disappointingly small, the different parts of the house being but meagrely filled. In *The Man Who Missed the Tide*, the actors, after the favourable reception of the first night, showed themselves more in sympathy with their respective parts, and, as a result, the performance went with a smoothness and ease that won complete acceptance. . . .

With the production of *The Piper* the temper of the audience underwent a marked change. Towards the close, exclamations of "Stage Irishman," "It's a shame," "Where is Yeats?" and "It's a vile insult," were indulged in, and as the curtain fell the occupants of the pit booed vigorously. Afterwards the writer, Mr. Norreys Connell, appeared before the footlights and said: — "I thank you, ladies and gentlemen, for allowing my play, which seems to have displeased you so much, to proceed." For a brief space there was renewed booing, and the audience afterwards separated.[42]

The *Piper* situation, coming directly on the heels of the Fays' departure, had all the elements of another *Playboy* row. One Abbey Theatre raconteur, Peter Kavanagh, rather romantically depicts Yeats's reaction:

Yeats must have realized that *The Piper* was a bad play, but it was important to convince the public they were incapable of forming judgment. Accordingly, it was essential that he defend it. In a leader, *The Irish Independent* of Saturday, February 15, appealed to Yeats to withdraw the play "now that it got a fair hearing." This, to Yeats, was a challenge to continue the play. He arranged that it be repeated the following week, with a matinee performance included. This was the final defeat for the Abbey Theatre audience and for the Dublin press. Obviously Yeats could not be intimidated. The audience, not Yeats, learned its lesson, and for the next seventeen years the public conducted itself in a humble manner.[43]

Although Yeats did keep the play on for another week, he also, by a letter to the press, by a programme note, and by several speeches to the audience, took pains to avert a riot by interpreting the play in the most patriotic light. This gambit was quite successful, and the play was listened to with patience. What Yeats did was not to infuriate his audience to the point of another confrontation, but to placate it so that the play could be heard. There is, incidentally, no reason at all to infer, as Kavanagh did, that Yeats thought *The Piper* a bad play. Everything that Yeats said about it indicated that he thought it worthy and interesting. For instance:

Before the curtain rose on *The Piper*, Mr. W. B. Yeats, the managing director of the theatre, came to the footlights and asked the audience to listen to a few words from him about Mr. Norreys Connell's play. He had no right to tell them what the author's idea was in writing the play. The play itself was Mr. Norreys Connell's explanation of his attitude, and it was for the audience to judge whether he had explained himself clearly (cries of Playboy). But he (Mr. Yeats) thought he had a right to tell them what the play meant to him when he read it, and why it seemed to him it should be staged. The play, to his mind, meant a satire upon the nine years of the Parnellite split, years of endless talk, endless rhetoric and futile drifting; years which were taken out of the history of the nation and made nothing of. Further, his imagination went back to the rebellion of Robert Emmet, the folly that surrounded him, the slackness that was as bad as treachery, which brought that heroic life to nothing (applause). That also, he said, was satirised in the play. And he thought they were all agreed that it was worthy of satire, the most bitter satire; and that a national theatre was right in satirising upon the stage that endless, useless talk through which the lifeblood of the nation was wasting away. There was only one possible difference between the audience and himself — whether that had been done in this play — and it was for them to judge. He saw, moreover, that Mr. Norreys Connell had not missed the

216

heroism underlying these movements. He (Mr. Yeats) saw the ceaseless, eternal, heroic aspirations of the Irish people embodied in the character of the piper; and he saw a figure which deeply impressed his boyhood in the character of Black Mike. He saw in that character Charles Stewart Parnell (applause). He saw that angry, heroic man once again as he saw him in his boyhood, face to face with Irish futility. He saw in the whole play simply a satire on all that dreadful epoch. And he thought the day had not yet come when the men of Dublin did not desire to see that satirised upon the stage (applause). Nor did he think the play less worthy of attention because the Englishman in it was not ignoble, nor unaware of the heroism which he had fought, and which, for good or evil fortune, he had overcome (applause).

The play was then proceeded with, and had on the whole a favourable reception, the author being called for and applauded at the close, although there was a considerable expression of dissent.[44]

Holloway, who heard Yeats's speech at the Saturday matinee, remarked, however:

The Piper was listened to with astonishing patience, and followed by some applause, but I fear the explanation scarcely cleared the atmosphere of mystery which surrounds the idiotic doings of the group of caricature, scare-crow Irish peasants which people the stage.[45]

On 20 March The Freeman's Journal reviewed the Abbey's new triple bill:

Last night in the Abbey Theatre, three new plays were presented for the first time by the National Theatre Society. There was not a very large audience, but most of the regular patrons of the theatre were present, and there was enough in the bill to interest any person with a genuine and serious interest in the drama. Mr. Yeats apologized for the absence of Mr. Arthur Darley, whose playing of traditional Irish airs at this theatre has been an ever-welcome feature. Mr. Darley is ill, but it is hoped he may be able to once more delight his listeners before the run of the present programme is over. . . . The first play submitted last night was Teja, described as a historical episode in the Gothic invasion of Italy.

It is the first production in English of a play by H. Sudermann, translated from the German by Lady Gregory. From every point of view it was a success. The idea is good — the effect of woman upon warrior. The method is excellent —

because the warrior is apparently a heartless butcher until a woman, his newly wedded wife, teaches him that he has been human all the time, and that she understands him. And the acting all through was not only impressive but exhibited some study of history in its interpretative note. The chief players were:—Teja, J. M. Kerrigan; Bathilda, Máire O'Neill; Bishop Agilla, Arthur Sinclair; Ildebad, King's spear-bearer, Fred O'Donovan. The two first-named were most admirable, the lady particularly presenting a convincing picture of a woman in a Gothic camp, slavish yet loving. The second piece was *The Pie-Dish*, by George Fitzmaurice. It is a comedy of peasant life in Kerry. The Kerry dialect is a subject on which no one dare dogmatise, but it seems that the attempt to reproduce the vernacular, though it might pass muster in a literary form, was overdone when spoken. In the case of the priest it was unnatural to a pronounced degree. The acting, too, had all through a certain amount of crudeness. The Kerry peasant is not uncouth; rather the opposite; the dramatist who will do him justice will write a very entertaining and finished comedy. . . . It is a sermon on the vanity of human wishes preached with considerable humour, but somehow the touch of artificiality was too distinct all through to enable people to enjoy the lesson of a very happy fancy. . . . The third piece was *The Golden Helmet*, by Mr. W. B. Yeats. It is billed as a heroic farce, but perhaps it would be better to take it seriously. Briefly, the story is that of a supernatural personage who throws discord into an Irish community, but drowns the man who makes the greatest sacrifice. The play is exceedingly interesting, and perhaps important, because it shows Mr. Yeats as a practical dramatist at last, telling a story in direct, plain language, presenting incident after incident, and leading up to a happy, yet imperfect, climax; all the poetic mysticism has disappeared. Mr. Yeats was called before the curtain, but he simply bowed his acknowledgment. . . . The acting all round in this piece was first-class, though there was the disadvantage that there had been during the night a considerable duplication and triplication of parts.[46]

'Sinn de Ceat' had nothing good to say of any of the plays in *Sinn Féin*; of *Teja*, he wrote, 'It seems a pity that the translator's work should have been lost on a piece which has little to show spectacularly, little to defend it intellectually, and little interest dramatically.' Of Fitzmaurice's compelling little grotesque *The Pie-Dish*, he wrote:

The play, by virtue of the farcical incident with which it begins, viz. — the old man being trundled while asleep into a settlebed, and his amaze on waking at finding himself there, amuses for a while, but whatever chance the author had of making his playlet interesting fritters away gradually before the plethora of colloquialisms with which he crowds his dialogue. The effect on the audience becomes more and more wearisome, and interest may fairly be said to lapse long before the melodramatic denouement which brings it to a conclusion striking, if whimsical.[47]

He thought that Yeats's treatment of his subject in *The Golden Helmet* was puerile, and that the actors were too constricted in their movements and too monotonous in their intonation.

J. H. Cox in *The Irish Independent* thought that, 'Lady Gregory was happy in her selection; tasteful and vigorous in her translation.' He considered *The Golden Helmet* 'weird and realistic', whatever that may mean, and remarked, 'It clings to the mind, and its meaning will go on expanding.' However, he had nothing good to say of *The Pie-Dish*: 'In conception it is ugly and untrue. In treatment it is clumsy; the early talk is quite unintelligible. And the action is sheer fuss. The absence of elementary sympathy with his theme has betrayed the author, apparently, into the grotesque and inhuman.'[48]

The reviewer of *The Dublin Evening Mail* had little good to say of any of the plays. *The Golden Helmet* was 'disproportioned and unharmonious'. The language of *Teja* was wrong: 'Why it should be turned into the strange sing-song of Kiltartan rather than into plain good English is more than I can see, and I think it helped to spoil the whole performance.' And *The Pie-Dish* was 'a wretched nothing very well acted. . . . The only thing in the play is the speech, and surely in itself a cheap dialect in which nothing is said wise or bright or tender or cheerful or cunning, is hardly enough to make a comedy.'[49]

On 3 April Holloway attended the dress rehearsal at the Abbey of *The Rogueries of Scapin* and of *Hyacinth Halvey*. He said:

Synge after the rehearsal told me "that a fortnight ago the work was only put in rehearsal." Mac (Sinclair) he thought would be very good as Scapin. "All the company worked very hard to have the work as perfect as possible." I asked him how did *Hyacinth Halvey* go? And he said, "Fairly. Frank Fay was at his best as Halvey. There was a fantastic grotesqueness about his playing of this part that could not be matched."[50]

Lady Gregory's translation received rather scant attention in the press. However, *The Freeman's Journal* opened its review with a good-natured eulogium:

> No matter what differences of opinion may arise from time to time as to the matter contained in some of the plays produced at the Abbey Theatre, there can be no second view as to the courage and earnestness shown by the moving spirits of the National Theatre Society. Whatever else they may lack, they are most assuredly not wanting in confidence and a whole-hearted devotion to the "cause" which they have taken in hand. Workers in a field such as they have chosen must needs be content to rest satisfied to a great extent with their belief in the justice of their movement, for the public as a rule do not go much out of their way to support them, and the attendance is by no means encouragingly large. . . . Lady Gregory's translation of *Les Fourberies de Scapin* is most admirable in every respect, and this is saying a great deal, when one remembers how completely the dash and go, the life and soul of these comedies depend upon vivacious dialogue with its keen wit, its sprightly sarcasms, its epigrams, and words and phrases for which English equivalents are not by any means readily to hand.[51]

The Irish Times also commended the beauty of diction and prophesied that the play would be one of the more popular pieces in the Abbey repertoire. Arthur Sinclair, it continued, was 'the great success of the performance. If his enunciation was occasionally somewhat lacking in clearness and deliberation, his work on the whole was deserving of very high praise. He is a comedian of great promise.'[52]

On 20 April the Abbey presented four short plays, one of which, *The Workhouse Ward*, was seen for the first time. Of the production, *The Freeman's Journal* wrote:

> Visitors to the Abbey Theatre last night were presented with a quartette of plays, three of which have already made their first bid for public favour, and met with varying degrees of success. The fourth was a new production, a comedy in one act, entitled *Workhouse Ward*, by Lady Gregory, who can justly claim to be the most prolific and in the opinion of the majority of the patrons of the Abbey Theatre is recognised as the healthiest and most attractive of the writers for the National Theatre Society. The comedy can scarcely be truthfully described as a new production, for it is practically a

revision or recasting of *The Poorhouse*, which was written by Lady Gregory, in collaboration with Dr. Douglas Hyde. In the preparation of the latter the plot was supplied by Lady Gregory, the dialogue being by Dr. Hyde. In an explanatory note accompanying the programme, Lady Gregory states that, "for certain practical reasons, I tried to manage it for three players only, but in doing this I found it necessary to write entirely new dialogue, the two old men in the old play obviously talking at an audience in the ward, which has now been taken from them." The alteration is decidedly for the better, inasmuch as it presents the situation in a more dramatic and striking fashion, and brings out with increased strength and boldness the two old bedridden paupers.[53]

On 29 May there was another quadruple bill at the Abbey. Two of the items, Lady Gregory's *Workhouse Ward* and *The Jackdaw*, were among the more popular of the theatre's one-acts, but as *The Freeman's Journal* remarked:

A farce by Richard Brinsley Sheridan and Lady Gregory's *Dervorgilla* were the principal items in a quadruple bill at the Abbey Theatre last night. Though Sheridan's play *The Scheming Lieutenant*, is familiar to every student of the drama, it has been practically unknown to theatre-goers, and the National Theatre Society have made a decided hit in adding it to their repertoire. It is a most entertaining piece, with amusing situations and a sparkling dialogue. Mr. Arthur Sinclair gave a good presentation of the part of Justice Credulous last night, and the other parts were also well filled. Mr. J. M. Kerrigan was Lieutenant O'Connor, and Mr. Fred O'Donovan, Dr. Rosy; Miss Maire O'Neill, Lauretta; and Miss Sara Allgood, Lauretta's mother, the loquacious Mrs. Bridget Credulous. Following Sheridan's amusing farce, during which the house was in constant laughter, there came the deep tragedy, in which Lady Gregory treats of the first coming of the Normans to Ireland. . . . This play would be well worth seeing at any time, but now, especially, with Miss Sara Allgood in the part of Dervorgilla; it is one which nobody who takes an interest in the drama should miss. There probably is no play in which Miss Allgood appears to better advantage than she does in this tragedy, and there certainly is no actress on the stage at present who could fill the part of Dervorgilla in such a satisfying manner as she did last night.[54]

The Irish Independent complained of both plays and the intervals between them:

221

. . . the Abbey Theatre people dished it up like a racecourse luncheon. You know those racecourse luncheons — first you get a plate with nothing on it, then something from somewhere to put on your plate, then a knife, then a fork. Then follow more bits and scraps which are duly disposed of as they come, and last of all a liberal supply of sauce. The sauce comes late — too late.

The Scheming Lieutenant is a dramatic dish which undoubtedly went down well with last night's audience, but it would please our tastes more if we hadn't to wait so long between the helpings. Those tedious intervals take the edge off our appetite.[55]

On 24 September Holloway had a chat with W. F. Casey[56] about his new play:

His "business" was about the title for his new "mild satire" about Rathmines. He had selected The Suburban Groove, and the Directors did not like the title. Lady Gregory suggested The Circular Road, which he thought would be mistaken for the thoroughfare of the name. Yeats had sent up quite a list of names — The Old, Old Story, The Sheep Path, etc., none of which met with Casey's approval. . . . Yeats thought his title, Suburban Groove, too like a newspaper heading. Casey could not understand Yeats's expressed dislike for newspapers. He seemed to despise them and yet read with avidity what they had to say on the plays and players, and quoted anything favourable he came across in them, and said they did not know anything of what they were writing about if unfavourable.[57]

The Abbey re-opened after its summer break on 1 October, and the following announcement which appeared a few days before in the press testified to the Directors' concern with sparse houses:

The directors of the Abbey Theatre have arranged for the production of a series of plays during the months of October, November, and December. It is proposed to issue special subscription tickets at a considerable reduction, which entitles holder to a reserved and numbered stall for ten performances, the bill for each being entirely different. The tickets may be taken for Thursday or Saturday nights or for Friday matinees. The price of one guinea is a reduction of 50 per cent on the usual charge. This has been done with the view of filling the dearer seats, which were not fully occupied during last season. . . . During the period twenty-six different plays will be produced. An important announcement is that Mrs. Patrick Campbell will fulfill her promise made last year, and appear in the Abbey Theatre for one week in the title role of Deirdre, W. B. Yeats's verse drama in one act.[58]

The theatre re-opened with Connell's *The Piper* and the new play by Casey, *The Suburban Groove*, which proved a great success.

However, the anonymous review in *Sinn Féin* harshly but justly was titled 'Inanities at the "Abbey" ' :

> The directors of the National Theatre Society, Limited, of the Abbey Theatre, have often prided themselves upon the fact that they do not represent a commercial undertaking. . . . It may be that the directors have changed their policy in the last few weeks. . . . Whatever the explanation is, there is no doubt of the fact that Mr. Yeats, Mr. Synge, and Lady Gregory are responsible for the production in Mr. Casey's *The Suburban Groove* of the most trifling attempt at drama that it would be possible to see outside the limits of the school-room of an old-fashioned Seminary for Young Ladies. There is not a single original speech in it, much less a single original idea. There is not even an attempt at a fresh arrangement of worn-out devices. Everything in it might have been picked out of the pockets of Mr. Casey's grandmother's apron, scrawled down at her leisure on the back of her butcher's and grocer's bills. Even the bright intelligences of the dramatic critics of the Dublin daily papers had to admit that the plot was of the slenderest type, that the incidents were like the currants in a penny bun, few and far between, and that the denouement was unsatisfactory.
>
> And yet the audience enjoyed it thoroughly and applauded vigorously. Rightly viewed, the whole affair is the greatest tragedy that has yet been enacted at the Abbey Theatre. It means that the directors of that institution who have, though in a very mistaken way, definitely tried, for some years past, to develop a genuine native drama in connection with their Theatre have either become intellectually incapable of continuing the effort or have decided to give it up. . . .
>
> But what about the roars of applause in the auditorium? It was, indeed, laughter, but the laughter not of a drama-appreciating crowd, but of a *Tit-Bits* educated, "Tivoli" frequenting audience. They enjoyed the excellent foolery of Mr. Sinclair transformed for the time being into a music-hall serio-comic artist, the familiar despondency of Mr. O'Donovan as the hen-pecked husband, and the somewhat over-acted

fussiness of Miss Allgood as the nagging, scolding, interfering wife. All regulation, stock, music-hall types!

To criticise the play seriously would be impossible. It affords excellent material for amateur dramatic societies. That is all. But to see it seriously put forward in a theatre exclusively endowed for the development of real drama can only send anyone who has the faintest conception of what a play should be into despair. Its place is with the charade-book and the family Christmas entertainment, and it should be allowed to remain there. Let us remind the directors of the Abbey Theatre that they have produced plays — real plays — by Mr. Boyle, Mr. Colum, Mr. Synge, in the past, and that if they have nothing on similar lines to offer it would be much more dignified and wholesome to keep their theatre shut.[59]

The Daily Express thought that, '*The Suburban Groove* will take rank with the very best of the plays in the repertoire of the Company. . . .' 'Cairbre in *The Peasant and Irish Ireland* was probably more accurate in saying, 'But if Mr. Casey has given us a trivial play, he has given us a very realistic, if somewhat superficial, portrayal of a middle class home. . . . In the hands of mediocre actors such a play would have been an utter failure. Instead of being funny it would have been ridiculous.' M. O'D, (probably Michael O'Dempsey) in *The Evening Mail* thought *The Piper* was 'that gust of proud and angry irony', and went on to say:

Mr. Casey's second play is, in execution as well as in conception, an advance on his first, though as yet the execution falls far behind the aspiration. But the intense spiritual reality of Mr. Norreys Connell's "Unended argument," intensifies all that is commonplace and ignoble in *The Suburban Groove*. Yet the new Abbey play is undoubtedly entertaining; it carries the audience with it, hitting straight home at many of the little foibles of the suburban bourgeoisie. . . . Mr. Casey has not yet got the art of making his audience see the root idea. He is, in the present writer's opinion, a little too anxious about the technical effect of his plays; he has not the art of subordinating the accidental to the essential, nor of hiding what is merely technical. Many of his exits and entries are very obviously worked up, and the main idea of the play seems quite swallowed up in a profusion of local hits. It seems to the present writer necessary to advert to Mr. Casey's love-scenes, which are painfully amateurish. One's general advice to a young dramatist would be to avoid love scenes in modern comedy. . . .

224

The Piper has already been dealt with in these columns; of it one must only remark that Mr. Sinclair's acting is becoming steadily more finished. A curious light upon the intense "inwardness" of this short Irish piece is the fact that an English actress seated near the present writer, was delighted with its humour, and laughed at it most merrily. Tears seem a more appropriate gift to this, the saddest and the fiercest of the Abbey satires, hardly excepting even Mr. Synge's plays.[60]

The success of Casey's *The Suburban Groove* was in sharp contrast to the reception the next week of *The Clancy Name*, a short, stark tragedy by a young man from Cork, Esme Stuart Lennox Robinson, who was to become one of the Abbey's most prolific dramatists and for years a member of its Board of Directors. On 5 October, however, Holloway wrote:

Henderson told me he knew so little of Robinson who wrote *The Clancy Name* that he had written to him to ask were he a Mr., Mrs., or Miss. His handwriting was distinctly feminine in character. He proved to be a Mr., and is coming up to Dublin tomorrow to see a rehearsal. The piece will only last nine minutes and is about a murder. . . . Mr. Casey's stage directions are very elaborate and often amuse the company. "Open your mouth and then close it again to express surprise" is one of them.[61]

The usually kind *Freeman's Journal* called Robinson's first Dublin production 'a most fatal fiasco':

. . . which, it is sincerely to be hoped, will not long burthen and be a blot on the stage. It is the production of such a play that not only discourages all earnest well-wishers, but which is calculated to create a positive aversion to the place. The idea of this play is that an Irish peasant commits a foul murder; his mother, by no means apparently concerned about the barbarity of his crime, is anxious to prevent his giving himself up to the police, and to urge him to marry a decent girl, all to clear the "Clancy name." Has it come to this, that acceptance to the ranks of writers at the Abbey Theatre is subject to the writer black-guarding his countrymen and countrywomen, setting up to the public a shocking and libellous picture of their methods and characteristics, and making Irish actors and actresses play parts which they know to be worse than travesties of their countrymen or countrywomen? The incident of a man lying in bed, supposed to be dead, like *The Shaughraun*, and listening to his wife's interlude with a lover, and her ultimate departure with a "Stranger," might be said to be so absurd as to relieve it of its disgustingness. And so that phrase of the colleen, "Let the doctor have a go at him," when a dead man is brought in, might be said to be too ridiculous to be referred to at all. But the whole thing is a shame and a disgrace. Now that a judge is occasionally sitting to hear pressing motions, one can see no just reason why a representative member of the distinguished family whose name has been so flagrantly and gratuitously mentioned in connection with this so-called play, should not apply at once for an injunction to stop the further perpetration of a libel on the good house of Clancy, and, if possible, have the ultimate determination as to the fate of the author referred in the usual way to the worthy Sub-Sheriff of the city. Seriously, there ought to be some sort of censorship applied to those things, and to find that incomparable artiste, Miss Allgood and her other gifted colleagues, faced with the ordeal of struggling through such stuff and nonsense, is a thing that every well-wisher of the Abbey Theatre must resent, as indeed they did last night. The worst of such an experience is that it takes from the audience that frame of mind by which they would enjoy the other admirably-performed plays, such as Sheridan's *Scheming Lieutenant*, and *Dervorgilla*, in the latter of which Miss Allgood achieves a success of quite a transcendant character.[62]

The Daily Express thought that, 'It is a gruesome sort of business, and as dull and melancholy as it is lacking in dramatic form.' The intelligent M. O'D. in *The Dublin Evening Mail* wrote, 'Whatever the author's conception of the dramatisation of sorrow at its most poignant — in the home — he has only succeeded in producing the very worst melodramatic sketch among the few melodramas produced on the Abbey boards.' 'Cairbre' in *The Peasant and Irish Ireland* wrote:

It seems like the synopsis of a long play, or the first act of one with the death tacked on as an ending. The whole picture is blurred and indistinct. It would need a lot of strengthening to make it even a third-rate sensational play. The piece is practically devoid of merit. It has no ingenuity of construction, no brilliance or naturalness of dialogue. It shows neither insight nor talent for a dramatic presentation of ideas; it neither excites the audience nor arouses their sympathy. On Thursday people were laughing right through, and at the most solemn moment when John was dying a general titter

226

was caused by a girl being made to say, "Wait till the doctor has a go at him." [63]

But Stephen Gwynn also wrote to *The Freeman's Journal* the following expression of protest:

> I read this morning your notice of *The Clancy Name,* and to-night I saw the play. Will you allow me one sentence of protest against what I think your injustice to Miss Allgood's superb piece of acting — the best thing I have seen her do — and to a very vigorous piece of dramatic composition, written, as I was glad to see, by quite a young man. [64]

On 10 October Holloway called in at the Abbey and saw that:

> Thomas MacDonagh was conducting a rehearsal of his play *When the Dawn is Come.* . . . I was speaking to George Fitz-maurice, and he said that he thought *The Clancy Name* the strongest bit of drama in the Abbey repertoire. Robinson will do something big in drama yet. There is material for a three act drama in his first effort. He then asked me what I thought of Casey's play, and I said I did not think it by any means as effective as his first piece, *The Man Who Missed the Tide.* He was surprised that such a piece as *The Suburban Groove* was played at the Abbey, but couldn't tell me why. The swell, Claude Callan, seemed to puzzle him as to why he was introduced. There was not sufficient in the "plot" to carry over three acts, he thought, and the construction was faulty. He owned up, however, that Casey was the most popular dramatist at the Abbey at present. . . . Fitzmaurice is of the opinion that *Dervorgilla* without Sara Allgood in the title role would be excessively tedious. [65]

On 15 October the Abbey produced a play which was to prove strangely prophetic, Thomas MacDonagh's *When the Dawn is Come.* MacDonagh, a young writer of great promise, was both a poet and a critic as well as a lecturer in English at University College Dublin. He was associated with Padraic Pearse in founding St. Enda's College and also in the Irish Volunteers. He was one of the signatories to the Proclamation of Easter Week in 1916, and after the Rising he was executed with the other revolutionary leaders. His son Donagh MacDonagh was to become well known as a poet and verse dramatist. His play dealt with Ireland's final struggle for independence, and *The Freeman's Journal* reviewed it as follows:

227

The first production of an original tragedy, written by Thomas MacDonagh, took place in the Abbey Theatre on Thursday night to a well-filled house. Its title is *When the Dawn is Come*. The time is fifty years hence. An Irish insurrectionary army is in the field. . . . The language of the play is well chosen throughout, though some of the speeches are spun out too much for soldiers. Some excellent passages contrast the views of the old man and the young man upon terms of peace. The same scene serves for the three acts, and considerable ingenuity has been displayed in developing a complicated story and study within this irksome limitation, but "excursions and alarms" are frequent. Three characters stand out boldly, those of Turlough, the man of brain; of O'Sullivan, the man of action; and of Ita, one of the ladies of the council who loves Turlough, and, being in his confidence, nearly shares his fate. As Turlough, Mr. Kerrigan gave a fine study of the thinker, forced by chance to be resolute for once. Mr. Arthur Sinclair, if he rather over-emphasized the bluntness of O'Sullivan, was very effective, the whole machinery of the plot being practically in his control. Miss Sara Allgood was Ita. . . . A few of the long orations might be usefully condensed or divided up, and some of the councillors given more to say and do at the expense of those who are overburdened. These are the only criticisms which need be offered upon a first production, which, if not an epoch-making success, was certainly above the average, both in idea and workmanship, of the Abbey plays.[66]

Padraic Colum reviewed MacDonagh's play in *Sinn Féin* with interest, but with several misgivings. He thought that MacDonagh was 'reticent when he should be explanatory', and that, 'The dialogue is not properly of the stage, one speech does not lead inevitably to another. . . .' Also, he thought that 'the play was not written in simple and concise prose; its prose is often verse disguised.' H.S.D., in *The Dublin Evening Mail*, was even sterner:

When the Dawn is Come is, it seemed to me, very thin drama, very cold literature, and, as a peep into the future entirely unsatisfying. . . . All the dialogue is vapid, uninteresting talk, entirely unredeemed by literary distinction, by observation of the world, by knowledge of men and affairs. . . . It is not drama, and does not display much promise of drama. The characters are terribly undeveloped.[67]

'Jacques' in *The Irish Independent* wrote:

There was a big audience to welcome it. And they welcomed it, and they called the author. And the author, who is a young man, and looked nervous and bashful, went on the stage and bowed. He looked just the kind of young man who would write this play. Many of us, though, felt sorry that the youthful, clever author didn't say a few words, explaining what it was exactly his play was meant to convey. Because, to tell the truth, it was a bit difficult to follow. There were words, and words, and words. Even on the stage I have rarely heard so many words spoken in the space of an hour. And after digging down into the depths of the verbiage, I don't feel quite sure that I have fished up the proper meaning — the lesson that Mr. MacDonagh wishes to teach across the footlights.[68]

On 17 October Holloway was at the third evening of *When the Dawn is Come*, and wrote:

W. B. Yeats had a word with O'Donoghue and me as we came out. He told us of Douglas Hyde abusing the play right and left when it was being acted, and then loudly calling for "author" at the end, and getting the house to join in the applause; and when Yeats asked him why he called for the author, he said, "Because I had never seen him and wanted to see what he was like." O'Donoghue said Douglas Hyde was such a kindly soul that he would not offend anyone. . . . In the vestibule I met Guinan, and he asked if I was with anyone, and I said no. Then he said he would sit by me. We lingered for awhile to see the people arrive. Yeats wore a velvet coat and chatted with MacDonagh. . . . Miss Colum sold books of the play, and Colum of the weirdly untidy locks rushed about. Mrs. MacBride's majestic form accompanied by Miss Ella Young then glided in. Her head and shoulders were enveloped in a mantilla of veiling, and as soon as Yeats saw her he was dancing attendance on her. . . . Yeats got seated beside her, and the pit on discovering her identity applauded. . . . Guinan told me that MacDonagh's play was the first produced at the Abbey that was not approved by Yeats. Pressure was brought to bear on him to have it presented, and he gave way.[69]

On 22 October the Abbey presented a revised version of Casey's *The Man Who Missed the Tide*, and Lady Gregory's *The Jackdaw*. *The Freeman's Journal* critic took the opportunity to praise Sara Allgood.

Miss Sara Allgood, as Mrs. Broderick, raises the question whether she is not finer in comedy than in tragedy. In this piece nothing could appear to be more simple and spontaneous than her impersonation of a sorely tried country shopkeeper. Surely, one would say, she never was anything else but a character comedienne; yet this is the actress, the awe of whose voice thrills an audience in pieces like *Kathleen Ni Houlihan*, and who was the embodiment of young matronly dignity early in the evening as Mrs. Quinn.[70]

On 27 October Holloway was, as usual, at the Abbey.

Lady Gregory was in the front row of the stalls rehearsing *Kincora* as I passed to and fro. Henderson was in the office. He showed me a telegram from Miss Horniman refusing to allow a play of George Moore's to be performed on the Abbey stage for copyright purposes. Her dislike for Moore dates back to the time he wrote in *Dana* that "at last W. G. Fay had found an admirer in Miss Horniman," and she took it up that he meant that they were "carrying on," as the saying goes, and was rightly indignant. Probably Moore never meant anything of the kind. The lady had her own thoughts on the matter and loathes Moore ever since. Refusing to be introduced to him and all that sort of thing. . . . MacDonagh was not at all pleased with Colum's article on his play in *Sinn Féin*. Colum is a bit of a "hedger." . . . He wrote several letters of indignation for the Abbey Company "billing" his play *The Land* without his permission, and at last gave them permission to play it. He doesn't want to break with the Abbey, and yet wants to appease the Theatre of Ireland folk at the same time.[71]

The event of the year for the Abbey was not the production of a new play, but the revival of Yeats's *Deirdre* with Mrs. Patrick Campbell appearing in the title role, which had previously been taken by Miss Darragh and Mona Limerick. The piece was produced on 9 November.

. . . there was a very large audience in the Abbey Theatre, far larger than the audiences which are seen at even the most popular plays of the National Theatre Society. There were some vacant seats in the balcony, but every other seat in the house was occupied. . . . Never before have the beauties of this play been brought out as they were last night with Mrs. Patrick Campbell in the principal part. . . . Deirdre is on the stage throughout the entire play, and the different elements of her nature are revealed to us in poetic language, sparkling with brilliancy. At one moment she is full of tenderness, recalling to Naisi's memory some incident of their love, at another her voice hardens as she grows fearsome of the fate before her and her lover, and at another her eyes flash and her voice is full of passion as she utters defiance at her captor, or recoils with scorn from his advances. All these varying emotions were interpreted last night by Mrs. Campbell in a manner which held the audience spellbound. The beautiful words were beautifully spoken, and not only in her speech, but in her every motion, Mrs. Campbell gave us a Deirdre full of life, vigour, the majestic beauty, such as would seem to have been the author's conception of the part. Mrs. Campbell has had many great triumphs in her long connection with the stage, but those who have seen her in many parts say that she surpassed herself last night.[72]

After the performance on 10 November, there was a dinner for Mrs. Campbell at the Gresham Hotel. Holloway attended and noticed all of the toasts and speeches.

> Yeats commenced by saying that for once in his life he had nothing to say, and then went on to say it at some length, while he crucified himself with strange, weird, angular gestures many times. He said when he was a child he dreamed of a number of purple clouds in each of which beautiful white angels appeared. These were the passions. Tonight he thought of Mrs. Campbell as one of those angels as he saw her realise the passions of his *Deirdre* on the stage. It was worth writing to be so perfectly interpreted.
>
> Lady Gregory appointed Dr. Hyde, who sat beside her, to be her spokesman, and he burst forth in a flood of amorous eloquence in Gaelic to the guest of the evening, and fairly mystified us all by the wonderful flow of soft sounding, almost cooing words. Lady Gregory then arose and translated what Hyde had said in the golden speech of the Gael, and amused us all by the extravagance of the Doctor's loving words; it was truly a love song of Connaught born in a moment of inspiration.
>
> A silver loving-cup with Gaelic inscribed was presented to Mrs. Campbell from the Abbey, and it was passed and touched by the lips of all present. Then Lady Gregory called on Miss Susan Mitchell for her "Wearing of the Green" song about George Moore which she sang with much "go." Later on she sang of "The Metropolitan Police" with equal humour,

Judge Ross enjoying both songs immensely. Sara Allgood sang "The Shan Van Vocht," and gave a startlingly beautiful rendering of "Kathleen Mavourneen." Her exquisite, sweet tones rang out like a birdsong without effort; nightingales, were they by, would have stopped to listen, and pick up some new notes to charm the night with sweeter song. Miss Florence Farr repeated one of Yeats's shorter lyrics—the one composed to Maud Gonne years ago in which the poet bids her brush her hair with a golden brush — in her best chant-like tones. As it was approaching two in the morning by this time, many stood up to go, and then all arose and chatted in groups for a time. Miss Mitchell sang a verse of "God Save Ireland" and then with general "good-byes" a pleasant function was over. . . .

Miss Máire O'Neill's hair caught fire from one of the torches used in *Deirdre* on Tuesday. I did not notice the incident myself. It was Kerrigan who told me afterwards at the Gresham, and she was annoyed to think that the other players saw what had happened and did not tell her for fear of spoiling the stage picture.[73]

*   *   *

W. B. Yeats, probably throughout his long career, was regarded by his countrymen with both admiration and dislike, with both respect and distrust. As one symptomatic example, in January there was a flurry of letters in *The Evening Mail* between Yeats and W. J. Lawrence, writing under the pseudonym of 'W'. The resignation of the Fays was much in the news, and Lawrence charged that the company was now in a state of 'mutiny':

It is understood that the final rupture was occasioned by the policy pursued by the directorate in shelving plays that drew audiences, and in insisting upon the performance of others towards which the public evinced no great liking. . . . Nothing remains now, if the organization is to be saved from wreck, but for the present directorate to retire in favour of a reading committee of three, who shall be selected from among the cultured residents of the city, and who, while being men of approved literary taste and dramatic judgment, shall not be in themselves playwrights.[74]

The next day Yeats replied:

I see no necessity to discuss in public details or organization and re-organization, for our plays concern the public, the rest

232

ourselves. You make one statement, however, which challenges the justice of our administration in the selection of plays, and that needs an answer. You state that we have not given "a fair field and no favour," and imply that we have suppressed excellent plays in the favour of our own work or of our friends' work. I challenge you to appoint three persons chosen from the literary men of this city, who shall invite rejected dramatists to send them their plays. If they find amongst the plays rejected by the Abbey Theatre during the last twelve months any play which they consider worthy of production we will produce it for three nights at the Abbey Theatre and allow the public to judge.[75]

Lawrence answered the following day:

. . . Mr. Yeats in limiting his challenge to the last twelve months has an uneasy suspicion that some of the plays rejected by the Abbey directorate at a remoter period had merit on their side. However, under the unnecessary limitations, I take up his challenge. Without consulting the gentlemen mentioned I name as a reading committee Mr. D. J. O'Donoghue, Dr. Tyrrell . . . and Mr. Sheehy-Skeffington. None of the three is an aspiring dramatist, and none has any axe to grind. I ask only that one rejected play should be submitted to them. It was sent in to the Abbey Theatre, if I mistake not, during the past twelve months, and came from the pen of a Dublin author who has recently risen into sudden fame as the writer of "Irene Wycherly." I have not read this rejected play, and do not personally know "Anthony Wharton," but I very much doubt if the budding dramatist whose work made the success of 1907 on the London stage could (if he tried) write as bad a piece as some of those produced at the Abbey from the pens of the powers that be. Let the standard of comparison for my reading committee be *The Shadowy Waters* and *The Canavans*, and I feel assured that Mr. Wharton's rejected piece will run the gauntlet with flying colours.

If Mr. Yeats will be so good as to waive his limitation of time, and let his challenge apply to the period which has elapsed since the first opening of the Abbey, I will ask my committee to consider the claims of a second play. It is a well-known fact that *John Bull's Other Island* was especially written for the Irish National Literary Theatre at the instance of Mr. Yeats. Bernard Shaw has stated as much in the preface to the play. Will Mr. Yeats explain to us what was his reason

233

for his rejection of that gem of quizzical dialectics? I have only heard one plausible explanation of the decision arrived at in that instance. It was said that the Abbey Company possessed no players with the necessary temperamental qualifications for the part of Broadbent. In other words the ship was spoiled for lack of the proverbial ha'porth of tar. To engage a professional English actor to play Broadbent would have involved an outlay of some £5 per week. The prospect was "most tolerable and not to be endured." But mark the subsequent inconsistency of the Abbey directorate. Money was no consideration when Mr. Yeats's *Deirdre* came to be produced. That was a different pair of shoes. An English actress, vastly inferior in spirituality to Miss Máire Walker or in technique to Miss Sara Allgood, was engaged to play the part of the Irish Helen, and at a salary, mark you, treble that of any regular member of the company.[76]

On the next day, Yeats replied:

I have asked Dr. Sigerson, President of the National Literary Society, if he will ask his Society to make the necessary arrangements for the judgment of plays, and to bring the matter to the knowledge of the authors concerned. It is essential from the point of view of the Abbey Theatre that some responsible newspaper or association should appoint the judges or give them authority. The production of a play means several weeks of rehearsal, and costs a good deal of money, and the contest would be useless from our point of view if the public did not believe in its reality. They will only do that if the details are arranged by some body like the National Literary Society. My challenge was given to the *Mail*, but as it will not take the matter up, I am glad to find that Dr. Sigerson is ready to do so, and I know that if your correspondent would go to see him, Dr. Sigerson will consider his suggestions. I am satisfied with the judges your correspondent has suggested, but one or more of them may refuse to act, and another judge or judges have to be chosen. The terms of the challenge as given by me and accepted by your correspondent are . . . P.S. I have just seen Maunsel and Co., and they undertake to publish the play selected by the judges, at the time of its performance. This will secure an appeal to an even larger public than could performance.[77]

In reply, Lawrence wrote in the next day's *Mail*:

Mr. Yeats is as elusive as a fen-fire and as vacillating as a weathercock. One wonders what fickle planet rules his horoscope. In the beginning he made no attempt to reply to the gravamen of my charge, preferring in his shuffling way to issue a challenge on a point not touched upon in Monday's article. Not a single word was said in that arraignment concerning the rejection of unperformed plays, but since Mr. Yeats's conscience seemed uneasy on that score, and it happened that I (as a journalist), had some special information on the point, I ignored his quibbling and accepted his clearly-expressed challenge on the terms stated.

Mr. Yeats's next move is to execute a right-about-face. Not content to be the challenger, he thinks he should have the right also to name the weapons. In the matter of the reading committee, he admits having no fault to find with the three nominees of my selection — one of whom, by the way, is a prominent member of the National Literary Society — but thinks he should have the right to choose his own jury. This is really too much. Equally with Mr. Yeats, I am spoiling for a fight, but it irks my ruggedly independent spirit to slake his insatiable thirst for domination. Moreover, it would not be fair to those of our dramatists whose plays have been unjustly rejected by the Abbey directorate to accept the amended terms. What guarantee have we that the play or plays upon which the proposed committee should put the hall-mark of their approval would meet with adequate representation in the Abbey Theatre. Not only have leading members like Mr. and Mrs. W. G. Fay, Mr. Frank Fay and Mr. Vaughan recently left the organisation, but other withdrawals from the seriously depleted company are on the cards. Does Mr. Yeats really think he will readily replace all these secessionists to the immediate satisfaction of the public, especially at the meagre salaries paid by the Society? No self-respecting dramatist would re-submit his play on the off chance of having its value completely destroyed by the inefficiencies of a number of raw amateurs. It would, therefore, be a sheer waste of time and energy to proceed further in the matter. I wash my hands of Mr. Yeats and his challenge, and with all possible equanimity leave the Mutual Admiration (alias the National Literary Theatre) Society to run headlong on that rapid dissolution which will not righteously be its due.[78]

Finally, on 18 January, Yeats wrote to the *Mail*:

> I have no desire to slake my "insatiable thirst for domin-
> ation" upon your correspondent's "ruggedly independent
> spirit," and should he change his mind again, and carry his
> suggestions to Dr. Sigerson, he will find that so far from
> appointing my own judges, I will object to no one and suggest
> no one. Should he, upon the other hand, prefer, to the National
> Literary Society, some other association of like authority, it is
> all one to me, so long as I hear from him, or it, in the next
> few days. In any case I hope he will bring his "ruggedly
> independent spirit" to the Abbey Theatre, when it re-opens
> some three weeks hence with new plays by new writers. We
> have confidence in our company, and know that whatever has
> been lost they have still humour, charm, and sincerity.[79]

As another symptomatic example of the distrust of Yeats, there
was the meeting of the National Literary Society on 10 February,
when James O'Neill read a paper on 'The Dublin Stage in the
18th Century'. W. B. Yeats arrived late, and missed the paper, but
gave a speech of his own.

> Mr. W. B. Yeats, in the course of his speech, stated that
> he was late owing to the fact that he had been attending a
> dress rehearsal in the Abbey Theatre, where they were going
> to produce new plays by new writers, with whom he believed
> they would be pleased. They should not believe what they
> read in the papers about the Abbey Theatre. They would find
> that newspapers were always wrong about those things of
> which one had personal knowledge. The Abbey Theatre might
> be doing many wicked things — probably it was — but they
> did not know (laughter). The President [George Sigerson] had
> just quoted a reference from some author about "Art for
> Art's Sake." When he (Mr. Yeats) wrote *Kathleen ni Houlihan*
> he did not write it to make rebels. All he meant was that he,
> like every other artist, wrote that play to express his own
> feelings at a certain moment, to express them without thought
> of anybody else, to express them as the bird expresses itself
> when it sings. The bird was not trying to preach to anybody;
> the bird did not moralise to anyone; it gave no lessons — it
> merely sang its song. All artists were precisely the same. "Art
> for art's sake" meant art for the sake of sincerity, for the sake
> simply of natural speech coming from some simple, natural
> child-like soul. Ireland at this moment was running the danger
> of surrendering her soul to the bourgeoisie, and to a worse

bourgeoisie than ever fought in France — to an ignorant, undisciplined bourgeoisie. The bourgeoisie of France was disciplined and it had great qualities. The bourgeoisie in Ireland had no past, no discipline, no good qualities. If they were to make the people great, the first to be fought was the bourgeoisie, so that the latter might get disciplined. They, artists, stood not for some pleasure, but for the laborious, disciplined soul, because all fine art — everything in which there was a personal quality — was the result of long labour. "Art for art's sake" was an intolerable toil. Any man could make himself popular if he took a few moral sayings, a few conventional moral platitudes, and put them into pictures, verses, or stories. But such a man would be forgotten in ten years, although during that ten years he would be popular and would gain wealth.[80]

Another example of the antipathy to Yeats was the reaction to a speech which he made on 4 September, when the Abbey gave a special programme on the occasion of the visit of the British Association to Dublin. His speech was merely a summary of the theatre movement up to 1908. He said:

> To some of you, who may perhaps have heard of the Abbey Theatre for the first time, it is necessary that I should tell a little how it all came about.
>
> Some years ago a group of Irish writers, among whom were Lady Gregory and myself, noticing that the Irish people cared more for oratory than for reading (for a nation only comes slowly to the reading habit) resolved to express ourselves through a Theatre. At first we brought over English Actors, because there was no Irish Company in existence; but there was always something incongruous between Irish words and an English voice and accent. Presently with the help of a very able actor, who has lately left us, an electric light fitter by occupation, we got together a group of young men and young women here in Dublin, who were prepared to give their entire leisure to the creation of an Irish Theatre. They worked for their living during the day, and for their art during the evening. At first we played in little inconvenient halls, but after a few years a generous friend gave us the use of this Theatre, and, finding that our people were becoming over-worked, gave us enough money to free them from their shops and offices. In this way, quite apart from the traditions of the ordinary Theatre, we had built up an art of acting which is perhaps peculiar to ourselves; our players, instead of

237

specialising, as most other actors do to represent the life of the drawing-room, which is the same all over the world, have concentrated themselves upon the representation of what is most characteristic in one nation. I think I can say with perfect sincerity that, until our people learnt their business, what is most characteristic in Irish life had never been set upon the stage at all. I doubt if the Irish accent had ever been accurately spoken there. It does not seem to us any drawback that we have limited ourselves, with the exception of a few foreign masterpieces, to the expression of the life of our own country. Art has, I believe, always gained in intensity by limitation, and there are plenty of other Theatres for the other things. In rehearsing our Plays we have tried to give the words great importance; to make speech, whether it be the beautiful and rhythmical delivery of verse, or the accurate speaking of a rhythmical dialect, our supreme end, and almost all our play-wrights in the same way give to the vividness and picturesqueness of their style a principal consideration. We believe words more important than gesture, that voice is the principal power an actor possesses; and that nothing may distract from the actor, and what he says, we have greatly simplified scenery. When we wish to give a remote poetical effect we throw away realism altogether and are content with suggestion; this is the idea of the Japanese in their dramatic art; they believe that artificial objects, the interior, let us say, of some modern house, should be perfectly copied, because a perfect copy is possible; but when you get to sea and sky they are content to put before you merely a pattern of waves. Good realistic scenery is merely bad landscape painting, an attempt to do something which can only be done properly in an easel painting; but if you are content to decorate the stage, to suggest, you create something which is peculiar to the stage, for you put before your audience a scene that only wakes into life when the actors move in front of it. *The Hour Glass* was our first experiment of this kind and our simplest; but I think the effect of the purple dresses against the green may have interested you. This play, by the way, is one of our very earliest, and I notice, somewhat to my alarm, that it means one thing to myself, and often quite a different thing to my audience. To me it is a parable of the conscious and the subconscious life, an exposition of ideas similar to those in Ernest Myer's great book; but the other day it converted a music hall singer, and kept him going to Mass for six weeks, after which he relapsed, and was much worse than before.

238

But we are not always so orthodox. We have been denounced at one time or another by every party in Ireland. One of the plays which we give to-night, *The Rising of the Moon*, has roused the enmity of two parties. A daily paper described it as a slander upon the police, for it represented a policeman letting off a Fenian prisoner, whereas some nationalist friends of mine were equally indignant because they said it was an unpatriotic act to represent a policeman as capable of any virtue at all. How could the Dublin mob fight the police, I was asked, if it looked upon them as capable of any patriotic act, and, Are not morals more than literature? At another time we were offered support from what are called "the classes," and at a time we greatly needed it, if we would withdraw my own play, *Kathleen ni Houlihan*. We have always refused to listen to any of these demands, for we claim always the entire independence of the artist from everything except the high traditions of his craft. And our trouble has not always come from Ireland.

Any of you who have heard of us at all will have heard how a year and a half ago some hundreds of police were called out to quell a riot over one of our plays. We brought that play to London, and a little while before we produced it there we received a letter from your Censor — (we have no official censor in Ireland) — saying that as the play, though harmless in itself, was likely to raise a riot, he was consulting the Home Office as to whether it should be forbidden. Now your English Censor is a very much worse person than our Irish censors are, for your man has got the police on his side. However, actors and authors consulted together, and after calculating ways and means and raising sufficient capital, we decided, if necessary, to give an illegal performance in London, and all go to prison. However, the Home Office had more sanity than your Censor, and we were allowed to give our play, which was taken very peaceably.

That play has been our "Belfast Address"; for just as history has shown that you are not the peaceable people you look, we are not either. No matter what great question you take up, if you are in earnest about it, you come to the great issues that divide man from man. Everything is battle. All the highest business of man is to do valiantly in some fight or other, and often when one looks into it, battles that seem fought about the most different things change their appearance and become but one battle.

When I was coming up in the train the other day from

239

Galway, I began thinking how unlike your work was to my work, and then suddenly it struck me that it was all the same. A picture arose before my mind's eye: I saw Adam numbering the creatures of Eden; soft and terrible, foul and fair, they all went before him. That, I thought, is the man of science, naming and numbering, for our understanding, everything in the world. But then I thought, we writers, do we not also number and describe, though with a difference? You are chiefly busy with the exterior world, and we with the interior. Science understands that everything must be known in the world our eyes look at; there is nothing too obscure, too common, too vile, to be the subject of knowledge. When a man of science discovers a new species, or a new law, you do not ask the value of the law, or the value of the species before you do him honour; you leave all that to the judgment of the generations. It is your pride that in you the human race contemplates all things with so pure, so disinterested an eyesight that it forgets its own necessities and infirmities, all its hopes and fears, in the contemplation of truth for the sake of truth, reality for the sake of reality.

We, on the other hand, are Adams of a different Eden, a more terrible Eden perhaps, for we must name and number the passions and motives of men. There, too, everything must be known, everything understood, everything expressed; there, also, there is nothing common, nothing unclean; every motive must be followed through all the obscure mystery of its logic. Mankind must be seen and understood in every possible circumstance, in every conceivable situation. There is no laughter too bitter, no irony too harsh for utterance, no passion too terrible to be set before the minds of men. The Greeks knew that. Only in this way can mankind be understood, only when we have put ourselves in all the possible positions of life, from the most miserable to those that are so lofty that we can only speak of them in symbols and in mysteries, will entire wisdom be possible. All wise government depends upon this knowledge not less than upon that other knowledge which is your business rather than ours; and we and you alike rejoice in battle, finding the sweetest of all music to be the stroke of the sword.[81]

The antipathy to Yeats may be seen by this criticism of his speech, which appeared in *Sinn Féin*:

It is probably too late now to mend to any extent the misleading statement of Mr. Yeats. But . . . it might be well

240

to correct a few of the most incomplete statements. . . .

The statement that they brought over English actors to Dublin in 1898 [*sic*] is, indeed, quite true. But this in itself cannot be regarded as exactly an epoch-making event, as the thing had been done for years before that by other people, and is still being continued weekly by other Dublin theatre managers. Indeed, one doubts a little Lady Gregory's implication in the matter. But the statement that the "movement out of which the Abbey Theatre and the Abbey Theatre Company began in 1898" is quite wrong. . . . The fact of the matter is that Mr. Yeats had nothing whatsoever to do in getting together the group of young men and women. This was due entirely to the efforts of Mr. W. G. Fay, the unnamed actor, and his brother, Mr. Frank Fay. In fact, Mr. Yeats held himself decidedly aloof from them, until he saw that by joining himself with them he could get the use of an amount of unpaid and very high quality labour in acting and general stagecraft. . . . When Mr. Yeats joined them, owing to his previous reputation as a Nationalist, and his position as a man of letters, they felt highly honoured, and very foolishly, as subsequent events proved, elected him President of their Society. Then commenced his "glorious" career, during which he has succeeded in driving out, one after the other, all the most talented members of the original group. . . . The Abbey Theatre Company stands only for Mr. Yeats and his personal ideas.[82]

P. S. O'Hegarty, whose bibliographies of Irish writers were in later years to be an important feature of *The Dublin Magazine*, wrote to refute this attack:

The cold shoulder which has for some years past been given in Nationalist circles in Dublin to the National Theatre Society, and the constant depreciation of Mr. Yeats, have been not a little puzzling to those who live outside Dublin. In the current issue of *Sinn Féin* your correspondent "S" makes statements regarding Mr. Yeats which require explanation and proof, statements which should not have been lightly made. We are told that Mr. Yeats only joined the National Theatre because "he saw that by joining himself with them he would get the use of an amount of unpaid and very high quality labour in acting and general stagecraft which it was impossible for him otherwise to produce." I ask any fair-minded person whether this is the kind of thing which any sincere Nationalist could write under an anonymity, and without adducing one particle of evidence in support. Where has "S" been all these years since the formation of the Society that he did not denounce Mr. Yeats in the early days? Can he get a single member of the original company, or a single individual of trustworthiness in the dramatic movement, to support this statement of his or to adduce any evidence. Mr. Yeats is also accused of "driving out, one after another, all the most talented members of the original group." Can "S" back this up by evidence, in the shape of statements from those alleged to have been driven out? . . . "S's" article, is, perhaps, the most regrettable and indefensible yet: it is an accusation against the greatest living Irish poet of having been insincere in his Nationalism and in his work in the dramatic movement.[83]

To all of which, Arthur Griffith tersely replied, 'The facts are as stated by "S".'

*   *   *

In November, Lady Gregory gave a rare public lecture:

Lady Gregory's lecture, "Some Thoughts on the Drama", at the Ard Craobh on Monday night, was a thought-provoking one. . . . Greek tragedy, the plays of Molière and Racine, and Goethe and Schiller, of Shakespeare, and other English playwrights were referred to in the course of her address. At the outset she paid a tribute to the Gaelic League, and added that though she had been invited by other associations to lecture for them she had not done so. She was glad to lecture when she received the invitation of the Gaelic League. She first dealt with exaggeration in the play. There must be exaggeration on the part of the writer. A miser, for example, in ordinary life, reveals his character through his actions, but he also does many things such as talk of the weather and the crops in doing so. These things must be dispensed with — on the stage. The exigencies of time compel this. The leading lines should be seized and made use of. To hold the mirror up to nature was more for the actors than the writers. A selection would have to be made of the traits required, and these should then be delineated. . . .

Passing on to the more immediate Irish considerations, Lady Gregory wished that a company of players could tour the towns and villages presenting historical plays. The expenses and the difficulties in the way of halls, etc., she feared, however, would not admit of this. So local companies suggested themselves. . . .

Father Dinneen, Padraic Colum, W. B. Yeats, and others took part in the discussion which followed. We understood Padraic Colum to say that as religion was now divorced from the stage, and as we could not go back to the old gods like the old tragedians, we had not the elements for great tragedy. What of the tragedy of modern civilization, a Phadraic?[84]

*　　*　　*

In January, Synge's play *The Tinker's Wedding* was finally published. Sensibly, it was not produced by the Abbey, for it would certainly have created another demonstration of *Playboy* proportions. Indeed, even the publication caused considerable outcry. On 26 January, for instance, Holloway wrote:

> . . . The Poster:— THE WRITER OF THE PLAYBOY OF THE WESTERN WORLD INSULTS THE PRIESTHOOD caught my attention as I walked downtown in the afternoon, and I was determined to possess a copy of the poster. Failing to get one in the news shop, I called at the office and was successful in securing one. The article was headed "THE PLAYBOY OF THE WESTERN WORLD, FAMOUS PLAY OUTDONE IN NEW PIECE, A VULGAR ATROCITY, GROSS LIBEL ON THE PRIESTHOOD OF IRELAND." The writer starts with — "Not content with his achievement in the direction of *The Playboy of the Western World*, Mr. J. M. Synge has perpetrated a still greater atrocity in the new play *The Tinker's Wedding*. The thing is an abominable libel upon the Irish priesthood. No such travesty has even been penned before. And it is safe to say that if the precious production is ever presented on an Irish stage the consequence will put the exciting scenes witnessed at the performance of *The Playboy of the Western World* completely in the shade." The writer goes on to describe the plot and winds up, "This may be 'art'; it may be 'comedy' in Mr. Synge's opinion. But it is safe to say once more that if this scurrilous 'comedy' is ever played before an Irish house, the actors who play it and the people who sanction its production will be taught a lesson that will make them sadder, if wiser, men.[85]

Synge's health was rapidly deteriorating, and he decided to postpone his wedding to Molly Allgood and go into Elpis nursing home for a second time for an operation. On 4 May Synge wrote the following self-explanatory note to Yeats:

Dear Yeats,

This is only to go to you if anything should go wrong with me under the operation or after it.

I am a little bothered about my "papers." I have a certain amount that I think would be worth preserving, possibly also the I and III acts of *Deirdre*, and then I have a lot of Kerry and Wicklow articles that would go together into a book. The other early stuff I wrote I have kept as a sort of curiosity but I am anxious that it should *not* get into print.

I wonder could you get someone — say MacKenna who is now in Dublin — to go through them for you and do whatever you and Lady Gregory think desirable. It is rather a hard thing to ask you, but I do not want my good things destroyed, or my bad things printed rashly — especially a morbid thing about a mad fiddler in Paris which I hate. Do what you can.

Good luck,

J. M. SYNGE.[87]

The operation was not a success, for the tumour was found to be impossible to remove. Synge's health temporarily improved, but he had not much longer to live.

*   *   *

The relations of probably any theatre with its writers are often a tender and sensitive business, but the Abbey seemed to have a particular talent for bringing out the, not always latent, irascibility of its writers. A good case in point is that of William Boyle, the popular playwright who had withdrawn his works from the Abbey repertoire as a protest against *The Playboy*. Yeats attempted to woo Boyle back, but the problem was difficult, for Boyle's usual dislike of Yeats had now boiled up into violent antipathy. Consequently, Yeats wrote to Henderson on 2 August from Coole Park:

I am astonished at the letter which Boyle has permitted his Agent to send us. I see nothing for it now but a publication of Boyle's signed agreement. The whole thing is scandalous. He signed a statement undertaking to leave his plays with us during the Patent period. He did this because he understood that the production of his plays cost time, money, and that we had all united in a patriotic movement, and that we all bound ourselves to receive nothing for our work until the players were properly paid and the Theatre was paying its way. I told him when he signed this statement that precisely because our movement was of this kind I would not legally enforce the agreement, it was as it were a debt of honour. After *The Playboy*, he withdrew the play on conscientious grounds. I made no use of the agreement in public or in private. Having heard lately that he was inclined to give back his plays, we communicated with him through O'Donoghue, and he replied that we could have the plays on condition that we made some payment to his Agent to compensate him or her for their trouble, he himself taking nothing. And now we get this preposterous document. There is no longer apparently any question of conscience, it is an affair of money. Of course we refuse his terms, remembering that all our authors, some of whom are in need of money, at least as much as Mr. Boyle, give their work for nothing. Meanwhile, though not through any act of ours, there have been statements in the papers that we are getting back Boyle's plays. This will make a public statement necessary.

One is slow to disbelieve a man's word, and we had as you know decided that Boyle's plays were to be put in rehearsal at once. This of course alters one's plans considerably. I will come to Dublin tomorrow, and put *The Sequel* into rehearsal. I will bring up *The Clancy Name*, and *The Miser* will soon follow. Would you write to Mac Donagh and telephone to him and get him to come round to me tomorrow evening at the Theatre, or else at the Nassau Tuesday morning. I want to go carefully through the play with him. On second thoughts I send *Clancy Name*. You can have parts typed as soon as possible.[88]

Later in the year, on 1 October, Yeats discussed the matter with Holloway:

The letter Boyle had written could not be answered. "You know what an angry Irishman can say when he is vexed," said Yeats. Such was Boyle's last letter to them. . . . As to the money Boyle's agent asked per performance, the theatre funds could not afford to give it to him, but Yeats had a private fund which he could draw on if Boyle would never tell he was receiving payment for his work. Yeats said he could never agree to the 30 performances or to producing the plays on tour.[89]

Holloway relayed the information to Boyle, who replied:

What a crooked person W. B. Y. must be to think that I would enter into a conspiracy of silence with him after what has passed! If he has any penetration he would have seen that,

245

when I would negotiate with him only through an agent, any such scheme as that he hinted at was out of the question. Enough of him and his schemes.[90]

Another disgruntled playwright was John Guinan who worked in the same office with George Fitzmaurice, with whom he collaborated on an unpublished play. In later years, Guinan was to have several works performed by the Abbey, but in 1908 he was still unproduced, and his reaction to Abbey criticisms of plays may be seen in the following comments to Holloway:

> The Directors of the Abbey think the enclosed would not play. The objection is that the third act is not a natural development of Acts 1 and 2. The first two derive their power from characterization, the third from a dramatic anecdote. All the objections resolve themselves into this one. Yeats says I have such a splendid gift for dialogue and characterization that I allowed it to outweigh other considerations. . . . If you are convinced that the objection does not hold, I propose challenging Yeats in the press openly as was done a few months ago. Be as hard on the piece as you like and let me know.
>
> . . . Of course, I would be only too willing to meet the views of the Abbey folk if they had any suggestions to make; but they hold that the one objection on which they rely — so to speak — is insuperable. . . . Yeats has asked me twice to try a play in one act, as he considers it a discipline for the author in unity of action of the most rigorous kind. He said Synge who had gone through this discipline himself had asked him to impress this fact on me.
>
> . . . I am afraid I said rude things to Yeats about his criticism. His constant talk about "uninteresting young couples" exasperated me. I said I rather welcomed severe criticism so long as it was relevant, but that I was afraid he read the little play under the impression that it was another anecdotal comedy.[91]

On 16 April Holloway borrowed Gerald MacNamara's two-act play, *An August Day*, which had been sent in to the Abbey. He thought everything was truly mad in it. On the 18th, he returned the script to Henderson who said:

> . . . that he did not think the Directors would produce *An August Day*. Synge was dead against it. (The new dramatist treads on his corns too much for his taste, I suppose). The poetic strain running through it delighted Henderson. . . .

246

Henderson told me two or three new plays had been sent in by outsiders. . . . Guinan has completed his three act play and sent it on. I wonder did he take Fitzmaurice's advice . . . and pepper the dialogue with strange oaths to suit the taste of the Abbey trio.[92]

About a month later, Holloway wrote:

Had a long chat with Mr. Guinan at the Conversazione of the National Literary Society about his new three act play. He told me Synge had read it and told him Act 3 was much better than the others. He was to return it to him, but went into Hospital next day. The Ms. was at the Abbey just now, and he was awaiting decision. Yeats liked the first act. . . . Lady Gregory thought the play too redundant of talk. Between the three they will fire it out as usual, I have no doubt. Speaking of the three act play he and Fitzmaurice wrote together, Yeats asked him who was it wrote the part in pencil at the end of the second act, for said he, "It was the most dramatic bit I ever read." Guinan owned up to having written it. Yeats said he wanted all the new plays they could get for the coming season. Why, oh why, don't they accept them when they get them is what I and many want to know.[93]

Despite Fitzmaurice's remark that the way to get a play accepted at the Abbey was to pepper it with oaths, Yeats does not seem to have been looking for plays that were provocative in language or in content. He did not produce *The Tinker's Wedding*; he did not produce Anthony Wharton's new play, *Nelly Lehane*, about the question of female suffrage; and according to information Holloway gleaned from a conversation with Kerrigan and Sinclair:

Yeats wanted Fitzmaurice to take the "dead and damned" speech out of the mouth of the priest, and the author wouldn't hear of it. Said it would spoil the strength of his play. Yeats said no priest would say such a thing at such a moment.[94]

Yet despite all of the hostile criticism, the theatre did struggle on to some prosperity. In April, Yeats had to write to John Quinn that, 'We are producing new plays at a great rate but drawing as bad houses as usual.'[95] But in October he was able to write:

The Abbey has been doing very well lately; for the last three months or so it has even been paying, and if it can keep on like this, which I doubt, we'll be able to do without a subsidy. The curious thing is that in spite of all the attacks upon us we have nothing but a pit and that is always full now. The stalls won't come near us, except when some titled person or other comes and brings guests. All the praise we have had from the intellectual critics cannot bring the Irish educated classes, and all the abuse we have had from the least intellectual cannot keep the less educated classes away. I suppose the cause of it all is that, as a drunken medical student used to say, "Pitt decapitated Ireland." [96]

In November, after the visit of Mrs. Patrick Campbell, Yeats was able to add, '*Deirdre* has been played with triumphant success — great audiences and great enthusiasm. . . . There has not been one hostile voice here and I am now accepted as a dramatist in Dublin.' [97]

*　　*　　*

1907 is a year that might leave the impression that the Abbey Theatre was constantly seething with turmoil, dissension, dissatisfaction, anger and riot. Of course, this was not the case; and so, as an antidote to much that has gone before in this chapter, here is Sara Allgood in a genial mood of reminiscence:

> What a quaint collection of people fastened themselves to the Abbey. There was Miss Bushel, a quiet little mouse of a woman, who sold programmes. Later she was promoted to the selling of tickets in the box office. She had the strangest complex I've ever heard of; she lived in a tiny room out by Inchicore (a suburb of Dublin) getting hardly a pittance from the Abbey. We, the actors, were the highest paid, and Three Pounds a week was, by this time, the top salary. Miss Bushel went out of her way to adopt small babies, some that were abandoned. She simply adored doing this, and at times I have known her to have a couple of small babies to take care of. How she fed and clothed them I do not know. She had the "mother" complex so strong that she was never happier than when she'd hear of some baby being left on a doorstep, and off she would go to try and get it. I, in all the early years of the Abbey, never knew her first name, and I didn't until this day (1948: Have just received a cutting from a Dublin paper. Miss Bushel died a few weeks ago. Her first name was Nellie. She was a weaver of poplin).
>
> Then we had Mrs. Martin, our charlady, a wonderful woman, harried to death by a ne'er-do-well husband, a large family, and very little money. I think she got about Ten Shillings a week to clean the theatre in the early days. Later she was made charlady in chief, and had two or three other

women under her for help. I remember her so well, rushing into the theatre in the early morning, putting on her canvas apron, dashing round with her duster, brush and pail, sweeping and washing up. In fact, I modelled my "Juno" in *Juno and the Paycock* on her. I gave her some money to get and make me a canvas apron, like she used to wear doing her work.

Then came Barney Murphy, a young man who was our prompter, and he was a stage-hand as well. The son of a well-to-do lawyer, who had come down in the world through drink, Barney was a most intelligent person, although brought up in a slum. I will never forget one night when he was prompting. I was a Queen and I had to begin my line with "It's a queer thing. . . ." I forgot what I had to say suddenly; there was a rather long pause, and from the side came Barney's voice saying, "It's a quare thing . . ." and without a moment's hesitation, I heard my queenly voice saying, "It's a quare thing . . . ," etc. When I realized what I was saying, I nearly died laughing, and Barry Fitzgerald, who was the King, looked completely mystified at his Queen coming out in such strong "Dublinese." The play was *The Dragon*, a children's play by Lady Gregory.

Then there was Peadar Kearney, our property man; his claim to fame is that he composed and wrote the Volunteers' "Soldiers' Song," which is now Ireland's National Anthem.

I am leaving almost to the last our stage carpenter and scene-shifter, Shaun Barlow, a curious young man, hardly ever smiled, taciturn, rather bad-tempered. He would be asked to make a chair or a table for a scene, and every difficulty in the world he would make as to why it could or should not be made the way it was wanted; till finally the Fays or the Directors would give up in despair and leave him, and then to their complete surprise, at the appointed time, up would come the article in dispute, beautifully made, and ready for what it was wanted for.

Adolphus Wright should not be considered as a stagehand, although he, too, helped in setting the scenes, and also acted small parts in plays. "Dossie," as we affectionately called him, was an electrician by trade. Well I remember when we were staging *The Green Helmet* by W. B. Yeats: he, Yeats, wanted a special red light for the entrance of the Green Man from the Sea. Dossie tried his best, but could not get the right effect for Mr. Yeats; suddenly a terrific red blaze appeared in the doorway. Yeats, who was in the stalls directing, shouted,

249

"That's it, that's the light I want. Keep it in."

"I can't, Mr. Yeats, sir," said Dossie, "the bloody scenery is on fire." . . .

Another member of the Abbey Theatre Company was Arthur Sinclair, a young man with a genius for comedy. I learned from watching him that acting does not depend on education, it is purely an instinctive art, and sometimes education is a handicap. If Sinclair understood a part in his first reading, you could leave him alone, and he would generally give a superb performance, but if he had any difficulty in characterizing a character, he was lost. To me, he did not appear to be able to "dissect" a part, as some actors can, and make a characterization out of it. He and Mollie, my sister, were given charge of the Wardrobe. Their duties were to give out the clothes to the other actors each week for the different parts, collect the clothes, and send them to the laundry or cleaners after the play finished; do small mending, pack the theatrical baskets when we were going on tour. For this they were paid Ten Shillings a week. One day they both demanded a raise. After some dispute, they got Two Shillings and Six-pence, which brought their salaries up to Twelve Shillings and Six-pence a week, and this covered their duties as Wardrobe Master and Mistress, as well as acting their parts.

Sinclair was quite a dandy, rather good-looking, a little on the Oscar Wilde type (of beauty, I mean). He had, as a young man, very lovely golden hair, which he wore divided in the centre and plastered down each side of his head with hair-oil to keep it absolutely flat. He also wore extremely tight trousers, I think they were the fashion at that time. One day, Sinclair and Mollie were packing up preparatory to going out on tour. They were both in the ladies' dressing-room — in those days we only had two large dressing-rooms, one for the ladies, and the other for the men (later the Abbey was able to purchase a house on the other side, and six dressing-rooms were constructed) — and I happened to be in the dressing-room also, getting ready my make-up case. They had packed the basket and Sinclair stooped to lock it; suddenly there was a terrific tearing sound, and a yell from Sinclair, "Don't look! Oh, don't look! Get me a dressing gown." We rushed and got the gown. There was poor Sinclair holding on to his britches; they had got split down the back. He wrapped his gown round him and dashed for the men's dressing-room, where I suppose he repaired the damage. Mollie and I nearly died laughing.

A few years ago Sinclair married my sister, Máire O'Neill, but I am afraid it has not been as happy an association as their earlier one, when they were both young and carefree.[98]

*   *   *

On 1 April, Holloway recorded that:

> The Theatre of Ireland gave a successful house warming at their new rooms, 95 Harcourt Street. . . . At one point of the evening, Mr. James Cousins mounted on a chair . . . discoursed on the Theatre of Ireland and its aims and objects in a concise and lucid manner, and then read a circular, that was afterwards distributed amongst those present, inviting membership at a subscription of 10/- per annum for non-acting members and 5/- for acting members. The Count Markievicz was the first to hand in a subscription for himself as a non-acting member and his wife as an acting member.[99]

On 22 and 23 May, the Theatre of Ireland rented the Abbey, and *The Freeman's Journal* reviewed their offerings as follows:

> The only new piece last night was a one-act drama by Padraic Colm entitled *The Miracle of the Corn.* . . . It is impossible to describe the play, because — even when sitting close to the stage — scarcely a word could be heard, all the performers speaking in subdued and muffled tones. From the acting and accompaniments it could be guessed that the weather was bad, that corn was scarce, that the farmer was a hard man, that his wife was lavishly charitable, that she gave to the poor the last of the corn in the bin, that she feared her husband's wrath, and that, by some miraculous power, the empty bin was filled with corn, and the husband's heart was softened. All the characters appeared to be oppressed by some terrible dread, but from what cause this arose could not be divined.
>
> The second piece was Mr. Edward Martyn's *Maeve* in two acts, described on the bills as a psychological drama. . . . As the two sisters, Máire Nic Shiubhlaigh (Maeve) and Caitía Ní Cormac (Finola) bore the burden of the drama, and nothing could be better done than the sharp contrast they drew in appearance and cast of mind. Both, in fact, acted with great skill and made admirable efforts to give life to the author's creation, but the whole work abounded in glaring incongruities that would make futile the very highest dramatic powers. . . .
>
> The third piece was a comedy in two scenes by Lewis Purcell, which had already been produced in Belfast. The

251

title is *The Enthusiast*. . . . The fun of the piece lies in the faithfulness of nearly all the characters to their prototypes in Co. Antrim.[100]

In *Sinn Féin*, 'Scrutator' gave *Maeve* the following critical yet perceptive notice:

> Of Mr. Martyn's *Maeve* much could be said. As seen last week one was especially struck by two things. The wealth of splendid material in the play, practically wasted owing to bad handling on the part of the author, and the extraordinarily beautiful and convincing interpretation by Miss Máire Nic Shiubhlaigh of the part of Maeve O'Heynes, unique in its combination of insurmountable difficulties to any ordinary actress. . . . Máire Nic Shiubhlaigh acted with a natural fervour, a sincere intensity, that pulled Mr. Martyn's somewhat disjointed play together, and gave it life and force, and a definite meaning. None of the inadequacies so plentifully sprinkled through the performance could obliterate the outstanding merit of her work. From the first sweet sound of her voice in the opening scene, until she disappears with the Queen of the Land of the Ever-living, she dominated; Maeve superb, Maeve sorrowful, Maeve stricken, Maeve triumphant. The slightest wrong touch, the slightest false note, and she would have been merely theatrical, pantomimic. But her intuitive grasp of the part saved her from every pitfall. It was the most notable piece of acting — the most characteristic and the most Irish — ever seen at the Abbey Theatre. Of the others, that very capable and excellent actor, Mr. P. Mac Siubhlaigh, though hampered by a somewhat grotesque costume, did very good work as The O'Heynes. It is great praise to him that he steered so resolutely and so successfully clear of the comic. The audience were dying to laugh at him, but he never gave them a chance.[101]

In the same issue, Ella Young, later known for her retelling of Irish legends in such volumes as *Celtic Wonder Tales* and *The Wonder Smith and His Son*, wrote, 'I never hoped to see *Maeve* played as well. . . . Miss Walker played the part with the stillness, the curious, apathetic intensity that Maeve demands. Her beautiful voice, the clear-cut lines of her face, the almost impersonal charm of her personality — all these made a magic through which the Maeve of the play took being.'[102]

The Theatre of Ireland again rented the Abbey on 23 and 24 November, to produce a revival of Rutherford Mayne's *The Turn*

of *the Road* and a new play by Seumas O'Kelly. 'Iberian' in
Sinn Féin remarked judiciously:

> *The Turn of the Road* . . . is not great drama. Our Sophocles,
> our Shakespeare, our Goethe, even, have still to come. If any
> should dispute whether it *is* drama in the ultimate sense I
> should pause before entering the lists against him. We need
> for plays like *Kathleen ni Houlihan* and *Riders to the Sea* and
> *The Turn of the Road* some word which shall differentiate
> them from the orthodox three act drama as the short story is
> distinguished from the novel. They are more than dramatic
> episodes; but the mantle of traditional drama sits all too
> loosely on them. We can only call them — plays. *The Turn of
> the Road*, as one sees it first, is a good play; well conceived,
> well constructed, capable in its psychology, capital in its
> situations, its dialogue, its climax. The critic may object that
> there is no climax. . . .
>
> One mistake is very likely to be made about *The Turn of
> the Road*, especially by Dublin audiences. It is not a comedy.
> The second performance, in which Rutherford Mayne himself
> acted, made this even more evident than the first. One could
> nearly wish that Miss Fitzpatrick — whose excellence of voice,
> gesture, idiom, accent, pose, everything in a word that one
> calls acting, could hardly be overpraised — had not portrayed
> the part of the auld wife of shrewish tongue, cantankerous
> temper, and narrow heart so faithfully. The audience halted
> between amusement and disdain, and, being good-natured,
> chose the first. . . .
>
> I have left no space in which to criticise *The Flame on the
> Hearth*, partly, perhaps, because I do not take its merits or
> shortcomings as seriously as some with whom I have spoken.
> It is just a dramatic episode, a little rhetorical in phrases,
> though containing some graceful speeches. As a narrative of
> fact it strikes one as improbable, although the programme
> refers us to a true incident for the basis. . . . I feel that
> Seumas O'Kelly, from whom we expect much good work in
> the future, should take his next serious play more seriously.[103]

Rutherford Mayne was at this time acting professionally with
William Mollison's Company, which was playing during the week
at the Gaiety. When Mollison saw a matinee of the Theatre of
Ireland, he invited the company to appear with his own at the
Gaiety. However, his Thursday newspaper advertisement stated
that members of the Abbey Theatre Company would perform
The Turn of the Road. Mollison had, of course, the best intentions,

but his confusion of the Abbey Company with the Theatre of Ireland Company irritated Miss Horniman, who then wrote the following letter to the press:

> Sir — During last week a certain body of people calling themselves "The Abbey Theatre Company" were advertised in the Dublin papers. Common courtesy, not to say decency, would demand that the permission to use the name should have been asked from the lessee of that building.
>
> To avoid further confusion in the public mind I am instructing Messrs. Cramer and Wood that neither "The Abbey Theatre Company" nor "The Theatre of Ireland" is to be permitted to hire my theatre again. I do not know whether these are two different societies or one body with two names.[104]

On the same day, Seumas O. Connolly and James H. Cousins both replied for the Theatre of Ireland. Connolly's letter was the more combative:

> Dear Sir — Miss Horniman has written to the Press stating that she will not allow the use of the Abbey Theatre to the Theatre of Ireland in the future. The reason she gives for doing so is in order to "avoid further confusion in the public mind" between the Abbey Theatre Company and the Theatre of Ireland.
>
> Will you allow me to say?
>
> (1) That there is no body named "The Abbey Theatre Company" in existence. Therefore there can be no confusion in the public mind on this point.
>
> (2) That the Theatre of Ireland is in no way whatsoever responsible for the confusion of names. The error arose only in connection with Mr. Mollison's preliminary announcement on November 25th last of a performance of *The Turn of the Road* at the Gaiety Theatre by the Theatre of Ireland. This was corrected immediately by us, not only in the advertisements, but by letters to every paper in which it occurred.
>
> (3) That I have before me a letter addressed by Mr. Yeats to the seceding members of the original National Theatre Society (now the Theatre of Ireland) stating that — "Miss Horniman will be glad to let them the theatre on the usual conditions." This constituted one of the most important conditions in the contract between Mr. Yeats and the seceding members. Is Miss Horniman about to endeavour to rescind this now in an arbitrary fashion? It is a curious coincidence that this attempt to withdraw from the original agreement

should occur immediately after the most successful performances of the Theatre of Ireland that have yet taken place. Will Mr. Yeats permit this violation of an agreement to which his name is attached?

Yours,
SEUMAS O. CONNOLLY,
Secretary, Theatre of Ireland[105]

A few days later, Mayne, who was now with Mollison's company in England, wrote to the Press requesting the publication of the following letter to Miss Horniman:

Dear Madam — I have received a copy of *The Freeman's Journal* containing a letter sent by you in which you state that the Theatre of Ireland is not to be permitted to hire the Abbey again.

I think if I perhaps explained the circumstances under which an error arose in the advertisements referred to, you will see that you have acted somewhat harshly towards the above Society.

Mr. Mollison's company, of which I am at present a member, were playing in Dublin the week commencing the 23rd November.

It so happened that the Theatre of Ireland were that same week playing *The Turn of the Road* at the Abbey Theatre, and Mr. Connolly, on behalf of his Society, extended an invitation to Mr. and Mrs. Mollison and their Company to a matinee performance given on the 24th ult. Mr. Mollison very kindly came, and was so pleased with the production of *The Turn of the Road* that he asked me that same evening at the Gaiety if it would be possible for the Theatre of Ireland to give a performance there the following evening after *Garrick*.

The Theatre of Ireland, through their Committee, consented, on conditions that the preliminary notices and advertisements clearly denoted that it was their members who were taking part, and laid particular emphasis on this point.

I informed my management of this; but unfortunately, through some error, the advertisement appeared that the play would be performed by the Abbey Theatre Company.

I need not say that as soon as the advertisement appeared Mr. Connolly informed the management, who immediately took steps to correct the matter, and notices to that effect, as well as a letter from Mr. Connolly, were inserted in all the papers.

255

The Theatre of Ireland are blameless. They, indeed, were particularly anxious that no mistake should arise about names. A similar error arose, I believe, at the Galway Exhibition this summer when the National Theatre Company were billed as "The Theatre of Ireland."

I think it very hard on the Theatre of Ireland that they should be obliged to suffer for a mistake altogether outside their control. . . . I had charge of the arrangements between Mr. Mollison and the Theatre of Ireland. If any blame is to be given to any person I will take the responsibility. . . .

Yours sincerely,
RUTHERFORD MAYNE[106]

Miss Horniman was not mollified.

*   *   *

On 24 April the Ulster Literary Theatre produced two new plays in Dublin at the Abbey. *Leader of the People* by James Winder Good, who used the pseudonym of Robert Harding, was another attempt to transplant Ibsenism to Ireland, and dealt with an election in Ulster. *The Drone* by Rutherford Mayne was a folk play of the type that later came to be called kitchen comedy. The reviews of both plays were very mixed. F.M.A. in *The Dublin Evening Mail* said of *Leader of the People*:

The play is vague, the dialogue is without distinction, and the ideas hidden in a mist. . . . Elewyn is very unconvincing, and speaks in a dreadfully whining voice for a supposed leader of men. . . . The poet is an incredibly offensive creature, and no one has ever met him, I hope, North or South. I could have wished that the players had known their parts better, but something may be forgiven in a first performance.[107]

'Jack Point' in *The Evening Herald* thought, 'Mr. Harding undoubtedly can write, and his dialogue is often decidedly clever; but one cannot but regret that he in common with many another modern Irish dramatist, has fallen so completely under the influence of Ibsen and mistaken the stage for the platform or the pulpit.' He thought that *The Drone* was 'in no sense an ambitious venture', but Seumas Connolly in *Sinn Féin* called it 'a masterpiece of comedy of life and manners', and the critic for *The Irish Independent* raved that:

Anything finer than the manner in which a play called *The Drone* was presented at the Abbey Theatre last night I have never seen at the hands of amateurs. It must have made the audience sit up, shake itself, and gape with astonishment.... The whole thing came very near to what we commonly call genius, and when I say so I don't gush. . . .

There was another piece produced called *Leader of the People*. It's poor stuff. It was poorly played.[108]

*   *   *

The Annual Oireachtas celebration was held early in August in the Round Room of the Rotunda by the Gaelic League. The League had sponsored a playwriting contest, and the four prize-winners were produced. First prize was won by Pádraig O Conaire, who was still a civil servant in London. In later years he was to take to the roads in Ireland and become a remarkable writer of short stories in Gaelic. His play was produced on the first night, and *The Freeman's Journal* reviewed it as follows:

> Pádraig O Conaire's play, *Bairbre Ruadh*, which was awarded the first prize, was performed by a company of members of the Gaelic League of London. It is a simple little play, dealing with an incident in the life of a young Galway girl, a farmer's daughter, who is in love with the servant boy, and for whom her brother, Máirtín, has made a match with a widower named An Brúnach, who has a publichouse in Galway. The action of the play takes place in the girl's house, and turns on the manner in which she elopes with her lover, Cuimin, on the morning that she is to be introduced to An Brúnach. Her sister, Cáit, however, accepts the Galway publican, and accompanies him and her brother to the pattern. Whether it was the fault of the building or of the actors, the voices were very indistinct, and very little of the play was heard by those who were any distance away from the stage. The author himself, in the part of Máirtín, was good; but the best actor of the company was Máirtín Mac Donnchadha, who filled the part of the Galway publican. The other parts were filled as follows: — Cáit, Sinéad Ní Phaidín; Bairbre, Caitlín Ní Shiothcháin; and Cuimin, E. I. O'Sullivan.[109]

The other plays were by Father O'Kelly, Pádraig O'Shea, and Máire O'Kennedy.

*   *   *

The year also saw the formation of the Independent Dramatic Company whose leading spirit was Count Casimir Dunin-Markievicz, a Polish nobleman who had married Constance Gore-Booth. The Count's plays were not usually Irish in subject matter, and

257

considering his command of the language it is even remarkable that they were in English. He was, however, a well-known man about town who, in addition to his theatrical interest, was an able amateur painter, the founder of a fencing club, and a convivial pub companion. The Countess, although her time came to be ever more taken up with politics, was still in 1908 an enthusiastic amateur actress. She had played in the Theatre of Ireland's revival of *Deirdre* in December 1907, and she was a leading actress in her husband's company. The productions of the Independent Dramatic Company were not remarkable for their polished professionalism, and of the company's first production one of the Countess's biographers remarked, 'It was the height of the Dublin social season, and since Count and Countess Markievicz were still very much in Castle society, the production was more a social than a theatrical event.'[110]

The company's first production was given at the Abbey on 9 March. The piece was a problem play by the Count, *Seymour's Redemption*, and *Sinn Féin* gave it a notice replete with heavy-handed irony:

> Consciously or unconsciously Count Markievicz is a master of irony. . . . The finest appreciation of the play came from a badly filled pit. Part of the stalls was reduced to an unspeakable state of thinking: I never saw so many furrows on so many noble brows. The heads of the actors, I noticed, were mostly bald and grave, and reverend. The staging and hairdressing were beyond all praise, and the drawingroom "supers"—! Well, any of them might give us valuable lessons in deportment.[111]

The Countess's acting was described later by Jacqueline Van Voris:

> Her speech, too, was a problem; she was not always clearly understood. She had a strong, Anglo-Irish clipped drawl which at first aroused suspicion among Irish nationalists. Also, her voice was shrill, good, no doubt, for hallooing in a chase or haranguing a crowd, but grating on the stage. She was vital and emotional, but lacked the control and restraint necessary to be a first-class actress. She was responsive to the words and situations and later showed a sense of comedy, but most of the plays she acted in and later wrote were intense and didactic. She was always direct, honest, and sincere, on stage as well as off, but her most successful performances were off stage.[112]

258

In December the Count's company took over the Abbey for three evening performances and a Saturday matinee. The plays were the Count's *The Dilettante,* and *Home Sweet Home* by him and Nora Fitzpatrick. *The Freeman's Journal* observed of *The Dilettante* that:

> In the first act seven ladies indulge in some criticism of men and their ways, which would have been more interesting if it could have been followed, but there were so many pauses and so much indistinctness, due to a first night, that they did not receive justice. . . . Miss Constance Gore had a congenial part in Althea. She looked it, and acted with spirit, though a little restraint here and there would have been better. She carried her infatuation beyond the bounds of probability, and some of the laughter in the wrong place was pardonable. . . . As Ella Watt, Máire Nic Shiubhlaigh proved herself once more an actress of uncommon power. Her conception of the part is consistent throughout, her simple pride was beautifully expressed in tone and gesture, and it was only in the sudden turn of affairs at the end that, through no fault of hers, she was incomprehensible. . . . To sum up, it is a play that cannot be described as a success, but it is good enough to be licked into better shape. The staging of the first act was very prettily done.
>
> The second piece was *Home, Sweet Home,* described as "a Belfast farce in one act," by Nora Fitzpatrick and Casimir Dunin Markievicz. Here again are all the elements of success, but a more distinct failure to properly compound them.[113]

*   *   *

Among the notable productions at the Gaiety were a special matinee of Sarah Bernhardt in *La Dame aux Caméllias*; Mr. Leigh Lovel's Company in an Ibsen week, and two appearances of Miss Horniman's Company under the management of Ben Iden Payne. In the company were Nigel Playfair, Lewis Casson, and Sybil Thorndike. In their two visits they played Shaw's *Candida* and *Widowers' Houses*, as well as plays by Stanley Houghton, W. Kingsley Tarpey, and Charles McEvoy.

During the year, The Royal produced its fourth Hippodrome season, one attraction of which was 'De Gracia's Assam Elephants, so well remembered in their Famous Cricket Match'. In September, Lena Ashwell appeared in her London success *Irene Wycherly* by the Dublin writer 'Anthony Wharton'. In November, the Vedrenne-Barker company played *Man and Superman* and *Arms and the Man*, although Barker himself was prevented at the last moment by illness from appearing. Also in November, the Royal opened its 'Winter Garden', and in the afternoon one could now visit the theatre and see the latest Living Pictures and have afternoon tea, all for a shilling.

On 11 September *The Evening Mail* stated that the proprietors of the Royal had just purchased the Gaiety from the executors of the late Michael Gunn:

> The new proprietors, it is said, regard the Gaiety Theatre as specially suitable for light comedy, and society plays, and, generally speaking, for that type of play which demands less staging accommodation, and appeals to the class of people which does not always make numerically the largest audience. . . . Mrs. Gunn, it is said, will have no interest in the new theatre, and will retire from active participation in theatrical affairs in Dublin, where she has long been a notable and popular figure.
>
> Mr. Frederick Mouillot, Mr. David Telford, Mrs. David Allen, and Mr. Sam Allen are the directors of the syndicate.[114]

The changeover was to take place in about six months.

On 13 February there was a story in *The Freeman's Journal* stating that the Queen's was to be re-opened under new management. The new management was an unnamed London firm which intended, however, to use Irish labour and materials in the re-building and maintenance of the theatre. On 1 March *The Freeman's Journal* stated that the Queen's was re-opening on 3 March under the management of the Colonial Picture Company and was to show cinematograph entertainments. Finally, on 6 August, the paper carried a long story detailing the theatre's history and stating that Frederick Wentforth Marriott Watson, a manager, actor and writer who used the stage name of Brooke Warren, had applied for a patent for the Theatre. The theatre's patent had expired on 25 March 1907, and had not come back into the possession of Trinity College, which owned the land, until 29 September 1908. That was the reason why the theatre had been used in the interim for bioscope pictures and variety. Watson now planned to spend £5,000 in repairs and to re-open the theatre as a legitimate house.

*　　*　　*

In 1908 a meeting was held in Cork to discuss the founding of a new dramatic society. The minutes were taken by Daniel Corkery:

> A meeting of those interested in Drama was held in the Dun on Sunday, November 1st at 1 o'clock. Mr. L. de Roiste

presided, and Mr. D. Corkery acted as Secretary. Those present were Mr. D. Harrington, Mr. P. Higgins, J. Higgins, S. Meade, P. Harrington, R. Linehan, D. Breen, T. McSwiney B.A., J. Jennings, T. O'Gorman, E. Lynam B.A., J. P. Conlon.

The Chairman explained that some preliminary meetings had been held at which the question of establishing a society for the purpose of encouraging Drama was discussed. The present meeting was the outcome of these discussions. It now remained to be seen whether such a society should be established. He would be glad to hear any suggestions.

Mr. D. Corkery then explained that he thought it would be wiser to establish an Art Club rather than a purely Dramatic Society. He thought the number of people interested in Drama in Cork was rather small, and that such a society would hardly continue to exist. The same statement applied to Painting; in fact, to every Art except Music. He thought the Art students should be got interested in the work; they might assist in the mounting of the plays etc., while those interested in Drama might help the art students by arranging an annual exhibition of sketches, etc. He also suggested that in the event of a Dramatic Society being established, the society should make it a rule to confine their attention to original work and to translations from such languages as French, German, etc.

The sense of the meeting was against the establishing of an Art Club; but in favour of establishing a Dramatic Society on the lines of Mr. Corkery's second proposal. Several of those present spoke in this strain; and finally on the proposition of Mr. D. Breen, seconded by Mr. T. Higgins, the society was established. Mr. D. Breen then proposed the following names as suitable committee: Mr. L. de Roiste, Mr. E. Lynam, B.A., Mr. and Mrs. F. Healy, Mr. T. O'Gorman and Mr. D. Corkery. The meeting unanimously adopted this proposal, Mr. P. Higgins having seconded it. It was unanimously agreed that the Committee should continue in office for one year, that it should have powers of co-opting others, and that the sum of 5/- payable annually entitles to membership. Some discussion took place as to a suitable name. The name, "Cork Dramatic Society," was finally agreed on, Mr. D. Breen proposing and Mr. D. Corkery seconding.[115]

A few days later, on 7 November, the group held a second meeting:

Mr. Liam de Roiste in the chair; also present: Mr. T. O'Gorman and Mr. D. Corkery; subsequently Mr. E. Lynam attended.

Mr. Liam de Roiste was elected Chairman on Mr. T. O'Gorman's proposition, seconded by Mr. D. Corkery, D. Corkery was appointed Secretary on the proposition of Mr. L. de Roiste, seconded by Mr. T. O'Gorman.

Mr. Corkery proposed that a typed statement of aims be got ready and circulated amongst those likely to be interested in the society. This was agreed to; Mr. L. de Roiste undertook to have it done.

The meeting spent some time in considering the question as to whether an acting manager should be appointed but was unable to come to any decision. It was decided to leave the question open for the present.

It was decided to get such people as would probably help in the way of acting together on Sunday, November 15th at 12.30 in the Dun when an outline of the scheme of the Society would be laid before them.

The next meeting was fixed for Friday, November 13th, at 10 o'clock in the Dun.[116]

The statement of aims issued by the Society was a single printed sheet, which read:

> The Dun,
> Queen Street
> Cork

At a Meeting recently held in the Dun of those interested in the development of a native school of dramatists in Ireland, a Society called the Cork Dramatic Society was established.

The Society intends to confine its attention to the production of two classes of plays:

(a) Original plays written by the Society,

(b) Plays specially translated for us from foreign languages.

This scheme of work gives the Society a province of its own, and serves to distinguish it from dramatic societies already in existence in the city.

The Society has entered into arrangement with the Committee of Management of the Dun, whereby the large hall in their premises is to be fitted up as a theatre; the Society has got a corps of actors together, and is actually engaged in rehearsing a play which has been specially written for it. Other original plays are promised as well as some translations from the French and German. The Society hopes to do for Cork what similar societies have done for Dublin and Belfast.

We earnestly desire your help in this work. You may become a member on paying an annual subscription of 5/-. This subscription admits to all performances during the twelve months for which it is paid.

Faithfully yours,

Liam De Roiste, Chairman
Thomas O'Gorman, Treasurer
E. W. Lynam, B.A.
M. F. Healy, B.A.
T. McSweeney, B.A.
D. Corkery, Hon. Sec.[117]

The Cork Dramatic Society staged its first production, Daniel Corkery's *The Embers,* in 1909. Although it never did produce translations of foreign plays, it did produce about seventeen new plays by its own members. No masterpieces emerged from the Cork Dramatic Society, but a group which staged the first plays of Daniel Corkery, Terence McSwiney, Lennox Robinson, T. C. Murray, J. Bernard McCarthy, and Con O'Leary made a significant contribution indeed to the Irish drama.

1909

On 24 March, after an extended illness, J. M. Synge died in a Dublin hospital. Despite all of the angry controversy that had swirled around him and his plays, the press on the occasion of his death was almost uniformly eulogistic. *The Evening Mail* wrote, 'It will be known with feelings of the sincerest regret that Mr. J. M. Synge, the brilliant young Irish playwright and author, is no more. He passed away this morning in a Dublin hospital, at the early age of thirty-eight years. . . .' *The Evening Herald* wrote, 'In the presence of death all the controversies which raged round Mr. Synge's play are at an end, and it is but bare justice to his memory to state that all the best informed dramatic critics were loud in their praises of it as a play apart from the tendency, which it undoubtedly had, to wound the susceptibilities of a big section of the Irish people. . . .' *The Irish Times* wrote, 'The death of this gifted dramatist and writer when just entering on the fulness of his powers leaves a gap in our midst which will not be easily filled. . . .' *The Irish Independent* wrote, 'There will be throughout the country a consciousness that Ireland and her reviving drama have alike suffered a loss by the untimely death of Mr. Synge, which the very uniqueness of his talent renders only the more acute.' *The Northern Whig* wrote, 'In the four years that have elapsed since the production of *Riders to the Sea* he has achieved a record of work that establishes his fame on a sound foundation, and his death at thirty-seven on the threshold of a great career is a national loss, as tragic in its way as that of Thomas Davis.' *The Manchester Guardian* wrote, 'His greatness lies not in promise but in achievement, and he will one day be recognised by the many, as he has already been by the few who knew him and his plays, as one of the greatest men of our time — certainly as standing among the foremost English-writing playwrights.'

The Evening Herald secured an interview with Yeats:

Asked generally as to what he thought of Mr. Synge as a writer, he replied, with emphasis — "I think he was a great dramatic genius, and one of the foremost prose writers of his time."

And then he went on to deplore what he described as the unjust treatment meted out to Mr. Synge by his fellow-countrymen. "He was probably," said Mr. Yeats, "worse treated by his country than any writer, not even excepting Keats. The reviews of Keats's works in the *Quarterly* were infamous, and the treatment of Synge by a section of the Irish press will be equally infamous."

Speaking of Mr. Synge's works, Mr. Yeats said — "Synge was almost entirely occupied by this country, with its problems and with its life. He wrote for it. Although many of his plays were successfully performed on the Continent, he never saw any of the performances. The very nature of the form he selected—the dialect drama—showed his pre-occupation with Ireland, for only Irish actors could play it." [1]

The Independent published a reminiscence by D. J. O'Donoghue:

My own acquaintance with him began about ten years ago. In a letter I received from W. B. Yeats in the year 1899, just as I was about to start for Paris, the latter called my attention to the fact that in the hotel where I always stayed there was then living "an Irishman named Synge," who was well worth knowing, and who was anxious to meet fellow-countrymen with literary tastes. Yeats had just returned from his first visit to France. Like many other Irishmen, he stayed at a small hotel in the Rue Corneille, opposite the Odeon Theatre, which has an interesting history, too long to narrate here. It has been somewhat transformed internally of late years, but externally and, indeed, in other particulars, it still remains the Bohemian resort it used to be. Readers of *Trilby* will recall that it was the hotel of Little Billee. It was for many years the residence of John O'Leary and other notable Irishmen. . . . As it happens, I did not meet him [Synge] on the occasion of the 1899 visit, for he had left the hotel for a small room near by, where he was able to make more of his slender means than in any hotel, however moderate.

As was the general custom with students, he furnished his small room (in a house in the Rue d'Assas, facing the Luxembourg Gardens) by a few purchases in the Montparnasse quarter, and there lived his rather lonely life for several years, broken only by his yearly visit to the Aran Islands, where he was studying Irish at possibly its purest source. I met him in Paris in the following year, and sat for many hours each day with him in his little room or in a small neighbouring cafe, talking over the possibilities of literary life, and perhaps building castles in the air, a pastime than which no career offers more opportunities to the optimist. When talk lagged Synge would take down his violin, one of his few consolations, and play over many mournful Irish airs, melodies which appealed to his somewhat sad nature. Then as always, though a most charming and kindly companion, and Irish of the Irish in his sympathies, his outlook was a little morbid, and decidedly cosmopolitan. . . . I do not think Synge loved the glare and crash of the battle, his essentially kindly and modest nature shrinking from such publicity. It cannot be said that he unduly forced himself on anyone, nor do I believe he ever wished anybody else to thrust him too prominently before the public. Now that the smoke of the battle has lifted to some extent, even those whose outlook on Irish life was not the same, will regret the death of a notable Irishman, while his friends will always deplore the disappearance of one of the most engaging and delightful personalities of our time.[2]

T.P.'s Weekly early in April printed the following reminiscence by Thomas MacDonagh:

The day was a stormy, "wuthering" day, a day fit for the death of J. M. Synge, one of the most lonely spirits of our time. Synge was nervous, quiet, and shy, full of pity and charity, yet with something unquiet in his soul — in love with the things of an older age that still linger on — very original, and, for all his tenderness, brave and steadfast to this thought. People who knew him a little wondered how he could have written *The Playboy of the Western World*; "he was so different from that," they said. This gentleness was the difference — a difference purely superficial. No dramatist of the age has more certainly contributed great things to literature, because none has written with more sure touch of things which "are not of an age, but for all time." "One never hears from Mr. Synge's people," wrote Mr. Yeats in *Samhain* in 1905, "a thought that is of to-day and not of yesterday. He has written of the peasant as he is to all the ages, of the folk imagination as it has been shaped by centuries of life among the fields or on the fishing grounds."

Synge has not completed his thirty-eighth year; he was already thirty-two when he first came before the public as a dramatist and writer. His life till then had been full of wandering and adventure in strange places. After leaving Trinity College, Dublin, where he was educated, he spent many years on the Continent, in France, Germany, and Italy; then in the West of Ireland, living in close intimacy with the Irish-speaking peasantry and fisher-folk. His first plays, *Riders to the Sea* and *In the Shadow of the Glen*, were produced in 1903; *The Well of the Saints* followed in 1905; then, two years later, came *The Playboy of the Western World*, the cause of great

267

controversy and bitterness and strife in Ireland. *The Tinker's Wedding* has been published, but not played. Meanwhile he had been writing that wonderful book, *The Aran Islands*, and a series of papers on phases of life in remote parts of Ireland, published in *The Manchester Guardian*, and *The Shanachie*, all full of the same qualities that gave to his plays their peculiar value. He has left behind him, unfinished, a play, *The Sorrows of Deirdre*, which is said to be his masterpiece, and a book of poems.

I have looked up an old note-book and found a diary entry of my first meeting with Synge: "To-day went to Abbey to meet Synge. Very like painting and sketches of him by J. B. Yeats, yet with something unexpected in his complexion, which has a kind of dark pallor. Head large and massive, face serious and fine. Reminds me strongly of certain pictures of Oliver Cromwell. His utterance seems at first indistinct. Can now understand what D. meant by saying Synge does not speak Irish well; would say, no doubt, he does not speak French well, or, indeed, English. Very courteous and thoughtful. Gentle in every sense, I am sure, yet has the bearing of a strong man. I wonder if he is musical." (Now, since his death, I have learned that he was a fine musician and that he first attempted musical composition.) My next note is of a visit to his lodgings. There he read me some translations he had made of Petrarch's sonnets into that wonderful rich language of his, with the tang of the Irish on it — so splendidly different from the hackneyed speech found in other translations of the poet. It was not only the language of that people he acquired. David Christie Murray said of himself that he had lived the life of Tommy Atkins, gone "dahn tahn" with him and the rest, yet had missed doing with Tommy Atkins what Kipling did, just because he had not the simple genius to do it — to pick it up. So some writers in Ireland may say of themselves when they read Synge's work. They know every phrase in it; they know that language, that people, well. But they have not had the simple genius to do what Synge did.

Leconte de l'Isle, writing to Verlaine of his first poems said that his work would gain for him the hatred and the injuries of the fools who praise only what resembles themselves; and Baudelaire was congratulated on having invented a new shudder. To me the work of these two poets seems artificially weak compared with that of Synge — at least, the things in them that might win the hatred or bring the shudder. Synge has, with that new sarcasm which Mr. Yeats claims for him, a new "tang", a new savour of both matter and speech. People disliked his work not because it did not resemble themselves, but because it did resemble things that they knew, and resembled them as their own thought showed them, whether they were conscious of that or not. He has died young, "with all his music in him," but he has left work full of nature, reticent strength. He wrought so well, with such clear care, that his work always remains vivid and firm, of a harsh beauty, perhaps, but great with the rich power of real life and of the elemental.[3]

On 28 May James Cousins gave a lecture at the Sackville Cafe entitled 'J. M. Synge: his Art and Message'. As *The Freeman's Journal* reported:

Mr. W. J. Lawrence, who presided, said that it was a good thing to be able to hear something of Mr. Synge's work from one of the early dramatists of the present movement.

Mr. Cousins said that Mr. Synge's attitude towards the drama was that it should be a didactic presentation of reality — of actual persons who would go through a series of actual events and speak actual language. It was a curious situation to find that in the old age, so to speak, of Ireland they were busying themselves in building up a national drama which would portray truly the life of the country. Mr. Synge had been in the forefront of that movement, and had been regarded as its brightest star; he came to it with all the manhood of the English and Continental drama, and he appeared in the movement as having an old head on young shoulders — a Triton among the minnows. Mr. Synge had deliberately adopted a certain patois, and had stated that he took most of his dialogue direct from life. That might give some light in regard to the curious mixture of feelings evolved by the production of his plays. To the lecturer his plays were something other than drama merely — his genius was essentially lyrical and only secondarily dramatic; but that did not mean that he was undramatic. The special patois adopted by him obscured what might otherwise be revealed. If instead of going to the Aran Islands he took the same extraordinary quality of fine art, and worked on it, and had given them something of himself, Mr. Cousins believed that he would have given to the world something infinitely more valuable, whereas the lecturer feared that the work of Mr. Synge as bequeathed to the Irish people would have a certain evanescent power at present, and then a more or less academic interest for those who meddle in dramatic things in years to come. The weakness in Mr. Synge's work, and in a good deal of other work presented in Ireland, was the preoccupation of technique and language, and an insufficiency of teaching in the truest sense of the drama. It was futile to be told that everything had to be accepted on the plea that art was a law unto itself. The uplifting of Ireland by ideals, by teaching, was more important than the artistic idea of actuality. Their imagination should be lifted up, and they should be sent away from a play with feelings of exaltation rather than abasement. The lecturer said that he greatly enjoyed the way things were taken in the Abbey Theatre on the previous night at the performance of *The Playboy of the Western World*. It showed a great advance of mutual understanding.

On the motion of Mr. Sheehy-Skeffington, seconded by Mr. F. Ryan, a vote of thanks was passed to the lecturer.[4]

The view of another of the playwrights was William Boyle's, 'To my mind he was essentially a foul-mouthed person who hated mankind at large and his own country people in particular.' [5]

*   *   *

Norreys Connell who, after the death of Synge, became the managing director of the Abbey for a short time, was a prolific and distinguished man of letters whose real name was Conal Holmes O'Connell O'Riordan. He was born in Dublin in 1874 and educated at Clongowes Wood College. He went to London in his teens, contributing to various journals and publishing his first book, *In the Green Park*, in 1896. He acted for J. T. Grein's Independent Theatre where he made the acquaintance of Shaw. He was active in the Irish Literary Society where he knew Yeats. He lived a full and eventful life and achieved a reputation as a witty and spirited writer. Neither his plays nor his many novels are much read today, but this is quite an injustice, for his *Adam of Dublin* tetralogy and his four volumes about the Irish soldier David Quinn would repay attention.

On 8 April Miss Horniman wrote to Connell:

Mr. Yeats tells me that you wish me to write to you that I am willing for you to become a Director. I am not only willing, but glad, yet we must all feel sad that the reason for the change is the sad death of Mr. Synge.

I believe that you have read my letter of February 9th to which I still hold. . . . You have my sympathy in regard to wishing to feel that your labours would be towards making a permanency. Yet as things stand at present it is impossible for anyone to know how matters will work out during the next few months. You might find the position untenable or that it would be impossible to overcome the various difficulties.

The leases run out in April 1910 and the Patent in December 1910, and next November I have arranged with my lawyer to decide whether I shall renew them for another term or whether for only one year.

I propose that at the end of next October you shall decide whether you feel that it would be of any use for you to remain at the Abbey. I shall know how the accounts stand up to August 31st and how the performances have succeeded during September and October and then I shall be able to make the offer to the Directors or to refuse to do so for reasons I consider to be good.

The performances I saw at Manchester lately did not encourage me in the idea that I should make the offer eventually. Your becoming a Director, bringing in practical knowledge of the professional stage and releasing Mr. Yeats from part of his burden, gives me the hope that it may be possible for me to make this offer next October.

It would be a great satisfaction to me for the Abbey venture *to live*, but I will not extend its life in a moribund condition a week more than I am obliged.[6]

Seán Barlow wrote of Connell:

About the beginning of 1909, Mr. Norreys Connell (Conal O'Riordan) came to the Abbey as manager and producer, and he was one of the most courteous and considerate men I have ever met, always cheerful, and painstaking at rehearsals, polite to everyone; although he could be sarcastic when necessary.

He remained at the Abbey for about eight months, during which time he produced two of his own plays, *An Imaginary Conversation* and *Time*. While we were on a visit to Cork, he wrote a letter of advice to the players, to be read by Mr. Henderson, who was the secretary at that time, and the reading was very unfavourably received by the members of the Company. Soon after Mr. Norreys Connell left the Abbey.[7]

The letter was written on 18 April, and in its upper corner Yeats added, 'Connell wants you to read this to company. Lady Gregory and I think well of what he suggests and are of course in agreement generally. I should have sent it before.   W.B.Y.'

Dear Mr. Henderson,

. . . With regard to the performances of *The Heather Field* last week I consider that they were on the whole, bearing in mind the difficulties presented by the play and the youth and limited experience of the performers creditable to the Company. There were indeed moments when I felt the play was going for all it is worth. On the other hand there were quite as many moments when it hung fire badly.

It is highly desirable that the company should make a regular habit of reading aloud good, modern intimate prose. Take a novel, let us say, by John Galsworthy and let each member in turn read a chapter of it to the others — the tendency to gabble and mispronounce will very quickly be checked by listeners unable to understand. Only the interruption must not be impertinent, no listener must appear to take it for granted that he is right and the reader wrong. It will be best to follow some such formula as "I beg your pardon, please read that again."

It is the desire of my co-directors and myself not only to make our performances at the Abbey as perfect as is within our power but also to train a school of actors who, even if one by one they should leave us to seek a wider field, or if the Abbey itself should cease to be, will, wherever they go, prove a credit to us, to themselves and above all to their country. We want the term "Irish actor" to be a term of commendation and not as it too long has been, one of reproach.

We are therefore determined to tolerate no artistic snobbishness, among the members of our company. Apart from the sheer question of seniority, all are equal in our eyes and there can be no question however much we may value his or her performance, of any one actor or actress being starred above the rest — unless the Directors decide that it be fitting with regard to some exceptional event.

From time to time it may be that I shall be able to play some part big or little in the plays we stage at the Abbey, and it is clearly to be understood that on these occasions I fall into rank as actor with the rest of the company. Same as director, I know no distinction between the last recruit and myself.

Be good enough to communicate this letter to every member of the company.

Faithfully yours,
NORREYS CONNELL.[8]

272

In June the theatre was in London for a season at the Royal Court. Sara Allgood had become friendly with Mrs. Patrick Campbell during the production of Yeats's *Deirdre* and stayed at Mrs. Campbell's house. Mrs. Campbell suggested that Sally read a short story at a meeting, possibly for women's suffrage, which was being organised by Mrs. Edith Lyttleton. When Miss Horniman learned of this, she immediately erupted, had a lengthy and furious scene with Yeats, and fired off letters to Lady Gregory and Norreys Connell, neither of whom knew anything about the affair. Her letter of 1 July to Connell read:

> Dear Mr. Connell,
> Mr. Yeats has been told by me this evening that his taking no action on Sunday night to prevent Miss Sara Allgood from taking part in a political meeting was a distinct breach of the ground understanding that politics should be avoided in connection with the Abbey Theatre. Unless the Directors, Miss Sara Allgood and Mrs. Alfred Lyttleton each separately apologise to me for their action in this case, the subsidy will not be paid on September 1st (and up to Christmas 1910) and the Abbey Theatre will be let to a permanent tenant or else be put completely in the hands of Messrs. Cramer on that date.
> Yours sincerely,
> A. E. F. HORNIMAN[9]

The next day Connell wrote to Yeats:

> 218, Pittshanger Lane,
> Ealing. W.
> 2nd July 1909
>
> My dear Yeats,
> Here is Wade's balance sheet for our season at the Court, which I believe to be quite in order and of a highly satisfactory nature.
> This morning I had an incomprehensible letter from Miss Horniman from which I gather that she commands me to apologise to her because you did not restrain Sara Allgood from abetting Mrs. Lyttleton in a political demonstration.
> I cannot imagine what politics Sally has in common with Mrs. Lyttleton, but I am quite certain that this is the last straw upon the camel's back and that I have finally done with the Abbey Theatre. Please delete my name from the list of directors and believe that I shall always be proud to have been associated with you in this work.
> If you will suffer me to give you a piece of advice, it is

this — Take in Hone as co-director and bring back the Fays. They will be good in Lady Gregory's plays and I understand they are good in yours. If Miss Horniman is going to withdraw her subsidy, her aversion from them does not matter.

I am, with all good wishes,

As ever,

Yours,

NORREYS CONNELL[10]

There were then more accusations from Miss Horniman and explanations from everybody, and the result was that Miss Horniman finally received letters of apology from Yeats and Lady Gregory, Sara Allgood, Mrs. Lyttleton, and Mrs. Patrick Campbell. All of these letters retained considerable dignity, and Mrs. Campbell's was a small masterpiece of tact and charm. Miss Horniman's reply to Mrs. Pat does her as little credit as any letter she ever wrote, and so possibly it is best left unpublished.

The real loss of the whole sorry, silly affair was Norreys Connell who perhaps could have been a major Irish dramatist. He, however, was busy directing his new light comedy *Thalia's Teacup, or the Delights of Deceit*, which opened at the Royal Court on 24 July. And so, like many Irish dramatists before him, and at least St. John Ervine after him, Connell was divorced from the Irish stage.

*   *   *

Despite the disruptions of Synge's death and Connell's brief tenure, the theatre managed to mount new productions.

Lady Gregory's *The Miser*, adapted from Molière's *L'Avare*, was first presented on 21 January. *The Irish Times* applauded the adaptor's adroitness and noted the great amusement of the audience, but, nevertheless, remarked, 'It is not easy at times to associate certain phrases of the English, or rather Irish, version with the polished grace of the author, and putting such sayings as "Shure it's yourself is looking grand" into the mouth of a French dame is hardly convincing.' The main character of Harpagon was played by Arthur Sinclair, of whom *The Irish Times* said, 'Occasionally he was a trifle too vigorous when restraint was necessary, but nevertheless, his acting was in keeping with his reputation, and carried conviction.' The other roles were 'creditably sustained' or 'given a special word of praise' or 'an important factor in the success of the performance.'[11]

Jacques in *The Irish Independent* was both more critical and more specific:

274

There is one criticism to pass upon the production of Lady Gregory's translation of Molière's *L'Avare*. It was not Molière. If you take a Shaw's sausage, squeeze out the contents, and then fill the skin with all-spice and tit-bits of your own, you may achieve a very respectable home-made sausage, but though it has Shaw's skin, it's not Shaw's sausage. Molière's play as done last night at the Abbey Theatre was a home-made delectable with the brand "Molière's *Avare*" on the outside. It was well spiced by Lady Gregory, and the Abbey Theatre Company added the tit-bits. And to tell the truth, the small audience seemed to enjoy it. They laughed heartily over it. . . .

There's no need to labour criticism on last night's performance. The players gave us a few hours of comedy, but it was not French comedy. The dresses worn by Miss Sara Allgood, Miss Máire O'Neill, and Miss Eileen O'Doherty (a very clever young lady) were a feast for feminine eyes. The gorgeous outfit, with its trimmings of gold and lace, in which Mr. Fred O'Donovan was ever-present would have dazzled all the Mariannes in Paris. On the whole the gentlemen did more for the entertainment than the ladies. Messrs. Sinclair (the Miser), Kerrigan ("Valère"), and Eric Gorman (valet) entered right merrily into the spirit of the thing. But they did not, and they could not, give us the "atmosphere." Neither did they give us the clash between characters who embody different points of view, upon which comedy depends.[12]

A revision of *Kincora* was produced on 11 February. *The Irish Independent* wondered, 'Does this re-dressing of old themes serve any useful purpose?' To *Sinn Féin*, the answer was a most emphatic 'No!':

> O, where, Kincora! is Brian the Great?
> And where is the beauty that once was thine?
> O, where are the princes and nobles that sate
> At the feast in the halls and drank the red wine?
> Where, O Kincora? . . .

These lines of Mangan haunted me as I sat in the Abbey Theatre last week listening to the revised version of Lady Gregory's play, *Kincora*. All through the greater portion of the first Act there was jabbering and snarling among the servants of Kincora. I don't object to servants, but when I am led to believe that Kincora was mainly remarkable for its cantankerous servants with a steady flow of Kiltartan English,

I have a queer feeling that I am being had. . . . Once or twice Arthur Sinclair as King Brian lifted up the tone of the drama. But for hopelessly flat acting and deplorable stage management the rest of the thing beat all Abbey records. The degeneracy of the Abbey Theatre is painful. Not even in the matter of make-up was there a scrap of art displayed. King Brian had two daubs of black on his otherwise youthful cheeks to account for his advancing years in the third act. It looked as if he had given up washing. . . .

The presentation in revised form of *Kincora* should have the effect of establishing two things: that historical subjects cannot be handled by dramatists who have narrow conceptions, and that players who have abandoned all attempts to act are not privileged to call themselves artistes. If Lady Gregory wants to write historical drama (and I think she ought to leave it alone) she must bring, if she can, some treatment to bear upon it different to that which she brought to bear on her *Jackdaw* and *Workhouse Ward*. If James Clarence Mangan had been in the Abbey Theatre last week he would have considered his lines on Kincora prophetic. He would have repeated his question when he had witnessed the national and artistic degradation of a great subject.[13]

On 11 March the Abbey produced for the first time *Stephen Grey*, a one-act play by D. L. Kelleher about the almost inevitable Irish subject of love and land. *The Freeman's Journal* remarked:

At the Abbey Theatre last night the programme consisted of three items — the first production of a new one-act play by D. L. Kelleher, a lecture on Molière by Prof. Maurice Gerothwohl, D. Litt. (Professor of Romance Languages, Trinity College), and Lady Gregory's translation of Molière's three-act comedy, *The Rogueries of Scapin*. . . . With regard to the first item, Mr. Kelleher has presented in what may be described as tabloid form one of the familiar love tragedies of rural life in Ireland. The entire performance occupies only a very brief period. Nevertheless the author succeeds in *Stephen Grey*, "A Dream and an Incident," in telling a story that reeks of the turf fire, and is eloquent of that tragedy of poverty which has for so long hung like a pall over the rural community.[14]

The Irish Times remarked with an enigmatic pithiness, 'Mr. Kelleher's work occupied but a very small time in performance,

276

but it augurs well for much success when he will essay more ambitious flights as a playwright.' [15]

On 1 April, in *The Evening Herald*, 'Jack Point' reviewed Lennox Robinson's *Crossroads* and Norreys Connell's *Time*:

> Mr. Robinson has begun well, will do much better, and may even fill the place left vacant by the lamented death of Mr. J. M. Synge. A clever little piece by Norreys Connell, concerning a privateer, a girl, and Father Time, the scene being the road — a high road — to Rome was capitally played by Mr. Kerrigan, Miss Máire O'Neill, and the author himself. Mr. Kerrigan as the painter — a bounder of the worst type — was most amusing. Miss O'Neill made a charming model, and Mr. Connell was very effective as Father Time. [16]

'Jacques' in *The Irish Independent* wrote of *Crossroads*, 'It is a powerful play, powerfully acted. . . . There was a one-act piece entitled *Time*. The author calls it a passing phantasy. The author is right. Only it doesn't pass quick enough.' However, H.S.D. of *The Evening Mail* wrote:

> If there should be in the mind of any worthy citizen of Dublin a doubt, however diminuendo, that the Abbey theatre has justified itself by faith and works, let him give himself the benefit of that doubt, and book a seat for tonight's performance of the *Crossroads*, Mr. S. L. Robinson's new play. He will not regret it. It would not be fair to Mr. Robinson to say that his play is a great play, or that it sounds the depth of human passion. But if its subject has no alluring charm or novelty or profundity, it is at once to be admitted that the young author handles it well, that he holds his audience as the Ancient Mariner held the wedding guests, and leads up to a really strong scene in the last act, closing his high, if sometimes shaky argument, with the curtain at once artistically effective and dramatic, and finely resisting the temptation of the happy ending that would spare our feelings and spoil his play. . . .
>
> There followed a fantasy by Mr. Norreys Connell, in which the author plays the part of Time. An artist and his lass are trudging on foot to Rome, and they sit down to rest by an old well at the roadside. At the well sits an old man, who, of course, is Time. With a cold and bloodless cynicism he listens to the posturing artist, bragging of what he is and will be. It must, of course, be entertaining to Time, the Avenger, to sit where he saw Caesar leading his troops across the Rubicon,

277

and watching the little puppets of an hour, who have their day and cease to be. Time, doubtless, appreciates the sorrow of woman, denied the love she craves for by the devotee of art, building, not for Time and Eternity, but for the dustbin of oblivion. The little fantasy is conceived in a delicate vein of poetic irony. . . . Mr. Connell's delivery of his lines was something at once musical, scholarly, and delightful. Miss O'Neill was excellent as the young girl. Mr. Kerrigan, full of the ichor of life, as the artist, but a little too jerky at times. . . .[17]

The Freeman's Journal gave only a sentence to Norreys Connell's Time, but thought Crossroads 'one of the cleverest plays that has ever been produced at the Abbey Theatre.' Of the acting, the reviewer remarked:

Ellen McCarthy is a brilliant character study, and the part lost nothing in Miss Sara Allgood's interpretation of it last night. Miss Allgood was very pleasing as the young girl setting out for the country, with all the optimism of youth and great ideas, but she was at her best in her quiet, subdued dignity in the tragic closing scene. Arthur Sinclair was perfectly natural as the farmer Tom Dempsey, and Fred O'Donovan filled the part of Brian Connor creditably.[18]

On 15 April, under Norreys Connell's stage direction, the Abbey revived Edward Martyn's The Heather Field. But although the play was praised by The Freeman's Journal, The Irish Times, and The Evening Mail, it was not really a success. Probably the general reaction of the audience was that of 'Jacques' in The Irish Independent:

It may be quite the proper thing to pretend to like a play of the order of The Heather Field, a work in three acts, by Edward Martyn, revived last night at the Abbey Theatre. If you would be numbered among the intellectual and literary you will praise it, and only speak of it in bated breath of admiration. It didn't hit me that way a bit, so I suppose I'm done for intellectually. Fact is, I can't pretend I liked it the least. If there was much more of it, it would have given me the jumps. The spectacle of Mr. Arthur Sinclair elocutionising like Martin Harvey and attitudinising like Mazinini the Marvellous Mesmerist, through three long acts, and goodness knows how many flamboyant speeches, didn't appeal to me. Of course, Mr. Sinclair was trying to show us (and hide it from the people in the play) that he was off his chump. The people in the play didn't see this till the last act, which was really a pity.

How splendidly Mr. Fred O'Donovan is coming on. He gave us the part last night of a landowner. In make-up, speech, gesture, he was tip-top. Mr. O'Donovan is the most improved actor of this exceedingly clever Abbey troupe. Sara Allgood fumed, fretted, sobbed, sighed, and scolded in her part, and Máire O'Neill looked just stunning in her Lady Shrule Directoire and walking costumes. But, as for the Play — no, I'd rather not.[19]

On 29 April the Abbey presented Lord Dunsany's mordant one-act fantasy *The Glittering Gates*. Unfortunately, on the same evening the Theatre of Ireland, playing at the Rotunda, produced for the first time Seumas O'Kelly's *The Shuiler's Child* and Rutherford Mayne's one-act comedy, *The Gomeril*. Dunsany's play, despite its later fame and popularity, went almost unnoticed.

Norreys Connell's one-act, *An Imaginary Conversation*, was produced on 13 May. The play is little more than its title suggests, an imaginary conversation between Robert Emmet, Tom Moore, and Tom's sister Kate. There is some talk, some songs, and a final moment of Emmet weeping about his country. 'Jacques', despite the patriotic elements of the play, could not refrain from noting:

> As the conversation is only imaginary, I suppose I may not ask how it could happen that a melody not published by Moore until 1807 (The melodies appeared between 1807 and 1834) could be used as a national anthem by Emmet, who was executed in 1803. The audience did not stop to think of that. They cheered the work and the author . . . most enthusiastically.[20]

The reviewers for *The Evening Mail* and *The Irish Times*, as well as 'Jacques', took issue with the dialogue given to Moore:

> That there was an interview of such a character has been pretty well established, but there is equally clear evidence that the Moore family were possessed of rather more culture than the author credits them with. That Tom Moore, referring to his musical compositions, should speak of "one of them" old things, and in other instances do equally glaring violence to the English language is most improbable.[21]

The Evening Mail added that 'the picture given of Moore is in some respects rather that of a jackeen of the period than of a young man of genius and refinement whose soul is fired with literary ambitions.'[22]

279

Connell's play was preceded by Synge's *The Well of the Saints*, somewhat revised, and all of the papers complained of:

> . . . unconscionable delays between the acts of Mr. Synge's play, and, worst of all, in the interval that elapsed after its conclusion, and which lasted for fully 25 minutes; it was close on half-past 10 o'clock when the curtain rose on *An Imaginary Conversation*.[23]

Connell's play appeared again on the programme two weeks later, this time in conjunction with a revival of Synge's *The Playboy of the Western World*. Despite the sympathetic press on the event of Synge's death, there was some opposition to the revival of *The Playboy*. One of the most vehemently opposed was, predictably, W. J. Lawrence, who wrote:

> Not since the death of Charles Stewart Parnell has Ireland had a leader in any department of public life of so magnificent an obstinacy as Mr. W. B. Yeats. . . . Throughout his disturbing career as leader of the Irish dramatic movement he has steadily pursued the suicidal policy of jeering at public opinion. . . . Willy-nilly, Synge's forbidding comedy is to be forced down our loathing throats, if need be, possibly, at the end of the baton. . . .[24]

The revival was directed by Connell; Fred O'Donovan took W. G. Fay's role of Christy; Sydney Morgan now played old Mahon; and J. M. Kerrigan took Frank Fay's role of Shawn Keogh. The new production was greeted with some booing and hissing on the fall of the curtain, but there was no demonstration and there was considerable applause. The reaction of the press was similarly mixed. *The Evening Mail* thought that the play had been revised and its coarser language eliminated, and *The Irish Times* recorded a cautious approval:

> . . . there was always the haunting suspicion that the outbreak of hostility on the former occasion had given *The Playboy* a fictitious value, and that it is really inferior to other plays written by Mr. Synge. With this qualification, *The Playboy* must still be regarded as displaying considerable dramatic ability; there are many bright flashes of humour to illumine the unwholesome picture, and if the audience are not edified, they are frequently amused.[25]

'Jack Point' in *The Evening Herald* thought that the original objection to the word 'shift' was childish and ridiculous, but that

280

the play was still 'little short of a slander on the people, especially the women of the West'. He went on to say:

> Even the London critics — never safe guides as to Irish plays — recognise that, taken as a serious study of Irish manners, it was decidedly rough on the people of Connaught, and tried to discover a highly-entertaining and original farce, brimful of humour, and picturesque in dialogue. I fail to see where the farce comes in, and where exists the wonderful dialogue, and, indeed, am of the opinion that *The Playboy of the Western World* is the poorest stuff in every respect Mr. Synge ever wrote.[26]

The most vitriolic account was that of *The Evening Telegraph* which, although unsigned, sounds in content and style as if it had been written by W. J. Lawrence:

> No useful purpose can be served by obtruding on the notice of playgoers this unique mixture of vulgarity, coarseness, sensuality, brutality, and profanity. Apart from its viciously libellous character, it is essentially unhealthy in tone. Nor has it any redeeming merit in dialogue, construction, or dramatic situation. On its worth as a play it could not hold the boards for a single week. . . . It is, perhaps, a good thing that it was heard from beginning to end, and that a full opportunity was thus given to all of discovering its inherent wretchedness as a play, and of getting the full whiff of its sickening squalor. There have been some alterations made, if we recall the text aright, but no treatment could disinfect the piece. It is as repulsive and unwholesome as ever.[27]

Lawrence, however, was not the theatre's only critic.

It was on 29 May that the Abbey Theatre was visited by Mr. Malachy Macfadden, who had drink taken. As Conal O'Riordan described the incident:

> He wandered on into Brunswick Street to see what was doing at the Queen's. It was closed, so he turned back again and crossed Butt Bridge and Beresford Place. There was a crowd there, a very modest one, listening to a short man with a black moustache who addressed them from the steps of Liberty Hall, using language not in Mr Macfadden's vocabulary. So Mr Macfadden just roared "Libertymyelbo" at him and passed on into Abbey Street. . . . There on his left hand he caught sight of yellow bills, such as those which had attracted Adam's curiosity many months before. They stood

outside a building he still remembered as the Morgue. He used to go there often when he was a lad, to see the coroner's jury sitting on sailors and women dragged out of the river, or murdered down the quayside as far as the North Wall. . . . Now the place was turned into a queer sort of theatre, not a real theatre like the Queen's, where you could see a railway engine running over a policeman, or the British Army scuttling for life from a patriot in a green tie, but where they spouted like street preachers and see-sawed with their hands. He remembered once on a Bank Holiday, seeing the word, *Kincora* on the bills. He was with two other fellows who had a sup taken and they all thought Kincora must be about a lad drinking Mooney's whiskey, and either getting funny on it or going grand and mad, so they all paid sixpence each and went in. But sure it was nothing of the kind. The place was as dismal as a methody chapel and not a soul scarcely in it but an old Protestant clergyman asleep in the stalls. As for the play, you couldn't make head or tail of it, except that the leading character let on to be called King Brian Boru, and talked as if he were tipsy, but he said nothing about drinking Kincora; and the whole thing being obviously a fraud, at the end of the first act they threatened to wreck the theatre unless they got their money back, and so came away and spent their sixpences on real Kincora in Marlborough Street.

But the placard now in front of him was different. That said, *The Playboy of the Western World*. He scratched his head to think. He seemed to remember hear tell that was an immoral play, a play insulting to religion and decency, that had been hissed off the stage years ago. . . . Was it possible they had the impudence to put it on the stage again after Marlborough Street had declared against it? He knew he had heard of something grossly indecent in it, but could not recall what it was, being a bit moidered by the drink and the contrariness of everything to-night . . . he was curious to know was this really the same play . . . he fumbled six coppers out of his pocket and went in.

Rotten hole the Abbey Theatre, you couldn't swing a cat in it, and yet not half full. How did they make it pay? Was it subsidised by Dublin Castle to corrupt the people? The audience dotted about were mostly young men, reading books or papers, without a spark of excitement in them. They didn't seem to care if the curtain never went up. Mr. Macfadden was the old enthusiastic style of playgoer: he stamped for thirteen minutes until the orchestra came in, and quieted him with familiar airs, he dozed a little until they ceased, and then stamped, like a giant refreshed, until the curtain at last rose. The play was not at all what he had been led to expect: two gentlemen and a lady in queer old clothes talked gibberish to each other as politely as if they lived in Rathmines. One of them was called Robert Emmet, but he was no more like the Robert Emmet that lived in Mr Macfadden's spiritual world, than was the Brian Boru of *Kincora* like Mr Macfadden's Brian Boru, that was done to death by Strongbow on Mud Island. The whole story might have been *Kincora* over again, only for trifling differences in the costumes and scenery, and the presence of a queer sort of piano-organ that played "Let Erin Remember," when there was no one near enough to lay hand or foot on it. Then Robert Emmet burst out crying because it wouldn't let him get a word in edgeways and the curtain came down.

"Is that tripe what you call *The Playboy of the Western World*?" Mr Macfadden shouted to the nearest group of young men.

They laughed shyly, and one of them, consulting his programme, answered that it was called *An Imaginary Conversation*.

"Conversationmiyelbo," cried Mr Macfadden. "I paid my money to see *The Playboy of the Western World*, and if they can't show me that I'll take it somewhere there's a bit of fun."

"If you wait long enough you'll see the *Playboy* all right," they answered, and gradually sidled further from him, not fancying his truculent tone. So he led off his heels again and kept at it, orchestra or no orchestra, until he fell asleep and snored solidly through the first and second acts. But the clatter of the last act woke him and he gazed around resentfully.

"What the hell is all this hullabaloo?" he demanded in a voice that drowned the simulated bass of old Christy Mahon. But the actors, inured to interruption, took no notice nor halted in the wild business of the tragic farce. Mr Macfadden was enthralled: half a dozen men were holding another down that had his teeth buried in yet another's calf, and a young girl was trying to get at one or other of them with a pair of red-hot tongs. Mr Macfadden clapped his hands: he had never seen anything half so good on the stage before. A fellow in a nightshirt chasing a girl in pyjamas was poor fun compared with this. "There's a bit of humour for you," he called delightedly to his neighbours, who affected not to hear but huddled still farther away. Louder grew the riot on the stage, overwhelming at last even his approving voice, and he gazed spellbound, forgetful even of his injured honour. Then suddenly there was a hush: a half animal form crawled in from the back of the scene, reared up, and revealed a hairy monster of a man with a clotted bandage round his skull. Mr Macfadden gathered that he was the father of the young lad with the nippy teeth, the others were holding down and the girl going to burn with the tongs. Mr Macfadden was annoyed with him as a kill-joy, and hissed and hooted, but still the actors went on acting imperturbably: no one there or in the audience took the smallest notice of him. It was maddening in itself for so big a man to be ignored. . . . But a moment later he could stand it no longer; for the young lad was no sooner released from his captors, at his father's instance, than he turned on the latter and drove him with violence off the stage.

This was the last straw. Mr Macfadden leaped on to his seat and howled at the top of his voice, "I call the Almighty to witness that this play is a bloody scandal to good Catholics. . . . Playboymiyelbo! Playboymiyelbo!" But still the performance went on, until against his own roar he could hear the girl shrieking as though it were a personal matter between her and himself which should have the last word: "My grief I've surely lost him now, the only playboy of the Western World!" And the curtain fell amidst applause chiefly intended to smother Mr Macfadden's language.[28]

*　　　*　　　*

With this production the Abbey then closed until August, in order to go on tour in England. Actually, this was the second English tour of the year. On 20 February *The Freeman's Journal* had reported on the first:

The Abbey Theatre Company has made another great success in Manchester. The *Guardian*, in a long and admirably written study of their work, has nothing but enthusiastic praise for the actors and for the plays. Mr. George Fitzmaurice's play, *The Piedish*, is praised most warmly. "In Mr. Synge, Mr. Fitzmaurice has gone to school with a good master. He has caught the secret of the greatest pieces that the Abbey Theatre has staged: that is to say, he has that imaginative reach which gets deep down into the elementary terrors and desires, and hopes and fears, of the world; that insight which pierces through the surface of common life and sees into the great forces beneath." Praise is given in a curious way to the speaking of the actors. The writer says that at first the play, *The Piedish*, was not easy to follow. "No doubt this was due in some measure to our unfamiliarity with the beautiful and rhythmical diction of the players, which our brute ears, accustomed to the harsher, less melodious sounds of every day, take a little time to follow. . . ." Mr. Norreys Connell's play, *The Piper*, stirs the critic to words of real beauty about Ireland's National cause; however that play has been taken here, abroad it carries the sense of the grandeur of Ireland's hope, even in defeat and present failure.[29]

The critic of *The Guardian* was James Agate, who had this to say about the acting and staging of *The Well of the Saints*:

> It was good to see Mr Arthur Sinclair manage so tactfully and surely the compromise between naturalism and a consciously beautiful treatment of the lines. His Martin was both cunning and childishly wondering. He *was* the old blind beggar, calling a halt to deliver the rhythmic cadence of a fine passage without ceasing to be the beggar, in the way that a great Macbeth can spout his thirty lines of splendid irrelevancies without ceasing to be Macbeth. His recognition of each man after the healing was full of the new wonder of sight, and his wooing of the girl amazingly fine in conception and certain in execution. It was a pity that he was not sure of all his lines; perhaps greater certainty will strengthen his voice, for we are afraid that people who did not know the play missed a good many fine things. Miss Sara Allgood was, as she always is, perfect both in vigour and bent submission. We thought Miss Máire O'Neill's Molly of extraordinary value. There is an absolute sureness of execution about everything she does that puts our *ingenues* to shame. Indeed, one does not like to use so stagey a word in connection with these players. Miss O'Neill had radiance as well as the good looks with which many of the young ladies over here would put us off. Beautiful, too, the staging — a few purposely shabby wings, a simple back-cloth, a single green bush, a daring orange sky, and a frame of red — a summary, not a representation, of Irish scenery, as the play is the spirit rather than the bodily likeness of the Irish poor.[30]

On 7 June the Abbey opened at the Royal Court Theatre in London, and the critic of *The Sunday Times* found a good many flaws in the productions:

. . . having seen a good many performances of this company
. . . I have come to the conclusion that there is a tendency to
over-estimate the quality of both plays and acting. Some of
the plays are nothing more than elaborated jokes.[31]

On the acting of *The Workhouse Ward*, he wrote:

The acting remains fairly competent, and especially Messrs.
Sinclair and O'Donovan and Miss Sara Allgood display much
versatility in their several parts which they represent. But the
stage management is not by any means as efficient as it
used to be.

This was particularly noticeable in *The Well of the Saints*
when the miracle happened. Instead of betraying such emotion
as would be natural in the vividly imaginative mind of the
Celtic race, those actors who had nothing to say made either
doll-like movements or stood about like logs, so that the
picture lost much of its effect. The rank and file of the
company still bear the impress of dilettantism, which at one
time was rather a quality than the reverse, for the actors sup-
plemented by ardour what they lacked in craft; but since the
company is no longer an amateur society but more or less a
regular theatre, the enthusiasm has somewhat suffered by
routine and individual crudeness is more obvious than before.[32]

*　　*　　*

The great quarrel of 1909 was not over the revival of *The Playboy*, but over a new play by Bernard Shaw, *The Shewing Up of
Blanco Posnet*. The play was to have opened in late May in London, but the Lord Chamberlain refused to licence it.

Discussing the prohibition with a representative of *The
Daily Chronicle*, Mr. Shaw said:— "I do not want to make
any detailed statement yet, but the news is certainly true, and
I may perhaps confess that what baffles me about the Censor's
action in this case is that he has refused to licence *The Shewing
Up of Blanco Posnet*, not because it is irreligious, but because
it is religious. What Mr. Redford demands is practically that
I should cut out the play. So I am afraid there will be nothing
for it but to abandon the production." [33]

Actually, there was at this time a very considerable controversy
in England about the powers of the Lord Chamberlain. A Joint
Committee of both Houses of Parliament was meeting during
August to hear testimony from many well-known producers,

writers, actors and critics about the effect of the English censorship. There was, however, no official censor for the Irish theatre, and it was to the Abbey Theatre that Shaw turned for a production of his banned play.

The Abbey announced that it would re-open on 24 August with a production of *The Playboy*, and then on the following night it would give the first production of *The Shewing Up of Blanco Posnet*. This announcement caused a flurry in Dublin Castle, and the following exchange of letters:

Dublin Castle, 20 August, 1909.

Dear Lady Gregory—I am directed by the Lord Lieutenant to state that his Excellency's attention has been called to an announcement in the public Press that a play entitled *The Shewing Up of Blanco Posnet* is about to be performed in the Abbey Theatre.

This play was written for production in a London Theatre, but its performance was disallowed by the authority which in England is charged with the censorship of stage plays. The play does not deal with an Irish subject, and it is not an Irish play in any other sense than that its author was born in Ireland. It is now proposed to produce this play in the Abbey Theatre, which was founded for the express purpose of encouraging dramatic art in Ireland, and of fostering a dramatic school growing out of the life of the country.

The play in question does not seem well adapted to promote these laudable objects, or to belong to the class of plays originally intended to be performed in the Abbey Theatre, as described in the evidence given on the hearing of the application of the Patent.

His Excellency, after the most careful consideration, has arrived at the conclusion that in its original form the play is not in accordance with the assurance given by those interested when the Patent was applied for, or with the conditions and restrictions contained in the Patent as granted by the Crown.

As you are the holder of the Patent, in trust for the generous founder of the Theatre, his Excellency feels bound to call your attention, and also the attention of those with whom you are associated, to the terms of the Patent, and to the serious consequences which the production of the play in its original form might entail.

I am to add that the Lord Lieutenant would deeply regret should it become necessary to take any action which might inflict loss upon the public-spirited lady who founded a home for the Irish National Theatre, or which might result in depriving the Society, that has already done good work for Irish dramatic art, of the means of prosecuting a worthy enterprise with which his Excellency is in entire sympathy, and which, if judiciously pursued, may do much to refine and elevate the literary taste of the community. — I am, yours most truly,

J. B. DOUGHERTY.

Nassau Hotel, 20th August, 1909.

Dear Sir James — Thank you for your letter. Please explain to His Excellency that the play is not in its original form as refused by the Censor. The printed version is not in that form, our modified stage version is still less in that form, and we are now taking out another passage in deference to His Excellency's opinion expressed to us yesterday.

I will not write at greater length, as I have just (11 o'clock) come back tired from a full rehearsal. — Believe me, sincerely yours,

AUGUSTA GREGORY

Dublin Castle, 21st August, 1909.

Dear Lady Gregory — I have received your letter, which I shall duly submit to the Lord Lieutenant. — I am, yours most truly.

J. B. DOUGHERTY.[34]

What happened next may be seen in the following story from *The Irish Times*:

A meeting of the directors of the Abbey Theatre was held on Saturday afternoon last for the purpose of considering what action should be taken with regard to the communication received by them from the Lord Lieutenant touching the production of Mr. G. B. Shaw's play, *The Shewing Up of Blanco Posnet*.

The meeting was conducted in private, and at its conclusion a communication was made to the Press, which stated: —

If our patent is in danger it is because the English Censorship is being extended to Ireland, or because the Lord Lieutenant is about to revive, on what we consider a frivolous pretext, a right not exercised for 150 years to forbid at his pleasure any play produced in any Dublin theatre, all these theatres holding their patent from him.

We are not concerned with the question of the English

Censorship, but we are very certain that the conditions of the two countries are different, and that we must not by accepting the English Censor's ruling give away anything of the liberty of the Irish theatre of the future. Neither can we accept without protest the exercise of the Lord Lieutenant's claim at the bidding of the Censor or otherwise. The Lord Lieutenant is definitely a political personage, holding office from the party in power, and what would sooner or later grow into a political censorship cannot be lightly accepted.

We have ourselves, considering the special circumstances of Ireland, cut out some passages which we thought might give offence at a hasty hearing, but these are not the passages because of which the English Censor refused his licence.

W. B. YEATS, Managing Director.

A. GREGORY, Director and Patentee.

On Sunday night the following explanation was issued on behalf of the Abbey Theatre Company:

The statement communicated to certain of Saturday's papers makes the following explanation necessary:—

During the last week we have been vehemently urged to withdraw Mr. Shaw's play, which had already been advertised and rehearsed, and have refused to do so. We would have listened with attention to any substantial argument; but we found, as we were referred from one well-meaning personage to another, that no one would say the play was hurtful to man, woman, or child. Each said that someone else had thought so, or might think so. We were told that Mr. Redford had objected, that the Lord Chamberlain had objected, and that, if produced, it will certainly offend excited officials in London, and might offend officials in Dublin, or the Law Officers of the Crown, or the Lord Lieutenant, or Dublin society, or Archbishop Walsh, or the Church of Ireland, or rowdies up for the Horse Show, or newspaper editors, or the King. In these bewilderments and shadowy opinions there was nothing to change our conviction (which is also that of the leading weekly paper of the Lord Lieutenant's own party) that so far from containing offences for any sincere and honest mind, Mr. Shaw's play is a high and weighty argument upon the working of the Spirit of God in man's heart, or to show that it is not a befitting thing for us to set upon our stage the work of an Irishman, who is also the most famous of living dramatists, after that work had been silenced in London by what we believe an unjust decision.

289

One thing, however, is plain enough, an issue that swallows up all else, and makes the merit of Mr. Shaw's play a secondary thing. If our patent is in danger, it is because the decisions of the English Censor are being brought into Ireland, and because the Lord Lieutenant is about to revive on what we consider a frivolous pretext, a right not exercised for 150 years, to forbid, at the Lord Chamberlain's pleasure any play produced in any Dublin theatre, all these theatres holding their patents from him.

We are not concerned with the question of the English censorship, now being fought out in London, but we are very certain that the conditions of the two countries are different, and that we must not, by accepting the English Censor's ruling, give away anything of the liberty of the Irish theatre of the future. Neither can we accept without protest the revival of the Lord Lieutenant's claim at the bidding of the Censor or otherwise. The Lord Lieutenant is definitely a political personage holding office from the party in power, and what would sooner or later grow into a political censorship cannot be lightly accepted.

We have ourselves taken out certain passages which we thought, considering the special circumstances of Ireland, might offend a hasty hearer; and one other as an act of courtesy to Lord Aberdeen, but these are not the passages because of which the English Censor refused his licence.

W. B. YEATS, Managing Director.
A. GREGORY, Director and Patentee.

Abbey Theatre, August 22nd, 1909.[35]

On Monday, 23 August, *The Evening Telegraph* carried the text of a letter from Shaw to Yeats, and an interview with the Lord Lieutenant:

LETTER FROM MR. SHAW

Mr. W. B. Yeats has received a letter from Mr. Bernard Shaw, dated August 22, which contains the following message: — "To-day the papers have arrived. . . . You can make a further statement to the Press that since the last statement Lady Gregory has written to me pointing out that a certain speech was open to misconstruction, and that I immediately re-wrote it much more strongly and clearly; consequently the play will now be given exactly as by the author, without concessions of any kind to the attacks that have been made upon it, except that, to oblige the Lord Lieutenant, I have consented to withdraw the word "immoral" as applied to the relations between a woman of bad character and her accomplices. In doing so I wish it to be stated that I still regard these relations as not only immoral, but vicious; nevertheless, as an English Censorship apparently regards them as delightful and exemplary, and the Lord Lieutenant does not wish to be understood as contradicting the English Censorship, I am quite content to leave the relations to the unprompted judgment of the Irish people. Also, I have consented to withdraw the words, "Dearly-beloved brethren," as the Castle fears that they may shock the Nation. For the rest, I can assure the Lord Lieutenant that there is nothing in the other passages objected to by the English Censorship that might not have been written by the Catholic Archbishop of Dublin, and that in point of consideration for the religious beliefs of the Irish people the play compares very favourably indeed with the Coronation Oath."

STATEMENT BY THE LORD LIEUTENANT

His Excellency the Lord Lieutenant accorded an interview to a representative of *The Evening Telegraph* yesterday afternoon on the subject of Mr. Bernard Shaw's letter and the publication of it by Mr. Yeats. Your representative having read for Lord Aberdeen Mr. Shaw's letter,

His Excellency remarked, laughingly — "It is characteristic, and its publication an excellent advertisement, to which, I suppose, neither of the gentlemen will object."

"But what about the suggestion that the word 'immoral' was struck out at the insistence of your Excellency?"

"The sentence," said his Excellency, with the slightest touch of temper, "in Mr. Shaw's letter on the matter is an absurd and rather gross misrepresentation of my views regarding this particular feature of the play. You will remember," he added, "what Sir Beerbohm Tree said about these passages regarding the relation of the sexes in this play. 'The passages,' he said, 'were rather too strong, and the Censor would be certain to strike them out.' "

"But, after all," added Lord Aberdeen, "Mr. Shaw's letter will deceive nobody. It is an attempt to make the objections to his play appear as if they were of a merely Puritanical character. I am rather astonished that such a letter should have been written under the circumstances, and, if written, that the whole of the letter had not been published by Mr. Yeats, rather than passages from it."

"Has your Excellency read the play?" your representative asked.

"Yes, I have," Lord Aberdeen said. "The publishers rather absurdly refused a copy, but a copy was got from another source."

"Of course," he said, "I have been acting throughout in concert with my advisors, legal and other."

"What about the reference to the exclusion of the phrase, 'Dearly Beloved Brethren'?"

"The use of the words," said his Excellency, "is of special significance in all Churches. The words are associated in the minds of the people with Divine Service. It is an expression sanctified by use, and one cherished by the clergy and the people."

His Excellency added that his letter to Lady Gregory on the subject of the play would be published. Copies were being prepared for the Press.[36]

On 24 August *The Evening Telegraph* carried a note from the Chief Secretary's office which said that the previous day's interview with the Lord Lieutenant was entirely unauthorised. It also carried a statement from Lady Gregory:

I see that my letter to Sir J. Dougherty of August 20th, in which I said that Mr. Shaw's play is not now in its original form, has been given by him to the Press. I have now to say that I wrote yesterday to the Lord Lieutenant on seeing Mr. Shaw's letter to W. Yeats telling him that the passage I had mentioned to him as having been struck out during rehearsal has now been re-written by Mr. Shaw, and enclosing a copy of the re-written passage, as put back in its place.

I did this that there might be no misapprehension, and to let him know that the play as it now stands is "exactly as by the author, without concessions of any kind to the attacks that have been made upon it," except by the withdrawal of the words "immoral" and "dearly beloved brethren" withdrawn by Mr. Shaw himself, as he has stated, "to oblige the Lord Lieutenant."

In further explanation, let me say that I wired to Mr. Shaw on the 13th saying the Castle asked him to cut out the passages he had offered to cut out for the English Censor. His answer was "what passages? Play as printed is as altered to make meaning clear to Censor. Specify page and line, and will reply at once." He sent a further wire next day on receiving my letter repeating the request made at the Castle. "The *Nation*

292

articles give particulars of cuts demanded, which I refused, as they would have destroyed the religious significance of the play. The line about immoral relations is dispensable." When, however, we took this telegram to the Castle the request for cuts was not repeated, and we were told — "We are in close official relation with the English officials, of whom the Lord Chamberlain is one. That is the whole question." We did not, therefore, offer to make the cut suggested by Mr. Shaw.

The passage which we ourselves took out seemed to us objectionable — not because of its meaning, but because we did not think it sufficiently clear and detailed to be intelligible at a first hearing — we thought it might be misconstrued. Mr. Shaw has since put it in a form which fully satisfies our judgment. We have been certain from the first that no one who understands Mr. Shaw's play will object to it.

I may add that we have received a letter from Miss Horniman approving of our action.

A. GREGORY.[37]

The story then continued:

The management of the theatre made the following statement to-day: —

An evidence of the wide interest taken in the first production of *Blanco Posnet* may be gathered from the fact that the following papers have sent special dramatic critics, or will be represented to-morrow (Wednesday) night: — *The Times*, whose dramatic critic has already arrived; *The Daily Mail*, represented by Mr. Beach Thomas; *The Daily News, The Daily Chronicle, The Standard, The Daily Telegraph, The Westminster Gazette, The Pall Mall Gazette, The Morning Leader, The Manchester Guardian, The Spectator, The Athenaeum, The Belfast News-Letter, New York Herald, Lady's Pictorial, Daily Graphic, Illustrated London News, Sporting and Dramatic News, Piccolo Della Sera*, and some German papers.[38]

On the day of production, the fifth number of *The Arrow* appeared. It was devoted entirely to the *Blanco Posnet* affair, and contained the Directors' statement of 22 August, Shaw's letter to Yeats, an article from *The Nation*, and a short note by Yeats called 'The Religion of Blanco Posnet'.

The meaning of Mr. Shaw's play, as I understand it, is that natural man, driven on by passion and vain glory, attempts to live as his fancy bids him but is awakened to the knowledge

293

of God by finding himself stopped, perhaps suddenly, by something within himself. This something which is God's care for man, does not temper the wind to the shorn lamb, as a false and sentimental piety would have it, but is a terrible love that awakens the soul amidst catastrophes and trains it by conquest and labour.

The essential incidents of the play are Blanco's giving up the horse, the harlot's refusal to name the thief, and the child's death of the croup. Without the last of these Mr. Shaw's special meaning would be lost, for he wants us to understand that God's love will not do the work of the Doctor, or any work that man can do, for it acts by awakening the intellect and the soul whether in some man of science or philosopher or in violent Posnet.[39]

On the same day, *The Irish Independent* carried an interview with Yeats:

> Mr. Yeats was interviewed by an *Irish Independent* representative at the Abbey Theatre yesterday.
>
> Questioned with regard to the interesting situation, and to the alleged interview with the Lord Lieutenant in a Dublin evening paper, Mr. Yeats said: — "Our fight is a fight against the extension of the English Censorship to Ireland. In our negotiations with the Castle we were met, again and again, with that fact. It was evident they were simply obeying the Lord Chamberlain."
>
> "You must remember," he went on, "that the Irish public and the English public are altogether different. A play objectionable in one country is not objectionable in the other. The religions of the countries are different, and the national characteristics of the countries are different."
>
> To illustrate his point, Mr. Yeats related how when the English Censor got *The Playboy* he passed it, but objected to one portion, which was as follows: —
>
>> I would not be fearing the lowsy Kharki cut throats and the walking dead.
>
> "That," continued Mr. Yeats, "the Censor said, should come out, and all other phrases derogatory to the army. That was his only objection, and one inferred from the whole nature of his letter that he was feeling vaguely about to find out what caused the trouble in Dublin, and —" Mr. Yeats smiled —"he came to the conclusion it must have been those phrases."

Then Mr. Yeats came to deal with the alleged interview with the Lord Lieutenant. His Excellency, he said, made a point of an opinion of Sir Beerbohm Tree as to a phrase in *Blanco Posnet* which had been kept out by Mr. Shaw in deference to the Lord Lieutenant.

Mr. Yeats then related an interesting circumstance. "There is," he said, "a play of Mr. Synge's which we refused to produce at the Abbey, because we considered it might give offence to religious feeling in Ireland. Well, Sir Beerbohm Tree wired to Mr. Synge's executors, and would have produced that play had we not objected. We considered it would have interfered with the success of our London tour, as it would have come out two or three days before we opened at the Court Theatre."

"You seem to believe," remarked our representative, "that there is a wide difference between the Irish and English peoples in their attitudes towards the stage?"

"Yes," replied Mr. Yeats, "the national characteristics differ in nothing more profoundly than in the attitude towards the stage. The English audience is made up of well-to-do people, who do not want to be disturbed in their composure. They resent any unexpected claim upon their intellects. They listen badly. They do not take the trouble to relate passages to their context — in other words, they resent being expected to understand.

"An Irish audience, on the other hand, resents not understanding. If it understands the main tendency of a play, or follows an argument, it will accept all incidental phrases and speeches necessary to put that argument with power and passion."

"You think, then, that a Shaw play would not be unpopular in Dublin?"

"I have said from the very start of our theatre, from the first writing of Mr. Shaw — *John Bull*, for instance — that a Shaw play would not be resented by an Irish audience. He has always a clear argument. One always sees what his satire strikes at. If he puts our teeth on edge for a moment, we know why he is doing it."

And then Mr. Yeats drew a comparison between Shaw and Synge. "Synge's work, on the other hand," he said, "is precisely the work that is dangerous with an Irish audience. It is very hard to understand, and, therefore, the very desire to do so makes them impatient with it. They have gradually come to know what he means, and to accept his work without resentment. But it has been a long fight. To him everything was capricious and temperamental, and he could not tell his secret quickly."

"That would not be so to-morrow night," Mr. Yeats impressed on our representative. "To-morrow night," he said, "*Blanco Posnet* will have a triumph. The audience will look at one another in amazement, asking what on earth did the English Censor discover objectionable. They will understand instantly. The root of the whole difference between us and England in such matters is, that though there might be some truth in the old charge that we are not truthful to one another here in Ireland, we are certainly always truthful to ourselves. In England they have learned from commerce to be truthful to one another, but they are great liars when alone. The English Censor exists to keep them from finding out the fact. He gives them uncompleted arguments, sentimental half-truths, and, above all, he keeps dramatists from giving them anything in sudden phrases that would startle them into the perception of reality." [40]

Sinn Féin was by this time opposed to anything that the Abbey might do, and so, even though the theatre was defying Dublin Castle, there were several articles criticizing the Directors' intention of producing the play. Griffith himself wrote:

. . . What the Abbey Theatre, which was instituted avowedly to give us Irish drama, hopes to achieve by producing a rejected English play which is very likely to offend the community here, we do not know. Mr. Bernard Shaw is a very brilliant Irishman who gave up his country to capture the British public. Now that he and the British public have quarrelled, there is no reason why we should take part in the squabble. When he returns to his country and renders it the services he owes it as an Irishman none will welcome him more heartily than we. Meanwhile, we point out that if an Irishman carries his talents to London and sells them to the British public and he later on falls out, the affair is none of us, and to use an Irish theatre, established to foster *Irish* drama, to produce a play written for the British public which the British public does not want is a very ridiculous thing. . . .

In this country the censorship of the drama exists, but not as in England. In that country a play before its production must be submitted to the Censor, who may order it to be altered or may prohibit it altogether. In our country a play has not to be submitted beforehand, but after its first production must be submitted to the Censor, who may order it to be altered or may prohibit it altogether. In our country a play has not to be submitted beforehand, but after its first production the British Lord Lieutenant has power to prohibit its further performance, and power to revoke the licence of the theatre that produced. The former of these powers has been exercised, but so long ago that it may be said to have fallen into desuetude, and it would be an almost impossible thing for a British Lord Lieutenant now to prevent a national play being performed in a Dublin theatre. The directors of the Abbey Theatre, however, by their blundering, have opened a road for the revival of the exercise of this disused power. . . .

Writing with knowledge we may say that the Castle has decided that if a disturbance takes place in the Abbey Theatre on the occasion of the production of the play, it will use that disturbance to interdict the play, and thus re-establish in full working order a machine with which hereafter to crush national drama.

Therefore any person who takes any part in disturbing this play is simply playing the Castle game, consciously or unconsciously. Any who think the play would be too much for their feelings should keep away. Anyone who goes to see the play and who disapproves of it, should manifest his disapproval only by silence.

The whole position is a very absurd one. The directors of the Abbey Theatre have, by their blundering, given the Castle one half its opportunity.[41]

On Tuesday evening, 24 August, the house was practically sold out, and on the programme were *The Playboy* and *The Rising of the Moon*. The performance of *The Playboy*, according to *The Freeman's Journal*, 'was not attended with anything in the nature of a strongly hostile display, but in the concluding act there were frequent boos and expressions of disapproval.'[42]

Wednesday, however, was the night that everyone was waiting for. 'Jacques' in *The Irish Independent* thought that the play was 'flapdoodle', but vividly described the occasion:

Chock full was the Abbey. Around and about me were critics from far and near. From London and the provinces they came. Berlin, Munich, and Vienna were represented. So was America. Men near me made desks of their knees. They wrote and wrote. Telegraph messengers stood by in relays to speed with the "copy" to the telegraph office. The story of this night must go forth to the ends of the earth.

What a crowd! Had the poor little Abbey but life, its sombre sides would gasp, its floor would heave, its very foot-lights would blink in amazement. Never before had it seen the like of this. The people for the most part were people who would applaud a dramatist's work in just the spirit in which, had he started a racing stable, they would have backed his horses. There were other people, critical people, reasonable people, thoughtful people, who are not hidebound by theatrical tradition. And there were Horse Show people, with Horse Show clothes and Horse Show manners and Horse Show accents. To them novelty is as the breath of life. All were attentive and very appreciative, while we were being chilled and thrilled by Mr. Yeats's beautiful dream play *Kathleen Ni Houlihan*.

The curtain is up. We are in darkness — a vault-like dark-ness. The air feels thick with tenseness. The silence hangs heavy. The audience ooze excitement. The play begins. The scene is a town hall in the territory of the United States of America. There are women in the hall, and they talk. They try to talk American slang with American twang, and some of them trip worse when they twist back to say it all over again.[43]

The Freeman's Journal described the occasion like this:

The Shewing up of Blanco Posnet, after a preliminary disturbance such as few dramatic pieces have excited, saw the light at the Abbey Theatre last night. To say that intense interest was manifested in the production is to put the fact in a very mild form. Outside the theatre there were a big crowd and many policemen, and inside, the most brilliant-looking audience that has, perhaps, ever assembled in the house. We need not go into the agitation through which the piece had to fight its way to the stage. Banned by the English Censor, and scrutinised with apparently the keenest critical eyes by the Governmental authorities in Ireland, one would not have been very greatly surprised if Mr. G. B. Shaw's work had to content itself with publication in book form. But, now that it has been played, what everybody who saw it will probably ask is, what the extraordinary fuss was all about.

At the outset it may be plainly stated that there is really nothing in the drama as played last night that could give offence to any but the most thin-skinned spectator. On the contrary, it is a very real, a very vivid, a very instructive little piece, with a decent moral, and in every way worthy and characteristic of the genius of Mr. Shaw. . . .

Now, many people have felt uneasy to learn that Mr. Shaw proposed to produce a play based on the workings of conscience in a man of rough life, and it is surely fairly arguable that religious themes, except, at all events, when dealt with in the most reverent spirit, ought not to be encouraged on the stage. But it would be very hard to discover offence in this little one-act piece, which plays for just an hour. The language is rough and strong. This is probably a part that shocked the Censor: — "Take care, Boozy," says Posnet; "He hasn't finished with you yet. He has always a trick up His sleeve"; and the Elder replies, "Oh, is that the way to speak of the Ruler of the Universe — the great and Almighty God?" And Posnet continues — "He's a sly One. He's a mean One. He lies low for you. He plays cat and mouse with you. He lets you run loose until you think you're shut of Him; and then, when you least expect it, He's got you." Now this, read in cold print, may seem irreverently familiar, or familiarly irreverent, which you will. But the words are uttered while Posnet is discerned in the throes of conversion, and, as heard from the rough-looking fellow on the stage, and in the uncouth surroundings of the semi-civilised village, they do not shock the ear. Nay, it may be confessed that they strike the hearer as the natural way in which such a man, at such a time, in such a place would pour out his very soul. And that is one of the striking merits of this very impressive piece. The atmosphere is true; there is not the slightest incongruity either in speech or demeanour, and roughness has seldom been presented with a greater reticence. Posnet points the moral with queer, quaint eloquence. Posnet's language is not the language of a Saint. This is how Saint Augustine put it long ago: "Nemo Te demittit qui non dimittit, et qui dimittit quo it, aut quo fugit nisi a Te placido ad Te iratum?" "No one loseth Thee who sendeth Thee not away; and he who sendeth Thee away, whither goeth he or whither fleeth he save from Thy kindness to Thy wrath?" The curious in poetic parallels may find one more modern in Francis Thompson's glorious ode, "The Hound of Heaven." If that great ode had been a play, how startling the Censor would have found the title!

The reception of the piece could not have been more flattering. The curtain went down amid a vigorous outburst of applause. As a one-act piece it is deserving of great praise. The characters are sketched with a strong hand; they all stand out distinctly; they live and breathe; they are no mere puppets. The action is as swift as a hurricane. Dramatic compression could go no further. Rough fun, and serious roughness, alternate with bewildering speed. Cynicism and sarcasm pervade the dialogue, and with all the play of his many-sided fancy the dramatist never for an instant loses his grip on the main idea, on the central character, and the moral he is designed to emphasise.

A word or two as to the acting of the piece. The rehearsals must have been very thorough. Everybody in the cast was letter perfect, and some excellent character acting was seen. The Yankee accent beat some of the artistes, but Mr. Arthur Sinclair (Elder Daniels) made a very good compromise with it; while several of the performers judiciously shirked it altogether. But this had a somewhat incongruous effect, for some of the dialogue was spoken in passable American and some in unmistakable Irish. But it was not a great fault, and there were abundant merits in compensation. Mr. Fred O'Donovan cut a fine figure in the title role. He gave a splendid portrayal of the dare-devil whose heart was not really in his dare-devilry. Every phase of a character very powerfully drawn was brought out into the clearest light, and he both looked and acted the part most excellently. Miss Sara Allgood completely disarmed criticism as Feemy Evans. Her bold, vixenish demeanour, and her breakdown, were superb features in the representation. Miss Máire O'Neill played the Mother with fine restraint, and Mr. Sydney J. Morgan as Sheriff Kemp could not have been very much better. It is very satisfactory to be able thus to record a success for the play, and to still any uneasy feelings that may have been aroused lest Dublin should be identified with the production of an objectionable piece. The question remains whether such themes as a sinner's conversion might not with advantage be left to the churches; but if they are to be considered as proper to the theatre, then *The Shewing up of Blanco Posnet* is well entitled to audience. . . . It may be mentioned that when the curtain fell on Mr. Shaw's play there were loud calls for the author, and Mr. W. B. Yeats coming before the curtain, said he was not present, but Mrs. Shaw was, and would convey to her husband the enthusiastic way in which his drama had been received."

At the conclusion of the play, *The Irish Independent* secured some interviews:

The following wire was despatched from the National Theatre Co. to Mr. Shaw immediately the play had been brought to a conclusion: —

"Glorious reception. Splendid victory. Where is the Censor now?"

Mr. W. B. Yeats, seen by our representative immediately after the performance, said the play had been a triumphant success. "I have heard nothing but enthusiastic praise about it, and the artistes got curtain after curtain," he added.

"Of course," continued Mr. Yeats, "we ought to be all pleased with Mr. Shaw for having sought our judgment on this play, and it is very difficult to see now how they can avoid licensing it in England."

Asked if the play would be produced, as already arranged, in the Abbey Theatre each night during the week, Mr. Yeats replied that it would, and added that it would now go into the regular repertoire of the Abbey. . . .

Lady Gregory, on being interviewed, said that she never yet saw a play received with such great enthusiasm. . . .

Mr. Frederick Mouillot, managing director of the Theatre Royal and the Gaiety Theatre, who was present during the performance, said at the close to our representative: —

"This play of Shaw's is the best and strongest thing he has ever done. It went through without the slightest trouble." . . .

Some twenty policemen, under the direction of Inspectors M'Cabe and Gordon, were in attendance, but beyond controlling the traffic they had little else to do.[45]

Canon J. O. Hannay, who under the pseudonym of George A. Birmingham was a prolific and popular novelist, reviewed the play for *The Morning Leader*, arguing that:

. . . in Dublin, the most religious city in the world, the provincial visitors who put in an appearance during Horse Show week are incapable of understanding Shaw. Of course, he says, Dublin, having the Censor's authority behind it — religious Dublin, and Irish Society generally — still believes that *Blanco Posnet* is a blasphemy. Such of them as ventured to attend the opening performance do not know that they have been enticed to a theatre to listen to a sermon. When they find it out they will be very angry, indeed, and quite rightly, for it is a clear case of obtaining money under false pretences to advertise a blasphemy and produce a sermon.

We have Mr. Shaw's own authority for calling *Blanco*

Posnet a sermon. The play has a sub-title, "A Sermon in Crude Melodrama." I kick against the epithet "crude." The work is coarse, violent, terrible, but it is not crude. Otherwise, the description is true. The play is not a blasphemy, and it is not indecent. It is a sermon on the working of the spirit of God in the heart of a man. It is an extraordinarily powerful sermon, the sort of sermon which makes the intelligent listener, if he calls himself a Christian, writhe in his pew.[46]

Most of the critics, however, felt that the play was 'rather second-rate stuff', and that the action of the British Censor and then of the Lord Lieutenant had created a quite artificial excitement. The acting was generally praised, but a number of critics joined in slating Sara Allgood. For instance, *The Irish Times* wrote:

Miss Sara Allgood looked acutely uncomfortable as Feemy Evans. The part is quite outside her mental sympathies. She does not know how a woman of the type would look and act and think, and we have a shrewd suspicion that she does not want to know. In consequence, she is adequate, but never anything more. And her great scene, when she is faced with the strange woman, is spoiled by the manager's making her drop in voice. There is no use mincing a scene of this sort. It is a crude and violent scene, and has to be played in a crude and violent manner.[47]

Nevertheless, the audience's reaction had been vigorously enthusiastic, and the evening had passed off without disturbance. On the day after the production, Yeats and Lady Gregory issued the following statement to the press:

Now that the danger of interference is over, we wish to protest against the grave anxiety and annoyance we have been put to by the endeavour to force an incompetent and irrelevant Censorship upon Ireland. We were both dragged away from our work — days upon days were wasted in futile interviews and correspondence. One of the Castle lawyers warned our solicitors that if we produced the play, the Castle would use against us all the powers the law gave them, and many similar threats were made to us personally, by officials, who it is only fair to say, seemed ashamed of the task set them. We were forced into a position where we had either to abandon a principle which every worker, in our dramatic movement or in the Gaelic movement, looks upon as essential, or to risk by the closing of our theatre the livelihood of our players and the fruit of years of work. Just when our theatre was beginning to be self-supporting the Castle, or those it has to obey, did its utmost to fix upon us a charge of encouraging blasphemy and indecency; and all this in the assertion of a right of moral censorship which had not been used for a hundred and fifty years. And when this was done, not upon its own judgment, but upon the judgment of a discredited English official, and at a moment when that official's own employers had appointed a Commission to consider whether he should or should not be dismissed. For a moment the attempt to impose the English Censorship on Ireland has been defeated, and the entire Press justifies the play and our action; but it may arise again upon the report of a Special Commission. The result of the Commission will probably be some new form of Censorship — possibly more intelligent, but certainly as objectionable from the Irish point of view — and a proposal to make it apply to Ireland with, as is suggested, an Irish assessor. This will mean no change as far as the plays brought to Ireland by English companies are concerned, but it will mean the putting of the plays of our theatre and all plays produced by the Gaelic League, and similar societies, under the control of a Castle Official responsible to the English Censor. *Sinn Féin*, *The Irish Nation*, and the official organ of the Gaelic League have already made their protests. They and we are but little concerned with the question of the Censorship now being fought out in London, but very much concerned in keeping the liberty we possess.

W. B. YEATS
A. GREGORY.[48]

*   *   *

After these exciting events, the Abbey remained closed until 16 September, when it presented a new play, *The White Feather*. The piece was written under the pseudonym of R. J. Ray, by R. J. Brophy, a journalist from Cork. The play has not been published and was not particularly well received. The following short notice probably sums it up adequately:

> Act 1 is by far the best of the three. The others are virtually rather tedious dialogue, in which Michael John Dillon, a farmer, who is apparently a cowardly murderer, is exhibited in his true colours. Michael John is not only a person who is ready to wipe out obnoxious individuals but is quite oblivious to the pleadings of Mrs. Brady, who does her best to ensure that justice will be meted out to an innocent man.

303

The time of the play is in the old Land League days, and the action takes place in Martin Kearney's shop, Dillon's house and the county prison. Mr. Ray's present success should encourage him to do better.[49]

H.S.D. in *The Dublin Evening Mail* thought the play showed great promise, although the ending seemed 'morbid and unreal and cheap'. The acting, however, he thought 'superlatively good'.

There are no tricks in this acting, no "playing for the laugh," or posturing in the limelight, the stale devices of the commercial theatre. The thing is done in a quiet, restrained, suggestive way that presents, not the counterfeit, but the real. More competent acting could certainly not be seen in any theatre.[50]

What the author thought may be gleaned from the following letter which Ray wrote to *Sinn Féin*:

Sir, — I read in *Sinn Féin* the remarks made about *The White Feather*, and am surprised to find no mention of the players. The other daily papers have expressed appreciation of the fine quality of the acting, and, with your permission, I should like to state what great pleasure was afforded me as the play went from act to act, without any of those hitches which are stated to be inevitable at a first night's performance. A dramatic author who sits out the first night's performance of his play may well hope that the audience will be sympathetic at least, and the audience at the Abbey Theatre were sympathetic and appreciative, both, and when the curtain fell at the close of the last act, I felt a large degree of pleasure. But to the players I owe a great deal, and their painstaking study of the various parts, the clever interpretation and remarkable insight of the moods, feelings, and passions of the characters made me marvel, even though I have long since recognised their ability.

Your critic states that the play was received "with chilling courtesy." As a matter of fact at the end of the first act the curtain was twice, and at the end of the third act three times raised. Applause, too, was loud at appropriate points in the first act. The second act invites applause but little, and the third act not at all. I should have been surprised disagreeably if there had been applause repeatedly in the course of the second act, and applause in the third act would have made me regard the act as a failure. The second and third acts are written in a tense key, and they held the audience as I expected they would. This letter is altogether written in the interests of the Abbey Theatre, the players, and the audience, and the last afforded me a concrete example that the work of the Abbey Theatre is already fruitful of good results.

Sincerely yours,

R. J. RAY[51]

The Abbey's next new play was a one-act, *The Challenge*, by Winifred M. Letts, which was first produced on 14 October with a revival of Casey's popular *The Suburban Groove*. It received little notice and that was not favourable. 'Jacques' thought, 'It might make a nice short story in a penny novelette,' and *The Irish Times* wrote:

> The piece has very little to recommend it, and had it not been for the excellent manner in which it was presented it would have fallen very flat, indeed. The dialogue is capital, but the motif so far transgresses all human experience or likelihood that passages which were intended to be intensely dramatic and pathetic excited laughter only. The time is fixed at 1890, and an old gentleman, Charles Caulfield (Arthur Sinclair) is found sitting alone in a decayed house on the North side of Dublin. The chief glory of the neighbourhood had long departed. It had once been the chief centre of fashion, but the great families who resided in it had taken their departure, and the grand mansions had become squalid tenements, inhabited by degenerates. The old gentleman was, however, too conservative to think of detaching himself from his early home. His sentiment did not rest here, for on the evening when we first encounter him he is talking yearningly to his butler (J. A. O'Rourke) of a sweetheart of 40 years ago, whose diary has just come into his possession. The conversation is interrupted by the arrival of an old acquaintance, James Buchanan (Mr. Fred O'Donovan), whose name has just been mentioned. Buchanan's presence strangely affects the old man, who talks of the possibility of the death of one of them that night, and the butler is summarily dismissed on an errand. Then a strange development takes place. Caulfield charges his friend with having gained the affections of the authoress of the diary, now dead, and declares that he had even gone so far as to kiss her. Buchanan admits the offence, but explains that innocent boy and girl flirtations are very common matters, and should not at any time merit tragic consequences, especially forty years afterwards. All his powers of persuasion are, however, useless, and he is forced to select a pistol for his

305

defence. The signal to fire is to be given by the tenth stroke of the clock. The opponents face each other with cocked weapons, but at the eighth stroke Caulfield drops dead of heart disease, and the curtain falls. The play was by no means satisfying, but in the hands of such capable artists even so grotesque a story was invested with a certain amount of interest.[52]

The production of Lady Gregory's new play, *The Image*, on 11 November, evoked this significant comment from *The Freeman's Journal*:

One of the most remarkable and interesting features in connection with the Abbey Theatre, it need hardly be said, is the fact that it provides new and wholesome plays, and in that sense presents — without meaning any offence to anybody — a distinct and agreeable contrast. The Abbey Theatre, therefore, deserves all the support that can be possibly given to a well-intended effort to purify the stage and make manifest the fact that it is possible to have good plays without indecency, clean plays without ladies with a past, or anything of the more or less humdrum monstrosities which the more recent dramatic degeneracy suggests.[53]

A remarkable comment, considering the theatre's reputation in the very recent past, but one which seems symptomatic of a new tolerance toward the Abbey. The play was not hugely admired, but the acting of Máire O'Neill was particularly remarked:

It should, perhaps, be said that though the object and purpose of the prolonged sketch was somewhat vague, the cleverness of the dialogue was manifest, and afforded an excellent opportunity to the artistes. But the purpose of it was too remote; the colloquies and interchanges too laboured; and, if one might say so without offence, the application of the pruning knife would have been a great relief. But what is one to say about the really delightful performance of Miss Máire O'Neill as old Peggy Mahon? In its own particular way it is the best thing this very gifted artiste has done, and that surely is saying a good deal. The part is an odd and peculiar one. It might be made ridiculous; but one felt the influence of that charm which inevitably comes from the work of an actress imbued with the sense of her surroundings, and whose art of concealing art is illimitable.[54]

306

'Jacques' correctly enough interpreted the theme of the play: '. . . we waste time bickering over trifles. We pursue the shadow and lose the substance.' What he thought was wrong was that:

> There is very little action in the play. . . . There are three short acts of dialogue. Indeed, the piece might be briefly summarised thusly: Act 1, Talk; Act 2, More talk; Act 3, Same as Act 2.[55]

* * *

In 1909 Frank Fay was acting in England, but a couple of his letters to Máire Garvey, although a bit touched with spleen, contain some interesting judgments:

> Why didn't you tell me about *Kincora*? In my innocent days, I used to like the play. Now I know better. I noticed in *The Manchester Guardian* the usual preponderance of Lady Gregory's work and when they came back, there was more Lady Gregory in Dublin. These dear people don't know how to write plays: they can do dialogue and character, but except Boyle and Fitzmaurice, they don't know how to write what will *really* act. Synge gets nearest to it, after Boyle and Fitz. They all think too much of what they call "literature," and too little of the play. Lady Gregory's dialogue used to make my teeth ache by a sort of bread and milk quality in it, and in *The Unicorn from the Stars*, I got my fill. It's hard to keep one's temper and act in things like *The Jackdaw* I can tell you, and be praised and praised with insincerity, by people who have their own fish to fry.
>
> How is the "Colm and Joy" and the other litterateurs? Is Poetry still rampant? At Christmas I saw in Manchester Cousins' *Bell Branch* on sale, but I could not bring myself to buy it, knowing that it, too, was sure to be bread and milky. When will some one with "guts" and without pose arise in Ireland? All these young self-conscious people who are so sure they are making history and like Yeats have their eyes so firmly fixed on the future, are pitiable. And they are all anaemic (I hope that's spelled properly!); no fierce red blood runs in their veins. They are playing at being men of letters and writing about life without having lived. We are a nation of actors in real life. Even in Gaelic circles, they were playing at "nation-building" (and other miserable phrases) when I knew them. . . . What is Máire Walker doing? Has she given up acting? She was a disappointment to me. She got into the talking and posing set and lost herself.[56]

307

On 26 April Fay wrote:

> . . . The Abbey people should never have attempted *The Heather Field*. Let the cobbler stick to his last. They have neither the accent nor the manner of the class it purports to present. It's a bad play. I read it when they were thinking of doing it before and was not enthusiastic. They had much less reason for shelving *John Bull's Other Island*. But Yeats is an impossible creature to head a theatre. His complete ignorance of acting is in itself sufficient to incapacitate him and his impish faculty for making mischief in a small place like Dublin is another reason. But as I helped to put him in the saddle, I'd better say no more. Connell has acted and is to be stage manager, I hear. His dialogue in *The Piper* showed that he had "the stage Irishman" clearly before his eyes as he wrote, and I've little doubt that the intensely local acting that my brother developed, by knowing the usual theatrical tricks and avoiding them, will go by the board. At any rate he's better than having Sara pottering at stage management for which she never showed the least instinct.[57]

Willie Fay and Brigit O'Dempsey, after their return from America, did not at first prosper. However, on 17 September, Boyle wrote to Holloway:

> The Fays are right in at last. Mrs. Fay has the part of "Norah" — (is that the young woman's name?) in *John Bull's Other Island*, and Will has, I think, the Miller. . . . Their pluck in persisting during an eclipse of eighteen months one must admire. Had I been Will, I would have gone back to plumbing or whatever he was formerly at in half the time. I forgot to ask after Frank. He never came to see me when he was here idle which I think shows a petty spirit.
>
> Well, what is the Abbey's programme for the future? Any new light discovered? If so, he will soon have the sconce clapped on him for fear his light should outshine the Great Directorate. Have you heard the cause of the split with Norreys Connell? To be fair, I think he *did* set himself up a bit too much.[58]

On 12 October Boyle wrote:

> I have seen the Fays in *John Bull's Other Island* and regret to say that Mrs. Fay is very ineffective. I am much disappointed in her. She has all the natural qualities for the part, but doesn't seem to have acquired the art of acting yet.

She and her husband are, however, quite satisfied, and they tell me Granville Barker is highly pleased with her work. So be it then.[59]

On 16 October Boyle had news of a quite different sort:

I received Lady Gregory's readdressed letter by same post as yours this morning. I am quite agreeable to the terms offered and wish no more restraint put on their arrangements than that they should not put up a piece of mine *along with The Playboy*. I reserve the right of withdrawing my plays again should I feel that I am being unfairly treated. I have no fear of this but plain talk is best. . . .

I thank you and all my Dublin friends for your allegiance to me while I was sulking in my tent.

If Dublin wants plays from me I promise you I can let it have plenty. I have at least a dozen in my head but felt it waste of time to write them.[60]

*   *   *

Miss Horniman's volatile relations with the Abbey continued to fluctuate wildly. Her extraordinary exacerbation over the Sally Allgood-Mrs. Lyttleton affair would be counter-balanced by an equally extraordinary generosity. The paramount issue, of course, was what would be the future of the theatre when the Patent expired in 1910 and Miss Horniman's agreement to subsidise the theatre was at an end. Both sides made innumerable proposals and counter-proposals, and these were interspersed by hysterical edicts and ultimatums from Miss Horniman. Sometimes she was capable of a proposal which was neither quixotically generous nor callously mean. For instance, on 9 February, she wrote to Yeats:

You asked me to state in writing what I told you might be possibly my intentions for the future, but I explained as clearly as possible that I would make no promises at present. To put it shortly, I said that if I found as time goes on, the venture becomes such that there would be a prospect that it could go on without the subsidy and pay my Dublin expenses *in full*, that I would consider an arrangement by which you should have the use of the Abbey as it stands for what it costs me (making no charge for the capital put into the concern) all complete including income tax, etc. That would give you the profits of my letting of the building and also the rent of the house in Abbey Street. You would have to be responsible for all repairs and costs of every kind and to be certain that this

309

responsibility would be possible to you. I am anxious for the accounts to be clearly and fairly stated. If I were to let the building as a small Music Hall I should get something at least beyond my bare expenses and present outlay, so I am considering the possibility of making a future offer to you worth at least about £200 a year, the interest on the capital spent.

I do not think that it would be wise in my circumstances for me to propose this at all unless you had at least £1,000 clear savings without any liabilities.[61]

At another time she made this generous proposal:

If you could take over the whole next Dec. 1, 1909, and give me £428 down and a quittance for £1000, you would practically be paying the latter sum by instalments, and what is more important, you would gain in popularity by getting rid of the stigma of my English name, and also you would become free at once to let the Abbey to the Gaelic League with 6d seats and to make it up with the Theatre of Ireland.

You would also be able in that case to renew the Patent without difficulty as I should not be concerned in that matter.[62]

And then on 31 August, she wrote:

At the end of November 1909 I shall practically owe £100 for coming subsidy and £200 for Abbey upkeep. If the affair is taken over *then* of course I shall pay out nothing more, but shall receive £500 and quittance for above £100, that will be giving up the whole property and contents for less than the cost of those parts which have been bought by me. If necessary the £500 can be reduced a little, but it must be enough to make it clear that I am completely bought out and "banished." [63]

On 15 December she followed this with:

If you do not return me one of these [three] copies signed by both of you before December 31st 1909, I shall conclude that my proposal is finally refused, and I shall arrange to dispose of or let the Abbey Theatre immediately that the Patent has run out.[64]

Miss Horniman wrote hundreds of letters about the Abbey Theatre, and it would be fruitless to untangle their complexities and contradictions. There was no logic to her behaviour, for her motivation was obviously emotional and based on the daily fluctuations of her feelings for Yeats. Consider, for example, the following notes which she sent to him during the course of one week:

310

Dec. 25th/09

Dear Demon,

. . . Long ago I warned you that Supermen cannot prevent a revolt of slaves and the time has not yet come that the Supermen are completely paramount, or that revolt is impossible.

You seemed hurt the other day that I appeared to accuse you of what you call bad faith. . . . How glad I shall be when I am free of the Abbey and you will be no longer urged by Dublin atmosphere to exhibit Dublin ways in regard to me!

Yours,

ANNIE

Dec. 26th/09

My dear Demon,

. . . Even Super People cannot be expected to enjoy a revolt of slaves, but I have been driven to this. I suffered very acutely at first when you changed in your attitude towards me; gradually, very gradually it is true, after your return from America. I fought against this by trying to ignore your unkindness but, strive as I might, it grew and grew. No *additions* to *Samhain* could alter that mis-statement. I don't care for compliments; they only irritate me. Do you both [Yeats and Lady Gregory] consent to the proposal being *on* the application?

Yours,

ANNIE

Dec. 31st/09

My dear Demon,

Just a few lines to wish you a most prosperous and happy year in 1910.

May all the old worries take flight.

Yours,

ANNIE[65]

Poor Miss Horniman, she gave a good deal more than money.

And how did the recipient of all this intensity react? Rather formally. For instance:

July 27 1909

My dear Miss Horniman,

I think that you are quite right considering your changed feelings about the National Theatre Society (and your decision not to continue the subsidy after 1910) to cancel the codicil in your will. However, in your letter to your solicitor you base your decision upon your objection to endow "a scheme which cannot succeed." None of the directors take that view of the prospects of the Theatre. We think we have a chance of success even as things are. Entirely upon my own part I wish to remind you of something I used to say to you. I have said to you once or twice, once I think when you were risking what I looked upon as certain loss upon a tour, "I will tell you when I think the moment has come when by spending more money it may be possible to make the Theatre a success." In now telling you, that I believe the moment has come, you must not think that I am expecting you to do anything. I know that every penny of your spare income is engaged, and that you are giving us a very generous share. I think it only fair to myself however to say that if this theatre fails the probable cause will be the lack of the necessary capital at a critical moment. We have now a perfectly disciplined company as I believe. We have a very remarkable body of plays of a new kind, and we have created a school of acting made possible by the expenditure on your part of a great deal of money. Our chance of success must depend in all likelihood on our getting extra capital somehow. . . .[66]

Early in 1910, Miss Horniman estimated her expenses from the opening of the theatre in December 1904, up to January 1910, as £9,957, not including losses incurred on the English tours. Yeats could really be rather loathsome.

*   *   *

A theatre is a joint endeavour of temperamental and talented people, and it is easy, even irresistibly tempting, when writing the history of a theatre, to stress the fights and the factions. However, a theatre movement at its best inspires an intense loyalty to it from its members and a rare camaraderie among them. And so the examples of deplorable behaviour should always be counterbalanced by instances of people acting extremely well. To cite one instance, then, after the Abbey paid a visit to Cork during the year, its policies were strongly attacked in a public lecture; and immediately two of the young Cork realists sprang to the theatre's defence:

Ballymoney, Ballineen,
15th December, 1909

To the Editor, *Cork Sportsman*.
Dear Sir, — My attention has been called to the report of a speech delivered by Mr. James J. O'Neill, which appeared in

your issue of the 4th inst. In this some very strong criticisms are passed on the Directors of the Abbey Theatre, on their treatment of aspiring dramatists, and it is implied that I consider myself (or ought to consider myself) very much ill-used at the "selfishness and neglect" shown to me and my play, *The Cross Roads*. I emphatically deny any such selfishness or neglect. The facts of the case are these: My play was produced for the first time on the 1st April in Dublin; within three weeks it was played in Cork; it was played in Dublin in May; in Belfast in August; in Dublin in October; and two performances of it were given in Manchester the very week before Mr. O'Neill's speech. Does this look like selfishness or neglect? Since April I have made many alterations in the play; it has only now reached a form which fairly satisfies me. In this form it was played in Manchester (and will, I understand, be taken on tour in England next year), but it had not reached this form when the Company visited London last June, and the programme of their visit last month was selected by the Incorporated Stage Society.

I must thank Mr. O'Neill for the very flattering opinion he holds of *The Cross Roads*, but I cannot let the impression get abroad that I have any reason to be dissatisfied with the Directors' treatment of me. Both my plays owe much to their advice and help.

Yours, etc.,
S. L. ROBINSON

Cork, December 13, 1909

To the Editor, *Cork Sportsman*.

Dear Sir, — I cannot, with completeness, reply to the remarks made by Mr. O'Neill about the Abbey Theatre and its Directors at the close of his lecture on "The Early Cork Stage." Any man who, in any respect, important or other, undertakes to bear witness, should be careful to speak the truth, and not to be moved by spleen or ill-humour, or what not; but Mr. O'Neill seems to be quite indifferent about the statements he makes, that is to say, whether they are well or ill-founded. I form this opinion from his remarks about Mr. Robinson's clever play, *The Cross Roads*. Mr. Robinson's reply will certainly confound Mr. O'Neill.

Myself, I should like, as far as may be, to indicate the manner in which the Abbey Directors treat, to them, an unknown playwright. I, in August last, sent a play, *The White Feather*, in three acts, to Mr. W. B. Yeats, one of the Directors

313

of the Abbey Theatre. From him I had, within a week a letter accepting the play, and not as one who would make an author feel that he was insignificant; on the contrary, the letter was warmly appreciative. The play was "very remarkable," he said, and again, "full of real dramatic quality." Then, the play was specially and rapidly rehearsed, and opened the Abbey Theatre season at Dublin this year.

I saw the play at the Abbey, and, despite the flattering mark of appreciation contained in a call before the curtain, I decided upon revision. The Directors, before revision, arranged for a rehearsal of the original play; and if it did not take place, the blame is not to them. If all had gone well, the play would have been presented in Cork on the visit of the Abbey Company, and was included in the programme, but, for the reasons given, had to be omitted.

As I have said, I cannot, with completeness, reply to the remarks of Mr. O'Neill, but I feel, so far as I can reply, from facts within my knowledge, I ought to do so. My experience ought to be an encouragement, rather than a discouragement, to any one who thinks he can write a play which would be suitable for the Abbey Theatre.

Mr. O'Neill made one serious mis-statement, that in regard to Mr. Robinson's play, and so I, at any rate, set him down as one who, so far as this Theatre is concerned, has a tremendous big and somewhat unwieldy axe to grind, for men with such an axe are never fair-minded. What the particular axe is, and how it came to exist, or rather how long he has been grinding it, I know not. There are some others also so inclined against the Theatre, and this year, and every year, the edge of each axe shall show a dull and even blunted edge.

Sincerely yours,

R. J. RAY[67]

And, of course, sometimes the camaraderie of the theatre became more than camaraderie. As Sally Allgood wrote:

Thus it came about that in Ireland in 1908, 09, and 10, my life was one of routine rather than excitement — except for one or two little episodes; such as getting a proposal of marriage from J. M. Kerrigan, one of the famous Abbey actors, and with the proposal a wrist-watch. Later, in moments of jealousy, J. M. Kerrigan asked me to give him back the watch, and he dashed it on the floor of the Green Room, and crushed the inoffensive little watch into smithereens under his heel. A couple of years later, Arthur Sinclair gave me a wrist-watch. One day Lady Gregory remarked, "Oh, what a pretty watch." I told her it was a gift from Arthur Sinclair.

"Oh," said she, "am I to congratulate you?"

"What!" said I, "Does a present of a watch mean a proposal of marriage?"

She smiled. So, I took off the watch, and returned it to Sinclair. He was very hurt. Apparently that had been his idea, but I wasn't having any of it. I don't think I was really interested in the thought of marriage. I was completely happy in my work.[68]

*   *   *

The Theatre of Ireland revived several past productions during the year, but its most notable productions were those on 29 April of two new plays, Seumas O'Kelly's *The Shuiler's Child*, in which Máire Nic Shiubhlaigh had her most striking role, and a one-act comedy of Ulster by Rutherford Mayne, *The Gomeril*. *Sinn Féin* gave a great deal of space to the productions, but easily the most remarkable was Susan L. Mitchell's spirited essay 'Dramatic Rivalry':

Mr. Yeats, you have been a fool. Here is an actress born in Ireland, and the Abbey Theatre has no claim on her. I grind my teeth for you, Yeats, with your boneless tragedians. Why did you let Máire Nic Shiubhlaigh go? Máire Nic Shiubhlaigh was an Abbey player once, she looked beautifully there, though it may not have been her fault — God had made her so — and she spoke beautifully, for He also had given her the noble arch of the palate that makes the ringing note, and Frank Fay was the devoted servant of a great art, and what he learned he had a passion to impart. But Máire never acted at the Abbey; not Yeats, nor Lady Gregory, nor Æ revealed her to herself though it was through the noble words of Æ's Lavarcam that her voice was trained to the great cadence. In the early days of the Theatre of Ireland, among their imperfect and often laughable attempts at acting, some one put on Ibsen's *Brand*. There was good acting in it — I remember it well in a night of puerilities — and there I believe Máire Nic Shiubhlaigh first found herself. I remember her then; no Yeats's painted angel, no statuesque instrument for reciting beautiful words, but a tragic temperament for the first time struggling with the bonds of convention. I laughed at the Theatre of Ireland then, I have often laughed at them

315

since; they have done, as well as some conscientious, some desperately bad work; but they are getting into the stride now; they will do splendidly, and they have brought Máire Nic Shiubhlaigh to her own.

Oh, Yeats, Yeats! with your broken-kneed heroes and barging heroines, even your drawingroom Deirdre, tender, appealing, complex as she was, did not save you, who, with all your talk of tradition, have only succeeded in producing in Kiltartan French and pidgin English some few passably competent comic actors and actresses. I feel very sad for you and for your loss in the possibilities that your futile dictatorship flung away, certainties now, and you have lost them. Your company can act Lady Gregory's brilliant little comedies, but spare us *Kincora*. Is it not a comedy? Do not turn your clever rogue of a valet into Brian Boru; he is only a valet still. Do not dress your urban scold in the robes of a queen, though even her barging tones in the height of their passion may bring us the faint echo of a grander note, and though in the younger Miss Allgood you have a wistful suggestion of delicacy in acting. Give us no heroics any more; your heroic actors haven't in any sense a leg to stand on! Cultivate Lord Dunsany if you will. I will foresee something big in the empty bottles and the picklock at the door of heaven, but get him an audience, man, get him an audience. *The Glittering Gate* is no farce, and the empty bottle deserves more than an empty laugh. Pull yourself together, Man of Genius, save your theatre. There is yet a little time.

By foolishly withdrawing the right of acting in the Abbey from the Theatre of Ireland you have made of them formidable rivals. They act on the same nights of the week as you do. They have full houses; likewise you, empty houses. You have used a tongue and a pen, destined to nobler work than belittling their struggling art; you have failed to treat them with the courtesy due from one set of artists to another. Change all this. You should not be enemies, but united against a common enemy — the commercial theatre. Make no mistakes. The Theatre of Ireland can act; they have got the Abbey into a corner. It is for you, Yeats, to make the next move if you can. Let it be a worthy move.

I found nothing remarkable in Seumas O'Kelly's play, save that it made a good opportunity for some good acting. The parts were well done, and equable enough, though I felt that Tim O'Halloran struck an old chord in a new and masterly way. Andy was good; Constance de Markievicz has gained

316

in steadiness and conviction. Neili O'Brien will do even better yet. Caitia Ní Cormac is a child of promise. But the supreme moment in the night was Máire Nic Shiubhlaigh's. Was it hers or was it the writer's? I think it was hers, though Seumas O'Kelly has an illumination here that may make him into a playwright yet. Surely it was Máire who gathered up all the emotion that might, could, would, or should have been in Seumas O'Kelly's play — gathered it up as it were in that old shawl of hers — . . . in the one breathless moment of the Song of the Streets of Galway. . . . An actress has been given to Ireland.

Rutherford Mayne's *Gomeril*, though much less than a play and hardly an incident, made a good vehicle for some northern accents, and that bitter jesting that sharpens here and there to a point in the somewhat amorphous humour of the north. Norah Fitzpatrick is an extraordinarily clever impersonator. I have not seen her act. I feel sure she could act, and trust she will soon get her chance. In the meantime she is a valuable asset to any company.[69]

'Mise' in the same issue wrote:

> Cluithchéoirí na hEireann has produced its best play, and produced it well. *The Shuiler's Child* is the finest character-study seen on the stage in Dublin for several years, and the only play written by a living Irishman about the life of our day which can be called a tragedy. . . . The dramatist has projected himself into the woman's mind — the woman's soul — and has given us a tragedy. Incidentally he gave Miss Nic Shiubhlaigh her opportunity, and splendidly she seized that opportunity. Those who have seen Miss Nic Shiubhlaigh playing in characters drawn by men who quite believed they were drawing women know her to be a clever actress. Those who saw her in a real woman's part know her now to be a great actress.[70]

Another article in the same issue thought it encouraging 'to notice how the young poets and artists of Dublin are flocking to its [The Theatre of Ireland's] assistance. . . . There is a feeling of enthusiasm about the Society, a sense of adventure and token of that devotion to ideal aims, which springs from unjaded vitality.' But after noting how enthusiasm and a real capacity for character portrayal had contributed to a remarkable production, the writer then went on to criticize the play:

317

The chief defect of *The Shuiler's Child* is in its construction.
. . . Seumas O'Kelly did not give his subject the rigorous study
and analysis necessary in order to settle definitely in his own
mind what the fundamental motive of his play really was —
what was the central situation round which everything should
tend, and bear a distinct and definite relation. To me it seems
that there were two motives, either of which would have
served for this purpose — namely, the struggle, under the
influence of the awakening affection for her child to regain
her lost self-respect. But neither of these is made sufficiently
prominent to definitely mould the play one way or the other.
The primary struggle is not for the child, because the Shuiler
does not long for the boy as intensely as she longs for her
own restoration. Indeed, the boy is simply with her as a
means to this end. Neither is it for the Shuiler's regeneration,
for in this the other characteristics, with one incidental exception take no part. . . . Máire Nic Shiubhlaigh had a
splendid opportunity as Moll Woods, and made the most of it.
The tragic intensity she achieved particularly in the last act,
was quite remarkable. If anything, she was a little too ethereal
for the part. But if at times she failed to convey what would
seem to be an adequate idea of the depths of sordidness and
misery to which the Shuiler must necessarily have sunk, she
did not shirk the duty imposed upon her in the last portion
of the second act. The singing of the ballad there was certainly
the most direfully realistic piece of work she has ever done.
It was terrible and awful, and yet unfortunately, true to life.
The Theatre of Ireland scarcely realise the valuable asset they
have in Máire Nic Shiubhlaigh. There are certain ranges of
acting in which she is quite unique. She has shown in *The
Shuiler's Child*, by her success in a part for which she is
temperamentally unfit, proof of her possession of an almost
unsuspected versatility.[71]

*   *   *

On 26 November the Ulster Literary Theatre appeared at the
Abbey in Dublin, with the premiere of Gerald MacNamara's
The Mist That Does Be on the Bog, and with Rutherford Mayne's
popular comedy, *The Drone*, which was now expanded into three
acts. C.A. in *The Dublin Evening Mail* confined his attention to
The Drone because, as he explained:

> . . . I had seen it before and have, therefore, become through
> lapse of time, a more impartial critic; and, also because it
> monopolises most of the hours devoted to the Society's

318

performance. When I saw this play previously, if my recollection serves me, it ended with the second act. The third act was, therefore, new to me last night, but in the other two which, I understood, had been re-written, I was not able to detect any great change. We have yet to meet the . . . dramatist who can convert a two, into a three act play. Mr. Yeats is one of the few people who can improve a play by polishing it, and the reason for this is that he has always a fundamental idea beneath the surface, which reveals itself more and more the harder he works at his material. But the curse of most of the young Irish dramatists is multiplicity of small ideas, and the want of a single and primary conception. What they need is practice, and what they had better do is to consign their plays to the waste paper basket as fast as they are written and played, so as to gain the necessary experience to enable them to express themselves when they have really something to say. And all this has its application to *The Drone*. It is a successful comedy, as witness the continuous laughter of the audience. Mr. Mayne has the gift in common with some of our Abbey writers, of catching and expressing the ordinary life of the people of Ireland he knows best, in their phrase, customs and manners. He has also made a definite and clever character study in the person of "The Drone." It is possible, too, that the hero . . . stands for some ideal, but if he does it is lost in "The Drone's" nimble-minded trickery and elusiveness. To my mind, he stood for nothing more ideal than a certain indolent good-heartedness, being lovable, no doubt, but purposeless. As to the action which, after all, should be the groundwork of a play of this kind it is improbable and farcical. The play is one neither of action nor ideas. In point of fact it is really not drama in any true sense. There is no working towards a definite purpose, no subordination of action, or ideas, to a culminating action or idea. I cannot regard it except as a staged character sketch, humorous and interesting, but as far removed from drama as a series of cinematograph pictures is below a work of art. . . .

The plays give evidence of no real talent for acting, but this is hardly to be expected. Some of the actors, however, suit their parts admirably, and this is the most that can be said. This was particularly noticeable in Mr. Arthur Malcolm's interpretation of Uncle Dan in *The Drone*. Miss Seveen Canmer was also very successful as his niece, but she has lost much of her former fascination in the part.[72]

319

'Jacques' in *The Irish Independent* devoted most of his notice to *The Mist That Does Be on the Bog*:

> The author calls his work "A fog in one act." A most apt title. The little play is most obviously a skit on the kind of dialogue put into the mouths of Irish peasants by dramatists and novelists who deal with Irish peasant themes. A gentleman and his wife and his wife's sister (Cissy Dodd), all of the motor car society class, rent Michael Quinn's cottage in the West of Ireland for the purpose of picking up the real modes of speech of the Western peasants and of studying the poor people's ways and habits of living. They dress up to their parts. On the same quest comes one Clarence St. John, a Dublin playwright, disguised as a tramp. St. John and the other crowd meet. Each side plays the game of pretending to be peasants. They talk the most outlandish nonsense. St. John and Cissy Dodd, who calls herself Moira, fall in love. There are Box and Cox complications and explanations, and the curtain falls on a scene of burlesque on the sugary sentiment of ha'-penny novelette romances.
>
> The idea is capital, but the play must never again be done as it was done last night. The players got lost in the fog, and the point of the play was completely missed by many in the audience. Further rehearsing and a prompter's guidance will shed more light on things that at this first performance were lost or clouded.
>
> As for *The Drone*. To say anything of this most droll of droll stage pictures would be to mention laughter in every sentence. A third act dealing with a breach of promise action has been added. The continuous laughter of the audience paid tribute to play, players, and author. What really excellent artistes all those Ulster players are![73]

* * *

On 5 May *The Cork Constitution* reported the beginning of a new dramatic society:

> The dramatic movement in Ireland continues to make steady progress. Founded in Dublin, it now flourishes there under the auspices of more than one society. It soon reached Belfast, and the Ulster theatre in that city is now recognised as having in its repertoire a number of brilliant plays typical of life in the North, and little, if anything, below the level of the Dublin plays in point of art. The movement has at last reached Cork; it, however, remains to be seen whether Cork

320

can keep pace with Dublin and Belfast in these matters. The Cork Dramatic Society has been founded with the same aims, and with much the same ideals as the societies in Dublin and Belfast. Like them, it will produce only such plays as are written for the society; moreover, the plays must have at least the feeling of literature about them. The sensational, the specious, the spectacular will be avoided; the critical and the thoughtful study of the life of our people, or the imaginative seizing of movements and racial tendencies will be encouraged; while in the matter of acting the ideals aimed at will be the simplicity, cohesion, and harmony that such classes of plays demand. The Cork Dramatic Society makes its first appearance before the public on next Thursday and Friday nights in the Dun, Queen Street, when *The Embers*, a play in three acts, written by D. Corkery, will be produced for the first time. It is hoped that the many people who found the visit of the players from the Abbey Theatre such a pleasant experience will extend their patronage to the local effort.[74]

The play opened on 6 May, and *The Cork Constitution* gave it this review:

Those who appreciate the plays produced by the Abbey Theatre Company, and they attract more and more attention from year to year, should willingly extend their cordial support to the Cork Dramatic Society, which will perform plays written specially for it, and which demands that these shall have some semblance at least of the spirit of literature, and shall not even suggest what is stereotyped and conventional. They expect any dramatists for their theatre to write what they feel and think, to describe life as they find it, and not to seek to win commendation at the expense of truth and reality. Well, the Cork Dramatic Society has begun well. Yesterday evening, in the Dun, they produced a play in three acts by D. Corkery, with the title *The Embers*. Mr. Corkery would hardly make the claim that his play is of exceptional merit, but this merit at least it possesses, and it is something of which he may feel proud: it is singularly unconventional, and one is made to feel and know that his own individuality permeates it. One may agree or disagree with it, but that it is real and true no one can deny. *The Embers* is a capital title. The play opens at a period when Parliamentarianism was, so to speak, rampant. Here in brief is the plot:— Laurence Kiely is the son of a farmer. The position of Clerk to the Union in Cooladhue is vacant, and his father intends that he shall obtain it, so much so, indeed, that he bribes the guardians to vote for him. Then arrives home one John Witelaw O'Loughlin, an ex-political prisoner, and Laurence withdraws in his favour, and O'Loughlin secures the position. Somewhat later the position of "M.P." for the constituency becomes vacant, and Laurence is the popular candidate, but O'Loughlin has infused him with new thoughts and ideas, and Laurence flouts the Convention and declines to enter Parliament. His father is enraged, and turns him out of the house. Laurence goes, but finds shelter with O'Loughlin, who wins him over to aims and objects far from Constitutional. Twenty-five years elapse. Behold the Cooladhue Literary Club! Here are politicians of another generation. Daly [is the] son of an M.P., whose ideas would shock his father. This son is thoughtful, and would have the members deal with ideas, let them permeate down to the multitude, study life and its surroundings, etc.; but his companions are for action. A national public procession is to take place, and while they are discussing what action they shall take, enters Laurence Kiely, now aged. His treatment by the processionists, his words in general, excite them, and they decide to take part in the procession, and show the "old men" who have charge of it what their — the young men's — ideas are. Kiely has successfully fanned "The Embers," and the play ends, showing him weary and broken, but uttering praises of O'Loughlin. The different periods are well contrasted, and one is made to feel that the day of thought may, after all, promise best for the people. But, it may be, the author means something other.

Mr. P. O'Leary made an admirable farmer-shopkeeper; Mr. E. O'Shea was excellent as his son; Mr. D. Harrington was typical as the ex-political prisoner; Mr. C. Ronayne and Mr. W. Lanigan were good as local politicians; Miss D. Gilley as Mrs. Kiely, Miss M. J. Dixon as Mrs. Forde, and Miss A. Walshe as Nan Forde acted in a praiseworthy manner; Mr. D. Breen as Daly, and Mr. P. Higgins as O'Brien, "politicians of another generation," were very satisfactory. The acting and manner of speech follows the company at Abbey Theatre, Dublin. There is not overmuch movement, and the voice is given every prominence. Defects, of course, there were, but they were altogether outnumbered by the merits of the performance, which, it should be mentioned, was witnessed by a large audience. . . . The author was called before the curtain and suitably thanked the audience.[75]

The size of the audience was actually probably not much more than fifty or sixty, for only £2/8/6 was taken in receipts for the first night and only £2/11/4 for the second. The performances at the Dun Theatre were for only two or three nights, and the total receipts for a production never totalled more than £9. As the cost of mounting the productions usually came to about £15, the annual membership dues of five shillings were indeed a necessity for the society.

The Society's second production appeared on 2 and 3 December, and consisted of three one-act plays: T. C. Murray's *The Wheel of Fortune*, Daniel Corkery's *The Hermit and the King*, and Lennox Robinson's *The Lesson of Life*. These three writers were to be the best known of 'the Cork realists', and it is interesting to find them all on the same programme at the outset of their long careers. *The Cork Constitution* reviewed the plays:

Congratulations may be extended to the Cork Dramatic Society on the success which attended the presentation of three plays, each in one act, at the Dun Theatre yesterday evening. Two of the plays were Irish light comedy, and the third play symbolic.

Dealing with them in the order in which they were presented, there was first *The Wheel o' Fortune*, by Mr. T. C. Murray. This play was concerned with match-making in a rural district, and, in some respects, clearly defined the emotions and feelings aroused on these occasions. But Mr. Murray made no effort to indicate the sordidness, fierce quarrels and passions aroused, and, more particularly, when the whole affair takes place in a publichouse. However, one cannot expect perfection at a first attempt, and the assertion can be made that Mr. Murray has done very well. He manages dialogue with considerable skill, and the emotions and feelings he wants to make evident are not to be mistaken. The piece was so well received that the author received a call before the curtain, and responded. . . . The acting is modelled on Abbey Theatre lines, but, of course, as yet lacks the fine artistic touches and finish one observes in these players.

The Hermit and the King was the next piece presented. As stated, it is symbolic in treatment, suggesting rather than proving that the author may yet become acceptable to the Irish public as a dramatist of merit. Selecting an incident concerned with two brothers, one is made to learn a great deal about the merely material and spiritual side of life, and the play ends on a note not only triumphant for the spiritual, but leaving an impression of intrinsic worth and beauty not too quickly dispelled. In great part the phrasing is admirable and really poetic. The intoning was delightful, and, as the author had paid attention to assonance, none of the harmonious effects were lost. . . .

The Lesson of his Life was the last play presented. This was by Mr. S. L. Robinson. It deals with a rural youth of wild ways, and his reformation by ingenious means. The dialogue was capital, and the whole scene well arranged, but there was more than a suggestion of the farcical in the little play. There was real cleverness in the presenting of the several characters, and in particular of the mother of the youth and Sergeant Cantillon. . . . Miss Daisy Gilley was splendid as the mother, and should in due course prove the Miss Sara Allgood of the Society. Mr. P. O'Leary could scarcely have done better, but the acting all round was good.[76]

These three plays proved among the most popular of the society and were several times repeated in later years. Perhaps the most popular was Robinson's play, but as he was shortly to become involved with the Abbey Theatre as its young manager he wrote no more for the Cork group. T. C. Murray rewrote his play a few years later, and it was presented at the Abbey under the title of *Sovereign Love*.

*   *   *

The Oireachtas was presented this year at the Rotunda for a week beginning 31 July. On that day Father Thomas O'Kelly's heroic play *Deirdre* was produced; on 2, 3, and 5 August an opera in Irish was produced. It was called *Eithne*; its libretto was by Father O'Kelly and its music by Robert O'Dwyer. On 4 August, Thomas Hayes's *An Sgrabhadóir* (*The Miser*) was produced. All three productions were reviewed by Seumas O Conghaile in *Sinn Féin*:

The artistic performances at the Oireachtas have made the present year of 1909 the most memorable in the history of the festival. For years we have been delving in soil so long gone fallow, to recover traditions of artistic impulse so nearly dead, that the pessimists amongst us were able to deny us any creative vitality without too good a show of unreason. "There is no Gaelic tradition in drama. You cannot produce a great play. For all our boasted eminence in melody, you cannot produce an opera of any sort." . . . We can fling back its mean insult with a laugh. We can exult in choking their calumny and their lie. We can simply point to *Eithne* and to *Deirdre*, an opera and a play, whose respective productions have marked an advance, as yet incalculable, in the march of triumph of the Gael. . . . Father O'Kelly's *Deirdre* is the finest play in Irish the Oireachtas has yet given us. . . .

I had not intended to say anything about the acting, because I had something to do with the production of the play; but I cannot — and I am sure no one who saw it will accuse me of *parti pris* — help congratulating Máire Nic Shiubhlaigh on the beautiful way she interpreted the part. Not even in Æ's *Deirdre* has she acted so well, nor her voice been so poignantly emotional as in the farewell speech to Alba. . . .

An Scrabhadóir, by Tomás O hAodha, was the second prize play of the Oireachtas week. Tomás is an ardent and successful dramatist in Irish, whose *Seán na Sguab*, given at the Oireachtas some six or seven years ago, itself marked a milestone forward in Irish drama. I am glad to see that he has come back to comedy, for in the *Seabhac*, his last Oireachtas prize play, he did not seem to be at home. It was a rattling melodrama, and good enough of its kind, but not good enough from Tomás O hAodha.

In his present comedy (*The Miser*) he has been bold enough to handle a theme that Molière has made immortal. But Tomás has not gone to Molière for inspiration; rather has he sought it in the life he knows. The scenes are laid in West Clare.[77]

Among other amateur groups active during the year were the Irish Theatrical Club, which staged plays and gave readings in its rooms in 40 Upper O'Connell Street; the Metropolitan School of Art Students' Union, which rented the Abbey for three days in April to present Thomas King Moylan's comedy *Paid in his Own Coin* and Hugh Barden's *The Storm*; and the Players Club, which rented the Gaiety for the week of 15 March to present Flora MacDonnell in Pinero's *The Gay Lord Quex*.

The Irish Theatrical Club was West-Briton in sentiment, and its occasional original dramas took their inspiration from the English polite stage and from conventional fiction, and were rarely more interesting than the attempts of Count Markievicz or those at the turn of the century by Mary L. Butler. As one instance, the Irish Theatrical Club presented on 11 March two new plays by Captain W. E. Tolfrey Christie. The first, a one-act called *Made in Germany* was:

. . . an episode in which the principal actors were Lady Betty Beaumont (Miss Evelyn Power) and Miss Ethel Morton (Miss Gill), one, a dashing, athletic, somewhat slangy young woman, and the other the diametric opposite. Both are smitten with the charms of a German Count, and throw over their former respective admirers. The ladies soon, however, discover the perfidy of the foreigner, and reconciliation with the British lovers follows.

Briefly, the plot of *The Broken Reed* is this: — Brutal, drunken husband; long-suffering, plucky wife; sympathetic, pitying friend; result complications which are ultimately adjusted.[78]

*   *   *

On 5 May the Theatre Royal had its own riot. The occasion was the production of a pseudo-serious play called *An Englishman's Home*. The play, as *The Evening Telegraph* described it, depicted 'the horrible consequences of an invasion of England by the Army of "The Empress of the North," and gives a vivid picture of the unpreparedness for war of Britons.' Unfortunately, the Irish audience did not thoroughly sympathize with the efforts of the English hero, Mr. Brown, to repel the invaders from his home:

> There is hardly a line of the text of this exceedingly cynical production that could hope to live. But such of the audience last night as came to form a serious judgment on the question were certainly not afforded very much opportunity of doing so. The gallery occupants especially indicated their determination to welcome the invaders with wholehearted cheers and to drown the voices of those who were "on the other side." Once the racket commenced there seemed little chance of ending it. The curtain was rung down, whether at the end of an act or before it was finished could hardly be definitely said, for no one could very well follow what was being uttered or done on the stage. From the gallery came the chorus of "God Save Ireland" and the "Marseillaise," whilst in the pit a number of young persons formed a kind of Dutch chorus by singing the English National Anthem. One enthusiastic gentleman in evening dress in the balcony stalls gesticulated wildly, and cried out, "Hear the play, boys; we all paid our money, and when it's all over give hell if you like." Another yelled at stated intervals "God save the King," and when the curtain was raised for the second or third act, and comparative peace seemed about to be restored, a number of youths

326

started the "Anthem" once more. This was met by a counter-blast from the gods, and so deafening was the noise that it seemed for a time pretty obvious that the "show" could not proceed, and down again came the curtain. Then the police were called in, and a score or so of them placed themselves in the gallery, the occupants of which varied their methods by applauding with such vigour as to prevent even more effectively than before any coherent sentence being heard from the stage. Paper darts were thrown about, and what seemed to be a piece of plaster was flung down. One arrest at least was made, and for a long time the singular picture was presented of half the audience standing up and singing one thing, whilst the other half were singing something else, and the orchestra vigorously but vainly endeavouring to accomplish the impossible of throwing musical oil on the troubled waters by playing some fine old English melodies. Meanwhile the corridors and approaches to the boxes were crowded with more or less excited people. One amongst them, of very bellicose propensities, and who looked like "the very model of a modern Major-General," excitedly offered to go up and personally "clear that d--d gallery," but when some-one observed: "I'd like to see you try," he subsided and returned to the stalls to adopt the less warlike occupation of joining in the chorus of "God Save the King." . . . It is really questionable whether it is good judgment to bring to Dublin a work of the kind, having regard, especially to its reception elsewhere, and to the elements of discordant notes which it presents. . . . There is no use trying to reason with an audience who have strong views on both sides; and if those who are saturated with "Jingoism" will demonstrate — well, those who are not so afflicted may be expected to have their say.[79]

The Theatre Royal, having found that its Hippodrome season was quite popular, now devoted more time to Variety. Such performers as Cecilia Loftus, Little Tich, and the ex-heavyweight champion James J. Corbett now appeared there, as did also Consul (The Almost Man) 'in his Marvellous Delineation of the Darwinean Theory as Exemplified by him before His Majesty the King'. Consul was an educated ape. The Royal still produced musicals and light comedies and occasionally hosted an eminent celebrity like Caruso. In the afternoons, one could have tea in the theatre's Winter Garden and also see films.

Frederick Mouillot, the controlling director of the theatre, gave an interview in August, in which he remarked with some degree of truth:

Yes, I now control two theatres in Dublin, the Gaiety and the Theatre Royal. I also do the booking arrangements for Belfast and Cork, so I suppose I am really the censor for Ireland. Someone on the Joint Committee said that the Irish theatres are more riotous than the English. I should like to modify that statement. In my experience of many years past there have been two disturbances — one in connection with *The Playboy of the Western World*, at the Abbey Theatre, Dublin, and the other concerning *An Englishman's Home*, at the Theatre Royal, Dublin. The first was political, the second I don't understand; but the second night we raised the price of the gallery, and that quelled the riot. Now, *John Bull's Other Island* I was very much afraid of in Ireland; but, lo and behold! it captured them, and made a very wonderful success.[80]

Although the Gunn family relinquished the management of the Gaiety on 1 May to Mouillot and his group, the booking policy of the Gaiety remained the same as in previous years.

Late in September, the Queen's re-opened after extensive re-modelling. Some of the designing was done by John Ryan of the Irish Fibrous Plaster Depot, and his work was described by *The Freeman's Journal*:

Mr. Ryan has given the lead in the matter of decorations in public buildings. He has revealed new possibilities in Celtic tracery, and the result is a playhouse whose interior will be a feast to the eye.

Gazing towards the stage the eye is arrested by a beautifully modelled allegorical group — Erin laying a gilt laurel wreath before the bust of Moore — which occupies the centre of the top of the proscenium. On the left-hand side of it is a figure representing Music, on the right a figure representing Drama. Above each of these figures is a shield, surrounded by Celtic grotesques and tracery. The former shield bears the names "Sheridan, Sullivan, Griffin," the latter "Goldsmith, Boucicault, Balfe." Beneath the whole of this is the inscription in large Celtic letters, "CEAD MILE FAILTE." [81]

The Queen's re-opened on 27 September, and its first programme, *The 10.30 Down Express* produced by Mr. Horace Stanley's Company, made it clear that there was to be no essential change in its policy. It was still the Home of Melodrama.

On 23 August the Empire Palace was the scene of a disturbance. As *The Evening Telegraph* reported:

Last night an exciting occurrence took place in the Empire Theatre. As usual, the gallery was thronged. After Miss Elsie Kerry, a popular Irish artiste, was most enthusiastically received, and after responding to several encores, the "gods" insisted on her singing more. The programme was very lengthy, and this rendered it impossible for the lady to gratify the wishes of her admirers. Consequently another artiste came forward. The hurricane of almost every description of noise was now so overpowering that the "turn" was gone through in mere dumb show. A similar fate befell succeeding performers. The demonstrants eventually adopted even yet more active measures. They smashed woodwork and windows. The police on duty in the theatre, reinforced by many of the stalwart attendants, formed themselves into a phalanx, rushed the gallery, and cleared out the "gods." During the disturbance nearly all the electric lamps in various passages were more or less wrecked. No arrests were made.[82]

*   *   *

In May, James Cousins published an article on historical drama in which he remarked:

Some time ago it was declared, at a meeting of the National Literary Society, that the Irish stage was suffering from too much peasant. The city man was suggested. This might do very well if the most important consideration of "the Irish stage" was the gratification of the rudimentary desire for variety. But there is something more substantial to be done. . . . I have myself felt a need for something in the way of change. I have had a longing for the breath of romance. I think I want someone to write a new historical play. I want someone to get "back to the land" — not the ground, but the soul out of which the things of the present have grown. Delving there he may, more surely than among the fluctuating and conventional eccentricities of cities, dint his spade on the bedrock of nationality.[83]

In June, Henry Mangan, who had written a few seasons before an historical drama about Emmet, approved of Cousins's views and suggested a national touring company that would use some of the Irish actors on the professional stage, such as the Fays, Dudley Digges, and P. J. Kelly. Alice Milligan disagreed, thinking that it would be improper to encourage young women to join such a touring company, and also that the various amateur groups around the country were quite sufficient.

The Dublin Companies, even of the Abbey Theatre or the Theatre of Ireland, with the exception of two or three actors and actresses whom I will not here name, do not surpass in ability in any remarkable way the good amateur actors who are at work in the other cities and country towns and districts.[84]

She then mentioned that she received many inquiries about scripts, and thought that she might start a dramatic bureau to publish and disseminate plays. Of her own work, she wrote:

> I have written the following historical pieces myself: — *Brian of Banba* (short, poetical in form); *The Feast of the Fianna, Oisin in Tír na nOg, Oisin and Padraic,* the three forming a dramatic trilogy; *The Last of the Desmonds* (which tells the story of Red Hugh O'Donnell's wooing — has been produced in Cork), *The Escape of Red Hugh* (well-known in Dublin), *The Daughter of Donogh* (Cromwellian melodrama, published in *The United Irishman*), *The Harp That Once* (a '98 piece in one act), *The Green upon the Cape* (a short piece relating an incident of the visit of Wolfe Tone to the Hague), and *The French are on the Sea* (a '98 drama in five acts, unpublished).
>
> I have several others sketched, but don't write them, as my plays are so seldom acted.[85]

*   *   *

By the end of 1909, the Irish theatre was in a flourishing state. These were years of achievement. Although John Synge was dead, his theatre had firmly established itself. It had survived the attacks of the nationalists which culminated in the row over *The Playboy.* It had survived the suspicion of Dublin Castle which culminated in the row over *Blanco Posnet.* It had shown its independence of every shade of political or social or national or religious opinion. It had shown that its one allegiance was solidly to the art of the theatre.

From nothing it had developed a repertoire of distinguished plays, some of which had already taken their place in the drama of the world. Undoubtedly, the greatest play of this period was *The Playboy of the Western World,* which has become a classic of the modern drama. But there were also *The Well of the Saints, Riders to the Sea, The White Cockade, The Eloquent Dempsy, Hyacinth Halvey, The Gaol Gate,* Yeats's *Deirdre, The Rising of the Moon, The Country Dressmaker, The Piper, The Pie-Dish, The Golden Helmet, The Workhouse Ward, The Glittering Gate,* and the early work of Lennox Robinson.

330

The theatre had developed a group of actors who were better than any in the world for the task they had to do. Some of them left the Abbey and made names for themselves in London and New York and Hollywood, but all contributed the best of themselves to the creation of a mood of playing. Not perhaps really to a style of acting, but to a mood of high seriousness which, even when faced with the problems of comedy, elevated the craft of an actor to an art. Frank and Willie Fay, Sara Allgood, Molly O'Neill, J. M. Kerrigan, Arthur Sinclair all have their names indistinguishably linked with the characters they created — Cuchullain, Martin Doul, Pegeen Mike, Hyacinth Halvey, Jeremiah Dempsy. There can be no greater honour for an actor than that.

The theatre of Yeats and Synge and Lady Gregory had also developed a drama for the whole of Ireland. The Theatre of Ireland, with Mary Walker playing for it and with Seumas O'Kelly writing for it, was no contemptible rival. The Ulster Literary Theatre, founded in imitation of the Abbey, was developing the comedy of Rutherford Mayne and the whimsy of Gerald MacNamara. After one false start in 1906, the theatre in Cork brilliantly revived in 1909 with plays by Daniel Corkery, T. C. Murray, and Lennox Robinson all on the same programme.

The theatre in the Irish language was perhaps the only disappointment. After a most promising beginning, with the short comedies of Douglas Hyde and the sketches of P. T. MacGinley, it developed no new writers as fine.

Nevertheless, in 1909, after eleven years of labour, the drama in Ireland had risen from nothing to distinction.

Appendix : Anglo-Irish Drama, *a checklist* 1905-1909

This list attempts to give the date of first publication, the date of first production, and the original cast of the most significant plays of the Irish Dramatic Renaissance during these years. It includes only the most important plays written in the Irish language, and it omits, for the most part, plays which lack any tincture of literary or theatrical or historical merit.

The plays are listed chronologically by date of first production. When the plays were not produced or when the production date is uncertain, they are listed by the date of their first publication. The cast lists, whenever possible, are based upon the original programmes, rather than upon the sometimes variant cast lists to be found in the books of some published plays. Often, neither programme nor published book was available, and in such cases the cast lists have been formed by a comparison of available newspaper accounts.

MAURICE JOY

The Message,
a Drama in One Act.
No record of production.
First published: In *The United Irishman*, XIII (7 January 1905).

J. M. SYNGE

The Well of the Saints,
a Play in Three Acts.
First produced: 4 February 1905, by the Irish National Theatre Society, at the Abbey Theatre, Dublin.

CAST

Martin Doul, a Blind Man
W. G. Fay
Mary Doul, his Wife
Emma Vernon
Timmy   George Roberts
Molly Byrne   Sara Allgood
Bride   Maire Nic Shiubhlaigh
Mat Simon   P. MacSiubhlaigh
A Wandering Friar   F. J. Fay
Girls and Men
Directed by W. G. Fay
Scenery by Pamela Colman Smith
First published: London: A. H. Bullen, 1905.

SEUMAS MacMANUS

The Lad from Largymore,
a Farce in One Act.
First produced: 27 February 1905, at the Rotunda, Dublin; revived probably with much the same cast on 30 October 1905, at the Molesworth Hall, Dublin.

CAST
of 30 October Revival

Master of the House   J. Connolly
Margaret MacClenaghan
Miss K. Toomey
Constable MacGlory
Gerald O'Loughlin
The Lad from Largymore
Mr. Carolan
First published: Mount Charles, Co. Donegal: D. O'Molloy, n.d.

DELIA O'DWYER

All Souls' Eve,
a Play in One Act.
No record of production.
First published: In *The United Irishman*, XIII (4 March 1905).

JOHN O'LOUGHLIN

(pseudonym of John J. Horgan)
The Nation Builder
First produced: 6 March 1905, by the Cork National Theatre, in the Assembly Rooms, Cork.

CAST

John Murphy, a Tweed Manufacturer, Owner of the Kilbreeda Mills   J. Milroy
Joseph Murphy, his Son, Educated in England   W. Finn
Thomas Fitzgerald, M.D., Dispensary Doctor and President of the Kilbreeda Branch of the Gaelic League   J. Archer
Henry Gore Maxdale, Solicitor and Agent for Lord Kilbreeda
T. O'Gorman
Robert Mansfield, Accountant and Company Promoter from Leeds   J. O'Regan
Michael Barry, J.P., Chairman of the Rural District Council
H. Golden
Denis Twomey, R.D.C., a Merchant and Creditor of John Murphy   T. Murphy
Mary Murphy, Wife of John Murphy   Miss M. Cronin
Sheila Murphy, their Daughter
Miss A. Barry
No record of publication.

ALICE L. MILLIGAN

The Last of the Desmonds,
a Bi-Lingual Irish Historical Play in One Act.
First produced: 6 March 1905, by the Cork National Theatre, in the Assembly Rooms, Cork.

CAST

Sir George Carew, President of Munster   James Archer
Lord Wilfrid Crosby, an English Nobleman   J. O'Regan
James, Earl of Desmond
J. L. Sullivan
Mistress Abigail Pym, Wife of a Limerick Gentleman in whose House Joan is Lodged
Miss M. Cronin
Deborah Pym, her Daughter
Miss L. Barry
Maire Sheehy, an old Nurse
Miss M. Goulding

The Lady Joan Fitzgerald
Miss A. Barry
Costumes Designed and Executed
by Alice L. Milligan
First published: In *The United
Irishman*, XI (4 June 1904).

JAMES H. COUSINS
The Clansman,
an Irish Historical Play
in Four Acts.
No record of production.
First published: In *The United
Irishman*, Act I (18 March 1905);
Act II (25 March 1905); Act III
(1 April 1905); Act IV (8 April
1905).

LADY GREGORY
Kincora,
a Play in Three Acts and
a Prologue.
First produced: 25 March 1905,
by the Irish National Theatre
Society, at the Abbey Theatre,
Dublin.

CAST
Brian of the Tributes, King of
Munster, afterwards High King
F. J. Fay
Murrough, his Son
George Roberts
Malachi, High King of Ireland
Ambrose Power
Gormleith, his Wife, afterwards
Wife of Brian
Maire Nic Shiubhlaigh
Sitric, her Son by Olaf of the
Danes P. Mac Siubhlaigh
Maelmora, her Brother, King of
Leinster Seumas O'Sullivan
Servants of Brian:
Brennain Arthur Sinclair
Derrick W. G. Fay
Rury, Malachi's Servant
J. H. Dunne
Phelan, Maelmora's Servant
Udolphus Wright
Maire, Brennain's Daughter
Maire Ni Gharbhaigh
Aoibhell, a Woman of the Sidhe
Sara Allgood
Broader R. Nash
A Dane U. Wright
Directed by W. G. Fay
Scenery and Costumes by
Robert Gregory
First published: Dublin: The
Abbey Theatre, 1905; Being Vol-

ume II of the Abbey Theatre
Series.

WILLIAM BOYLE
The Building Fund,
a Comedy in Three Acts.
First produced: 25 April 1905, by
the Irish National Theatre Society,
at the Abbey Theatre, Dublin.

CAST
Mrs. Grogan, a Miserly Old
Woman Emma Vernon
Shan Grogan, her Son, Another
Miser W. G. Fay
Sheila O'Dwyer, her Grand-
daughter Sara Allgood
Michael O'Callaghan, an
Elderly Farmer F. J. Fay
Dan MacSweeny, a Young
Farmer Arthur Sinclair
Directed by W. G. Fay
First published: Dublin: Maunsel
& Co. Ltd., 1905; Being Volume
VII of the Abbey Theatre Series.

JOSEPH CAMPBELL
(Seosamh MacCathmhaoil)
The Little Cowherd of Slainge,
a Dramatic Legend in Verse
in Two Scenes.
First produced: 4 May 1905, by
the Ulster Literary Theatre, in the
Clarence Place Hall, in Belfast.
In the Cast, Josephine Campbell
played Fionnghuala, and the play
was produced by Fred Morrow.
First published: In *Uladh*, I (November 1904).

LEWIS PURCELL
(pseudonym of David Parkhill)
The Enthusiast,
a Comedy in Two Scenes.
First produced: 4 May 1905, by
the Ulster Literary Theatre, in the
Clarence Place Hall, in Belfast.

CAST
William John McKinstray,
a Farmer
James, his Son, Home from
Belfast on Vacation
Desmond Brannigan
Sam, Brother of James
John Campbell
Aunt Margaret, Housekeeper to
her Brother Alice O'Dea

Minnie, Engaged to James
Rab, a Servant Man
　　　　　　Rutherford Mayne
Produced by Fred Morrow
First published: In *Uladh*, I (May 1905).

THOMAS MARKHAM
The Trail of the Serpent,
a Comedy.
First produced: 28 May 1905, at the Banba Hall, Dublin.
No record of publication.

PADRAIC COLUM
The Land,
a Play in Three Acts.
First produced: 9 June 1905, by the Irish National Theatre Society, at the Abbey Theatre, Dublin.

CAST

Murtagh Cosgar, a Farmer
　　　　　　W. G. Fay
Matt, his Son
　　　　　Proinsias Mac Siubhlaigh
Sally, his Daughter　Sara Allgood
Martin Douras, a Farmer
　　　　　　F. J. Fay
Cornelius, his Son　Arthur Sinclair
Ellen, his Daughter
　　　　　Maire Ni Gharbhaigh
A Group of Men and a Group of Boys and Girls.

　　　　Directed by W. G. Fay

First published: Dublin: Maunsel & Co. Ltd., 1905, Being Volume III of the Abbey Theatre Series.

LIAM MacEIREANN
Cloc ar an mBothar,
a One-Act Play in English.
No record of production.
First published: In *The United Irishman*, XIII (10 June 1905).

SEUMAS MacMANUS
The Mullinafad Town Council,
a One-Act Comedy Sketch.
Date of production unknown.
First published: In *The United Irishman*, XIII (17 and 24 June 1905).

JAMES H. COUSINS
The Turn of the Tide,
a Play of Real Life in One Act.
No record of production.

First published: In *The United Irishman*, XIV (26 August and 2 September 1905).

ROSA MULHOLLAND, LADY GILBERT
Boycotting,
a Miniature Comedy.
First produced: 30 October 1905, by the National Players, at the Samhain Festival in the Molesworth Hall, Dublin.

CAST

Major O'Flattery	P. O'Connor
Charlie Thomond	
	Gerald O'Loughlin
Brian	P. White
Tim	J. Keegan
Pat	J. O'Reilly
Eileen O'Flattery	
	Miss C. Morrison
Miss Hart	Miss H. Molony
Hon. Mrs. Thomond	
	Miss Shortall
Katty	Miss T. Kirwan
Nancy	Miss E. Morrison
Bridget	Miss Dunne
Peggy	Miss Dillon

First published: Dublin: M. H. Gill, [1915] under the title *Our Boycotting*.

EDWARD MARTYN
The Tale of a Town,
a Play in Five Acts.
First produced: 31 October 1905, by the National Players, at the Molesworth Hall, Dublin.

CAST

Joseph Tench, the Mayor	
	Joseph O'Byrne
Jasper Dean	Daniel Laurence
Thomas Murphy	Valentine Foley
Ralph Kirwan	James Cassidy
Michael Leech	Gerald O'Loughlin
John Cloran	P. Reilly
George Hardman	
	Cathal MacGarvey
Miss Millicent Fell	
	Miss H. Molony
Miss Caroline Dean	
	Miss C. Morrison
Miss Arabella Dean	
	Miss May Dillon
Mrs. Bella Cassidy	
	Miss E. Morrison
Miss Sarah Leech	
	Miss E. Shortall

Also with J. Keegan, P. O'Connor, Brian MacAilindean, John Connolly, M. Carolan, and Joseph Reilly.

First published: In *The Tale of a Town and An Enchanted Sea*. London: T. Fisher Unwin, 1902; Kilkenny: Standish O'Grady, 1902.

DOUGLAS HYDE
Teach na mBocht,
a Play in One Act,
Translated by Lady Gregory as *The Poorhouse*.
The date of first production is uncertain, but an early production occurred on 31 October 1905, by the National Players, at the Samhain Festival in the Molesworth Hall, Dublin.

CAST
The Matron   Miss Lucy M'Kernan
Kate   Miss Rose Kavanagh
Sean Donn   C. O'Byrne
Padraig   John M'Glynn
Colum   John M'Glynn
The Porter   Joseph Hayes
First published: In *Samhain* (September 1903) in English and Irish; translation reprinted in Lady Gregory's *Poets and Dreamers* (1903), and in Vol. IX of the Abbey Theatre Plays: *Spreading the News and The Rising of the Moon*, by Lady Gregory, *The Poorhouse*, by Douglas Hyde and Lady Gregory (Dublin: Maunsel & Co., 1906); later rewritten as *The Workhouse Ward* by Lady Gregory and published in her *Seven Short Plays* (1909); published separately in Irish (Baile Atha Cliath: Oifig Díolta Foillseacháin Rialtais, 1934).

SEUMAS MacMANUS
The Woman of Seven Sorrows,
an Allegory in One Act.
First produced: 1 November 1905, by the National Players, at the Samhain Festival in the Molesworth Hall, Dublin.

First published: In *The United Irishman*, XIV (12 August 1905); published separately (Dublin: M. H. Gill, Ltd. and Mount Charles, Co. Donegal: D. O'Molloy, 1905).

MICHEAL UA DONNABHAIN
Making the Match,
a Comedy in One Act.
No record of production.
First published: In *The United Irishman*, XIV (4 November 1905).

LADY GREGORY
The White Cockade,
a Comedy in Three Acts.
First produced: 9 December 1905, by the National Theatre Society Ltd., Abbey Company, at the Abbey Theatre, Dublin.

CAST
Patrick Sarsfield, Earl of Lucan
  F. J. Fay
King James II   Arthur Sinclair
Carter, Secretary to King James
  J. H. Dunne
A Poor Lady
  Maire Nic Shiubhlaigh
Matt Kelleher, an Inn-keeper
  at Duncannon   W. G. Fay
Mary Kelleher, his Wife
  Sara Allgood
Owen Kelleher, his Son
  P. Mac Siubhlaigh
French Sailors   Walter S. Magee
  and Edward Keegan
1st Williamite   Ambrose Power
2nd Williamite   Udolphus Wright
Williamite Captain   M. Butler
First published: Dublin: Maunsel & Co., 1905, Being Volume VIII of the Abbey Theatre Series.

JAMES H. COUSINS
Sold,
a Comedy of Real Life
in Two Acts.
First produced: 27 December 1906, by the Cork National Theatre in Cork; revived 18 March 1907, at the Queen's Theatre, Dublin.

CAST
of the 1907 Production
William Mawhinney, a Farmer
  L. Ingoldsby
Molly, his Wife   Miss E. Moloney
Samuel Malone, a Pedlar
  M. Carolan
Thomas Hunter, a Solicitor's
  Clerk   F. Rigney
James Mansell, a Sherriff's
  Officer   L. Ua Dálaigh
Mr. Askin, a Solicitor   J. O'Reilly

Mr. Moneypenny, a Merchant
A. Lowe
Pullman, a Detective
M. MacAlaindin
Bib, Askin's Office Boy
F. Dowling
Directed by James H. Cousins
First published: In *The United Irishman*, VIII (27 December 1902).

JOHN HAMILTON

That Gossoon o' Mine,
a Drama of Irish Peasant Life
in Three Acts.
No record of production.
First published: In *The United Irishman*, XV, Act I (6 January 1906), Act II and Act III (13 January 1906).

MICHEAL UA DONNABHAIN

The Jokers,
a Short Drama,
in One Act and Three Scenes.
First produced: 16 January 1906, at Loughrea.
First published: In *The United Irishman*, XIV (16 December 1905).

WILLIAM BOYLE

The Eloquent Dempsy,
a Comedy in Three Acts.
First produced: 20 January 1906, by the National Theatre Society Ltd., at the Abbey Theatre, Dublin.

CAST

Jeremiah Dempsy, Publican and Grocer, County Councillor for Cloghermore   W. G. Fay
Mrs. Catherine Dempsy
Sara Allgood
Mary Kate, his Daughter
Brigit O'Dempsey
Dr. Bunbury, J.P.   F. J. Fay
Captain McNamara, J.P.
Arthur Sinclair
Mike Flanagan, a Workingman [spelled Flanigan in Gill, 2nd ed.]   J. H. Dunne
Brian O'Neill, in Love with Mary Kate   Udolphus Wright
Directed by W. G. Fay
First published: Dublin: Gill, n.d.

LADY GREGORY

Hyacinth Halvey,
a Comedy in One Act.
First produced: 19 February 1906, by the National Theatre Society Ltd., at the Abbey Theatre, Dublin.

CAST

Hyacinth Halvey   F. J. Fay
James Quirke   W. G. Fay
Fardy Farrell   Arthur Sinclair
Sergeant Carden   Walter Magee
Mrs. Delane   Sara Allgood
Miss Joyce   Brigit O'Dempsey
Directed by W. G. Fay

First published: In *Seven Short Plays* (Dublin: Maunsel & Co., 1906) and from the same plates as a separate booklet in the same year.

T. O'NEILL RUSSELL

Red Hugh, or Life and Death of Hugh Roe O'Donnell,
a Drama in Three Acts and in Blank Verse.
First produced: 17 March 1906, by students at St. Patrick's College, Carlow; revived 5 April 1909, by the Pioneer Dramatic Society, at St. Xavier's Hall, Upper Sherrard Street, Dublin, directed by Prof. Burke, B.A.

First published: Dublin: M. H. Gill & Son, Ltd., 1905.

LADY GREGORY

The Doctor in Spite of Himself,
a Farce in Three Acts by Molière, adapted by Lady Gregory.
First produced: 16 April 1906, by the National Theatre Society, Ltd., at the Abbey Theatre, Dublin.

CAST

Sganarelle   W. G. Fay
Martha, his Wife   Sara Allgood
Robert, his Neighbour
Arthur Sinclair
Valère, Servant of Géronte
Ambrose Power
Luke, the Same   Udolphus Wright
Géronte, Father of Lucy   F. J. Fay
Jacqueline, Nurse at Géronte's and Wife of Luke
Maire O'Neill (Molly Allgood)
Lucy, Daughter of Géronte
Brigit O'Dempsey
Leeane, Lucy's Lover
Arthur Sinclair

First published: In *The Kiltartan
Molière* (Dublin: Maunsel, 1910).

EDMUND LEAMY
Cupid in Kerry,
a Comedy in Three Acts.
First produced: 19 April 1906, at
the Queen's Theatre, Dublin.
Probably unpublished.

FELIX PARTRIDGE
An tAthrughadh Mór
(The Great Change),
a Bi-Lingual Play in One Act.
First produced: 9 August 1906,
by members of Craobh Bhealach
a' Doirin, the Western Players,
at the Rotunda, Dublin, for the
Oireachtas.

CAST

Nora O'Neill, Bean an Tighe
                  Annie Higgins
Máire, Inghean is sine
                 Miss K. Feeney
Nuala, Inghean is óige
                Una O'Kelly
Seaghán, Mac   James Gannon
Cathal, Mac atá tagaidhthe ó'n
   Oileán Ur   John Gaughan
Conn (Mac Og)   J. Cunniff
Tadhg O hEadhra (Cómharsan)
            Michael O'Rorke
Conchubhar Mac Mathghamhna
   (Cómharsan)   T. Cannon
Mártan Ua Tuathail, Cómharsan
            Patrick J. Ryan
First published: Dublin: M. H.
Gill & Son, Ltd., [1906].

LADY GREGORY
The Gaol Gate,
a Tragedy in One Act.
First produced: 20 October 1906,
by the National Theatre Society,
Ltd., at the Abbey Theatre,
Dublin.

CAST

Mary Cahel, an Old Woman
                Sara Allgood
Mary Cuchin, her Daughter-
   in-law   Maire O'Neill
The Gatekeeper   F. J. Fay
   Caoine by Arthur Darley
First published: In *Seven Short
Plays* (Dublin: Maunsel & Co.,
1909).

WILLIAM BOYLE
The Mineral Workers,
a Play in Four Acts
(Three acts, according to original
programme).
First produced: 20 October 1906,
by the National Theatre Society,
Ltd., at the Abbey Theatre,
Dublin.

CAST

Sir Thomas Musgrove
                Arthur Sinclair
Mrs. Walton, his Sister
                Sara Allgood
Stephen J. O'Reilly   F. J. Fay
Dan Fogarty   W. G. Fay
Ned Mulroy   A. Power
Mary, his Wife   Alice O'Sullivan
Patrick, his Son Udolphus Wright
Kitty, his Daughter Maire O'Neill
Uncle Bartle   J. A. O'Rourke
Casey, a Poor Law Guardian
                 H. Young
Dick, an Engine Driver J. Barlow
   Directed by W. G. Fay
First published: Dublin: M. H.
Gill & Son, 1920.

SEUMAS MacMANUS
Orange and Green,
a Play in Four Scenes,
Founded on Gerald Griffin's
Ballad of the Same Name.
First produced: 2 November 1906,
by the National Players, at the
Abbey Theatre, Dublin.
First published: Mount Charles,
Co. Donegal: D. O'Molloy, n.d.

W. B. YEATS
Deirdre,
a Play in Verse.
First produced: 24 November
1906, by the National Theatre Society, Ltd., at the Abbey Theatre,
Dublin.

CAST

Concobar   J. M. Kerrigan
Fergus   Arthur Sinclair
Naisi   F. J. Fay
Messenger   U. Wright
Executioner   A. Power
First Musician   Sara Allgood
Second Musician Maire O'Neill
Third Musician Brigit O'Dempsey
Deirdre   Miss Darragh
   Scenery by Robert Gregory
   Songs by Arthur Darley

First published: London: A. H. Bullen, 1907; Dublin: Maunsel & Co., 1907, Being Volume V of Plays for an Irish Theatre.

RUTHERFORD MAYNE
(Samuel J. Waddell)
The Turn of the Road,
a Play in Two Scenes and an Epilogue.
First produced: 4 December 1906, privately, at the Examination Hall of the Queen's University, Belfast, by the Ulster Literary Theatre; repeated 17-19 December 1906, in public performance, at the Ulster Minor Hall, Belfast.

CAST

William John Granahan,
  a Farmer   W. R. Gordon
Mrs. Granahan, his Wife
                Brigid O'Farrell
Their Sons:
  Samuel James
            Rutherford Mayne
  Robbie John   S. Bullock
Ellen, their Daughter Lily Coates
Thomas Granahan, Father of
  William John Granahan
             Arthur Gilmore
John Graeme, a Farmer
         Gerald MacNamara
         (Harry Morrow)
Jane, his Daughter Edith Lilburn
Mr. Taylor, a Creamery
  Manager   John Field Magee
A Tramp Fiddler   James Story
    Directed by Fred Morrow
First published: Dublin: Maunsel & Co., 1907.

LEWIS PURCELL
The Pagan,
a Comedy in Two Scenes.
First produced: 4 December 1906, privately, at the Examination Hall of the Queen's University, Belfast, by the Ulster Literary Theatre; repeated 17-19 December 1906, in public performance, at the Ulster Minor Hall, Belfast.

CAST

Crimall Ruadh, a Petty
  Chieftain of the Tribe of
  Ui Nial   S. Bullock
Nuala, his Daughter
       Miss F. Smith (or Smythe)

Gorman MacRory, a Petty
  Chieftain of the Cruithni
          Rutherford Mayne
Cellach, his Follower
        Gerald MacNamara
Turloch, a Fighting Man
           A. Gilmore
Congall, a Bard   J. Thompson
Maelcova, a Cleric
        John Field Magee
Feilech, a Bonds-boy
          Fred Hughes
  Directed by Fred Morrow
First published: Dublin: Maunsel & Co., 1907.

LADY GREGORY
The Canavans,
a Comedy in Three Acts.
First produced: 8 December 1906, by the National Theatre Society, Ltd., at the Abbey Theatre, Dublin.

CAST

Peter Canavan, a Miller
           W. G. Fay
Antony Canavan, his Brother
         J. A. O'Rourke
Captain Headley, his Cousin
        Arthur Sinclair
Widow Greely Brigit O'Dempsey
Widow Deeny   Maire O'Neill
  Directed by W. G. Fay
First published: In *Irish Folk-History Plays, Second Series—The Tragic-Comedies* (New York & London: G. P. Putnam's Sons, 1912).

SEAMUS UA GREGAIN
(James Gregan)
The Leprechaun,
a Comedy in One Act.
First produced: 15 December 1906, in the Workmen's Club Hall, York Street, Dublin; revived 10 April 1907, by the Sinn Féin Dramatic Society, at the Molesworth Hall, Dublin.

No record of publication.

JOSEPH FORD
The Bailiff of Kilmore,
a Romantic Drama in Three Short Scenes.
First produced: 15 December 1906, in the Workmen's Club Hall, York Street, Dublin.
Unpublished.

SEUMAS O'KELLY

His Father's Son,
a Play in Three Acts.
No record of production.
First published: In *Sinn Féin, I,*
Act I (15 December 1906), Act II
(22 December 1906), Act III (5
January and 12 January 1907).

J. M. SYNGE

The Playboy of the Western World,
a Comedy in Three Acts.
First produced: 26 January 1907,
by the National Theatre Society,
Ltd., at the Abbey Theatre,
Dublin.

CAST

Christopher Mahon   W. G. Fay
Old Mahon, his Father,
  a Squatter   A. Power
Michael James Flaherty,
  a Publican   Arthur Sinclair
Margaret Flaherty (called
  Pegeen Mike), his Daughter
               Máire O'Neill
Shawn Keogh, her Cousin,
  a Young Farmer   F. J. Fay
Widow Quin   Sara Allgood
Small Farmers:
  Jimmy Farrell   J. M. Kerrigan
  Philly Cullen   J. A. O'Rourke
  Sara Tansey   Brigit O'Dempsey
  Susan Brady   Alice O'Sullivan
  Honor Blake   Mary Craig
Some Peasants Udolphus Wright,
              Harry Young
   Directed by W. G. Fay
First published: Dublin: Maunsel
& Co., 1907.

LADY GREGORY

The Jackdaw,
a Comedy in One Act.
First produced: 23 February 1907,
by the National Theatre Society,
Ltd., at the Abbey Theatre,
Dublin.

CAST

Joseph Nestor   F. J. Fay
Michael Cooney   W. G. Fay
Mrs. Broderick   Sara Allgood
Tommy Nally   Arthur Sinclair
Sibby Fahy   Brigit O'Dempsey
Timothy Ward   J. M. Kerrigan
   Directed by W. G. Fay.
First published: In *Seven Short
Plays* (Dublin: Maunsel & Co.,
1909).

LADY GREGORY

The Rising of the Moon,
a Play in One Act.
First produced: 9 March 1907, by
the National Theatre Society, Ltd.,
at the Abbey Theatre, Dublin.

CAST

Ballad Singer   W. G. Fay
Policeman X   J. A. O'Rourke
Policeman Y   J. M. Kerrigan
Policeman Z   Arthur Sinclair
[later changed to the Sergeant]
   Directed by W. G. Fay
First published: In *The Gael* (New
York, November 1903); in *Samh-
ain* (December 1904); first book
publication in *Seven Short Plays*
(Dublin: Maunsel & Co., 1909).

GERALD O'LOUGHLIN

The Rapparee,
a Play in One Act.
First produced: 18 March 1907,
by the National Players' Society,
at the Queen's Theatre, Dublin.

CAST

Connor O'Hagan, a Soldier of
  King James   E. Keegan
Tadhg Ruadh, an Innkeeper
               F. Rigney
Feidhlemidh, Servant Boy
           P. Ua Dalaigh
Williamite Officers:
  Colonel Ellison
        Gearóid O'Lochlainn
  Captain Brooks
        B. MacMenamin
Remy Dubh, Captain of
  Rapparees   S. MacConghaile
Probably unpublished.

PADRAIC COLUM

The Fiddler's House,
a Peasant Play in Three Acts,
a Later Version of *Broken Soil.*
First produced: 21 March 1907,
by the Theatre of Ireland, at the
Large Concert Hall, the Rotunda,
Dublin.

CAST

Conn Hourican, a Fiddler
         Joseph Goggin
Máire Hourican, his Daughter
     Máire Nic Shiubhlaigh
Anne Hourican, a Younger
  Daughter   Eileen O'Doherty
          (Annie Walker)

Brian MacConnell, a Young
  Farmer   Edward Keegan
James Moynihan, a Farmer's
  Son   P. Mac Siubhlaigh
    Directed by Fred Morrow
First published: Dublin: Maunsel
& Co., 1907.

WINIFRED M. LETTS
The Eyes of the Blind,
a Play in One Act.
First produced: 1 April 1907, by
the National Theatre Society, Ltd.,
at the Abbey Theatre, Dublin.

CAST

Mrs. Doyne   Máire O'Neill
Theresa Doyne Brigit O'Dempsey
Lawrence Shaughnessy W. G. Fay
Blind Phelim, a Beggar F. J. Fay
    Directed by W. G. Fay
Unpublished.

DOUGLAS HYDE and LADY GREGORY
The Poorhouse,
a Comedy in One Act.
First produced: 3 April 1907, by
the National Theatre Society, Ltd.,
at the Abbey Theatre, Dublin.

CAST

Colum   W. G. Fay
Paudeen   Arthur Sinclair
The Matron   Máire O'Neill
A Country Woman
        Brigit O'Dempsey
    Directed by W. G. Fay
First published: In *Samhain* (September 1903).

WILFRID SCAWEN BLUNT
Fand,
a Play in Verse, in Two Acts.
First produced: 20 April 1907, by
the National Theatre Society, Ltd.,
at the Abbey Theatre, Dublin.

CAST

Cuchulain   F. J. Fay
Conchubar   Arthur Sinclair
Laeg, Cuchulain's Charioteer
        J. M. Kerrigan
Friends to Cuchulain:
  Laeghaire   Ernest Vaughan
  Lugaid   J. A. O'Rourke
Emer, Cuchulain's Wife
        Sara Allgood
Fand, a Fairy Wife, to
  Manannan   Maire O'Neill

Eithne, a Poetess, Beloved of
  Cuchulain Maire Ni Gharbhaigh
Attendants: Brigit O'Dempsey,
        Annie Allgood.
  The Music to the Songs
Composed by Arthur Darley
First published: as *Fand of the
Fair Cheek,* a 3 Act Tragedy in
Rhymed Verse, Written for the
Irish National Theatre Society.
Privately Printed, 1904.

T. D. FITZGERALD
The Passing,
a Play in One Act.
No record of production.
First published: In *The Shanachie,*
II (Winter 1907).

GEORGE FITZMAURICE
The Country Dressmaker,
a Comedy in Three Acts.
First produced: 3 October 1907, by
the National Theatre Society, Ltd.,
at the Abbey Theatre, Dublin.

CAST

Julia Shea, a Country
  Dressmaker   Sara Allgood
Norry Shea, her Mother
        Brigit O'Dempsey
Matt Dillane, their Next-door
  Neighbour   F. J. Fay
Min, his Daughter Máire O'Neill
Pats Connor, a Returned
  American   J. M. Kerrigan
Edmund Normyle J. A. O'Rourke
Michael Clohesy, a Strong
  Farmer   Arthur Sinclair
Maryanne, his Wife
        Máire O'Neill
Their Daughters:
  Babe   Eileen O'Doherty
  Ellie   Kathleen Mullamphy
Jack, their Son   T. J. Fox
Luke Quilter, the Man from
  the Mountains W. G. Fay
    Directed by W. G. Fay
First published: In *Five Plays*
(London and Dublin: Maunsel &
Co., 1914) and also separately from
the same plates in the same year.

LADY GREGORY
Dervorgilla,
a Tragedy in One Act.
First produced: 31 October 1907,
by the National Theatre Society,

Ltd., at the Abbey Theatre, Dublin.

CAST

Dervorgilla, once Queen of Breffney Sara Allgood
Flann, an old Servant F. J. Fay
Mona, his Wife Máire O'Neill
Owen, a Young Man J. M. Kerrigan
Mamie, a Girl Brigit O'Dempsey
Other Young Men and Girls Arthur Sinclair, J. A. O'Rourke, Kathleen Mullamphy
A Wandering Songmaker W. G. Fay

First published: In *Samhain* (1908); first book publication in *Irish Folk History Plays. First Series—The Tragedies* (New York and London: G. P. Putnam's Sons, 1912).

MISS L. McMANUS

O'Donnell's Cross,
a Play in Three Acts.
First produced: 31 October 1907, by the National Players, for the Samhain Festival, at the Rotunda, Dublin.
First published: Dublin: Sealy, Bryers and Walker, 1909.

R. G. WALSH

Before Clonmel,
a Dramatic Sketch in One Act.
First produced: 1 November 1907, by the National Players, for the Samhain Festival, at the Rotunda, Dublin.
Unpublished.

W. B. YEATS and LADY GREGORY

The Unicorn from the Stars,
a Play in Three Acts, a Revision of *Where There is Nothing.*
First produced: 21 November 1907, by the National Theatre Society, Ltd., at the Abbey Theatre, Dublin.

CAST

Father John Ernest Vaughan
Thomas Hearne, a Coachbuilder Arthur Sinclair
Andrew Hearne, Brother of Thomas J. A. O'Rourke
Martin Hearne, Nephew of Thomas F. J. Fay
Johnny Bacach, a Beggar W. G. Fay
Paudeen J. M. Kerrigan
Biddy Lally Máire O'Neill
Nanny Brigit O'Dempsey

First published: *The Unicorn from the Stars and Other Plays,* by W. B. Yeats and Lady Gregory (New York: The Macmillan Co., 1908).

SEUMAS O'KELLY

The Matchmakers,
a Comedy in One Act.
First produced: 13 December 1907, by the Theatre of Ireland, at the Abbey Theatre, Dublin.

CAST

Larry Dolan, a Matchmaker Frank Walker (P. Mac Siubhlaigh)
Ellen Dolan, his Wife Máire Nic Shiubhlaigh
Mary Noonan, his Neice Honor Lavelle
Tom O'Connor, another Matchmaker M. Carolan
Seán O'Connor, his Brother Séamus O'Connolly (James Connolly)
Kate Mulvany, a Neighbour Nora Fitzpatrick

Directed by Fred Morrow
First published: Dublin: M. H. Gill & Son, Ltd., 1908.

LEWIS PURCELL and GERALD MacNAMARA

Suzanne and the Sovereigns,
an Extravaganza in Four Acts.
First produced: 26 December 1907, by the Ulster Literary Theatre, in Belfast.
Unpublished.

W. F. CASEY

The Man Who Missed the Tide,
a Play in Three Acts.
First produced: 13 February 1908, by the National Theatre Society, Ltd., at the Abbey Theatre, Dublin.

CAST

Dr. Gerald Quinn Arthur Sinclair
James Walsh Fred O'Donovan
Martin Kelly J. M. Kerrigan
Mrs. Gerald Quinn, Moira Sara Allgood

Sheila Kennedy, her Sister
Máire O'Neill
A Housemaid   Eileen O'Doherty
A Barmaid   Eileen O'Doherty
Directed by Sara Allgood
Unpublished.

NORREYS CONNELL
(Conal O'Riordan)
The Piper,
an Unended Argument in One Act.
First produced: 13 February 1908,
by the National Theatre Society,
Ltd., at the Abbey Theatre,
Dublin.

CAST

The Piper   Sara Allgood
Larry the Talker   J. M. Kerrigan
Black Mike   Ambrose Power
Tim the Trimmer   J. A. O'Rourke
Pat Dennehy   Sydney J. Morgan
Captain Talbot   Arthur Sinclair
An English Ensign   U. Wright
Soldiers   Stuart Hamilton,
T. J. Fox, Harry Young
Rebels   Fred O'Donovan,
J. J. Seymour,
Dermott Robinson,
Harry O'Neill

Directed by Norreys Connell

First published: In *Shakespeare's
End and other Irish Plays* (London: Stephen Swift & Co., Ltd.,
1912).

LADY GREGORY
Teja,
translated by Lady Gregory from
the German of H. Sudermann,
a Play in One Act.
First produced: 19 March 1908,
by the National Theatre Society,
Ltd., at the Abbey Theatre,
Dublin.

CAST

Teja   J. M. Kerrigan
Bathilda   Máire O'Neill
Amalaberga   Sara Allgood
Bishop Agilla   Arthur Sinclair
Theodimer   Sydney J. Morgan
Eurich   Udolphus Wright
Two Councillors   T. J. Fox,
Dermott Robinson
Haribalt, a Watchman
J. A. O'Rourke
Ildebad, King's Spear-bearer
Fred O'Donovan

Two Guards   Ambrose Power,
Stuart Hamilton
Directed by J. M. Synge
First published: Lady Gregory,
Collected Plays, Vol. IV. Gerrard's
Cross: Colin Smythe, 1971.

GEORGE FITZMAURICE
The Pie-Dish,
a Play in One Act.
First produced: 19 March 1908,
by the National Theatre Society,
Ltd., at the Abbey Theatre,
Dublin.

CAST

Leum Donaghue   Arthur Sinclair
Daughters to Leum:
  Margaret   Sara Allgood
  Johanna   Máire O'Neill
Sons to Margaret:
  Eugene   J. A. O'Rourke
  Jack   Sydney J. Morgan
  Father Troy   J. M. Kerrigan
First published: In *Five Plays*
(Dublin: Maunsel & Co., 1914).

W. B. YEATS
The Golden Helmet,
an Heroic Farce in One Act.
First produced: 19 March 1908,
by the National Theatre Society,
Ltd., at the Abbey Theatre,
Dublin.

CAST

Cuchulain   J. M. Kerrigan
Conal   Arthur Sinclair
Leagerie   Fred O'Donovan
Laeg, Cuchulain's Charioteer
Sydney J. Morgan
Emer, Wife of Cuchulain
Sara Allgood
Conal's Wife   Máire O'Neill
Leagerie's Wife   Eileen O'Doherty
Red Man   Ambrose Power
Scullions and Horseboys and
  Blackmen   Stuart Hamilton,
T. J. Fox, Udolphus Wright,
Dermot Robinson, T. O'Neill,
J. A. O'Rourke, Peadar Kearney
First published: New York: John
Quinn, 1908.

LADY GREGORY
The Rogueries of Scapin,
an Adaptation of Molière's
Comedy *Les Fourberies de Scapin,*
in Three Acts.
First produced: 4 April 1908, by
the National Theatre Society, Ltd.,
at the Abbey Theatre, Dublin.

Argante, Father of Octave and
Zerbinette   Sydney J. Morgan
Géronte, Father of Leandre and
Hyacinthe   J. A. O'Rourke
Octave, in Love with
Hyacinthe   Fred O'Donovan
Léandre, in Love with
Zerbinette   J. M. Kerrigan
Hyacinthe Máire Ní Gharbhaigh
Scapin, Valet of Léandre
Arthur Sinclair
Silvestre, Valet of Octave
Ambrose Power
Nérine, Nurse of Hyacinthe
Eileen O'Doherty
Carle   Stuart Hamilton
Two Porters   T. J. Fox,
Dermot Robinson
Directed by J. M. Synge
First published: In *The Kiltartan
Molière* (Dublin: Maunsel & Co.,
1910).

LADY GREGORY and DOUGLAS HYDE
The Workhouse Ward,
a Comedy in One Act
(a Revision of Lady Gregory's
Translation of Hyde's *Teach
na mBocht*).
First produced: 20 April 1908, by
the National Theatre Society, Ltd.,
at the Abbey Theatre, Dublin.

CAST

Mike MacInerney Arthur Sinclair
Michael Miskell Fred O'Donovan
Mrs. Donohoe, a Countrywoman
Máire O'Neill
First published: In *Seven Short
Plays* (Dublin: Maunsel & Co.,
1909).

ROBERT HARDING
(James Winder Good)
Leaders of the People,
a Play in Two Scenes.
First produced: 24 April 1908, by
the Ulster Literary Theatre, at
the Abbey Theatre, Dublin.

CAST

Loftus Rankin, Candidate
J. P. Campbell
Andy Wilson, Organiser
A. Gilmore
Mary Hamilton, Engaged to
Rankin   Miss J. Campbell
Timothy M'Grath, a
Nationalist M.P. R. H. Leighton

Ned Leslie, an Ulster
Politician John Field Magee
Paul Glenwood, a Poet
Cahal Byrne
Hugh Elewynn Rutherford Mayne
Unpublished.

RUTHERFORD MAYNE
The Drone,
a Comedy Originally in Two Acts,
Later Expanded to Three.
First produced: 24 April 1908, in
two acts, by the Ulster Literary
Theatre, at the Abbey Theatre,
Dublin.

CAST

John Murray, a
Farmer   G. A. Charters
(A. Gilmer)
Daniel Murray,
his Brother   Arthur Malcolm
(Sam Bullock)
Mary Murray,
John's Daughter Seveen Canmer
(Josephine Campbell)
Kate, a Servant Girl
in John Murray's
Employment   Máire Crothers
(Edith Lilburn)
Sam Brown, a Labourer in
John Murray's Employment
Rutherford Mayne
Andrew McMinn, a
Farmer   John Field
(John Field Magee)
Sarah McMinn, his Sister
Bridget O'Gorman
Alick McCready, a Young
Farmer   Ross Canmer
(J. P. Campbell)
Donal Mackenzie, a Scotch
Engineer   Robert Henry
(R. H. Leighton)
First published: Dublin: Maunsel
& Co., 1909.

PADRAIC COLUM
The Miracle of the Corn,
a Play in One Act.
First produced: 22 May 1908, by
the Theatre of Ireland, at the
Abbey Theatre, Dublin.

CAST

Fardorougha, a Farmer
Ambrose Power
Sheela, his Wife   Honor Lavelle
Paudeen, a Fool
P. Mac Siubhlaigh

344

Aislinn, a Child
Una Nic Shiubhlaigh
Shawn, a Poor Man   H. Sinclair
Directed by Fred Morrow
First published: In *The United Irishman*, XI (9 April 1904); reprinted in *Studies*, Being Number Two of the Tower Press Booklets, Second Series (Dublin: Maunsel & Co., 1907).

RICHARD BRINSLEY SHERIDAN

The Scheming Lieutenant,
a Farce in One Act.
First production by the Abbey Theatre Company: 29 May 1908, at the Abbey Theatre, Dublin.

CAST

Lieutenant O'Connor
J. M. Kerrigan
Doctor Rosy   Fred O'Donovan
Justice Credulous   Arthur Sinclair
Sergeant Trounce
Sydney J. Morgan
Corporal Flint   J. A. O'Rourke
Lauretta   Máire O'Neill
Mrs. Bridget Credulous
Sara Allgood
Soldiers   Ambrose Power, Stuart
Hamilton, Udolphus Wright,
Eileen O'Doherty
Directed by Sara Allgood

W. F. CASEY

The Suburban Groove,
a Mild Satire in Three Acts.
First produced: 1 October 1908, by the National Theatre Society, Ltd., at the Abbey Theatre, Dublin.

CAST

Dick Dalton   J. M. Kerrigan
James O'Connor   Fred O'Donovan
Mrs. James O'Connor
Sara Allgood
Jack O'Connor, their Son
Udolphus Wright
Una O'Connor, their Daughter
Máire O'Neill
Claude Callan   Arthur Sinclair
Directed by W. F. Casey
Unpublished.

S. L. ROBINSON
(Esmé Stuart Lennox Robinson)
The Clancy Name,
a Tragedy in One Act.
First produced: 8 October 1908,

by the National Theatre Society, Ltd., at the Abbey Theatre, Dublin.

CAST

Mrs. Clancy   Sara Allgood
John Clancy, her Son
Arthur Sinclair
Mrs. Spillane   Máire O'Neill
Eugene Roche   Fred O'Donovan
Jerry Brien   J. A. O'Rourke
Mary Brien   Eileen O'Doherty
Father Murphy   J. M. Kerrigan
Michael Dempsey
Sydney J. Morgan
[There is some doubt about whether this is the original cast. It is listed in Robinson's *Ireland's Abbey Theatre* as the original cast, but listed in the Maunsel edition of the play as the cast of 30 September 1909.]
First published: In *Two Plays: Harvest, The Clancy Name* (Dublin: Maunsel & Co., 1911).

THOMAS MacDONAGH

When the Dawn Is Come,
a Tragedy in Three Acts.
First produced: 15 October 1908, by the National Theatre Society, Ltd., at the Abbey Theatre, Dublin.

CAST

The Seven acting as Captains of the Irish Insurgent Army, and Members of the Council of Ireland:
Thurlough MacKieran
J. M. Kerrigan
Hugh MacOscar
Sydney J. Morgan
Reamonn O'Sullivan
Arthur Sinclair
Father John Joyce   Eric Gorman
Alexander Walker
Fred O'Donovan
Rory MacMahon   Ambrose Power
Patrick Ryan   Udolphus Wright
Ita MacOscar, Daughter of
Hugh, Member of the Council
of Ireland   Sara Allgood
Sheela O'Hara, Member of
the Council   Máire O'Neill
Connor O'Gatry, a Ballad
Singer, a Spy   J. A. O'Rourke
MacEamonn, a Spy   J. H. Dunne
Irish Soldiers as Guards
G. H. Fitzgerald,
Maurice McCall

Directed by Thomas MacDonagh
First published: Dublin: Maunsel
& Co., 1908, Being Volume XI of
the Abbey Theatre Series.

RUTHERFORD MAYNE
The Troth,
a Play in One Act.
First produced: 31 October 1908,
by William Mollison's Company,
at the Crown Theatre, Peckham,
London; produced by Mollison's
Company in Dublin on 25
November 1908, at the Gaiety
Theatre.

CAST

Ebenezer McKie, a Farmer
                    W. A. Mackeray
Mrs. McKie, his Wife
            Josephine Woodward
Francis Moore, a Neighbour
                    Whitford Kane
John Smith, a Labourer in
    McKie's Employ
                    Murray Graham
First published: Dublin: Maunsel
& Co., 1909.

LIAM DE ROISTE
The Road to Hell,
a Realistic Drama of Irish
City Life.
No record of production.
First published: In *The Road to
Hell and Fodhla* (Cork: The Shan-
down Publishing Co., 1908, and
Dublin: Gill and Eason, 1908).

SEUMAS O'KELLY
The Flame on the Hearth,
later retitled *The Stranger,*
a Play in One Act.
First produced: 23 November
1908, by the Theatre of Ireland,
at the Abbey Theatre, Dublin;
revived on 19 March 1909, by the
Theatre of Ireland, at the Rotunda, Dublin.

CAST
of 19 March 1909 Revival

Peter Williams P. Mac Siubhlaigh
Margaret Williams
            Máire Nic Shiubhlaigh
A Stranger   George Nesbitt
Sergeant of the Yeos
            Arthur Owen Orett
First published: In *Three Plays
by Seumas O'Kelly* (Dublin: M.
H. Gill & Son, 1912); possibly

there was an earlier periodical
publication which we have been
unable to trace.

SEUMAS MacMANUS
Bong Tong Come to Balriddery,
a Farce.
First produced: December 1908,
by the Chapelizod Dramatic Class.
First published: Mount Charles,
Co. Donegal: D. O'Molloy, n.d.

NORA FITZPATRICK and
CASIMIR DUNIN
MARKIEVICZ
Home Sweet Home,
a Belfast Farce in One Act.
First produced: 3 December 1908,
by the Independent Dramatic
Company, at the Abbey Theatre,
Dublin.
Unpublished.

ARNOLD GRAVES
Stella and Vanessa,
a Drama in Four Acts.
First produced: 10 December,
1908, by the Irish Theatrical Club,
at 40 Upper O'Connell Street,
Dublin.

CAST

Dr. Delany   Arnold Graves
Swift   Maurice Gerothwohl
Stella   Deena Tyrrell
Vanessa   Miss St. Clair Swanzy
            And Others.

Publication uncertain.

LADY GREGORY
The Miser,
an Adaptation of Molière's
Comedy *L'Avare* in Five Acts.
First produced: 21 January 1909,
by the National Theatre Society,
Ltd., at the Abbey Theatre,
Dublin.

CAST

Harpagon, Father to Cléante,
    in Love with
    Marianne   Arthur Sinclair
Cléante, Harpagon's Son, Lover
    to Marianne   Fred O'Donovan
Valère, Son to Anselme and
    Lover to Elise   J. M. Kerrigan
Anselme, Father to Valère and
    Marianne   Udolphus Wright
Master Simon, Broker
            Sydney J. Morgan

Master Jacques, Cook and
  Coachman to Harpagon
               J. A. O'Rourke
La Flèche, Valet to Cléante
               Eric Gorman
Brindavoine, Lackey to
  Harpagon   Udolphus Wright
La Merluche, Lackey to
  Harpagon   Richard Boyd
Commissionaire
               Sydney J. Morgan
Clerk   F. J. Harford
Elise, Daughter to
  Harpagon   Eileen O'Doherty
Marianne, Daughter to
  Anselme   Máire O'Neill
Frosine, an Intriguing
  Woman   Sara Allgood
First published: In *The Kiltartan
Molière* (Dublin: Maunsel & Co.,
1910).

DANIEL LAURENCE KELLEHER

Stephen Grey,
a Dream and an Incident
in One Act.
First produced: 11 March 1909,
by the National Theatre Society,
Ltd., at the Abbey Theatre,
Dublin.

CAST

Stephen Grey, Former School-
  master of Bawnamore
               Fred O'Donovan
Margaret Mary O'Neill, his
  Worshipper, called Maggie
  May   Máire O'Neill
Mrs. N. O'Neill, her Mother
               Elaine Wodrow
               (or possibly Woodrow)
Mike O'Neill, her Father
               Sydney J. Morgan
Ellen, Household Servant
               Eileen O'Doherty
Stephen Swanton, Widower,
  Vintner of Bawnamore Cross
               Arthur Sinclair
Father Canavan, a Young
  Curate   J. A. O'Rourke
Dan Sullivan, a Neighbour's
  Son   J. M. Kerrigan
Possibly unpublished.

HUGH BARDEN

The Storm,
a Play in One Act.
First produced: 18 March 1909,
by the Students' Union, at the
Metropolitan School of Art; revived at the Abbey Theatre on
22 April 1909.

CAST
of 22 April 1909 Revival
James M'Gragh   William Pearse
Bridget   Ethel Rhind
Tom   Hugh Barden
Mary Doran, a Neighbour
               Margaret Crilly
Tim, a Sailor Edward M'Loughlin
Neighbours and Sailors
  May Barden, Miss Hayden,
               Mr. Long
Produced by Fred Morrow
Probably unpublished.

THOMAS KING MOYLAN

Paid in his Own Coin,
a Comedy in Three Acts.
First produced: 18 March 1909,
by the Students' Union, at the
Metropolitan School of Art; revived at the Abbey Theatre on
22 April 1909.

CAST
of 22 April 1909 Revival
Katie Sweeney   Alice Halpenny
Michael Guinan George Cogan
Michael John   Denis O'Meagher
Brian Cleary   James Golden
Mrs. Duffy   Julie Hayden
Biddy Norris   May Barden
Frederick Egan Harry Clarke
Henry Brown   Fred McDonald
The Judge   Thomas King Moylan
Produced by Thomas King Moylan
First published: Dublin: James
Duffy & Co., n.d.

KATHARINE TYNAN

The Stepmother,
a Playlet.
No record of production.
First published: In St. Patrick's
Day Double Number of *The
Weekly Freeman* (20 March 1909).

JOHN GUINAN

The Fairy Follower
No record of production.
First published: In St. Patrick's
Day Double Number of *The
Weekly Freeman* (20 March 1909).

S. L. ROBINSON

The Cross Roads,
a Play in a Prologue and
Two Acts.

First produced: 1 April 1909, by the National Theatre Society, Ltd., at the Abbey Theatre, Dublin.

CAST OF PROLOGUE

James O'Reilly Sydney J. Morgan
Sydney Doyle   Eric Gorman
Brian Connor   Fred O'Donovan
Henry Blake   J. A. O'Rourke
Ellen McCarthy   Sara Allgood

CAST OF PLAY

Ellen McCarthy   Sara Allgood
Mrs. McCarthy, her Mother
                Máire O'Neill
Mrs. Desmond Eileen O'Doherty
Mike Dempsey   J. M. Kerrigan
Tom Dempsey, his Son
              Arthur Sinclair
Brian Connor   Fred O'Donovan

First published: Dublin: Maunsel & Co., 1910, Being Volume XII of the Abbey Theatre Series.

NORREYS CONNELL
Time,
a Passing Phantasy in One Act.
First produced: 1 April 1909, by the National Theatre Society, Ltd., at the Abbey Theatre, Dublin.

CAST

A Young Painter J. M. Kerrigan
A Young Girl   Máire O'Neill
An Old Man   Norreys Connell
   Directed by Norreys Connell
No record of publication.

WILLIAM BOYLE
The Confederates,
a Duologue.
First production: 3 April 1909, by the Irish Literary Society, London. W. G. Fay and Bridget O'Dempsey comprised the cast.
Unpublished.

SEUMAS O'KELLY
The Shuiler's Child
First produced: 29 April 1909, by the Theatre of Ireland, at the Large Concert Hall, the Rotunda, Dublin.

CAST

Moll Woods
      Máire Nic Shiubhlaigh
Andy O'Hea, a Farmer
            Austin Martin

Mary O'Hea   Nelly O'Brien
(changed to Nannie O'Hea on publication)
Sara Finnessy, a Neighbour
(changed to Sarah on publication)
        Caitia Nic Cormac
Tim O'Halloran, a Poor Law
  Relieving Officer Stephen James
         (James Stephens)
Miss Cecilia, a Lady Inspector
of the Local Government
Board Constance de Markievicz

First published: Dublin: Maunsel & Co., 1909.

RUTHERFORD MAYNE
The Gomeril,
a Farcical Comedy in One Act.
First produced: 29 April 1909, by the Theatre of Ireland, at the Large Concert Hall, the Rotunda, Dublin.

CAST

Hans Mullen, a Farmer C. Brady
Andy, his Son   Frank Lowry
Tommy Hughes, a Servant Man
             Ian Gilbert
Eliza Macken, a Spinster
        Nora Fitzpatrick
  Directed by Fred Morrow
Publication uncertain.

LORD DUNSANY
(Edward John Moreton Drax Plunkett, 18th Baron Dunsany)
The Glittering Gate,
a Play in One Act.
First produced: 29 April 1909, by the National Theatre Society, Ltd., at the Abbey Theatre, Dublin.

CAST

Jim, Formerly a Burglar, Since
  Hanged   Fred O'Donovan
Bill, Also a Burglar, Since Shot
        Norreys Connell
  Directed by Norreys Connell
First published: In *Five Plays* (London: Grant Richards, 1914; New York: M. Kennerley, 1914).

DANIEL CORKERY
The Embers,
a Play in Three Acts.
First produced: 6 May 1909, by the Cork Dramatic Society, at the Dun, Queen Street, Cork.

Laurence Kiely   E. O'Shea
Mr. Kiely, his father   P. O'Leary
John Witelaw O'Loughlin
              D. Harrington
Mrs. Kiely   Miss D. Gilley
Mrs. Forde   Miss M. J. Dixon
Nan Forde   Miss A. Walshe
Daly   D. Breen
O'Brien   P. Higgins
Unpublished.

NORREYS CONNELL

An Imaginary Conversation,
a Play in One Act.
First produced: 13 May 1909, by
the National Theatre Society, Ltd.,
at the Abbey Theatre, Dublin.

CAST

Tom Moore   J. M. Kerrigan
Robert Emmet   Fred O'Donovan
Kate Moore   Sara Allgood
   Directed by Norreys Connell
First published: In *Shakespeare's
End and Other Irish Plays* (London: Stephen Swift & Co., 1912).

GEORGE BERNARD SHAW

The Shewing-Up of Blanco Posnet,
a Sermon in Crude Melodrama
in One Act.
First produced: 25 August 1909,
by the National Theatre Society,
Ltd., at the Abbey Theatre,
Dublin.

CAST

Babsy   Eileen O'Doherty
Lottie   Cathleen Mullamphy
Hannah   Sheila O'Sullivan
Jessie   Mary Nairn
Emma   Annie O'Hynes
Elder Daniels   Arthur Sinclair
Blanco Posnet   Fred O'Donovan
Strapper Kemp   J. M. Kerrigan
Feemy Evans   Sara Allgood
Sheriff Kemp   Sydney J. Morgan
Foreman of Jury   J. A. O'Rourke
Nestor, a Juryman   A. J. Goulden
The Woman   Máire O'Neill
Waggoner Joe   Eric Gorman
Jurymen, Boys, etc.
   Udolphus Wright, J. Dunne,
     J. Fitzgerald, H. Harford,
     J. Downes, Hugh Barden,
     P. Murphy, J. O'Brien, etc.
   Directed by Lady Gregory

First published: In *The Doctor's
Dilemma, Getting Married and
The Shewing-Up of Blanco Posnet*
(London: Constable & Co., 1911).

ALICE L. MILLIGAN

Return of Lugh,
a Pageant Play in Verse.
First produced: 25 August 1909,
in the woods of Marino, Clontarf.
Probably unpublished.

R. J. RAY (R. G. Brophy)

The White Feather,
a Play in Three Acts.
First produced: 16 September
1909, by the National Theatre
Society, Ltd., at the Abbey Theatre, Dublin.

CAST

Martin Kearney, Publican and
  Shopkeeper   J. A. O'Rourke
William Pat McCarthy, an Estate
  Bailiff   Sydney J. Morgan
James Cassidy, a Cattle
  Dealer   J. M. Kerrigan
Michael John Dillon,
  a Farmer   Arthur Sinclair
Mrs. Margaret Dillon,
  his Mother   Eileen O'Doherty
Sergeant Barton, R.I.C.
           G. H. Fitzgerald
Mrs. Brady, Wife of a Small
  Farmer   Máire O'Neill
Warder A   Fred O'Donovan
Warder B   A. J. Goulden
Governor of County Gaol
           Eric Gorman
Unpublished.

WINIFRED M. LETTS

The Challenge,
a Play in One Act.
First produced: 14 October 1909,
by the National Theatre Society,
Ltd., at the Abbey Theatre,
Dublin.

CAST

Charles Caulfield   Arthur Sinclair
James Buchanan   Fred O'Donovan
Terence, a Butler   J. A. O'Rourke
Unpublished.

LADY GREGORY

The Image,
a Comedy in Three Acts.
First produced: 11 November
1909, by the National Theatre So-

ciety, Ltd., at the Abbey Theatre, Dublin.

CAST

Thomas Coppinger, a Stone
  Cutter   Arthur Sinclair
Mary Coppinger, his Wife
            Sara Allgood
Malachi Naughton, a Mountainy
  Man   Fred O'Donovan
Brian Hosty, a Small Farmer
        Sydney J. Morgan
Darby Costello, a Seaweed-
  gatherer   J. M. Kerrigan
Peggy Mahon, an Old
  Midwife   Máire O'Neill
Peter Mannion, a Carrier
        J. A. O'Rourke
  Directed by Lady Gregory
First published: Dublin: Maunsel & Co., 1910.

J. M. SYNGE

The Tinker's Wedding,
a Play in Two Acts.
First produced: 11 November 1909, for the Afternoon Theatre at His Majesty's Theatre, London.

CAST

Michael Byrne   Jules Shaw
A Priest   Edmund Gurney
Mary Byrne   Clare Greet
Sarah Casey   Mona Limerick
  Directed by Edmund Gurney
First published: Dublin: Maunsel & Co., 1908.

GERALD MacNAMARA

The Mist That Does Be on the Bog,
a Fog in One Act.
First produced: 26 November 1909, by the Ulster Literary Theatre, at the Abbey Theatre, Dublin.

CAST

Clarence St. John Ross Canmer
Fred Magill   G. A. Charters
Gladys Magill   Mary Crothers
Cissy Dodd   Seveen Canmer
Michael Quinn J. M. Harding
Bridget Quinn
      Margaret O'Gorman
  Directed by David Parkhill
Unpublished.

T. C. MURRAY

The Wheel O' Fortune,
a Play in One Act.
First produced: 2 December 1909, by the Cork Dramatic Society, at the Dun Theatre, Queen Street, Cork.

CAST

Donal Lucey   P. O'Leary
Ellen, his Daughter
        Miss Lily Gilley
Katty, his Daughter
        Miss Daisy Gilley
Jeremiah Dempsey, their
  Uncle   J. Gilley
William Carroll D. Harrington
Maurice Carroll, his Son
        C. Ronayne
Jim Daly, a Matchmaker
        R. S. O'Brien
Mrs. Hickey, a Publican
        Miss M. Dixon
Humphrey Cooney, a Yank
        J. Goold
Unpublished, although later revised and produced at the Abbey under the title of *Sovereign Love.*

DANIEL CORKERY

The Hermit and the King,
a Play in One Act.
First produced: 2 December 1909, by the Cork Dramatic Society, at the Dun Theatre, Queen Street, Cork.

CAST

Manus, the King Eugene O'Shea
Courtiers:
  Cairbre   P. Kenefick
  Conan   C. Ronayne
  Breasil   J. Gilley
Colman, a Hermit D. Harrington
Rory, a Boy Friend
      Master Ernest O'Shea
First published: As *King and Hermit* in *The Yellow Bittern and other Plays* (Dublin: The Talbot Press, 1920; London: T. Fisher Unwin, 1920).

LENNOX ROBINSON

The Lesson of his Life,
a Comedy in One Act.
First produced: 2 December 1909, by the Cork Dramatic Society, at the Dun Theatre, Queen Street, Cork.

CAST

Mrs. O'Donoghue Daisy Gilley
Barty, her Son   C. Ronayne
Sergeant Cantillon P. O'Leary
Jerry Burke   D. Harrington
Patrick Dunne   J. Gilley
Unpublished.

Notes

1905

1 W. B. Yeats, 'J. M. Synge's *The Shadow of the Glen*', *The United Irishman* (28 January 1905), p. 1.
2 [Arthur Griffith], *Ibid.*
3 Yeats, letter in 'All Ireland' column, *The United Irishman* (4 February 1905), p. 1.
4 [Griffith], *Ibid.*
5 Yeats, letter in 'All Ireland' column, *The United Irishman* (11 February 1905), p. 1.
6 [Griffith], *Ibid.*
7 Joseph Holloway, *Impressions of a Dublin Playgoer*. Ms. 1803, National Library of Ireland.
8 *Ibid.*, 11 January 1905.
9 Letter of F. J. Fay to J. Holloway. Holloway Ms. 4455, National Library of Ireland.
10 'Emma Vernon' was the stage name of Vera Esposito.
11 'Irish National Theatre, Mr. Synge's New Play', *The Freeman's Journal* (6 February 1905), p. 5.
12 [Griffith], 'All Ireland', *The United Irishman* (11 February 1905), p. 1.
13 'Irish National Theatre', *The Irish Times* (6 February 1905), p. 71.
14 F. McC., 'Irish National Theatre', *The Evening Herald* (6 February 1905), p. 3.
15 R.M., 'At the Abbey Theatre', *The Dublin Evening Mail* (6 February 1905), p. 2.
16 L. J. M'Quilland, 'Mr. Synge's New Play: Pinero by the Liffey', *The Belfast Evening Telegraph* (14 February 1905).
17 George Moore, Letter to the Editor, *The Irish Times* (13 February 1905), p. 6. Moore's defence irritated Miss Horniman extremely, and on 9 February she wrote to Yeats, using her ordinary salutation:

> Dear Demon,
>
> I want you to clearly understand that though I acknowledge that I have no right to interfere with your social life yet that I am publicly connected with the Irish National Theatre Society.
>
> If by any writings of your "friend" they appear to be his "protectors" in any way I shall look upon it as a public insult offered to me by the whole Society severally and collectively unless those writings are publicly repudiated. I shall carry out all the promises I have made most scrupulously, and I shall alter the stage costumes to the best of my ability, but in that case I shall do no more. It is your duty to carry out what you think best for your country, and if pleasing Mr. Quinn and your "friend" will serve your aims better than what I can do, I have no right to blame you. But I will not raise a finger, beyond carrying out the pledges I have already given, to anything with which your friend is allowed to connect himself in any way, without public protest from the Society.
>
> Yours sincerely,
> A. E. F. HORNIMAN.

This letter is contained in the Yeats papers in the National Library of Ireland, Ms. 13,068. Yeats, in a letter of 15 February to John Quinn, wrote:

Moore has written to the *Irish Times* saying that it [*The Well of the Saints*] is a great play, more remarkable than any original play produced in England during his time. I wonder what has converted him, for he abused the play when he saw an act of it in rehearsal some months ago. He has also praised the acting in the same strenuous way. I imagine that his dislike of our work was artificial and that he has gradually come to feel that he would make himself absurd. He is now unbounded in his enthusiasm, both in public and private, which makes Miss Horniman perfectly furious. She threatens us with all kinds of pains and penalties should we accept any help from him.

In *Letters of W. B. Yeats*, ed. Alan Wade (London: Rupert Hart-Davis, 1954), pp. 446-47.

18 Holloway, *Impressions*, 11 February 1905.
19 'Kincora', *The Freeman's Journal* (25 March 1905), p. 4.
20 'Chanel', [Arthur Clery] 'Kincora', *The Leader* (1 April 1905), pp. 90-91.
21 'Lady Gregory's *Kincora*', *The Freeman's Journal* (27 March 1905), p. 5.
22 [Griffith], 'All Ireland', *The United Irishman* (1 April 1905), p. 1.
23 Holloway, *Impressions*, 27 March 1905.
24 Lady Gregory, *Our Irish Theatre* (New York & London: G. P. Putnam's Sons, 1914), p. 107.
25 Letter of W. Boyle to G. Roberts, dated 13 April 1905. In Roberts Ms. 8320, National Library of Ireland.
26 'Abbey Theatre, a New Irish Play', *The Freeman's Journal* (26 April 1905), p. 5.
27 [Griffith], 'All Ireland', *The United Irishman* (6 May 1905), p. 1.
28 Holloway, *Impressions*, 29 April 1905.
29 Letter of W. B. Yeats to J. M. Synge, dated 15 August 1905. In Synge Microfilm 5380, National Library of Ireland.
30 Letter of J. M. Synge to W. B. Yeats. In Fay Ms. 10,952 National Library of Ireland.
31 Letter of J. M. Synge to F. J. Fay, dated 8 September 1905. In Fay Ms. 10,952, National Library of Ireland.
32 Letter of Padraic Colum to Máire Garvey. In Roberts Ms. 8320, National Library of Ireland.
33 'The Irish National Theatre, New Play: *The Land*', *The Freeman's Journal* (10 June 1905), p. 8.
34 'The Land Hunger', *The Daily Express* (10 June 1905), p. 8.
35 'The Abbey Theatre', *The Irish Times* (3 October 1905), p. 5.
36 Holloway, *Impressions*, 16 June 1905.
37 Lady Gregory, 'Notes [to *The White Cockade*]', *Selected Plays* (New York: Hill and Wang, 1963), p. 173.
38 'The White Cockade', *The Freeman's Journal* (11 December 1905), p. 6.
39 'The White Cockade', *The Evening Mail* (11 December 1905), p. 4.
40 'The White Cockade', *The Daily Express* (11 December 1905), p. 6.
41 W. J. Fay & C. Carswell, *The Fays of the Abbey Theatre* (London: Rich & Cowan, Ltd., 1935), p. 185. A portrait of Sinclair as King James, painted by Robert Gregory, hangs in the Abbey Theatre.
42 Gerard Fay, *The Abbey Theatre, Cradle of Genius* (Dublin: Clonmore & Reynolds, Ltd., 1958), p. 100.
43 Peter Kavanagh, *The Story of the Abbey Theatre* (New York: Devin Adair, 1950), p. 51.

44 Letter of A. E. F. Horniman to W. B. Yeats, dated 26 September 1905. In Roberts Ms. 13,272, National Library of Ireland.

45 Yeats does some injustice to Æ, whose real opinion was:

> I feel rather sorry I ever helped to get up the Irish National Theatre Society. If I had foreseen the vortex it created drawing in half a score of good writers to it and [to] write plays which don't interest me I would have seen it perish in babyhood before I would have spent so much precious time and energy on it.

In *Letters from Æ*, ed. Alan Denson (London, New York, Toronto: Abelard-Schuman, 1961), p. 56.

46 *Letters of W. B. Yeats*, p. 461.

47 Letter of W. G. Fay to W. B. Yeats. In Fay Ms. 13,068, National Library of Ireland.

48 Letter of Padraic Colum to W. B. Yeats, dated 3 June 1905. *Ibid.*

49 Letter of W. G. Fay to W. B. Yeats. *Ibid.*

50 Letter of F. J. Fay to J. M. Synge, dated 14 September 1905. In Synge microfilm 5381, National Library of Ireland.

51 Letter of W. B. Yeats to Máire Garvey, dated 18 December 1905. In Roberts Ms. 8320, National Library of Ireland.

52 Fay & Carswell, p. 100.

53 Holloway, *Impressions*, 19 December 1905.

54 *The Sunday Sun* (London), (3 December 1905).

55 Letter of A. E. F. Horniman to J. Holloway. In *Impressions*, 19 December 1905.

56 'The Week', *The Nationalist* (7 December 1905), p. 183.

57 Oliver St. John Gogarty, 'The Irish Literary Revival, Present Poetry and Drama in Dublin', *The Dublin Evening Mail* (4 March 1905), p. 2.

58 Maurice Joy, 'The Irish Literary Revival: Some Limitations and Possibilities', *The New Ireland Review* (July 1905), pp. 257-66.

59 'Lee' [Daniel Corkery], 'Mr. Yeats in Cork', *The Leader* (30 December 1905), pp. 313-14.

60 Holloway, *Impressions*, 28 October 1905. Holloway also has an interesting footnote to this performance. On 5 November, he wrote:

> In chatting to W. J. Lawrence, he told me Father Dinneen did not like to take the call for "author" after his play *Faith and Famine* at the Abbey on Saturday, October 28, as "The theatre had such a bad name for irreligion he did not wish to associate himself with it in any way." I met Mrs. McHardy Flint on Saturday, November 4, in Eason's news depot, and she also told me of a lady who held up her hands in holy horror at the mention of the Abbey Theatre. "Her idea of it was a hotbed of sedition and all sorts of dreadful things." However, she promised to patronise the Flints' show at the end of the month. I suppose the poor dear thing will put herself under police protection on the occasion!

61 [Griffith], 'All Ireland', *The United Irishman* (4 November 1905), p. 1. Lady Gilbert, under her maiden name of Rosa Mulholland, was a prolific writer of romantic Irish fiction for the popular press.

62 [Griffith], 'All Ireland', *The United Irishman* (11 November 1905), p. 1.

63 'A Powerful Allegory', *The Irish Independent* (2 November 1905), p. 2.

64 J. W. [Good], 'The Ulster Literary Theatre', *Uladh* (February 1905), pp. 4-8.

65 J. W. [Good], 'The Theatre and the People', *Uladh* (May 1905), pp. 13-14.

66   Forrest Reid, Letter to the Editor, *The Northern Whig* (6 May 1905), p. 11.
67   [Griffith], 'All Ireland', *The United Irishman* (13 May 1905), p. 1.
68   Untitled note, *Uladh* (September 1905), p. 2.
69   Seosamh de Paor, 'The Ulster Literary Theatre', *Uladh* (September 1905), pp. 5-10.
70   [Griffith], 'All Ireland', *The United Irishman* (25 March 1905), p. 1.
71   'Chanel', [Arthur Clery] 'The Cork Plays', *The Leader* (18 March 1905), pp. 55-56.
72   As a note upon contemporary manners, the following advertisement from the programme of *Pelléas and Mélisande* is irresistible: 'Ladies and Gentlemen Can have a Permanent Natural BLUSH put on the Face. Absolutely no Pain. Tattooing. Sperin North, Japanese Tattoo Artist, 28, Up. Ormond-quay. Patronized by Nobility.'
73   'Mr. George Moore on Dublin', *The Dublin Evening Mail* (6 December 1905), p. 3.

1906

1   Fay and Carswell, p. 210.
2   Letter of A. E. F. Horniman to W. B. Yeats, dated 9 January 1906. Ms. 13,068, National Library of Ireland.
3   Letter of W. B. Yeats to J. M. Synge, dated 6 January 1906. Microfilm 5380, National Library of Ireland.
4   Letter of A. E. F. Horniman to J. M. Synge, dated 7 January 1906. Microfilm 5381, National Library of Ireland.
5   Letter of Lady Gregory to Padraic Colum, dated 7 January 1906. Microfilm 5380, National Library of Ireland.
6   Letter of Lady Gregory to Padraic Colum, dated 9 January 1906. Microfilm 5380, National Library of Ireland.
7   Letter of Lady Gregory to J. M. Synge, dated 10 January 1906. Microfilm 5380, National Library of Ireland.
8   Letter of Lady Gregory to J. M. Synge, dated 20 February 1906. Microfilm 5380, National Library of Ireland.
9   [Arthur Griffith], 'All Ireland', *The United Irishman* (10 March 1906), p. 1.
10 'National Theatre', *The Freeman's Journal* (17 April 1906), p. 9.
11 W. B. Yeats, 'A Note on *The Mineral Workers*', *The Arrow* (20 October 1906), p. 9.
12 'The Abbey Theatre', *The Irish Times* (22 October 1906), p. 8.
13 Lady Gregory's *The Canavans* was also to have received its first production on this night, but was postponed because of the illness of one of the cast.
14 Miss Darragh was the stage name of Laetitia Marian Dallas, who, after leaving the Abbey, founded the first repertory theatre in England, the Liverpool Repertory Theatre.
15 Micheál O Conaire, 'The Death of Deirdre', *Sinn Féin* (4 December 1906), p. 3.
16 Fay and Carswell, p. 208.
17 W. B. Yeats, *'The Shadowy Waters'*, *The Arrow* (24 November 1906), pp. 3-4.
18 'Sinn Dicat', 'The Drama in Dublin', *Sinn Féin* (15 December 1906), p. 3.
19 'New Plays at the Abbey Theatre', *The Freeman's Journal* (10 December 1906), p. 10.
20 *Ibid.*
21 Memorandum of A. E. F. Horniman. Ms. 10,952, National Library of Ireland.
22 Memorandum of A. E. F. Horniman. *Ibid.*
23 Letter of J. M. Synge to Lady Gregory. Ms. 10,952, National Library of Ireland.
24 Letter of A. E. F. Horniman to W. B. Yeats, dated 12 June 1906. Ms. 10,952, National Library of Ireland.
25 Letter of A. E. F. Horniman to W. B. Yeats, dated 21 June 1906. *Ibid.*
26 Letter of A. E. F. Horniman to W. B. Yeats, dated 23 June 1906. Ms. 13,068, National Library of Ireland.
27 Letter of J. M. Synge to W. B. Yeats, dated 2 July 1906. Ms. 10,952, National Library of Ireland.
28 Letter of A. E. F. Horniman to W. B. Yeats, dated 4 July 1906. Microfilm 5381, National Library of Ireland.

29 Letter of A. E. F. Horniman to W. B. Yeats, dated 13 July 1906. Ms. 13,068, National Library of Ireland.
30 Letter of A. E. F. Horniman to W. B. Yeats, dated 16 July 1906. Ms. 10,952, National Library of Ireland.
31 Letter of A. E. F. Horniman to W. B. Yeats, dated 17 July 1906. *Ibid.*
32 Letter of A. E. F. Horniman to W. B. Yeats, dated 22 July 1906. *Ibid.*
33 Letter of W. B. Yeats to W. G. Fay, dated 13 August 1906. *Ibid.*
34 Undated letter of W. G. Fay to W. B. Yeats. Ms. 5977, National Library of Ireland.
35 Letter of A. E. F. Horniman to W. B. Yeats, dated 30 August 1906. Ms. 13,068, National Library of Ireland.
36 Letter of A. E. F. Horniman to W. B. Yeats, dated 3 September 1906. Ms. 10,956, National Library of Ireland.
37 Letter of Miss Darragh to W. B. Yeats, dated 22 September 1906. Ms. 10,952, National Library of Ireland.
38 Letter of A. E. F. Horniman to W. B. Yeats, dated 26 October 1906. *Ibid.* Miss Horniman's remark refers to a statement Shaw made to an English reporter about his Irish play, *John Bull's Other Island*: 'Here's a play by an Irishman on Ireland as original as anything could be, as sympathetic with the genius of the people and in every way racy of the soil. Why don't the National Theatre people give it? Shall I tell you? Well, one reason is that the blinding of naked truth in that outburst of an English valet would so enrage all Nationalist auditors that they'd rise as one man at it, and burn the house down.' Gerard Fay, in whose book this remark is quoted, justly writes, 'This made a good headline but there was no truth in it. The play had been offered to the Abbey before it was given to Granville Barker for production in London. The first objection, and it was a serious one, was that there was no actor in the Abbey company who could have made even a reasonable shot at Broadbent' (p. 110). Willie Fay who journeyed to London during the run of the play especially to see it thought that, 'our company could not do it adequately in their present circumstances. Their experience was far too limited. To my thinking the play depends on having a Broadbent who can carry the weight of it. . . . Besides, he must both look and sound English, and we had nobody who could do that. . . . The rest of the cast I might have managed, though my people were really too young for the parts. Rather reluctantly I had to advise against attempting the play.' Fay and Carswell, pp. 206-207.
39 Letter of A. E. F. Horniman to W. B. Yeats, dated 14 November 1906. Ms. 10,952, National Library of Ireland.
40 Letter of A. E. F. Horniman to W. B. Yeats, dated 26 November 1906. *Ibid.*
41 Memorandum of W. B. Yeats to Lady Gregory and J. M. Synge, dated 2 December 1906. Microfilm 5380, National Library of Ireland.
42 Memorandum of W. B. Yeats to Lady Gregory and J. M. Synge, probably written on 2 December 1906. *Ibid.*
43 Undated memorandum of J. M. Synge. *Ibid.*
44 Letter of A. E. F. Horniman to W. B. Yeats, dated 3 December 1906. Ms. 13,068, National Library of Ireland.
45 Letter of A. E. F. Horniman to W. B. Yeats, dated 10 December 1906. *Ibid.*
46 Letter of A. E. F. Horniman to W. B. Yeats, dated 12 December 1906. *Ibid.*

47 Undated letter of Lady Gregory to J. M. Synge. Microfilm 5380, National Library of Ireland.

48 Letter of J. M. Synge to Lady Gregory, dated 15 December 1906. *Ibid.*

49 Undated memorandum of J. M. Synge. *Ibid.*

50 Letter of A. E. F. Horniman to W. B. Yeats, dated 17 December 1906. Ms. 13,068, National Library of Ireland.

51 Letter of A. E. F. Horniman to Lady Gregory, dated 19 December 1906. Microfilm 5380, National Library of Ireland.

52 Letter of Lady Gregory to J. M. Synge, dated 20 December 1906. *Ibid.*

53 Letter of A. E. F. Horniman to Lady Gregory, dated 26 December 1906. *Ibid.*

54 Undated memorandum either by Yeats or Lady Gregory, *Ibid.*

55 Letter of W. B. Yeats to J. M. Synge, dated 28 December 1906, *Ibid.*

56 Letter of A. E. F. Horniman to W. B. Yeats, dated 31 December 1906. Ms. 13,068, National Library of Ireland.

57 Letter of A. E. F. Horniman to W. B. Yeats, dated 31 December 1906. Ms. 10,952, National Library of Ireland.

58 Fay and Carswell, pp. 194-96.

59 Holloway, *Impressions*, 15 May 1906. Ms. 1804, National Library of Ireland.

60 Letter of Thomas Keohler and Padraic Colum to Joseph Holloway, dated 16 May 1906. Unnumbered collection of Holloway letters, National Library of Ireland.

61 Minutes of the Theatre of Ireland, dated 18 May 1906. Ms. 7388, National Library of Ireland.

62 [Arthur Griffith], 'The National Theatre', *Sinn Féin* (22 December 1906), p. 1.

63 Letter of Máire Garvey to James H. Cousins, undated. Ms. 8320, National Library of Ireland.

64 'Sinn Dicat', 'The Drama in Dublin', *Sinn Féin* (15 December 1906), p. 3.

65 The Queen's was in 1906 still under Whitbread's management, and his own company played there frequently in Boucicault and Whitbread melodramas, with James O'Brien and Mrs. Glenville usually in the casts. Kennedy Miller, who, although born in Glasgow, had long maintained a company of Irish players, died this year on 3 March. Among the notable popular touring companies which played at the Queen's in 1906 were Miss Kate Vincent and Company who opened on 22 March in 'the Greatest of all Sensational Dramas' *The Streets of London* by Boucicault; and Junius Booth, 'the Great American Actor' and a nephew of Edwin, in *Monte Cristo*.

The halls continued with their usual fare, such as Permane's Educated Bears, including the Famous Equestrian Bear, at the Tivoli, and Marzella's Bird's, Max Merlin 'the Human Crocodile', and Lora, the Marvellous Talking Bird at the Empire Palace. The Empire Palace also put on a play when George Gray's Company appeared in *The Fighting Parson*, which was described as 'The Rage of London! The Rage of the Provinces!!, 100 AUXILIARIES 100, Gorgeous Spectacle, Special Scenery, Dancing Effects, Tears, Cheers, Excitement, and Laughter.'

On 17 February the Theatre Royal was the scene of some disturbance. As *The Freeman's Journal* reported it two days later:

> The closing performance of the Pantomime, *Royal Cinderella*, at the Theatre Royal on Saturday night was the occasion of a series of disorders, which resulted in numerous objections and one

arrest. At 7.45, when the curtain was raised, and a number of artistes took their place on the stage, there was immediately a shower of flowers, boxes, papers, and miscellaneous articles thrown across the footlights. The front rows of the parterre stalls were occupied by a number of noisy youths, and as the performance advanced, the actions of these interrupters drew the attention of the gallery, which was crowded. The youths in the parterre cheered, waved handkerchiefs and sticks, and otherwise asserted themselves, and in certain vital efforts they were assisted by occupants of the gallery. All the artistes did their utmost to come to terms with their tormentors, but nearly all had to retire without a proper hearing.

After more uproar, the police were finally summoned and they made an arrest, whereupon many people left the parterre.

Later in the year the Theatre Royal was brought to court by one of its rivals, the Star Theatre of Varieties. *The Freeman's Journal*, on 6 March, in its most jocular tone gave the disagreement extensive coverage.

The Rolls Court, under ordinary circumstances a prosaic place where nothing but heavy legal arguments about Chancery suits are heard, was yesterday a scene of some interest. The court was thronged by members of the public, theatrical gentlemen, and barristers for the hearing of the application of the Star Theatre Company of Varieties, Ltd., against the Dublin Theatre Company, Ltd., in which the plaintiffs sought to restrain defendants from giving a hippodrome performance, which would include the "Globe of Life" and the performances of an elephant.

As previously announced, the elephant was at court this morning. He is a magnificent animal, and seemed, whether by reason of elephantic personal magnetism or otherwise, to attract a huge crowd of admirers.

The elephant is of light colour, though, indeed, not exactly a white elephant. He took up a prominent position in the courtyard, immediately outside the buffet, and there remained in sweet placidity while his character was being discussed by the gentlemen in wig and gown.

It was amusing to watch his antics. He eyed the crowd of spectators with the appearance of suspicion, and seemed to regard with a glance of contempt the lawyers who halted on their way from the dressing room to the courts to view his elephantship. . . .

When the result of the case was known there was a cheer given for him, and he tossed his head and trunk with an air of lofty indifference of the "I told-you-so" character.

11 June was the grand opening of the Royal's second Hippodrome season. Among the week's attractions were Madrali, the Terrible Turk, De Gracia's Assam Elephants, trick cyclists, and wrestlers. Later weeks included Marie Loftus, Herr Grais' Baboons, including Diavoleno the daring Baby Baboon, and what undoubtedly drew the greatest crowd at any Dublin theatre during the year, the second meeting of Hackenschmidt, the Champion Wrestler of the world, with Tom M'Inerney of local fame. Hackenschmidt had been appearing at the Royal, taking on all comers, when M'Inerney beat him, and so a

358

second meeting was arranged for 18 July at a matinee. *The Freeman's Journal* described the spectacle: 'Once inside the magnificent house a unique spectacle was presented. It is safe to say that there has never been a larger matinee audience in Dublin. The day was uncomfortably hot; nevertheless a sweltering audience, packed tightly from floor to ceiling, waited enthusiastically and excitedly for the coming of the two athletes. When the curtain rose at one o'clock there was not a seat empty. The gods shouted for their respective favourites, and some of the more humorous of the deities wagered across the house.' Hackenschmidt won in some twenty minutes, apparently by nearly pulling his opponent's arm off. The great excitement of this contest created a mode that was to last in several of the halls for a number of years.

The Empire Palace, for instance, during Horse Show week featured both boxing and wrestling. Pat Connolly, the Irish Champion wrestler, met all comers during the week, except at the Wednesday matinee when M'Inerney met the Indian Champion Ka Houta. On Thursday the Empire Palace featured a contest for the boxing championship of Ireland, between Jem Roche of Wexford and young John L. Sullivan of America. Sullivan lost.

66   Holloway, *Impressions*, 23 September 1906.
67   'Mr. Leamy's Play', *The Freeman's Journal* (14 April 1906), p. 7.
68   'By the Way', *The Freeman's Journal* (6 December 1906), p. 8.
69   'Queen's College, Two New Plays Presented, by Ulster Literary Theatre', *The Northern Whig* (5 December 1906), p. 9.
70   'The Irish Stage', *The Irish News and Belfast Morning News* (5 December 1906), p. 6.
71   'The Irish Peasant and the Stage', *The Freeman's Journal* (6 February 1906), p. 8.
72   Padraic Colum, 'Ibsen and National Drama', *Sinn Féin* (2 June 1906), p. 3.
73   'The Abbey Theatre', *The Freeman's Journal* (16 October 1906), p. 5.
74   Frank Dalton, Letter to the Editor, *The Freeman's Journal* (2 November 1906), p. 8.
75   Lady Gregory, 'A Note on *Spreading the News*', *The Arrow* (20 October 1906), p. 3.
76   *The Seething Pot* and *Hyacinth* were two novels by 'George A. Birmingham', the pseudonym of Canon J. Owen Hannay.
77   Stephen Gwynn, 'The Value of Criticism', *The Freeman's Journal* (27 October 1906), p. 5.
78   'Scrutator', 'Yeats of the Dramas', *Sinn Féin* (24 November 1906), p. 3.
79   Alice L. Milligan, 'Yeats and the Drama', *Sinn Féin* (31 December 1906), p. 1.
80   Padraic Colum in *The Irish Independent* (8 December 1906), p. 4.
81   'National Drama, Lecture by Mr. Colm', *The Freeman's Journal* (12 December 1906), p. 5.

1907

1 Holloway, *Impressions*, 23 January 1907. Ms. 1805, National Library of Ireland.
2 Lady Gregory, *Our Irish Theatre*, p. 133.
3 J. M. Synge, note to *The Playboy of the Western World*, printed in Abbey Theatre programme, 26 January 1907.
4 'The Abbey Theatre', *The Daily Express* (28 January 1907), p. 6.
5 'Disturbance at the Abbey Theatre', *The Daily Express* (29 January 1907), p. 5.
6 'The Abbey Theatre', *The Daily Express* (30 January 1907), p. 5.
7 Quoted in *The Evening Mail* (29 January 1907), p. 2.
8 'What Lady Gregory Said', *The Freeman's Journal* (29 January 1907), p. 7.
9 Editorial, *The Daily Express* (30 January 1907), p. 4.
10 'Last Night's Row at the Abbey', *The Dublin Evening Mail* (30 January 1907), p. 2.
11 'The Scenes at the Abbey Theatre', *The Daily Express* (1 February 1907), p. 7.
12 'The Abbey Theatre Disturbance', *The Daily Express* (2 February 1907), p. 7.
13 'The Abbey Theatre', *The Daily Express* (4 February 1907), p. 2.
14 'The National Theatre', *The Irish Independent* (31 January 1907), p. 4.
15 'Current Affairs', *The Leader* (2 February 1907), pp. 384-85.
16 'The Abbey Theatre', *The Daily Express* (4 February 1907), p. 7.
17 Ms. 13,068 (21), National Library of Ireland.
18 *Ibid.*
19 'The Abbey Theatre Disturbances', *The Daily Express* (5 February 1907), p. 8.
20 Letter of Padraic Colum to J. M. Synge, dated January 1907. Microfilm 5381, National Library of Ireland.
21 Letter of George Moore to J. M. Synge, dated 6 March 1907. *Ibid.*
22 George Roberts, 'A National Dramatist', *Shanachie* (1907), pp. 57-60.
23 Lady Gregory, 'An Explanation', *The Arrow* (1 June 1907), pp. 5-7.
24 *An Claidheamh Soluis* (9 February 1907), p. 7.
25 Letter of W. B. Boyle to W. B. Yeats, dated 31 January 1907. A typescript contained in W. A. Henderson papers, Ms. 1730, National Library of Ireland.
26 W. B. Yeats, 'The Controversy over The Playboy', *The Arrow* (23 February 1907), [p. 1].
27 W. Boyle, 'The Abbey Theatre', *The Freeman's Journal* (2 April 1907), p. 3.
28 Letter of W. Boyle to D. J. O'Donoghue, dated 14 January 1907. A copy in Holloway, *Impressions*, Ms. 1805, National Library of Ireland.
29 Letter of A. E. F. Horniman to Lady Gregory, dated 1 February 1907. Ms. 10,952, National Library of Ireland.
30 Letter of A. E. F. Horniman to Directors of the I.N.T.S., dated 1 February 1907. Ms. 13,068, National Library of Ireland.
31 Letter of A. E. F. Horniman to J. M. Synge, dated 10 February 1907. Microfilm 5381, National Library of Ireland.
32 Letter of A. E. F. Horniman to *The Evening Telegraph* (12 February 1907), p. 2.
33 Letter of J. M. Synge to W. B. Yeats, dated 9 January 1907. Typescript copy in Ms. 10,952, National Library of Ireland.

34 Letter of J. M. Synge to W. B. Yeats, dated 11 January 1907. Typescript copy in Ms. 10,952, National Library of Ireland.
35 Undated letter of Lady Gregory to W. B. Yeats. Typescript copy in Ms. 10,952, National Library of Ireland.
36 Letter of A. E. F. Horniman to W. B. Yeats, dated 11 February 1907. Ms. 13,068, National Library of Ireland.
37 *Ibid.*
38 Holloway, *Impressions*, 19 March 1907.
39 Letter of A. E. F. Horniman to W. B. Yeats, dated 27 March 1907. Ms. 13,068, National Library of Ireland.
40 Letter of W. B. Yeats to A. E. F. Horniman, undated. Ms. 10,952, National Library of Ireland.
41 Letter of A. E. F. Horniman to W. B. Yeats, dated 6 June 1907. Ms. 13,068, National Library of Ireland.
42 Holloway, *Impressions*, 17 May 1907.
43 W. B. Yeats, untitled note, *The Arrow* (1 June 1907), [p. 2].
44 Holloway, *Impressions*, 15 July 1907.
45 Undated letter of A. E. F. Horniman to W. B. Yeats. Ms. 13,068, National Library of Ireland.
46 Letter of W. B. Yeats to J. M. Synge, dated 15 August 1907. Microfilm 5380, National Library of Ireland.
47 Letter of W. G. Fay to W. B. Yeats, dated 22 August 1907. Ms. 5977, National Library of Ireland.
48 Proposal of W. G. Fay, dated 1 December 1907. Copy in Ms. 10,952, National Library of Ireland.
49 Reply of Directors, dated 4 December 1907. Copy in Ms. 10,952, National Library of Ireland.
50 Letter of W. G. Fay to W. B. Yeats, dated 17 December 1907. Typescript copy in Ms. 13,068, National Library of Ireland.
51 Letter of W. B. Yeats to J. M. Synge, dated 18 December 1907. Microfilm 5380, National Library of Ireland.
52 Letter of W. B. Yeats to J. M. Synge, dated 30 December 1907. *Ibid.*
53 Programme note signed 'A. G.' for Abbey Theatre programme of 23 February 1907.
54 'The Abbey Theatre', *The Freeman's Journal* (25 February 1907), p. 9.
55 'Abbey Theatre', *The Irish Times* (25 February 1907), p. 7.
56 'At the Abbey Theatre', *The Irish Independent* (25 February 1907), p. 7.
57 'Abbey Theatre', *The Irish Times* (11 March 1907), p. 7.
58 'The Abbey Theatre', *The Freeman's Journal* (11 March 1907), p. 4.
59 'F.M.A.', 'The Abbey Theatre', *The Dublin Evening Mail* (11 March 1907), p. 2.
60 W. M. Letts, 'Young Days at the Abbey Theatre', *Irish Writing* (September 1951), pp. 43-44.
61 'Scrutator', 'Private Theatricals in Excelsis', *Sinn Féin* (27 April 1907), p. 3.
62 'The Abbey Theatre', *The Freeman's Journal* (22 April 1907), p. 8.
63 'New Play at the Abbey Theatre', *The Dublin Evening Mail* (4 October 1907), p. 2.
64 '*The Country Dressmaker* at the Abbey', *The Evening Telegraph* (27 December 1907), p. 2.
65 W. B. Yeats, *Letters*, pp. 495-96.
66 Quoted in *The Freeman's Journal* (16 November 1907), p. 5.
67 'The Abbey Theatre', *The Freeman's Journal* (1 November 1907), p. 7.

68 'Jacques', 'Tragedy and Comedy', *The Irish Independent* (15 November 1907), p. 4.

69 W. B. Yeats, *Letters*, p. 503.

70 'Evan', 'The Unicorn and the Bard', *Sinn Féin* (30 November 1907), p. 3.

71 'New Play at the Abbey Theatre', *The Daily Express* (22 November 1907), p. 6.

72 'F.M.A.', 'The Abbey Theatre', *The Dublin Evening Mail* (22 November 1907), p. 6.

73 Sara Allgood, *Memories*. Typescript in the Berg Collection, New York Public Library.

74 'Maeldúin', 'The Ulster Literary Theatre', *Sinn Féin* (6 April 1907), p. 3.

75 W. J. Lawrence, 'The Ulster Literary Theatre in Dublin', *The Lady of the House* (15 April 1907).

76 'Ulster Literary Theatre', *The Irish News and Belfast Morning News* (27 December 1907), p. 8.

77 'Scrutator', 'Cluitcheoirí na hEireann', *Sinn Féin* (30 March 1907), p. 3.

78 Letter of Padraic Colum to W. G. Fay, dated 3 August 1907. Copy in W. A. Henderson papers, Ms. 1730, National Library of Ireland.

79 Máire Nic Shiubhlaigh, *The Splendid Years* (Dublin: James Duffy, 1955), p. 90.

80 'The Queen's Theatre', *The Freeman's Journal* (19 March 1907), p. 4.

81 James H. Cousins and Margaret E. Cousins, *We Two Together* (Madras: Ganesh & Co., 1950), p. 95.

82 'The Samhain Plays', *Sinn Féin* (9 November 1907), p. 2.

83 Edward Martyn, 'Suggestions to the Gaelic League', *The Freeman's Journal* (26 April 1907), p. 5.

84 Kathleen O'Brennan, 'Mr. Edward Martyn on the Theatre', *The Irish Packet* (18 May 1907), p. 182.

85 'New Irish Play', *The Freeman's Journal* (7 May 1907), p. 10.

86 'Freedom of the Theatre', *The Freeman's Journal* (7 February 1907), p. 9; and 'The Stage Irishman', *The Freeman's Journal* (15 October 1907), p. 9.

1908

1 Frank Fay was not always at his most congenial in these years either. He is sometimes described as moody by the other players, and although he is generally said to have followed the lead of his brother he too could apparently have his intractable moments. For instance, as Holloway once recorded:

> Sinclair told me of the company resenting always being referred to as composed of artisans and labourers and of their calling a meeting while in London over B. Iden Payne in an interview to *The Daily Chronicle* again referring to the company as such. The meeting was held under the stage in the Great Queen's Street Theatre, now the Kingsway. Lady Gregory and W. B. Yeats were present, and the latter was spokesman. As usual, he wandered away from the matter in hand, and Frank Fay hauled him up repeatedly, until at last Yeats declared the meeting over, and ran away as he always does from trouble, Frank Fay reminding him of the fact. Payne was crying, but the company offered him the hand of fellowship, as he never liked his coming into the company. Frank Fay was the only one who kept Lady Gregory in her place; he treated her with great disdain, as only he could when he so willed it. After Yeats's British Association speech, the company again called a meeting and censured Yeats for again referring to them as taken from the workshops and desks. Again he wiggled but had to hear them out. . . . Frank Fay one evening called Yeats into the dressing room and said to him, "I admire you as an artist, but despise you as a man. Now you may go!" and Yeats went, smiling to himself.

Holloway, *Impressions*, 1 December 1908. Ms. 1806, National Library of Ireland.

2 *Ibid.*, 3 January 1908.
3 *Ibid.*, 4 January 1908.
4 *Ibid.*, 9 January 1908.
5 Fay & Carswell, pp. 228-29.
6 *Ibid.*, pp. 230-31.
7 Letter of W. G. Fay to W. B. Yeats, dated 13 January 1908. Henderson Ms. 1731, National Library of Ireland.
8 Letter of F. J. Fay to W. B. Yeats, dated 13 January 1908. *Ibid.* W. G. Fay's wife, Brigit O'Dempsey, and Ernest Vaughan left at the same time.
9 'Mr. Yeats and His Critics, a Sporting Offer', *The Dublin Evening Mail* (14 January 1908), p. 3.
10 Holloway, 14 January 1908.
11 *Ibid.*, 15 January 1908.
12 *Ibid.*, 16 January 1908.
13 *Ibid.*, 18 January 1908.
14 Letter of W. Boyle to D. J. O'Donoghue, dated 17 January 1908. *Ibid.*
15 'F', The "Abbey" Ruins', *The Peasant*, ca. 14 January 1908, from W. G. Fay and Brigit O'Dempsey. Ms. 5975, National Library of Ireland.
16 Holloway, *Impressions*, 21 January 1908.
17 *Ibid.*, 22 January 1908.
18 Letter of W. Boyle to J. Holloway, dated 22 January 1908. *Ibid.*

19 *Ibid.*, 26 January 1908.
20 Letter of J. M. Synge to W. A. Henderson, dated 13 February 1908. Henderson Ms. 1731, National Library of Ireland.
21 Letter of A. E. F. Horniman to W. B. Yeats, dated 4 February 1908. Fay papers, Ms. 13,068, National Library of Ireland.
22 Holloway, *Impressions*, 5 February 1908.
23 *Ibid.*, 10 February 1908.
24 Postcard of F. J. Fay to James Montgomery, dated 19 February 1908. From an unnumbered collection of letters to J. Holloway, National Library of Ireland.
25 Letter of F. J. Fay to W. J. Lawrence, dated 19 February 1908. In Holloway, *Impressions*.
26 *Ibid.*, 20 February 1908.
27 Letter of W. Boyle to J. Holloway, dated 21 February 1908. *Ibid.*
28 J. Holloway, 2 March 1908.
29 *Ibid.*, 7 March 1908.
30 *Ibid.*, 8 March 1908.
31 *Ibid.*, 9 March 1908.
32 Letter of F. J. Fay to W. J. Lawrence, dated 17 March 1908. *Ibid.*
33 Letter of W. Boyle to J. Holloway, dated 30 March 1908. *Ibid.*
34 Letter of F. J. Fay to W. J. Lawrence dated 10 April 1908; *Ibid.*
35 Letter of W. Boyle to J. Holloway, dated 23 April 1908. *Ibid.*
36 Letter of W. Boyle to J. Holloway, dated 19 May 1908. *Ibid.*
37 W. B. Yeats, Letter to the Editor, *The Evening Mail* (21 May 1908), p. 5.
38 *Ibid.*
39 Letter of F. J. Fay to Máire Garvey, dated 27 May 1908. In George Roberts papers, Ms. 8320, National Library of Ireland.
40 Letter of W. Boyle to J. Holloway, dated 2 July 1908. In Holloway, *Impressions*.
41 'New Plays at the Abbey Theatre', *The Freeman's Journal* (14 February 1908), p. 5.
42 'The Abbey Theatre, Noisy Reception of "The Piper" ', *The Freeman's Journal* (15 February 1908), p. 5.
43 Kavanagh, p. 69.
44 'The Abbey Theatre', *The Freeman's Journal* (17 February 1908), p. 9.
45 Holloway, *Impressions*, 15 February 1908. As a postscript to the *Playboy* riots and the *Piper* disturbance, it might be noted that there was a theatrical disturbance of another kind in Galway on the evening of 14 November. As *The Freeman's Journal* reported it:

> On Saturday night there was a considerable uproar at the Court Theatre, Galway, owing to the failure of one of the parties in a boxing contest for £15 a side failing to put in an appearance. The students of the Queen's College, who attended in large numbers, started by throwing chairs from the auditorium to the stage, and the "gods" threw seats from the gallery. Later on the students and the "Gods" got into handigrips, with the result that the students were routed from the theatre and chased through the streets. A number of persons were struck with stones. The police dispersed the crowds in the street and escorted the students to their homes.

'Scene in Galway Theatre', *The Freeman's Journal* (17 November 1908), p. 8.

46 'Three New Plays at the Abbey Theatre', *The Freeman's Journal* (20 March 1908), p. 10.

47 'Sinn de Ceat', 'Three New Plays at the Abbey Theatre', *Sinn Féin* (28 March 1908), p. 3.

48 J. H. Cox, 'A Whole Range of History', *The Irish Independent* (20 March 1908), p. 5.

49 'New Plays at the Abbey', *The Dublin Evening Mail* (20 March 1908), p. 2.

50 Holloway, *Impressions*, 3 April 1908.

51 'The Abbey Theatre, *Hyacinth Halvey* and *The Rogueries of Scapin*', *The Freeman's Journal* (6 April 1908), p. 5.

52 'Abbey Theatre', *The Irish Times* (6 April 1908), p. 9.

53 'The Abbey Theatre', *The Freeman's Journal* (21 April 1908), p. 4.

54 'The Abbey Theatre', *The Freeman's Journal* (30 May 1908), p. 9.

55 'Sheridan's Farce at the Abbey', *The Irish Independent* (30 May 1908), p. 6.

56 After leaving Dublin, William Francis Casey worked for many years for *The Times* of London, and climaxed a long career by being appointed its editor in 1948.

57 Holloway, *Impressions*, 24 September 1908.

58 'Abbey Theatre, Special Subscription Tickets', *The Freeman's Journal* (28 September 1908), p. 4.

59 'Inanities at the "Abbey" ', *Sinn Féin* (10 October 1908), p. 3.

60 M. O'D., 'Two Ways of Satire', *The Evening Mail* (2 October 1908), p. 2.

61 Holloway, *Impressions*, 5 October 1908.

62 'The Abbey Theatre', *The Freeman's Journal* (9 October 1908), p. 10.

63 'Cairbre', 'An Abbey Play and Gaelic Actors', *The Peasant and Irish Ireland* (10 October 1908), p. 1.

64 Stephen Gwynn, Letter to the Editor, *The Freeman's Journal* (10 October 1908), p. 7.

65 Holloway, *Impressions*, 10 October 1908.

66 'A New Tragedy at the Abbey', *The Freeman's Journal* (17 October 1908), p. 10.

67 H.S.D., 'When the Dawn is Come', *The Dublin Evening Mail* (16 October 1908), p. 2.

68 'Jacques', 'Fifty Years Hence', *The Irish Independent* (16 October 1908), p. 4.

69 Holloway, *Impressions*, 17 October 1908.

70 'The Abbey Theatre', *The Freeman's Journal* (23 October 1908), p. 8.

71 Holloway, *Impressions*, 27 October 1908.

72 'The Abbey Theatre, Mrs. Patrick Campbell as "Deirdre" ', *The Freeman's Journal* (10 November 1908), p. 10.

73 Holloway, *Impressions*, 10 November 1908.

74 'W' [W. J. Lawrence], 'Abbey Theatre, Serious Rupture', *The Dublin Evening Mail* (13 January 1908), p. 3.

75 W. B. Yeats, 'Mr. Yeats and His Critics, A Sporting Offer', *The Dublin Evening Mail* (14 January 1908), p. 3.

76 'W' [W. J. Lawrence], 'Abbey Theatre, Mr. Yeats's Challenge Accepted', *The Dublin Evening Mail* (15 January 1908), p. 5.

77 W. B. Yeats, 'The Abbey Theatre, Mr. Yeats's Reply', *The Dublin Evening Mail* (16 January 1908), p. 3.

78 'W' [W. J. Lawrence], 'Abbey Theatre, Mr. Yeats and his Critics', *The Dublin Evening Mail* (17 January 1908), p. 3.

79 W. B. Yeats, 'The Abbey Theatre', *The Dublin Evening Mail* (18 January 1908), p. 5.

80 'The Drama in Dublin', *The Evening Telegraph* (11 February 1908), p. 2.

81 First printed in an Abbey Theatre programme published 8 September 1908, pp. 6-8.

82 'S', 'Mr. Yeats and the British Association', *Sinn Féin* (19 September 1908), p. 3.

83 P. S. O'Hegarty, 'Mr. Yeats and the British Association', *Sinn Féin* (26 September 1908), p. 1.

84 'Firin', 'Lady Gregory on Drama', *The Peasant and Irish Ireland* (21 November 1908), p. 5.

85 Holloway, *Impressions*, 26 January 1908.

86 Letter of J. M. Synge to Máire O'Neill, dated 3 May 1908, in Greene and Stephens, p. 285.

87 Letter of J. M. Synge to W. B. Yeats, dated 4 May 1908, in Fay papers, Ms. 10,952, National Library of Ireland. A portion reprinted in Greene and Stephens, p. 225.

88 Ms. 13,068 (22), National Library of Ireland.

89 Holloway, *Impressions*, 1 October 1908.

90 Letter of W. Boyle to J. Holloway, dated 15 October 1908. *Ibid.*

91 Letters of J. Guinan to J. Holloway, dated 4 June, 6 June, and 24 October, 1908. In Holloway Ms. 13,267, National Library of Ireland.

92 Holloway, *Impressions*, 16 April 1908.

93 *Ibid.*, 25 May 1908.

94 *Ibid.*, 1 April 1908.

95 Yeats, *Letters*, p. 510.

96 *Ibid.*, p. 512.

97 *Ibid.*

98 Sara Allgood, *Memories*, pp. 49-50, 56-57, in the Berg Collection, New York Public Library.

99 Holloway, *Impressions*, 1 April 1908.

100 'The Theatre of Ireland', *The Freeman's Journal* (23 May 1908), p. 8.

101 'Scrutator', 'Cluitcheoiri na hEireann', *Sinn Féin* (30 May 1908), p. 3.

102 Ella Young, '*Maeve*: An Impression', *Ibid.*

103 'Iberian', 'A Play and an Episode', *Sinn Féin* (28 November 1908), p. 3.

104 A. E. F. Horniman, 'The Abbey Theatre and the Theatre of Ireland', *The Freeman's Journal* (2 December 1908), p. 9. Miss Horniman's determination to keep her theatre free from the Nationalist movement is also apparent in this letter of 25 January 1908, which she wrote to an official of the National Players Society, who had written for permission to play in the Abbey:

I know many particulars as to the history of the National Players Society. If you will look at the number of *Samhain* containing my letter and its acceptance bearing the signatures of various people, you will see that they promised to help my scheme to carry out Mr. Yeats's ideas. They then withdrew after giving as much trouble as possible, without a word of explanation to me personally. They also extracted money and costumes from the venture they had promised in writing to assist, taking a mean advantage of a phrase in the Patent.

I have forbidden 6d seats to all paying tenants and when an

untruthful statement on the subject was sent to Messrs. Cramer by the Cumann na nGael, not one of you took the trouble to make any apology nor to offer any explanation.

I would willingly make a favourable arrangement with an amateur society with a reputable past and which did not pander to the curse of your country — that love of wicked politics, which teach you to hate each other so intensely, has spoiled my efforts at the Abbey Theatre. Decent people under the present circumstances are quite right in objecting to go there for they call it "a political theatre."

Fay Ms. 10,952, National Library of Ireland.

105 Seumas O'Connolly, 'The Abbey Theatre and the Theatre of Ireland', *The Freeman's Journal* (2 December 1908), p. 9.

106 Rutherford Mayne, 'The Abbey Theatre', *The Freeman's Journal* (7 December 1908), p. 8.

107 F.M.A., 'Ulster Literary Theatre', *The Dublin Evening Mail* (25 April 1908), p. 4.

108 'The Real Thing', *The Irish Independent* (25 April 1908), p. 4.

109 'Oireachtas Plays', *The Freeman's Journal* (7 August 1908), p. 8.

110 Jacqueline Van Voris, *Constance de Markievicz: In the Cause of Ireland* (Amherst: University of Massachusetts Press, 1967), p. 57.

111 'Cos', 'The Play Ironical', *Sinn Féin* (14 March 1908), p. 3.

112 Van Voris, pp. 57-58.

113 'The Irish Dramatic Company', *The Freeman's Journal* (4 December 1908), p. 11.

114 'The Dublin Theatres, Monopoly Again Threatened', *The Freeman's Journal* (12 September 1908), p. 7.

115 From a manuscript notebook entitled 'Cork Dramatic Society', among the Daniel Corkery papers in the library of University College Cork.

116 *Ibid.*

117 Contained in the Corkery papers in the library of University College Cork.

1909

1 'Death of Mr. J. M. Synge', *The Evening Herald* (24 March 1909), p. 2.
2 D. J. O'Donoghue, 'John M. Synge, a Personal Appreciation', *The Irish Independent* (26 March 1909), p. 4.
3 T.M. [Thomas MacDonagh], 'J. M. Synge: Irish Dramatist, Writer, Poet', *T.P.'s Weekly* (9 April 1909), p. 469.
4 'Mr. Synge's Art and Message', *The Freeman's Journal* (29 May 1909), p. 5. A full version in Cousins's own words is printed in *Sinn Féin* (17 July 1909), p. 1.
5 Letter of William Boyle to J. Holloway, dated 2 November 1909. In Holloway Ms. 13,267, National Library of Ireland.
6 Letter of A. E. F. Horniman to Norreys Connell, dated 8 April 1909. In Yeats papers, Ms. 13,068, National Library of Ireland.
7 Lennox Robinson, *Ireland's Abbey Theatre* (London: Sidgwick & Jackson, Ltd., 1961), pp. 76-77.
8 Letter of Norreys Connell to members of the Abbey company, dated 18 April 1909. In Henderson papers, Ms. 1732, National Library of Ireland.
9 Ms. 13,068 (9), National Library of Ireland.
10 Berg Collection, New York Public Library.
11 'Abbey Theatre', *The Irish Times* (22 January 1909), p. 9.
12 Jacques, 'A French Comedy', *The Irish Independent* (22 January 1909), p. 7.
13 A Visitor, 'Kincora', *Sinn Féin* (20 February 1909), p. 3.
14 'A New Play at the Abbey Theatre', *The Freeman's Journal* (12 March 1909), p. 8.
15 'Abbey Theatre', *The Irish Times* (12 March 1909), p. 6.
16 'Jack Point', 'A New Play', *The Evening Herald* (2 April 1909), p. 4.
17 H.S.D., 'At the Cross Roads', *The Dublin Evening Mail* (2 April 1909), p. 2.
18 'The Abbey', *The Freeman's Journal* (2 April 1909), p. 9.
19 'Jacques', 'Heather Field Blooms Again', *The Irish Independent* (16 April 1909), p. 4.
20 'Jacques', 'Something Old and Something New', *The Irish Independent* (14 May 1909), p. 6.
21 'Abbey Theatre', *The Irish Times* (14 May 1909), p. 6.
22 'The Abbey Theatre', *The Dublin Evening Mail* (14 May 1909), p. 5.
23 *Ibid.*
24 W. J. Lawrence, '*The Playboy of the Western World*, Proposed Revival at Abbey Theatre', *The Evening Telegraph* (19 May 1909), p. 3.
25 'The Abbey Theatre', *The Dublin Evening Mail* (28 May 1909), p. 6; 'Abbey Theatre', *The Irish Times* (28 May 1909), p. 6.
26 'Jack Point', 'The Playboy Again', *The Evening Herald* (28 May 1909), p. 4.
27 'The Abbey Theatre', *The Evening Telegraph* (28 May 1909), p. 5.
28 Conal O'Riordan, *Adam of Dublin* (London: W. Collins Sons & Co., 1920), pp. 123-27.
29 'By the Way', *The Freeman's Journal* (20 February 1909), p. 7.
30 Herbert Van Thal, ed., *James Agate, An Anthology* (London: Rupert Hart-Davis, 1961), p. 31.
31 J. T. Grein, 'Court: The Irish Plays', *The Sunday Times* (13 June 1909), p. 4.
32 *Ibid.*

33 Quoted in 'Censor and Bernard Shaw', *The Evening Telegraph* (22 May 1909), p. 5.

34 'More About Blanco Posnet', *The Evening Telegraph* (24 August 1909), p. 3.

35 'Mr. Shaw's Play', *The Irish Times* (23 August 1909), p. 7. The first letter had been printed by several papers on Saturday. See, for instance, 'Mr. Shaw's Play', *The Dublin Evening Mail* (21 August 1909), p. 5.

36 '*Blanco Posnet* at the Abbey', *The Evening Telegraph* (23 August 1909), p. 3.

37 'More About Blanco Posnet', *The Evening Telegraph* (24 August 1909), p. 3.

38 *Ibid.* The *Piccolo della Sera* correspondent was James Joyce.

39 W. B. Yeats, 'The Religion of Blanco Posnet', *The Arrow* (25 August 1909), [p. 7].

40 'Fighting the Censor', *The Irish Independent* (25 August 1909), p. 5.

41 [Arthur Griffith], 'The Castle and the Theatre', *Sinn Féin* (21 August 1909), p. 2.

42 'The Abbey Theatre', *The Freeman's Journal* (25 August 1909), p. 9.

43 'Jacques', 'A Shaw Spoof', *The Irish Independent* (26 August 1909), p. 5.

44 '*The Shewing Up of Blanco Posnet*, Mr. Shaw's Play at the Abbey', *The Freeman's Journal* (26 August 1909), p. 7.

45 'Triumphant Success', *The Irish Independent* (26 August 1909), p. 5.

46 George A. Birmingham [Canon J. O. Hannay], quoted in 'Press Views of the Play', *The Irish Independent* (26 August 1909), p. 5.

47 'Abbey Theatre', *The Irish Times* (26 August 1909), p. 7.

48 W. B. Yeats and Lady Gregory, 'Abbey Theatre and the Castle', *The Dublin Evening Mail* (26 August 1909), p. 5.

49 'New Play at the Abbey Theatre', *The Irish Independent* (17 September 1909), p. 8.

50 '*The White Feather*', *The Dublin Evening Mail* (17 September 1909), p. 8.

51 R. J. Ray, Letter to the Editor, *Sinn Féin*.

52 'Abbey Theatre', *The Irish Times* (15 October 1909), p. 6.

53 'The Abbey Theatre', *The Freeman's Journal* (12 November 1909), p. 9.

54 *Ibid.*

55 'Jacques', 'Lady Gregory's Secret', *The Irish Independent* (12 November 1909), p. 6.

56 Letter of F. J. Fay to Máire Garvey, dated 6 March 1909. In George Roberts papers, Ms. 8320, National Library of Ireland.

57 Letter of F. J. Fay to Máire Garvey, dated 26 April 1909. *Ibid.*

58 Letter of W. Boyle to J. Holloway, dated 17 September 1909. In Holloway papers, Ms. 13,267, National Library of Ireland.

59 Letter of W. Boyle to J. Holloway, dated 12 October 1909. *Ibid.*

60 Letter of W. Boyle to J. Holloway, dated 16 October 1909. *Ibid.*

61 Letter of A. E. F. Horniman to W. B. Yeats, dated 9 February 1909. In Yeats papers, Ms. 13,068, National Library of Ireland.

62 Letter of A. E. F. Horniman to W. B. Yeats, n.d., *Ibid.*

63 Letter of A. E. F. Horniman to the Directors of the National Theatre Society, Ltd., dated 31 August 1909. In Fay papers, Ms. 10,952, National Library of Ireland.

64 Ms. 13,068 (9), National Library of Ireland.

65 *Ibid.*

66 Ms. 13,068 (23), National Library of Ireland.
67 Contained in W. A. Henderson papers, Ms. 1732, National Library of Ireland, p. 256.
68 Sara Allgood, *Memories*, in Berg Collection, New York Public Library, n.p.
69 S.L.M. [Susan L. Mitchell], 'Dramatic Rivalry', *Sinn Féin* (8 May 1909), p. 1.
70 'Mise', 'The Shuiler's Child', *Sinn Féin, Ibid.*
71 'K', 'Theatre of Ireland', *Sinn Féin, Ibid.*
72 C.A., 'Ulster Plays at the Abbey', *The Dublin Evening Mail* (27 November 1909), p. 7.
73 'Jacques', 'Northern Drolleries', *The Irish Independent* (27 November 1909), p. 7.
74 'Drama in Cork', *The Cork Constitution* (5 May 1909), p. 8.
75 'Cork Dramatic Society', *The Cork Constitution* (7 May 1909), p. 5.
76 'Cork Dramatic Society', *The Cork Constitution* (3 December 1909), p. 6.
77 Seumas O Conghaile, 'Notes on the Oireachtas Opera and Plays', *Sinn Féin* (14 August 1909), p. 1.
78 'Duo of Pretty Plays', *The Irish Independent* (12 March 1909), p. 7.
79 '*An Englishman's Home* Produced at Theatre Royal', *The Evening Telegraph* (4 May 1909), p. 2. Ireland and England were not the only countries to have their self-esteem punctured in the theatre. On 13 January *The Freeman's Journal* had carried this story:

> The Comédie Française was again the scene of some disturbances last night during the performance of the play, *Le Foyer*. During the second act at the point where Baron Coubertin asks the Abbé whether he has decided to reveal secrets of the Confessional, M. André Gaucher, who was arrested on the occasion of the first disturbance some weeks ago, stood up in the box which he occupied with several friends and shouted, "I shall not permit Jews to attack the national religion." Protests were also raised by the occupants of other boxes, and the curtain descended amid the jeers and whistles of about forty persons in the gallery. The performance was resumed after some minutes, but there was another demonstration of hostility at the end of the act, and several disturbers, including M. André Gaucher and his brother, the well-known boxer, were arrested. They were subsequently released.

'Scene in Paris Theatre', *The Freeman's Journal* (13 January 1909), p. 7. On 27 January *The Freeman's Journal* reported that in Marseilles:

> At a performance of *Le Foyer* in the Théâtre du Gymnase yesterday evening, some of the audience belonging to Catholic and Royalist groups, disapproving of the tone of the piece, created a violent disturbance, which led to a counter demonstration. The demonstrators were ejected by the police, and some thirty persons were put under temporary arrest.

'Anti-Catholic Play', *The Freeman's Journal* (27 January 1909), p. 8.
80 'The Theatre in Ireland', *The Freeman's Journal* (16 August 1909), p. 7.
81 'The Queen's Theatre', *The Freeman's Journal* (6 September 1909), p. 5.
82 'Scene at the Empire', *The Evening Telegraph* (24 August 1909), p. 3.
83 James H. Cousins, 'A Word for Historic Drama', *Sinn Féin* (15 May 1909), p. 1.
84 Alice L. Milligan, 'Historical Drama', *Sinn Féin* (26 June 1909), p. 1.
85 *Ibid.*

Index

Abbey Theatre, 9-45, 54-55, 57-101, 113-115, 120, 122, 123-182, 193-251, 270-315, 330.
Abbey Theatre Series of Plays (Maunsel), 54.
Aberdeen, Lord. See Lord Lieutenant.
Adam of Dublin (C. O'Riordan), 270.
Æ. See George Russell.
Agate, James. Quoted, 285.
Allen, Mrs. David, 260.
Allen, Sam, 260.
Allgood, Molly. See 'Máire O'Neill'.
Allgood, Sara, 31, 32, 40, 66, 68, 73, 76, 77, 78, 85, 89, 125, 170, 171, 172, 177, 178, 179, 193, 194, 198, 206, 212, 213, 215, 221, 224, 226, 227, 228, 229-230, 232, 234, 273, 274, 275, 278, 279, 285, 286, 300, 302, 308, 309, 314-315, 316, 331. Quoted, 181-182, 211, 248-251.
Antigone (Sophocles), 81, 115.
The Aran Islands (J. M. Synge), 268.
Ard Craobh of the Gaelic League, 242.
Aristotle, 122.
Arms and the Man (G. B. Shaw), 259.
The Arrow, 65, 68, 82, 117, 156, 158, 201, 293.
Artistic-minded Tailor (W. Boyle), 210.
Ashwell, Lena, 259.
The Athenaeum, 293.
An tAthrughadh Mór (F. Partridge), 106, 107, 118.
An August Day (G. MacNamara), 246.
L'Avare (Molière), 274.

Bairbre Ruadh (P. O'Conaire), 257.
Balfe, Michael, 328.
Barden, Hugh, 325.
Barlow, Jane, 112.
Barlow, Seán, 101, 249. Quoted, 271.
Barrie, J. M., 204, 205, 207.
Baudelaire, Charles, 268.
Beaslai, Piaras, 132, 133-135, 150, 191.
Before Clonmel (R. G. Walsh), 189.
The Belfast Evening Telegraph. Quoted, 21.
The Belfast News-Letter, 293.
Bell, Mr., 70, 71, 72, 75.
The Bell Branch (J. H. Cousins), 307.
The Bending of the Bough (G. Moore and E. Martyn), 157.
Benson, F. R., 164. Quoted, 179.
Bernhardt, Sarah, 54, 259.
Birmingham, George A. Quoted, 301-302.
Blake, William, 11.
Blunt, Wilfrid Scawen, 115, 175, 177.
A Book of Irish Verse (W. B. Yeats), 11.
Bootle Branch of the Gaelic League, 189.
Boucicault, Dion, 54, 115, 116, 191, 328.
Boycotting (Lady Gilbert), 46.

371

Boyle, William, 9, 26-30, 43, 54-55, 65-66, 73, 78, 82, 89, 118, 119, 161, 197, 201-202, 203, 207, 224, 244-246, 307. Quoted, 27, 158-161, 198-199, 205, 208-209, 209-210, 212, 245-246, 308-309.
Brand (Ibsen), 106, 315.
Breen, D., 261, 322.
Brian of Banba (B. Hobson), 48-49, 51.
Brian of Banba (A. Milligan), 330.
British Association, 237.
The Broken Reed (W. E. T. Christie), 326.
Broken Soil (P. Colum), 185.
Brophy, Robert J. See 'R. J. Ray'.
The Building Fund (W. Boyle), 26-28, 32, 43, 54-55, 118, 158, 199, 202, 207, 208, 209-210, 211, 212.
Bull, Ole, 113.
Bushell, Nellie, 248.
Butler, Mary L., 325.

'Cairbre', 224. Quoted, 226-227.
Calderon, 88.
Callender, Brian, 45, 106.
Campbell, John, 51.
Campbell, Joseph, 50-51, 52.
Campbell, Josephine, 51.
Campbell, Mrs. Patrick, 54, 76, 90, 92, 101, 179, 223, 230-231, 248, 273, 274.
The Canavans (Lady Gregory), 68, 69-70, 81, 89, 233.
Candida (G. B. Shaw), 259.
Canmer, Seveen, 319.
Carleton, William, 112, 151.
Carr, Phillip, 88.
Casadh an tSugain (D. Hyde), 106.
Casey, W. F., 200, 212, 213, 222, 223-225, 227, 229, 305.
Casson, Lewis, 259.
Celtic Wonder Tales (E. Young), 252.
The Challenge (W. Letts), 305-306.
Chicago Sunday Tribune, 211.
Christie, Capt. W. E. Tolfrey, 325.
An Claidheamh Soluis, 36, 157. Quoted, 158.
The Clancy Name (L. Robinson), 213, 225-227, 245.
Clery, Arthur ('Chanel'). Quoted, 24. 53.
Clongowes Wood College, 270.
Cluithcheóirí na hEireann. See the Theatre of Ireland.
Coleridge, S. T., 68.
Colonial Picture Company, 260.
The Colleen Bawn (D. Boucicault), 116.
Colum, Miss, 229.
Colum, Padraic, 9, 28, 29, 30-33, 35-36, 45, 57, 58, 59-61, 63, 103, 104, 105, 107, 108, 112, 185-186, 187, 191, 202, 210, 212, 224, 229, 230, 243, 251, 307. Quoted, 30, 36, 102, 113, 120-121, 152, 186, 228.
Columb, Patrick (Sr.), 132.
Compton Comedy Company, 54.
Conlon, J. P., 261.
Connell, Henry. See Henry Connell Mangan.
Connell, Norreys (Conal O'Riordan), 193, 199, 200, 212, 213, 214-216, 223, 224, 270-271, 277-278, 279, 280, 285, 308. Quoted, 272, 273-274, 281-284.

Connolly, Seumas, 187, 202-203, 256. Quoted, 254-255, 324-325.
Consul, the Ape, 327.
Corbett, James J. (Gentleman Jim), 327.
The Cork Constitution. Quoted, 320-324.
Cork Dramatic Society, 53, 260-263, 320-324, 331.
Cork National Theatre Society, 9, 53.
Cork Sportsman, 312, 313.
Corkery, Daniel ('Lee'), 321, 323, 331. Quoted, 44-45, 260-263.
Cormac, Caitia Ní, 251, 317.
Cormac na Coille (P. Beaslai), 191.
Corneille, 167.
The Countess Cathleen (W. B. Yeats), 14, 17, 49, 120, 146, 152.
The Country Dressmaker (G. Fitzmaurice), 171, 177-179, 330.
Cousins, James H., 102, 106, 211, 251, 307. Quoted, 188-189, 269-270, 329.
Cox, J. H., 219.
Creideamh agus Gorta (Fr. Dinneen), 45.
Cromwell, Oliver, 268.
Crossroads (L. Robinson), 277-278, 313.
Cupid in Kerry (E. Leamy), 107.
Cymbeline (Shakespeare), 10.

The Daily Chronicle (London), 286, 293.
The Daily Express, 28, 65, 66, 67, 68, 224, 226. Quoted, 32, 34, 124-125, 126, 127-130, 130-132, 143-144, 144-152, 181.
Daily Graphic, 293.
The Daily Mail (London), 293.
The Daily News (London), 293.
The Daily Telegraph, 293.
Dale, Allan, 204, 205.
Dalton, Frank, 115. Quoted, 116-117.
D'Alton, Louis, 115.
La Dame aux Caméllias (A. Dumas fils), 259.
Dana, 93, 230.
Darley, Arthur, 68, 217.
Darragh, Miss (Letitia Marion Dallas), 67-68, 74, 76, 77, 78, 79, 81, 87, 89, 90, 91, 92, 96, 98, 198, 230. Quoted, 80.
The Daughter of Donogh (A. Milligan), 330.
Daughters of Erin (Inghinidhe na hEireann), 187.
David Garrick (T. W. Robertson), 255.
Davis, Thomas, 265.
Decameron (Boccaccio), 11.
De Gracia's Assam Elephants, 259.
Deirdre (Æ), 61, 110, 187, 258.
Deirdre (T. O'Kelly), 324, 325.
Deirdre (W. B. Yeats), 39, 49, 67-68, 76, 80, 90, 92, 167, 200, 223, 230-232, 234, 248, 273, 330.
Deirdre of the Sorrows (J. M. Synge), 244, 268.
Delaney, James, 135-139.
de l'Isle, Leconte, 268.
The Deliverance of Red Hugh (A. Milligan), 106.
de Roiste, Liam, 260-263.
Dervorgilla (Lady Gregory), 179-180, 221, 226, 227.
Dever, John (or Denvir, or Denveer), 107, 189.
Diarmuid and Grania (G. Moore and W. B. Yeats), 17, 42.

373

Fitzmaurice, George, 177-179, 210, 212-213, 218, 227, 246, 247, 284, 307.
Fitzpatrick, Nora, 253, 259, 317.
The Flame on the Hearth (S. O'Kelly), 253.
Forbes Robertson, J., 179.
Les Fourberies de Scapin. See *The Rogueries of Scapin.*
The Freeman's Journal, 64, 66, 67, 68, 107, 125, 130, 182, 187, 188, 189, 227, 229, 255, 260, 269, 278, 297. Quoted, 18-19, 23, 24-25, 27, 30-32, 34, 65, 69, 107, 108, 172, 174, 177, 179-180, 213-215, 220-221, 222-223, 225-226, 228, 230-231, 251-252, 257, 259, 276, 278, 284-285, 298-300, 306, 328.
The French are on the Sea (A. Milligan), 330.
Frohman, Charles, 193, 203, 205, 207, 208.

Gaelic League, 9, 15, 45-47, 75, 89, 105, 107, 113, 161, 179, 189, 190, 191, 242, 257, 303, 310.
Gaiety Theatre, Dublin, 54, 253, 259, 260, 301, 328.
Gaiety Theatre, Manchester, 167, 325.
Galsworthy, John, 272.
The Gaol Gate (Lady Gregory), 65, 66-67, 330.
Garvey, Máire, 30, 31, 38-39, 57, 58, 85, 103, 176, 307. Quoted, 104-106.
The Gay Lord Quex (A. W. Pinero), 325.
The Geisha, 16.
Gerothwohl, Prof. Maurice, 276.
Gilbert, Lady (Rosa Mulholland), 46.
Gilden, Miss, 70.
Gill, Miss, 326.
Gilley, Miss D., 322.
Giraldus Cambrensis, 11.
The Girl Who Took the Wrong Turning, 182.
Gisippus (G. Griffin), 54.
The Glittering Gate (Lord Dunsany), 279, 316, 330.
Goethe, 88, 242, 253.
Gogarty, Oliver St. John. Quoted, 42.
The Golden Helmet (W. B. Yeats), 213, 218, 219, 330.
Goldsmith, Oliver, 116, 328.
The Gomeril (R. Mayne), 279, 315, 317.
Gonne, Maud. See Maud Gonne MacBride.
Good, James Winder, 256. Quoted, 48-50.
Gore-Booth, Constance. See Countess Markievicz.
Gorman, Eric, 275.
Granville Barker, Harley, 259, 309.
The Green Helmet (W. B. Yeats), 249.
The Green upon the Cape (A. Milligan), 330.
Gregory, Lady Augusta, 9, 22, 23-26, 28, 29, 30, 33-34, 35, 37, 39, 40, 54-55, 62, 63, 64, 65, 66-67, 69-70, 71, 74, 76, 77, 78, 79, 81, 82, 89, 93, 98, 100, 120, 126, 128, 131, 137, 142, 166, 168, 171, 173, 179-180, 191, 195, 197, 201, 206, 207, 208, 213, 217, 219, 220-221, 223, 229, 231, 237, 241, 244, 249, 274-276, 292, 301, 306, 307, 309, 315, 316, 331. Quoted, 26, 59-61, 91, 117-118, 123, 130, 156-157, 163-164, 172, 242-243, 288, 288-289, 289-290, 292, 293, 302-303.
Gregory, Robert, 23, 26, 68, 71, 96.
Grein, J. T., 270.
Gresham Hotel, 231, 232.
Griffin, Gerald, 54, 328.